P9-APM-436

THE SIXTIES IN CANADA

971.0643 Six

The sixties in Canada.

PRICE: $24.99 (3559/he   )

THE SIXTIES IN CANADA

A Turbulent And Creative Decade

M. Athena Palaeologu, editor

BLACK
ROSE
BOOKS

Montreal/New York/London

Copyright © 2009 BLACK ROSE BOOKS

No part of this book may be reproduced or transmitted in any form, by any means electronic or mechanical including photocopying and recording, or by any information storage or retrieval system—without written permission from the publisher, or, in the case of photocopying or other reprographic copying, a license from the Canadian Copyright Licensing Agency, Access Copyright, with the exception of brief passages quoted by a reviewer in a newspaper or magazine.

Black Rose Books No. NN371

National Library of Canada Cataloguing in Publication Data

The sixties in Canada : a turbulent and creative decade / M. Athena Palaeologu, editor

ISBN 978-1-55164-331-1 (bound) ISBN 978-1-55164-330-4 (pbk.)

1. Canada--Social conditions. 2. Canada--Politics and government--1963-1968.
3. Canada–Civilization–1945-. 4. Nineteen sixties. I. Palaeologu, M. Athena

FC625.S59 2009   971.064'3   C2009-900541-7

For permission to print material published elsewhere, we express our thanks: to Bryan D. Palmer for a different version of "New Left Liberations: The Poetics, Praxis and Politics of Youth" and the University of Toronto Press which published "Canada's 1960s: Ironies of Identity in a Rebellious Era" (2009). Also to the Canadian Historical Review (June 2009) for premission to reprint "They Smell Bad, Have Diseases and are Lazy: RCMP Officers' Reporting on the Hippies in the Late Sixties" by Marcel Martel.

Cover image: RCMP officer at Expo 67, Montreal.
Copyright: National Archives of Canada.

BLACK ROSE BOOKS

C.P. 1258	2250 Military Road	99 Wallis Road
Succ. Place du Parc	Tonawanda, NY	London, E9 5LN
Montréal, H2X 4A7	14150	England
Canada	USA	UK

To order books:

In Canada: (phone) 1-800-565-9523 (fax) 1-800-221-9985

email: utpbooks@utpress.utoronto.ca

In the United States: (phone) 1-800-283-3572 (fax) 1-800-351-5073

In the UK & Europe: (phone) 44 (0)20 8986-4854 (fax) 44 (0)20 8533-5821

email: order@centralbooks.com

Our Web Site address: http://www.blackrosebooks.net

Printed in Canada

Table of Contents

Preface

This spring a spate of new books have been published complaining that democracy in Canada is in deep crisis. Surprise, surprise. The subject matter of current concerns range from the centralization of power in the office of the Prime Minister, the marginalization of parliament, the defects of the current electoral system, which elects political minorities to rule like majorities, and recognizing political parties as instruments first and foremost aiming at power, and the shutting out of electors in between elections. All the more reason to turn our attention to the 1960s in Canada and to study what happened and why.

Recall that early in the decade the new radicals here and elsewhere had concluded that liberal democracy was in crisis and referred to it as a "consenting democracy." They had concluded that the dominate political institutions throughout society had lost legitimacy. Instead, the new radicals moved boldly away from all centralization of power and called for a participatory democracy. "All power to the people," became the rallying cry of that decade. They practiced new forms of democracy in the movement on a daily basis, while mainstream society and its main political and economic interests looked on nervously, thinking hard of how this movement was to be sidetracked.

Participatory democracy was, and is, the enduring legacy of the sixties.[1] Its impact was such that at meetings of the Trilateral Commission it was clearly stated that too much accommodation and too much democracy had been given over to citizens, and these changes, large or small, had to be clawed back.[2] The new radicals raised the level of social criticism and research in Canada beyond previous generations, especially before and after the 1930s. All forms of authoritarianism were confronted. A popular badge activists wore read "Question Authority." Corporate liberalism was demystified, while social democracy was found wanting.

It is difficult to recall the early sixties in mood and style. It was an intense period of considerable experimentation in almost every way, hence the "New," in New Left. The sterility of the Old Left encouraged the New Left to open up questions of both theory and look in a fresh undogmatic matter at "Root and Branch," as one magazine was named. Radicalism was taken to mean going to the root of a problem, and avoiding patchwork. When unemployment was discussed the very nature of work was questioned. When class was debated the whole range of youth as an agency for social change was raised. When the crisis of the urban question was placed on the agenda, the relationship between town and country was posed, as was the moral bankruptcy of capitalism, which let loose the ravaging real estate industry and its unqualified promotion of suburbia.

Empire was a major focus of the new radicals, with the dismantling of the U.S. and Soviet power blocks in favour of a third non-aligned association of countries as a goal. In all of these branches of concern, the root cause was thought to be the impotence of our worn-out political institution: the State. What has also not been grasped by enough researchers was, that in Canada, there were three and a half centres of action and intellectual activity. There was Montreal, where it all began, which was very much absorbed by the Left-wing nationalism of the day, with added influences from Britain, France, Germany, Italy and the U.S., with their many schools of thought and grassroots activism, all mixed into the a cultural and political mortar. There was Toronto, with offshoots in surrounding cities, and Kingston was very much influenced by Left-liberalism melded with the instincts of the Old Left and drew from the civil rights movement. There was also Saskatchewan, with its deep-seated CCF/NDP foundations, from which there were attempts at leftwards breakthroughs, and finally the social democratic tendency in Vancouver.

Each one of these centres, more oftentimes than not, analysed reality and its major problems differently. Given these different backgrounds and contexts, and in spite of and because of them, there were noble efforts to hold the movement together in a forward direction.

To those who do not look at the record carefully enough, it is simply wrong to say that the New Left had no programme, but simply a string of assertions. What the New Left was not was a political party or faction. It was a movement, a form that is difficult to understand today given the social fragmentation. The programmatic approach began as early was 1959, with significant policy proposals for new directions in Canadian foreign policy. This then matured into major overviews, manifestos if you will, reflected in a number of books and journals.[3]

Researchers have to search beyond the inadequate and incomplete archival material currently found in the McMaster University collection in Hamilton, Ontario, which has excluded material from the early part of the decade, and which has not sought out the contributions and writings of many veterans who are still about.

The Queen's University interdisciplinary conference in 2007, "New World Coming: The Sixties and the Shaping of Global Consciousness," was an imaginative and corrective experience. Canada has matured as an industrial/technological society to be sure, but the Left in this sub-continent of a country has yet to bring itself together even in a common forum of conversation, discussion and debate. While almost every country and continent on the planet has brought thousands together under the umbrella "Another world is possible" in response to the machinations of the World Trade Organisation, International Monetary Fund, and the annual Davos World Economic Forum, to date, no alternative has been dared in English-speaking Canada. Five thousand people gathered from across the province in last year's Quebec Social Forum, and many hundreds have gathered in five Citizen Summits on the future of Montreal. Activists are busy organising a new social forum in the fall. It is a common understanding here that isolation, fragmentation, must be overcome if alienation and cynicism is to be turned around. Let's not stop trying, the activists here insist. Hence the importance of this anthology.

Regarding solid scholarship, the investigation of what constituted the movement of the Sixties is crucial to any renewal of both theory and practice. Yet Canada has lagged behind in this work. The volume of investigations on the Sixties that has been, and continues to be, written and published annually in the U.S., Britain, France, Germany and Italy is simply amazing. Indeed, the quantity is hard to understand. In Canada, by comparison, the intellectual productivity has been minor, and this is not because comparable social and political actions did not take place in this country, a popular and self-fulfilling media assertion. A new generation of scholars have come forward with a real passion to dig up the roots of the movement and history in Canada. We can only open ourselves to this much-needed fresh air, and call out to them and others, that more is needed. We must remind all of that well-proven maxim, that at all times, grassroots social and political action for basic change will season research.

Dimitri Roussopoulos
Montreal, August 2009

Notes

1 *The Case for Participatory Democracy: Some Prospects for a Radical Society*, C.George Benello and Dimitri Roussopoulos, editors, Grossman Publishers, New York, 1969, and Vintage, New York, 1971. The first such book on participatory democracy. Revised edition, *Participatory Democracy: Prospects for Democratizing Democracy*, Dimitrios Roussopoulos, C.George Benello, editors, Black Rose Books, 2005.

2 *Trilateralism: The Trilateral Commission and the Elite Planning for World Management*, Holly Sklar, editor, Black Rose Books, 1980.

3 *The New Left in Canada*, Dimitri Roussopoulos, editor, Black Rose Books, 1970. Includes essays analyzing activism in every part of Canada, except Atlantic Canada, where the commissioned essay was interrupted. The book concludes with a sweeping overview, "Towards a Revolutionary Youth Movement and an Extra-Parliamentary Opposition in Canada." The publication of this book, originally contracted by a major Toronto publisher, was followed by country-wide speaking engagements. *Canada and Radical Social Change*, Dimitri Roussopoulos, editor, Black Rose Books, 1973. Includes the definitive critique of Canadian social democracy and moves on with several seminal essays including "Democracy and Parliamentary Politics" by Gerry Hunnius and concludes with a new formulation of the manifesto on an "Extra-Parliamentary Opposition." Also contributing to this anthology, amongst others, are James Laxer and Arthur Pape, George Grant, Mel Watkins, and Philip Resnick. Not listed here are the many programmatic articles in *Our Generation*, one of the leading international New Left journals, published in Montreal, 1961-1994. Not to be ignored is Myrna Kostash's book which also attempts a credible perspective for the future.

Introduction

As a member of a new generation of researcher/activist interested in the 1960s, I was invited by Black Rose Books to bring together this selected anthology. It is refreshing to acknowledge the level of interest in this decade, from its inception to its enduring impact on Canadian history.

There is now a growing critical literature, which is welcome, but much remains to be done. There is original work in this book. Some of it was presented for the first time at the Queen's University Conference on the Sixties, but some essays are also original to this book.

The archival material in Canadian university libraries, major public libraries and the National Library in Ottawa are tragically sparse. The large archives of the RCMP, the federal police, and some provincial police, are notoriously unreliable. The educational level, and particularly the political education, of the spies and infiltrators were so low that their reports are hilarious in their inaccuracies. When one compares this reporting with that of the French police in Paris on the mid- to late-19th century on the emerging French Left, the Canadian effort is wanting by far. The volume of these police reports nevertheless is evidence that a great deal was in fact going on in Canada, and international police records also show that the influence of the Canadian New Left was considered important and that it had an impact both in Western Europe and the U.S., particularly through the nuclear disarmament, anti-war and human rights movements.

To follow the role of the young Canadians in helping to organize the first non-aligned, independent international federation of peace organisations to counter the political machines of the pro-Soviet World Peace Council and its U.S. equivalents is fascinating. To read, for example, of the international meetings held in Ljubljana, in August of 1968, around the time of Warsaw Pact invasion of Czechoslovakia and the planned actions to help the resisters of the military occupation and to organize international solidarity is impressive. How many researchers know that the Canadian New Left organised strategic meetings between the Students for a Democartic Society (SDS) in West Germany, the SDS in the U.S., and others. I have come across little on these connections in Canada, but found material in the Geneva archives of the International Peace Bureau. All this, and much more, has to be mined for historical insights and for publication.

Myrna Kostash has correctly complained that unlike New Left activists in other countries, the Canadians have, on the whole, been silent. True, many of them have become part of the mainstream, but this alone should not prevent them from writing and publishing. Do we have to simply settle for extensive interviews with some of them? These people are not illiterates. Where are the biographies, autobiographies, memoirs, histories, by the key activists, or even those activists at large? Why the silence? Where are the writings on the Sixties by Anthony Hyde, Mike Rowan, Heather Dean, Liora Proctor, Cathy Wood, Peggy Morton, Joan Kuyek, Jim Major, Arthur Pape, Peter Boothroyd, Jim Best, Robert and Andre Cardinal, Richard Thompson, Jim Harding, Rocky Jones, Pat Uhl, Dennis McDermott, Clayton Ruby, Judy Pocock, Ken Druska, Nick Ternette, Harvey Shepard, Elsa Cohen, Stan Gray, Doug Ward, to mention a few. The list of key activists is long. Or from others activists in the Sixties who were not formally connected to the Combined Universities Campaign for Nuclear Disarmament (CUCND) and the Student Union for Peace Action (SUPA). Many of these people are now in their late fifties and sixties. We have to wake them up to their obligations to us and to Canadian history. We, the new generation of researchers, are hungry. Some of the veterans are no longer amongst us: Jim Jones, Anne-Marie Hill, Alan Marks, Henry Tarvienen and Matt Cohen.

This anthology has some very outstanding essays. The contribution of Myrna Kostash is a lament for a generation that did not, and does not, take seriously enough reflection and introspection. The contribution of Michael Maurice Dufresne provides new research, especially in the early emergence of the movement, and contains research often missing from the existing literature. The extensive essay by Bryan D. Palmer is a masterpiece by an exemplary historian/activist with an impressive capacity for both research and writing. It appears in a different form in a recently published book, which is extensive. The contribution of Sean Mills is a brilliant piece of original research and analysis, not only filling a large gap in the published literature, but also in the perception of almost all researchers. To understand the complexity and vitality of the movement of ideas and action in an important city like Montreal, with several political and ethnic languages, is truly impressive.

The essay by Marcel Martel, which also appeared in an academic journal after it was presented at the aforementioned Queen's University conference, highlights, in an impressive manner, how the State security apparatus in Canada understood and misunderstood the movement. John Cleveland brings forcefully to the fore a major campus uprising with widespread ramifications, which he ably demonstrates as an important a rebellion as many other student revolts in other countries. Kevin Brushett's essay on the Company of Young Canadians fills in some of gaps in Margaret Daly's book *The Revolution Game*, which is an incomplete story with serious omissions and factual errors. One insight has to be made, in retrospect, which is that the history of the New Left in Canada would have been entirely different—so different, in fact, that it is impossible even to guess where radicalism in this country might be now—if the Student Union for Peace Action had not been split down the middle over whether to cooperate with this government initiative. Who knows what sort of independent New Left might have developed by maintaining a critical or outright anti-Statist position. Instead, there is still no New Left movement today.

The essays by Kristin Ireland, Pat Smart, Gillian Helfield, Chris Harris and Eric Morton represent new research in various untapped areas of the impact of the Sixties. In revealing the impact of this extraordinary decade on Canadian society, each point of view is unique. Bu there is so much more to examine. The challenge is not only to cover the full range of events and issues, but also to keep in mind the deep differences of how various parts of Canada took up the goals of the new radicals.

What was the effect of all this activity on the mainstream student movement? The impact on high school students? The Sir George Williams University uprising had international echoes among black communities as far away as the Caribbean islands. McGill University, and the assault on it by Francophone nationalists with the Anglophone Left-wing allies, is an interesting case study also. The consequences on vocational education and the Glendon College affair are to be noted. The rise and fall of student syndicalism emerging in Quebec, how it was articulated in the rest of Canada and the U.S., is a fascinating subject: so are the Forest Hill student protest, from April/May 1969, to the protests in Newfoundland high schools from teacher colleges, to Cecile Rhodes and R.B. Russell Vocation School in Winnipeg.

The seeds of women's liberation in the late Sixties in Canada is worthy of a major study, to say nothing of the impact of the Sixties on the labour movement —another subject of considerable importance.

To gauge the impact of the counter-culture as it reached well beyond student youth would be a major study. Fifteen hundred workers at Ottawa's Civic Hospital voted by secret ballot to reject the recommended contract settlement proposed by their bargaining committee; the United Steelworkers staged a four-month strike against the Steel Company of Canada, in 1969, after rejecting a settlement recommended by their negotiating team; B.C. longshoremen, in the winter of 1969-70, rejected three separate recommended settlements that kept them on the picket line for a total of ten weeks. One observer estimated that one out of every seven collective agreements was overthrown by union members despite recommendations from the union leadership to accept them because of rising expectations among an increasingly militant number of younger workers influenced by the debate and actions in society as a whole. A seasoned unionist further observed, "

> These young workers are using contract rejection as means of repudiating what they consider are the injustices of the workplace and of their unions. We hear a lot these days about the generation gap: it exists between parents and children; between teachers and pupils; between the adult establishment and youth culture. But there is also a generation gap in the labour movement.[1]

The scope of the Sixties was much wider than is generally thought. Canada is no exception and lazy journalists who cut and paste nostalgic comments are not to be taken seriously. For the new generation of researchers, much more remains to be investigated from any number of angles. Hopefully this book helps this process along. We need to know more.

M. Athena Palaeologu

Note
1 *The Labour Gazette*, page 722, November 1971.

Notes on the Contributors

KEVIN BRUSHETT is a professor of history at the Royal Military College of Canada where he teaches courses in the social, political, and foreign relations history of both Canada and the United States. He has published in the area of Canadian urban and social history in the post World War II period. He is currently working on a history of the Company of Young Canadians, a program sponsored by the Pearson government, in 1965, to promote community development as part of Canada's "War on Poverty."

JOHN W. CLEVELAND, PhD, teaches social justice oriented Sociology courses at Thompson Rivers University. An activist in a series of 1960s groups including SUPA, Simon Fraser SDU, the Western Voice and En Lutte, he is currently writing a book on the English Canada student movement. He will use his 2010 sabbatical and a wiki-type web site to get former members of the main 1960s and 1970s groups to share in writing interpretative histories of their former groups.

MICHAEL MAURICE DUFRESNE studied history at Carleton University and did extensive research on the 1960s, conducting interviews with several of the principal activists. He entered the PhD programme in history at Queen's University, but decided not to complete this academic work, choosing instead to work as a writer and editor. Currently, he is working at Library and Archives Canada, in Ottawa.

BARBARA GODARD, Historica Chair of Canadian Literature Emerita of York University, studied at the Universities of Toronto, Montreal and Paris during the 1960s. She has translated a number of Quebec writers and written widely on Canadian and Quebec culture. Her most recent book is *Canadian Literature at the Crossroads of Language and Culture* (2008).

CHRIS HARRIS is a doctoral candidate in the Department of Sociology and Equity Studies in Education, Ontario Institute for Studies in Education, University of Toronto (SESE, OISE/UT). Harris is also a longtime organizer in Toronto who has worked with the Black Action Defense Committee (BADC) for eight years. As the program director at BADC, Harris currently facilitates anti-racist youth leadership training and hip hop healing arts therapy with street-involved youth in gangs in the west end of Toronto. Harris also works closely with BADC elders and former leaders in the Canadian Black Power movement (Dudley Laws, Norman "Otis" Richmond) to engage BADC youth activists in inter-generational learning for anti-racist change.

GILLIAN HELFIELD is a lecturer specializing in Film and Television Studies at York University in Toronto. Her PhD, which she received from the University of Warwick in the UK, was on the topic of Quebecois films of the Quiet Revolution, and she has written extensively on this subject. She is the author of *Representing the Rural: Space, Place and Identity in Films about the Land*. Prior to embarking on a full-time teaching career, Dr. Helfield worked in the Canadian film and television industry as a free-lance production coordinator and production manager.

ANNA HOEFNAGELS is an Assistant Professor of Music in Carleton University's School for Studies in Art and Culture. She has trained as an ethnomusicologist, completing her PhD at York University. She has published in *The Canadian Journal for Traditional Music*, and *Ethnologies*, and she contributed to, and co-edited *Folk Music, Traditional Music, Ethnomusicology: Canadian Perspectives, Past and Present* with Gordon Smith.

MYRNA KOSTASH is a Canadian writer and journalist who has written for many magazines including *Chatelaine*. She is a founding member of the Periodical Writers' Association of Canada and of the Writers' Guild of Alberta and has served as Chair of the Writers' Union of Canada. Kostash is the recipient of several awards. She is the author of *Long Way From Home: The Story of the Sixties Generation in Canada*.

MARCEL MARTEL is an Associate Professor and holder of the Avie Bennett Historica Chair in Canadian History at York University. A specialist of twentieth century Canada, he has published on nationalism, public policy and counterculture. His recent publications include *Not This Time: Canadians, Public Policy and the Marijuana Question, 1961-1975* (University of Toronto, 2006), with Yves Frenette and John Willis, and with Martin Pâquet, *Légiférer en matière linguistique* (Presses de l'Université Laval et CEFAN, 2008).

SEAN MILLS is currently a postdoctoral fellow at New York University, and holds an MA from McGill University and a PhD from Queen's University. He has published many articles on Quebec and Canadian history, and is co-editor of the forthcoming collection, *New World Coming: The Sixties and the Shaping of Global Consciousness*.

ERIN MORTON is an Assistant Professor in the History of Visual Culture at the University of New Brunswick. She recently completed her PhD in Visual and Material Culture Studies in the Department of Art at Queen's University. Her research examines the intersection of public history with visual culture, tourism, and processes of folklorization in Maritime Canada.

M. ATHENA PALAEOLOGU is a researcher on the Sixties internationally, with a particular interest in Canada. She has participated actively in the international meetings of the European Social Forum and in all the meetings of the World Social Forum and holds a PhD in cultural studies.

BRYAN D. PALMER, PhD, is the Canada Research Chair, Canadian Studies, Trent University, Peterborough. His areas of specialization are labour and social history, and he edits the journal *Labour/Le Travail*. His most recent book, *Canada's 1960s: The Ironies of Identity in a Rebellious Era*, was published by University of Toronto Press in 2009.

DIMITRI ROUSSOPOULOS is the author and/or editor of some eighteen books including *The Public Place* (1999), *Participatory Democracy* (2004), *The New Left* (2007) and *The Rise of Cities* (2009). He continues to work for urban democracy, ecological cities and world peace.

PATRICIA SMART is a Distinguished Research Professor of French at Carleton University, and the author of many books on Quebec literature, art and culture. Her feminist study of Quebec literature, *Écrire dans la maison du Père,* won the Governor General's Award for 1988 and her translation of it, *Writing in the Father's House: The Emergence of the Feminine in the Quebec Literary Tradition* was awarded the Gabrielle Roy Prize of the Association for Canadian and Quebec Literatures. She was an editor of *Canadian Forum* from 1989 to 1998, was elected to the Royal Society of Canada in 1991, and became a member of the Order of Canada in 2004.

Myrna Kostash

<table>
<tr><td>Chapter</td><td rowspan="2">*1*</td><td>Killing Me Softly</td></tr>
</table>

I

When my book, *Long Way From Home: The Story of the Sixties Generation in Canada* was published (by James Lorimer & Co.) in 1980, it provoked a flurry of disdain, scorn and denunciation from the mainstream press, and virtually no reaction from the Left.

I had steeled myself for the former but I was utterly unprepared for the latter.

The book opened with CUCND's march for nuclear disarmament in 1959, the first student demonstration in Canada since the end of the Second World War, and closed with the War Measures Act of 1970 and the collapse of the New Left Caucus; between these dates, the chapters covered *inter alia* student power, anti-war campaigns and draft resistance, hippie culture, Red and Black Power, the rise of Women's Liberation, and anti-colonialist struggle in Quebec. Schooled in the New Journalism, I made no pretence of "objectivity" but wrote a kind of full-tilt boogie prose which, admittedly, fit awkwardly with sober patches of analysis. As Ted Allan, for the *Winnipeg Free Press*, described my style, not unfairly: "It's by turn passionate, clumsy, comprehensive, inflated, zealous, hyperbolic and unequivocal." As it turned out, it had some few admirers.

I had told myself that I was writing this book "for" the English-Canadian Left; I fancied myself a bit of a heroine for having taken the trouble to launch this vividly-romantic but not uncritical history on the cusp of international Thatcher-Mulroney-Reaganism; and, considering that no one else in Canada—least of all the Left's own loquacious avant-garde—had yet bothered to write anything like as sweeping as *Long Way From Home,* I felt justified in expecting an enthusiastic response, or at least a warm welcome. Of course, I also girded myself for the inevitable critical appraisal of my arguments from activists, even those whom I had interviewed, who had been far more engaged in the New Left's *praxis* than I had been. Truth be told, I was always a more convincing hippy than Leftist activist (feminism was to change that).

II

"Publishing," said Marshall McLuhan, "is the self-invasion of privacy," and bad reviews were hanging out there for the world to see.

The *Winnipeg Free Press*, rather wittily describing me as an "auto-anthropologist picking over the navel lint of the 'Sixties," found the book "ineffably dull" with "hardened arteries." The Sarnia *Observer* also took me to task for "navel-gazing," and for vilifying "Anglo-Saxons," and producing "the nostalgic musings of a middle-aged revolutionary." (I was thirty-six.) The reviewer was deeply offended by the fact that I had received a grant from the Canada Council. "But she expresses no compunctions about tapping Establishment assistance for her opus—which might better have been compacted for compost." The reviewer at the *Ottawa Citizen* found the book "sometimes shallow and often breathless in tone. *Maclean's* hated how I ladled out the "leftist hagiographical hooey in syrupy globs" about the era's "tarnished icons," "dogmatic adolescents," and "LSD pillow talk": "If memories are made of this, let's forget the Sixties." The *Globe and Mail* ran a derisory review across the top of the book section—I imagined hundreds of thousands of Canadians reading and smirking—so mean-spirited that I never kept a copy of it and don't have one now.

The publisher sent me on a promotional tour. I kept notes. In Toronto, interviewed at CITY-TV and transformed by make-up, I shared the program "You're Beautiful" with two older women who were teaching Women's Studies somewhere; one of them declared the Sixties was "American" and "just a bunch of spoiled middle-class kids having a temper tantrum." At CHFI radio, the interviewer wanted to know "what happened after we lost Camelot?" *We*? The interviewer for the *Ryersonian* asked me what sort of childhood I had had and what the women's movement had "accomplished." I sold one book at a book-signing table at York University. In a Canadian Literature class at St Michael's College at the University of Toronto, a student challenged me to defend myself: "How can you talk about an anti-war movement when thousands of babies are being aborted every year?" I skated around this by firing off a dazzling rap about the need to integrate the questions of production and reproduction.

In Winnipeg, a freelance contributor to CBC Radio came to a party some friends threw in my honour, and went around the room with the question: "Did you protest in the Sixties?" The artist Esther Warkov: "Against what?" The artist Ted Howorth: "I was involved in one protest but I don't remember what it was about. We all went down to the Legislature but I don't remember why." Melinda McCracken, writer: "I didn't protest but I was involved in the music end of it. The coffee house was a centre for protest. A lot of runaway kids ran away to this coffee house." A CBC news reporter, Judy Waytiuk, remembered a protest at the University of Manitoba: "We ran a ring of cars around the administration building because the professors had parking spots close to the building and the students didn't." The bookstore owner, John Oleksiuk, was "never involved in any protest at all." But the printmaker Bill Lobchuk was, once: "It was the first time tuition fees had gone up and we were all standing around in the Rotunda of the Legislature building. The protest organizers demanded to see the Education minister, who refused to come out. Our guys said: 'Well, I guess that's it. Let's go home.' I couldn't believe it. We had a march down the streets, we had had a rally, and now we were all just going to go home? I figured if that's the level of protest at this campus, we're in a lot of trouble."

"To fit the occasion," the reporter went on, "music tapes filled the room with *You Can't Always Get What You Want, The Eve of Destruction,* and *Sounds of Silence.* The hostess had baked a carrot cake and decorated it with the peace symbol: brown icing on white. She brought it into the living room and ceremoniously gave it to Myrna to cut. Everybody tried to sing *We Shall Overcome* but nobody could remember the words."

In Calgary, the *Herald* wanted to know my position on federalism, and the *Sun*—a young woman who had missed the whole thing—whether there was anything left of the Sixties. To a full-house of students at Nelson's David Thompson University Centre I read from my chapter on the war in Vietnam; "Isn't it true," one of them asked, "that all the radicals have become chartered accountants?" In Vancouver, the photographer for the *Sun* wanted me to look "tough," "just like the Sixties." A live television appearance with the legendary Jack Webster, host and curmudgeon, made me anxious. He had "mellowed," I was assured, and he did indeed treat the guests who preceded me with gruff deference—a Social Credit cabinet minister, a senior bureaucrat, and Duke Redbird, Metis poet and social activist. But, having admitted he hadn't "really" read my book, he let loose a stream of abuse about the Sixties as an era of deadbeats, drug casualties, broken families, and anti-growth anti-capitalists. I was also unaccountably interviewed at a heavy metal FM station where neither Bob Dylan nor Gordon Lightfoot dared speak their names.

In Regina, not a single interviewer asked a question about the extraordinary role played by Saskatchewan activists in the New Left and NDP, and all the callers to a phone-in radio show, with one exception, hated the Sixties, holding the era's "Marxist-Leninist malarkey" responsible for all ills, including the rise in the crime rate, rampant VD, and lack of labour discipline. The exception was a Native man, who called the Sixties a "right-on decade." (Later in the afternoon, at a book-signing, I noticed a

Native man—perhaps my caller—hovering about a stack of my books at the cash register, and I felt an acute pang about the $17.95 price tag.) Invited to address a first year Political Science class at the University of Regina who were studying Canadian Government, I was confronted by students all seated in a pack by the doorway (for a quick getaway?) who returned my increasingly frantic "rap" about the Canadian Sixties with unblinking stares of complete blankness. I was unnerved, as though all the grievances behind the demands for Student Power of fifteen years earlier had come to roost again at the front of this classroom where it was now *I* who stood in solitary authority, and the "alienation" and "impersonality" of the university classroom took on an awful concreteness in that collective blankness. Actually, explained the professor, they weren't blank at all, they were all "stunned." An old radical himself, he had tears in his eyes.

By the time I "did" Edmonton, my home town, the questions and my answers had become predictable. And the questions did not necessarily derive from a reading of the book; reading the jacket copy would do. Where are all the radicals now? Why were the 1970s so apathetic? How were the Canadian Sixties different from the American? Why should hippies get government hand-outs?

At the end of the tour, and with the reviews all in, I may be forgiven for wondering if I had hallucinated the Sixties, at least as I had described them. Everyone else's "Sixties" seemed to be, at best, an occasion for rueful nostalgia, at worst a period of self-indulgent, anti-social, perverse, drug-addled and long-haired conspiracy against Western civilization. Thus, there were only two possible stances toward the era from the vantage point of 1980: misty-eyed reminiscence of one's wild, irretrievable youth; sarcastic, even hostile, dismissal of its agenda. No one, it seemed, took the Sixties seriously anymore.

I fought back for awhile. In *Alberta Magazine* I reminded readers of what had happened in just one year, 1969-70, in just one place, the University of Alberta:

> ...women run for student council office on a platform to 'end the brutal suppression of women as second-class citizens.' Two radical sociology professors are denied tenure and the Students for a Democratic University (SDU) raises a hullabaloo. A German new leftist visits; the posters announce: 'Humanity will not be free until the last capitalist is hanged with the innards of the last bureaucrat.' A united front of SDU, the Student Christian Movement, Maoists and freelance leftists protests the existence of the 'fascist' Law and Order (Disciplinary) Committee...The students'

council sponsors a teach-in on the American domination of Canada and Walter Gordon, Robin Mathews and Mel Watkins are there. You can hear a pin drop when Watkins says: 'Even if it could be done, it hardly seems worth the effort to build an independent capitalist Canada. The U.S. has given that option a bad name.'

This was nothing if not serious business.

In *Today* weekend magazine, I made the case for viewing the Sixties as unfinished business, in "lifestyle," the arts, the status of women, politics, Native land claims, the environment: "Do we let the economic despair and social nastiness of the '80s win the day, or do we keep the promise of the '60s?"

I would not have sounded so plaintive had I had the "left" in my corner. But the men and women of the organized New Left had gone MIA.

Only the people around *Our Generation* rallied around the book—I remember a friendly gathering at Black Rose bookstore—and, except for Duncan Cameron of the University of Ottawa who put up a spirited albeit unpublished defense in a letter to the *Globe & Mail,* no one on the Left came publicly to my defense as all the hostile notices arrived. Even the people I had interviewed remained silent as to my work's importance. This was completely bewildering to me. As I explained to the *Ottawa Citizen*, I believed that each one of my chapters could be expanded as a whole book, and I fully expected an entire bibliography of books about Canada in the 1960s to follow on my heels, by the people who themselves had fashioned it on the left. Instead, the immediate response was silence, which I could only interpret as indifference, if not disapproval, as if I were being chastized for something I was in the dark about. In following years, the book was never referred to in any Left forum that I was aware of nor included in any syllabi—although I was delighted to discover that a copy in Trent University's library was heavily marked with enthusiastic exclamation marks in orange marker pen—and technically it remains in print, although I've never earned out my modest advance.

For more than twenty-five years, I carried a mixed burden of shame and anger at this outcome. I shelved *Long Way From Home* and filed away all the papers bearing on it, and left them to moulder. I fled to Greece several winters in a row—they had just elected a social democratic government after decades of a junta and a right-wing party—where I set myself the task of trying to write a different kind of book henceforth, experiments in what is now called creative non-fiction. Then I began several years of travel in Eastern Bloc countries, displacing onto the Generation of '68 in Warsaw, Prague and Belgrade the unrequited love for my "comrades" back in Canada.

Then, in 2005, a quarter-century after the publication of *Long Way From Home*, the Queen's University historian, Ian McKay, published a fine little book, *Rebels, Reds, Radicals: Rethinking Canada's Left History*, and I was flabbergasted, and delighted, to read there that, in the opinion of this scholar almost a whole generation younger then me, my book is "an eloquent, underrated study of the radical 1960s in English Canada," and "indispensable." In 2007 I was invited to take part in the international conference at Queen's, "New World Coming: Canada and Global Consciousness"; and that year I also received a royalty cheque for sales of *Long Way From Home*, the first such, in twenty-seven years.

III

This was not the end of the surprises. In a phenomenon well-known to artists, because bad reviews are the only ones, deep in our hearts, we believe, only the bad reviews stick. And so it turned out that, on rereading all the reviews in preparation for the Queen's conference, I discovered that I had completely forgotten that my book had had its admirers. I had forgotten that June Callwood, for example, was a fan, writing in the *Edmonton Journal* that

> ... those [the '60s] were lively, lovely times ... there was prevailing decency, joy, democracy and ceaseless commitment to destroy Ghandi's old enemies, 'injustice, untruth, and humbug.' Myrna Kostash ends her tough, definitive, marvellous book with a memorable line: 'We should be so ridiculous again.' Soon, I hope.

And in Toronto's feminist paper, *Broadside,* Susan Cole concluded a long review essay, "Where have all the flowers gone?" with this assessment:

> But whether the actual political activity of the sixties was more than a brief spasm of outrage remains to be seen. I for one do not share Myrna Kostash's optimism concerning our generation. But you have to love her for the fact that she still believes.

Elsewhere, the book was judged "profoundly moving at times," "conclusive and worthwhile...a must for anyone mildly interested in recent political movements," "fascinating, well-researched," a "valuable social record," written with "flinty righteousness that is hard-earned," "an encyclopaedic review destined to become a classic." Some were overtly partisan:

> The reviews of Kostash's book to date have often been so unnecessarily negative in tone that one suspects many of the commercial media types have

vested interests for denouncing any book which suggests there were indeed some constructive and ongoing lessons to be taken from that period.

Finally, some were in deep identification with the subject: "In the end, the 60s changed the common coin of our lives...We are all changed."

At the *Montreal Gazette* the novelist Michael Dorland (identified as the author of *The Assassination of Leon Trotsky*) wrote of the Sixties that

> ...for the first time in a good long time, youth stopped acting like the jerks they are and said NO...Such beautiful presumption, such unmitigated gall...In *A Long Way From Home* Kostash has tried to keep that special 1960s spirit alive by blowing on the ashes...the alternative is living death.

And from another review, balm to a writer's esteem: "I stayed up late to finish it."

I now have a more balanced view of the fate of my book, but one answer still hangs over it: why did the Canadian Left ignore it?

In *Rebels, Reds, Radicals*, Ian McKay noted in one of his compendious footnotes that "remarkably we still lack in Canada one historical monograph that could be placed with confidence alongside [American and British] titles." And there precisely lay my problem, even back in 1977–9 when I was researching my book.

I had received a Canada Council grant for what was supposed to be essentially a literary project: a composite study, in the style of the New Journalism, of characters in the Canadian "movement." This bore faint resemblance to the book I eventually wrote. That literary project was sabotaged by the fact that, to my dismay and consternation, the secondary sources which I hoped to consult as preparation for my own project had not been written. Or barely. I mean the historical monograph(s) but also the memoirs, the biographies, the critical deconstructions, the correspondence, the celebratory memorabilia, that were issuing non-stop from British and American and French writers and activists. (What a treasure-trove *Rolling Stone's* oversize photo essay on the 1960s proved to be, just as a 'for instance.') Well, there were a few things, and several anthologies (along with Dimitri Roussopoulos, I often think of Canadian intellectuals being particularly susceptible to *anthologitis*, an inflammation of the organ of self-doubt) but there wasn't nearly enough for me to rely on as a "mere" writer who had not been much of an activist until the women's liberation movement but rather a sympathising hippy who had been "stoned" then politicized by two years in the USA, 1965–7.

The point is that I found myself having to do primary research—interviewing former activists, screening old TV footage, rescuing mildewed journals from basements, reconstructing events from the hodgepodge of people's disorganized files—because none of these glorious veterans, these "rebels, Reds and radicals," had sat down to write a comprehensive account of their own experience and their critique of it. (And they never have: where are the memoirs by Peter Boothroyd, Clay Ruby, Danny Drache, Marjaleena Repo, Jim Harding, Dimitri Roussopoulos, Judy Rebick…?) I felt, perhaps wrongly, that *I* somehow had to do it, when in fact I was ill-equipped to do so; that *I* had to assimilate all the disparate materials into a coherent political project as well as serve my original literary purpose.

Nor was it noticed among the literati. But this was less of a shock, as nonfiction in Canada has been decidedly déclassé. And, besides, I had abandoned my original project in order to write a political history that ended by overwhelming it. (In retrospect, I can see that there were other problems: my publisher should have sent the manuscript back to me for a rewrite, as one of its early readers, Patrick Watson, urged me to do, warning me the reviewers were going to hate it, as indeed some did, for its tortured phrasings as much as for its politics: instead, Lorimer glibly dismissed my fears with a "even bad reviews are publicity," which is a cruel deception foisted on writers by publishers who are already thinking about the next season's list.)

In fairness, by the time of the book's publication in the Fall of 1980, many true believers on the Left were full of skepticism and weariness about the romance of the '60s in the face of recession, unemployment, police repression and the looming struggle against Free Trade, and those who remained optimistic had hived off into the women's and gay liberation movements and the nascent environmentalism of the 1970s. Students, it had turned out, were not a revolutionary class: "The absolute last thing that the 1960s were was a crisis of capitalism," as one correspondent put it. Perhaps the potential lay in marginalized, diasporic, racialized subalterns?

I was a female writer from Alberta who had not been a Movement person-of-consequence, a freelance writer not a scholar. Eventually, word reached me that, among some of the men of the New Left, there had indeed been a reaction: "Who the hell does Kostash think she is?" Was this a fight over political memory? They would not grant my book the dignity of a response by writing their own accounts. Perhaps this was the rub: I had written a book and they hadn't.

Now in the early twenty-first century there is a whole library of books about Canada since the 1960s, many of them written by Sixties activists, but their own life and times as youthful "rebels, Reds and radicals" remain unexamined. It's the next generation that will have the last word.

Michael Maurice Dufresne

Chapter		"Let's Not Be Cremated Equal:"

Chapter 2

"Let's Not Be Cremated Equal:"
The Combined Universities Campaign
for Nuclear Disarmament 1959-1967

Introduction: The "Great Awakening," Eh?

The similarity of ideas and programs of the 1960s student movement in Canada and the United States has been widely remarked upon. The danger, however, is that the historical experience of Canadian students may be obscured or even lost in the recognition of the transnational existence and character of the movement. In the United States, for example, the struggle for the civil rights of Blacks may have been the most important issue effecting the "Great Awakening" of American students.[1] In Canada, however, it may have been the Diefenbaker government's decision to acquire from the United States the Bomarc B nuclear missile.[2] It was announced in early 1959 and was intended as a defence against Soviet planes flying over the Canadian north. The Americans were to supply the missiles, and the Canadian government was to build two bases: one in North Bay, Ontario, and the other in La Macaza, Quebec. On Christmas Day 1959, students marched on Parliament Hill for the first time since the end of the Second World War. They were members of three university chapters of the Combined Universities Campaign for Nuclear Disarmament (CUCND); in about a years time they expanded membership to include universities from across the country.

Hence, the origins and development of the Canadian student movement must be squarely placed in a domestic context if we are to understand its specific character. In a prominent textbook account, we are told that it was a time in which mass participation in politics was highly valued. Reflecting the tenor of the times the CCF became the New Democratic Party, and the convention theme of all three of the major federal political parties was popular involvement in a process open to everyone. There was "the spirit of public action" and a "willingness to test limits, a thirst to taste what was new."[3] It was in this context, seemingly favourable to grassroots participation, that Canadian peace groups emerged in opposition to the Bomarc. In addition to the CUCND, there was its "adult" counter-part, the National Committee for the Control of Radiation Hazards (NCCRH) that started in 1958; it changed its name in 1960 to the Canadian Campaign for Nuclear Disarmament (CCND). Other groups included, among many others, the Toronto Committee for Disarmament and the Voice of Women, both of which appeared in 1960.

The democratic spirit of the time encouraged the formation of these peace groups and likely created an expectation of their effectiveness in influencing the government's position on nuclear weapons. Coupled with this "democratization" of foreign policy was, as peace workers likely perceived it, the imperious threat of a nuclear war.

Thus the placard seen at many CUCND demonstrations that read "Let's Not Be Cremated Equal." It was a play on a Christian and liberal democratic aphorism and was symbolic of both their right to participate in the process of government and their apocalyptic fears that made the exercise of that right necessary.

Historiography: Neglecting the Contribution and Significance of Canadian Students to the Emergence and Development of a Canadian Student Movement in the Mid-60s

Student participation in the anti-Bomarc campaign between 1959 and 1965 suggests a line of inquiry that is undeveloped in the existing literature. We may ask: What was its significance to the 60s student movement in Canada? The student peace activists in the CUCND predated the more general student politics in Canada that emerged around the middle of the decade. When it changed its name to the Student Union for Peace Action in 1965, it also changed the content of its criticism and multiplied the areas in which they could justifiably express their dissent. It also became the only indigenous and country-wide organization of student activists. To the extent that Canadian experiences have been recognized in the existing literature, they are often considered to be of secondary importance to seminal developments in the United States in the mid-60s. Writers have tended to concentrate on the more visible years of student activism, and have largely ignored the crucial years of the early 60s that led up to a more generalized student movement. The appearance of a multi-issued student movement in the mid-60s cannot be adequately explained without going back to its formative years and examining the emergence and development of students within the peace movement. It was this experience that facilitated the acceptance of a more radical and holistic criticism of Canadian society that would lead to students questioning everything from the nature of the university to the legitimacy of parliamentary democracy. The focus on American influences is partially valid be-

ginning in about 1963; before this time, students in the peace movement were influenced by the British peace campaign. When the ideas taken from the British and
adapted to their Canadian situation failed, students began discussing and applying
ideas first used by American student activists. It was not a passive assimilation of
ideas, as some of the authors seem to imply, but an active and purposive adoption of
ideas to their own crisis. A crisis that, as we shall see, not only facilitated the acceptance of ideas of an American origin but gave a specific meaning to the activism that
would follow.

The literature is limited to three accounts: Cyril Levitt's *Children of Privilege: Student Revolt in the Sixties*, Kenneth Westhues essay, "Intergenerational Conflict in the
Sixties," and Myrna Kostash's, *Long Way From Home: The Story of the Sixties Generation
in Canada*. The fact that the body of literature on the subject is so small may itself be
an indication that the experience of Canadian students in the 60s has been thought
of in transnational terms. In contrast, the corresponding body of work in the United
States on American students has been enormous.

Levitt, a sociologist, argues that the underlying cause of the American, Canadian and German student movements in the 1960s was the "massification" of higher
education, a consequence of the post-Second World War need for trained personnel.
When this occurred, according to Levitt, middle-lass students suffered a sense of betrayal in the knowledge that the massification of the university entailed a loss of elite
positions they had been promised upon graduation. The result was a student protest
movement clothed in an anti-elitist disguise that was in reality, says Levitt, a means
of acquiring positions of influence and power. Thus, a structural change in the relations of production, according to Levitt, was the "crucible" of the student revolt.[4]

The cornerstone of Levitt's research was the interviews he conducted with former student activists. In most cases, the subjects of his interviews served in a leadership capacity from 1965-70. In the very choice of his material he ignored the possible
importance of the early sixties in the aborning student movement. He points uncritically to the 1964 Berkeley Free Speech Movement (FSM) as the starting point of a
"radical politics."[5]

Westhues, also a sociologist, sees the student movement in Canada exclusively
as part of an international phenomenon. He defines the nature of the movement as a
"broad ideology embracing a variety of protests and expressions of collective un-
rest." Specifically, it was a rejection, he wrote, of "industrial capital social orders, of
'establishments' of whatever kind, of the cult of consumer goods, and of the quest for

upward mobility." Participants wanted, according to Westhues, a society without alienation brought about by student control of universities, an end to racism and the war in Vietnam, and a return to nature.[6]

Like Levitt, Westhues gives prominence to a structural explanation for student revolt. First, the opportunity to mobilize the student population had to exist. This occurred with the rapid growth in both countries of the university population, placing students together in a setting that facilitated the communication of discontent and the mobilization of disaffected youth. He writes:

> The physical proximity of students on campuses, their freedom from daily contact with parents, the free time available to students, the availability of places for meetings and rallies, and other attributes of the university setting were all conducive to rapid mobilization of large numbers of students … The youth movement occurred not only because students were discontented but because their social situation was highly conducive to mobilization and gave them easy access to communication mechanisms.[7]

Second, that disaffection was a result, according to Westhues, of new child-rearing practices in upper-middle-class homes in both the United States and Canada. These parents stressed "independence, self-expression, permissiveness and democratic relations," a set of values embodied in the advice literature of American Doctor Spock.[8] Socialized as youth to be autonomous individuals, they met in a university setting that seemed to be treating them as faceless objects processed for industry. The ensuing clash of expectation and experience Westhues has called "institutional deficiency."

For him, the beginning of the movement occurred in the United States with the formation in 1964 of the Student Nonviolent coordinating Committee (SNCC) and the Campus Congress of Racial Equality (CORE). It was chapters of these student organizations, both members of the Free Speech Movement, that fought the administration at the University of California at Berkeley and "ushered in the new era of student revolt."[9]

Home for Kostash, a historian and journalist, is a metaphor for identity. *Long Way from Home: The Story of the Sixties Generation in Canada* is, in part, the story of her changing identity and the role of the decade in effecting that change. She writes,

> I 'came of age' in 1965: I turned twenty-one, and threw myself into the great learning about camaraderie, war, imperialism, rock 'n' roll, the Godhead, vagabonding, lust, appetite and woman power; and I consider myself blessed to have been young in a period when the vision of the good and true was up for grabs. In seeking our re-vision, thousands and thou-

sands of us wandered very far from "home," from our families, our communities, the values with which we were bred, the ideals with which we were entrusted, the country we were to inherit. Along the way we experienced corruption, disillusion, pain and death, as well as joy, but these were tracks to another 'home,' lives of our own construction.[10]

She stresses the importance of issues and the experiences of individuals in a romantic and highly sympathetic work. In contrast to Westhues's account, the FSM does not figure as the catalyst of the Canadian movement. It is there as an important event of the time, a kind of background to the foreground of Canadian happenings. There is no strong link of causality between the FSM or any other American event and the Canadian movement. The FSM is there, but so is the Quiet Revolution and the not-so-quiet activities of the FLQ, and so are events of the student movement in Europe and in Latin America.[11] But Kostash does not establish the importance of the peace movement as a radicalizing experience. It has a place in her chronology, but not as a causal link. For Kostash, it was important for student activists, but she has largely treated it as an isolated phenomenon divorced from subsequent student activism.[12]

Objectives

This essay will examine one aspect of the Canadian student movement from 1959 to 1967 in the student organization, the Combined Universities Campaign for Nuclear Disarmament (CUCND). The CUCND was the student component of the Canadian Campaign for Nuclear Disarmament (CCND), originally called the National Committee for the Control of Radiation Hazards (NCCRH). The purpose of this essay is to reestablish and to contribute to an understanding of one of the domestic origins of the Canadian student movement. It will ask the following questions: From what political context did the CUCND arise in 1959? How did students define their peace activism in the CUCND? How did their experience in the campaign to prevent the federal government's acquisition of the Bomarc missile contribute to a redefinition of that activism? And how, finally, the political culture born in the student peace movement was to influence the whole student political culture thereafter?

The rest of this essay will be divided into two sections. The second section will begin with a description of the political climate in the 1950s and its relationship to the Canadian peace movement. This will be used to explain the origins of both the CUCND and their adult counterpart, the Canadian Campaign for Nuclear Disarmament (CCND). It will also help to show the different natures of the CUCND's and the CCND's peace activism at this early stage of their separate actions. This essay will move to a description of the campaign from 1959 to 1963 to prevent the federal government's acceptance of the Bomarcs and then will look at the consequences of the Liberal party's 1963 election victory for both the CUCND and the CCND. It will also demonstrate the transformation of the CUCND to its successor organization, the Student Union for Peace Action (SUPA) in 1965.

Sources

The following sources were used: CUCND/SUPA archives held in the William Ready Division of the Archives and Research Collection, Mills Memorial Library McMaster University, Hamilton. The collection was especially useful in providing CUCND publications and in elucidating the North Bay '64 project, whose importance will soon be made clear. The CCND papers at the National Archives of Canada were supplemented with the papers of J.T. Thorson, president of the CCND from 1962-63. Also used were articles from movement publications. Newspaper accounts from the CCND/CUCND disarmament newspaper, Sanity, the editorials, published in the CUCND journal, Our Generation Against Nuclear War, and articles in the SUPA Newsletter and the New Left Committee Bulletin all proved valuable. Most of the other articles used came from the mainstream press and included the Globe and Mail and the North Bay Nugget. Maclean's Magazine was a notable source, especially the sympathetic coverage of the La Macaza demonstration by David Lewis Stein. My access to The Carleton provided me with material on the university's chapter of the CUCND as well as chapters on other campuses via the Canadian University Press. Unfortunately, Canadian newspapers from the period remain unindexed. When dates were known articles could be found with relative ease; when this was not the case, the papers of John Endicott and Rabbi Feinberg at the National Archives of Canada was invaluable. Endicott was the leader of the Canadian Peace Congress throughout the fifties and early sixties; Feinberg was one of the founders of the Toronto Committee for Disarmament, an affiliate of the Canadian Campaign for Nuclear Disarmament. Both collected clippings from various newspapers relating to disarmament. The Feinberg papers also contained some original publications of the CUCND.

Two requests were made using the Access to Information Act to acquire records of the RCMP as they related to both the CUCND and SUPA. Both were severely limited in scope because of the prohibitive expense of a more inclusive request. However, given the degree of censorship imposed upon the documents that have been released an exhaustive search may not reveal much more than is already known. Among the material that was released was a pot-pourri of innocuous written comments from Security and Intelligence (S. and 1.) officers of the RCMP. While much of the released material tells us very little about the perception of the group by S. and I., its volume does indicate a very strong interest in monitoring the activities of the group. The RCMP files did manage to provide some useful newsletters from the Carleton chapter of the CUCND.

The project provided the opportunity to supplement the documents with oral evidence. My proximity to Montreal, home of one of the most important and prominent former members, Mr. Dimitrios Roussopoulos, allowed me to conduct a personal interview with him. Roussopoulos initiated the CUCND in October 1959 in Montreal while on a pre-Christmas break from his graduate studies in Britain. He was Chairman of the CUCND, then Honorary Chairman of it and SUPA until its demise in 1967. He was conspicuously active at an intellectual level on the editorial boards of *Sanity*, the journal *Our Generation Against Nuclear War* (later called *Our Generation*). He also participated in the group's marches and in its later acts of civil disobedience.

A Quiet Decade for Political Activism

In the 1950s political activism appears to have been relatively limited. Part of the reason was that the Soviet Union provided a common enemy around which consensus appeared to have been built. There was very little dissent to the country's participation in the Korean "police action" beginning in 1950 or in its membership in the North American Treaty Organization from its creation in 1949.[13] A solid majority of Canadians believed peace was ensured by nuclear deterrence.[14] Contributing to the relative lack of dissent was an immigration screening process that weeded-out potential trouble makers,[15] and a robust economy that weakened left-wing opposition.[16] Coupled with this was a detachment from the public sphere. Sociologist, S.D. Clark has written of the rise and influence of the new suburban communities on the general political culture. Perhaps resulting from the recent war experience where the family unit was sacrificed to the needs of the collective, he wrote, the new suburbs found people who were concerned exclusively with the interests of their family, who had no vision of the good society and who largely eschewed public life. "It was not a society," Clark has written, in which people were alert to the important issues of the world."[17]

Students were no different than other segments of society. If there was political opposition the historical record is oblivious to its existence. In an anthology of historical papers on Canadian higher education purporting to be representative of Canadian historiography on the subject, there is nothing written on the 1950s. The two decades that do represent student dissent are the 1930s and the 1960s.[18]

A survey of institutional biographies reveals a similar trend. Where students are included at all in accounts of the 1950s their activities are invariably trivial and socially oriented; if they are at all rebellious, it was in a sophomoric and apolitical way. Of the immediate post-war years and the 1950s, one author has written that it was a time of snake dances, dorm raids, growing rowdyism at dances, and increased open drinking. Compared to the following decades, however, there was still a significant amount of control and restraint.[19]

Another writes of the annual social pattern, including such things as "the freshie dance, field day … and the graduation banquet." He continues: "Many of the most colorful stories told in reflection in this period involve ingenious skits."[20]

It was a time of the apolitical and the quiescent. Educators and journalists complained of student apathy. When a student was detained on Ellis Island for making a controversial speech, there was not a modicum of protest from students. Nor was there a demonstration or reaction when two professors from the University of Toronto and Queen's University were forbidden to enter the United States. It may be, as one writer later suggested, that the "McCarthy era, with its brutal assault on free institutions, generated nothing but a ripple in the stream of student consciousness."[21] It does not appear to have been fertile ground for the emergence of a student movement or any other.

The peace movement would eventually provide students with what they would apparently consider a legitimate area of political activity. But its adverse condition in the 50s had first to be overcome. In the Cold War atmosphere of the time the peace movement was especially vulnerable to suspicion; pacifism was political and dissent could be construed as a form of treason. Historian Lucille Marr writes:

> Not only had the war made it difficult to generate enthusiasm for any kind
> of peace project, but the anti-communist climate fed by McCarthyism in
> the United States … made peace groups suspect in the 1950s.[22]

In the late 40s and early 50s, demands for disarmament were associated by the general public with the Soviet Union's wish to weaken the West. The Soviet's had a defence policy less predicated on nuclear weapons, and had a larger number of conventional forces.[23]

A 1949 External Affairs publication exemplified the suspicion of Soviet peace proposals when it wrote of one disarmament offer "… another variation on the Soviet theme that the governments of all non-Communist countries are evil and should be overthrown."[24] The belief was enhanced by the fact the Soviets used Western peace movements as a vehicle to encourage the reception of their foreign policy objectives by Western governments. In 1949, communist parties were encouraged by the Cominform to focus their attention on the peace movement.[25] Whitaker and Marcuse write:

> … the peace movement was a leading target of the Cold War in Canada. The Canadian State intervened actively against it, and within certain sectors of Canadian society there were clear signs of a quasi-McCarthyite mentality that did not shrink from using extreme methods, including threats and occasional acts of violence, to intimate dissenters.[26]

According to historian Thomas Socknat, the former core of the peace movement had been unable to meet the problem of the "atomic age" and was criticized by many for being "unrealistic for the times."[27] The clearer minded Congress was thus able to push others to the sidelines to become the dominant group within the Canadian peace movement.[28] The CPC was a national umbrella organization that linked peace with Marxist ideology.

The CPC had been created a couple of years after the Grouzenko revelations, the same year of the coup in Czechoslovakia, the year in which Quebec's padlock law was reactivated and an alleged communist was refused entry to the British Columbia bar.[29] In 1948, it had risen from an amalgam of left-wing groups with some of its members from organizations like the Quakers, the Student Christian Movement, and the Women's International League for Peace and Freedom. Importantly, however, the majority of its members were from a defunct communist inspired organization, the League for Democracy and Freedom. An estimate of its long-time president, Dr. James Endicott, put the number of Communists at eighty-percent.[30] Endicott himself contributed to the CPC's reddish hue. He was an errant missionary who had been asked by his church to leave his post in China for his support of its Communist government.[31] Moreover, the CPC was affiliated to the communist sponsored and dominated World Peace Council.[32]

The CPC's unpopularity was manifest. The mass media was never sympathetic to its activities, even the left-leaning publication *Canadian Forum*.[33] Speaking tours were interrupted by problems with immigration, cancelled venues, violence and protesters shouting down the speaker.[34] All parties in the House of Commons shared the antipathy towards the group exhibited by External Affairs Minister Lester Pearson.[35] In a speech to a civil service union in 1950, he accused CPC members of having knowingly, or unknowingly, sold their souls to Moscow. In 1951, he told a young persons' current events club in Toronto to beware of the peace issue because it was communist inspired. The CPC, he said, "was a trap so cunningly baited by the Communists and their sympathizers." Responding to the group's call for the abolition of nuclear weapons, Pearson would tell the same group that it was suspicious because the "Soviet Union and its friends and satellites possess a great superiority in all other types of military powers."[36] A year earlier at the United Nations, the Congress had opposed Canada's vote against the abolition of nuclear weapons and as a result Pearson had refused to meet with them again[37]; the Common's External Affairs Committee would do the same a few years later.[38]

The National Committee for the Control of Radiation Hazards: Looking South for Inspiration

The condition of the peace movement is significant for the history of the NCCRH and the CUCND, since neither built on the organizational foundation of the Congress. The NCCRH had relatively conservative beginnings on the penumbra of the peace movement. It was created in response to anxiety over the health risks posed by exposure to radiation. In 1958, a United Nations Commission warned of the problems, and Nobel Prize winning scientist Linuis Pauling estimated that the fallout from atomic missile testing the previous year would result in one million defective babies and the death of two million newborns.[39] Western governments were concerned about the increase in world radiation levels and were themselves proposing greater research and the sharing of data.[40] In Canada, Radiation Services had been created in 1950 to ensure the protection of government employees working with radioactive material. In the mid-1950s, it began studying the effects of low-level radiation from A-bomb testing.[41] A lack of Canadian regulations permitted anyone in any province to buy and use an X-ray machine; people would develop skin ulcers after having unwanted hair removed with the machines; and shoe fitting fluoroscopes were uncontrolled with some stores permitting children to play with them.[42]

The NCCRH was founded on the American experience of SANE, also called the Committee for a Sane Nuclear Policy.

The Canadian group had autonomy from the American group, but the affinity of the two organizations meant that the NRCCH was able to draw on SANE speakers and literature. It began in early 1959 under the direction of Dr. Jan Van Stolk and his wife Mary, Americans living in Edmonton, Alberta, after trips to New York and to Los Angeles in 1958 and 1959 to consult the executive of SANE. Similar committees were organized in Toronto, Montreal and Vancouver. On 2 February 1960 the formation of a national committee was announced to the press consisting of local committees in Montreal, Toronto, Edmonton and Victoria.[43] Its first Chairman was Dr. Hugh Keenleyside, Chairman of the British Columbia Power Commission and the former Director-General of the United Nations Technical Assistance Administration.

The choice of Keenleyside was consistent with the strategy of the NCCRH to look respectable in a time when any criticism of nuclear testing was readily assimilated to communism. Like in its American counterpart, SANE, prominent and well esteemed people were asked to become "sponsors" and to serve on the national committee; their names would be placed on the group's literature and letterhead. By the first national committee meeting in Montreal in June 1960, some of the sponsors included prominent intellectuals Hugh MacLennan, Claude Bissell, Eugene Forsey, Andre Laurendeau and Frank Scott.[44] By January 1962 there were 12 local committees in major cities across the country.[45]

Its need to be dissociated from communism extended to its methods. Mrs. Van Stolk may have been alluding to the British CND when she disavowed the "usual weapons" of the ban-the-bomb movements: speeches on public platforms, marches and petitions. The NCCRH would change public policy by educating the public, "calmly and without raising voices." "We are not pacifists," she told *Globe* reporter Roderich Goodman, "We are not interested in politics. We don't think there is any need for a march on Ottawa."[46] A short time before, she explained to Rabbi Feinberg, Chairman of the Toronto Committee for Disarmament,[47] that the organization was not about "curing all the ills of the world, but rather views one practical problem in a practical manner." Its chief purpose was the distribution of literature; it would not "shake a fist at government."[48]

The British Influence on the Formation of the Canadian CUCND: Completing the North Atlantic Triangle

Like so many other times in Canadian history, British, American and Canadian ideas came together to shape the country's experience. The influence of the British anti-nuclear campaign on the formation of the CUCND completed this familiar triad. The organizational origins of the student group can be traced to Montreal in October 1959. Dimitrios Roussopoulos, a Canadian graduate student studying at the London School of Economies had been involved in both the campaign for Nuclear Disarmament and its universities arm, the CUCND. Several months after Diefenbaker announced the decision to acquire the Bomarc missile delivery system, Roussopoulos was visiting home in October. He broached the idea to friends of a Canadian organization modelled after the CUCND in Britain. A press conference followed at Sir George Williams University. The conference, unreported in the press, brought together students from Sir George Williams and McGill. They decided to contact students at the University of Montreal, draw up a petition and march on Ottawa.[49]

On Christmas Day 1959, about eighty students from the three universities rode in a cavalcade from Montreal to Parliament Hill. They left petitions for the Prime Minister and Governor General Vanier, and they laid a wreath at the National War Memorial.[50] After the demonstration a secretariat was established in Montreal and contacts were made with sympathetic campus groups including, among others, branches of the Student Christian Movement, CCF youth groups, and international relations clubs. In a few months time chapters were established at universities across the country.[51]

The quickness with which chapters were established should not obscure the obstacles some of them faced nor indicate wide student support. It took McMaster students two years to be approved by the Student's Council as a campus club.[52] To have their constitution ratified, students at the university of Western Ontario had to respond to unsympathetic councilors who believed universities should not be connected with the "radical" thoughts of the group.[53] When established as official campus clubs the problem of legitimacy continued. In 1961, the *McGill Daily* conducted a poll of students asking if they agreed with CUCND policy and methods. Of 800 students polled 649 disapproved; the paper reported that "several" of those who voted against the CUCND accused it of being influenced by communists.[54] Some chapters were denied places to meet. St. Michael's College of the University of Toronto refused the group the use of its rooms. President of the college, Father John Kelly, justified the decision on the grounds that the college supported the acquisition of nuclear weapons and that he suspected they had communist connections.[55] The CUCND at St. Paul's College of the University of Manitoba planned to counter charges of communist influence in a series of talks, but were refused rooms at the college in which to conduct them. St. Paul's student council voted almost unanimously to deny them space claiming it was "pacifist" and "Communist-tinged." CUCND members at the university complained of a "continuous smear campaign" by "fascist elements."[56] During the Cuban missile crisis in 1962, the Carleton CUCND picketed on Parliament Hill to protest the American decision to blockade the Island. Embarrassed about their association with Carleton, the student's council passed a resolution to make it publicly known to the people of Ottawa that their campus CUCND club did not represent the university. One council member expressed his opposition to the resolution when he declared that it was already "widely known that the group is not representative of the student body."[57]

The CUCND addressed themselves to charges of communist influence when the Toronto chapter expelled Danny Goldstick, the campus Communist leader, for refusing to condemn the Soviet tests of the hydrogen bomb.[58] When they became members of the adult campaign; they had the bulwark of its prominent sponsors. The only other documented response involves the CUCND and the Edmonton chapter of the executives on the local committee including Mrs. Van Stalk argued that admitting communist organizations to their membership would make them susceptible to smear campaigns. Several members threatened to quit if known communists entered the organization. After "a considerable amount of debate" throughout the year the issue was addressed at a combined meeting of the CUCND and the local committee. To counter charges of being communist organizations, they agreed to admit individuals only. This appears to have given them the ability to assess memberships on a case by case basis.[59] It's not known if anyone was turned down by a local committee for membership.

If the peace movement continued to have problems gaining legitimacy, it appears nevertheless to have taken students out of the political slumber of the 1950s. It did so because it was able to at least partly disassociate the peace movement from the CPC, for which students had only contempt, and link it to the more popular British campaign. The Christmas student march on Ottawa was the first since the end of World War Two[60] thus indicating a watershed in Canadian student history. They marched, in part, because the tradition upon which they drew encouraged it; the British campaign was clearly their source of inspiration. "In policy and method," they declared in a statement of policy in 1960, "we are one with the British Campaign and its Combined Universities for Disarmament."[61] Many of the tens of thousands of marchers in the British campaign's Aldermaston marches had been members of the British CUCND.[62] The peace signs carried at these protests now dotted the marches of the Canadian CUCND. In the fall of 1960, a meeting of the group's National Secretariat and representatives from each university branch created a "provisional Policy Statement" to inform the public of their nature and policy objectives. In the section entitled, "Background," they presented the formation and the effects of the British CND and the Canadian CUCND together. They wrote:

> January 1958 saw the formation of the British Campaign for Nuclear Disarmament. November 1959 saw the formation of the Combined Universities

Campaign for Nuclear Disarmament in Canada. Both found an immediate and startling response. Firstly individuals, then groups of individuals and soon, like in Britain and other countries, scores of thousands will become conscious of the monstrous weapons (nuclear and C.B.R.) of annihilation.[63]

Like its British counterpart, the Canadian CUCND was unilateralist. This meant renouncing the possession, control and use of nuclear weapons prior to seeking an international disarmament agreement, as an example to other countries. Hence, they asked for the removal of nuclear bases from the country; the cessation of storage, testing and the manufacturing of nuclear weapons in Canada; the end of H-Bomb patrol flights over the country; and the withdrawal from NATO and North American Air Defence Command (NORAD) because of their reliance on a nuclear strategy.

It is this connection to the British campaign that suggests a radical potential beyond their relatively limited objectives. Many members of the British CUCND were also members of the nascent New Left that eschewed both the old communists and the Labour party. The British New Left was nourished, wrote English Historian, Christopher Driver,

> ...by Hungary and Suez, which at one stroke turned the most sensitive minds of their generation equally away from communists leanings and from all forms of political bipartisanship within this country.[64]

The critique of the New Left extended beyond the issue of nuclear disarmament and was concerned with the issues and problems of British society."[65] Historian of the movement, Peggy Duff, suggests the existence of a radical pacifist current in the British CUCND:

> While the bomb was its main occasion and theme, it was much more than that. It was a mass protest against the sort of society which had created the bomb, which permitted it to exist, which threatened to use it—this is why so many of them were young, still free enough to reject it.[66]

The Canadian CUCND presents a confusing picture. Its affinity with the British campaign suggests a radical discontent. The Canadian group's policy statement, however, reveals that it arose out of the realization that the bomb was the problem, not the social system that created it. It saw itself as "an expanding pressure group" and not a social movement.[67] Below the level of policy, however, there was a realization that disarmament may be connected to social change. The documents do not reveal the nature or the breadth of change that some had broached at the executive level in

1961 nor why the addition of social issues to their agenda was refused.[68] In the same year that this occurred, the CUCND's journal, *Our Generation Against Nuclear War*, began its first full year of publishing. Its Statement of Purpose suggested more than the policy Statement arrived at a year earlier. It read, in part,

> We believe quite categorically that the greatest achievement of this generation will be the saving of the world from a nuclear holocaust. Our generation must be firmly committed to putting an end to war once and for all. The virtues, sentiments, and thinking of our generation are different from that generation of people that is bent on war because of its crippled thinking.

To prevent war it is necessary, it said, to reexamine economic and social structures.[69] In the preface to its inaugural issue, mentor Bertrand Russell wrote that nuclear disarmament was the first step in effecting a "radical change" necessary to guarantee human survival.[70] In the preface to the second issue, J.B. Priestly wrote that the bomb was a product of the anti-democratic influence of those in power and that the weapons diverted resources away from fighting poverty, disease, ignorance and prejudice.[71] Thus, there appears to have existed a radical current in the group masked by its policy objectives. The loss of the Bomarc campaign would later facilitate the expression of this current beyond the pages of the journal and, eventually, in the creation of a new student peace organization that multiplied its criticisms of society and helped bring about a more generalized student movement.

The nascent stage of the CUCND in 1959 allows us to question the findings of Westhues and Levitt. We do not know how the members of the CUCND were socialized by their families. As we have seen, this is what Westhues argues is central to the advent of Canadian student activism in 1964. But the evidence above suggests that they grew up in a society that seemed more conformist than one that encouraged the expression of individual autonomy. The dissent of the CPC proves the rule because they were held up by politicians and the media as an example of how not to behave. The American influence on the formation of the NCCRH, and the British influence on the creation of the Canadian CUCND suggested that the domestic peace movement had been effectively marked illegitimate.

Moreover, the issue to which students reacted was not the impersonal environment of the university, as Westhues suggested, or the "massification" of university education, as Levitt has argued. Student activism was a reaction to an issue that transcended the university and that was played out almost wholly outside of it. It was the perceived threat of nuclear war, i.e., the end of humankind, that moved students to act as peace activists, a perception undoubtedly strengthened by national civil defence exercises in 1961,[72] the building of bomb shelters throughout the early 60s, and global tensions like the Berlin blockade in 1958 and the Cuban missile crisis in 1962. Students shared this fear with many others and acted with them to lobby their parliamentary elites to take the lead in its prevention. They did not suggest the replacing of the elites with themselves or any others nor did they propose at this stage, as they would come to advocate later on, that the elites be stripped of their power to wage war. The crucible of the Canadian 60s student movement rested within the framework of an apocalyptic view of the future. As indicated earlier, "Let's not be Cremated Equal," was often seen on their placards during their annual Christmas demonstrations in Ottawa, a display of their anxiety and dread for the future, but also a call to action. It was significant because, a play on an aphorism at the foundation of modern liberal democracy, it justified participation in a protest movement that dealt with an issue that affected all and gave an urgency to citizen participation in their own governance. If all men are cremated equal, then all must have a say in governing in the atomic age. But if the fear of nuclear war moved them to participate in politics it was as lobbyists with no objective beyond influencing the formation of policy within the existing political system. As their provisional policy statement above indicated, the CUCND was not at this stage a radical organization that wanted to bring about fundamental change in the way the country was governed. It believed in the efficacy of protest and the possibility of positively influencing the circle of decision-makers entrusted with making the right decisions to prevent a nuclear holocaust. They accepted the political system as it was, but their actions suggested they could not assume their governing elites would make the right decisions as members of the CUCND understood them. By their actions they were implicitly defining the important role of the citizen in the nuclear age: a role limited, at this stage of the group's development, to protesting and mobilization of public.

Early Methods of Influence: Belief in the Efficacy of Protest and Lobbying in a Parliamentary Democracy

Thus, demonstrations continued to be an important tool in their peace activism. Their next demonstration seemed to reflect the influence of the British Aldermaston marches, focused as they were on that city's nuclear missile base. In the spring of 1960, the students went to North Bay, a small northern Ontario community of about 23 000 people. About eight miles north of the city's core, the first Bomarc missile base was in the process of being built.[73] As a long motorcade made its way there on 9

May 1960, readers of the *North Bay Nugget* were warned to expect 150 Peace Marchers' to stage a protest on Tuesday. Mimeographed pamphlets had been sent to universities asking students to participate in a three day protest. The pamphlets expressed their belief that students had a "vital part to play in calling for a Canadian initiative to stop the spread of nuclear weapons."[74]

Neither the local newspaper nor Mayor Merle Dickerson were interested in their message but were concerned that the demonstration be peaceful. "This is a free country," said Dickerson, "It's quite all right for them to come here to picket the base, as long as they don't break any laws of the city."[75] Earlier, the local Legion branch successfully lobbied the City Manager, T.A. Frair, to forbid the CUCND's use of Memorial Park, "objecting to use of dedicated ground to demonstrate against the government's decisions."[76]

Early the next morning, about one hundred students from the University of Toronto, Carleton, the University of Ottawa, the University of Montreal, McGill, Laval and Sir George Williams picketed the Bomarc construction site and handed out CUCND literature. Escorted by police, they sang peace songs and paraded at noon in the city's downtown stopping on Ferguson Street, between Main and Oak, for a public meeting. Some of the paraders gave speeches. Michel Boyer from McGill called the bases futile and implored the people of North Bay to write their MPs and protest the establishment of the bases in the city. Liz Makarchuk, the only woman from the University of Toronto to attend the protest, "blasted" Canadian women for their apathy.[77]

The media continued to show more concern for the effect of the marchers on the city than for their ideas, and pointed out the "university-level" spelling of "missle" on one of the CUCND's signs.[78] On the same day as the march, Dickerson was across town officially opening the construction site of the city's newest shopping mall, the Northgate Shopping Centre.

During a ceremony to lay a golden foundation stone, the Mayor lit a miniature Bomarc that exploded noisily and soared upwards. The *Nugget* titled the article, "Northgate Centre Gets off with a (Bomarc) Bang!"[79]

In sum, their first experience in North Bay showed the importance of the economic factor in encouraging the acceptance of the missiles and some conflicting notions of citizenship. As for the latter, their right to protest was accepted grudgingly, though their choice of venue was partly regulated by the local government, and the nature of their protest was reduced by the local newspaper and the Mayor to the maintenance of order. This was one of the earliest times that the efficacy of protest must have been impugned; it was early in the campaign, however, and if their confidence was shaken it did not lead to any change within the organization. As for the former, the community and the students seem to have had different ideas about the importance of the base. For this small community its significance was perceived in terms of the economic fallout it was apparently expected to bring; not the "fallout" with which peace activists had been concerned. As we will see later in the paper, the students returned to the city to address the economic importance of the base and adopted another means of precipitating change while dropping the tool of the demonstration altogether.

In the meantime, the CUCNP conducted its second Christmas Day demonstration in Ottawa in 1960. The number of students attending the Parliament Hill protest reflected the CUCND's rapid expansion on to university campuses. Where 80 students from three universities stood in front of the Peace Tower on Christmas Day 1959, there were now 450 from 17 schools. The day was chosen because of its symbolic importance as the day of peace, and it was meant to demonstrate the depth of their conviction.

They paraded through Ottawa and arrived at Centre Block expecting to meet members of the government and the opposition. They were met instead by a few RCMP officers and the House of Commons protective staff. Some students gave speeches competing with the carillon in the Peace Tower sounding Christmas songs. Leaving the Hill they marched to Governor General Vanier's residence. He was not home and so a member of his staff received their petition.

In March 1961, about two years after the creation of the Canadian CUCND, the NCCRH adopted a policy opposing the acquisition of nuclear weapons by any country not already possessing them, including Canada. By that time the peace group the Voice of Women (VOW) had been formed and *Maclean's Magazine*, *Saturday Night*, the *Globe and Mail* and the *Toronto Star* expressed oppositions against the weapons. The two opposition parties, the CCF and the Liberals, were also against the acquisition of the weapons. Support for non-acceptance appeared widespread. But the NCCRH had a little trouble transcending its conservative tradition. It had been created not to encourage disarmament, but to encourage controls on the use of radiation technology. Not only this, but as described by its founder, Mary Van Stolk, it held to a narrow view of appropriate strategy to influence government decisions. The NCCRH had never marched or gathered signatures for a petition. It took two votes and six months for opposition to the missiles to become official policy of the NCCRH and local affiliated groups.[80] In press announcements, they justified the new policy on the grounds that "an increasing number of Canadians" including the Official Opposition Liberals and the third party CCF opposed the spread of nuclear weapons.[81]

There is some evidence the CUCND had something to do with the expansion of the NCCRH's mandate. Gerry Hunnuis, a founding member of the CUCND, was now the executive secretary of the National Committee of the adult group.[82] It is not known when the CUCND began to work with the NCCRH. What seems to have occurred is that before the NCCRH changed its name to the Canadian Campaign for Nuclear Disarmament (CCND) to better reflect its new policy in 1961, the CUCND had been working within the group to capitalize on the prestige of its banner membership. Formed in 1959, the student group was the first among the newly created peace groups to come out against the Bomarc. They soon realized that they needed alliances with others if they were going to influence government policy. They turned to the NCCRH which had a network of country-wide local affiliates and a banner membership not unlike the British CND. To convince the NCCRH to change its policy they tried to legitimate the ideas and protest methods of the British group by introducing CND literature and by pointing to its well-known members, including people like Bertrand Russell and J.B. Priestly.[83]

It was at the behest of the CUCND that the NCCRH changed its name to the CCND and adopted the CND's emblem; the black and white peace sign.[84] In the same year, the CCND began publishing the newspaper *Sanity* modelled after the British CND's publication of the same name. The purpose of the paper was to provide news on other groups in the country and around the world and to proffer articles on peace related issues. Its editorial board consisted primarily of students including its Editor-in Chief, Dimitrios Roussopoulos, and included, among others, Harvey Feit, and Art Pape. We do not know enough at this point to state with much precision the organizational links between the CUCND and the CCND. It was clear that they discussed policy, worked on one major national campaign together, shared the undoubted benefits of the CCND's list of prominent members printed on both group's letterhead, and that they worked together in the publication of *Sanity*. It is also clear that they were able to work together with sometimes divergent policies. The CCND, for example, never advocated unilateral disarmament or quitting military alliances as had the CUCND. Nevertheless, there is some evidence that suggests the relationship was close, even hierarchical. A report of the RCMP on the CCND in 1962 noted that the students worked "very closely" with and were "in some cases directed" by them.[85]

The direction of which the report speaks may be referring to the CCND's one big national campaign. With the help of the CUCND, they organized a country-wide petition to convince the government to refuse the missiles.[86] The CPC had sponsored the last nation-wide anti-nuclear petition in 1948; in 1950 it merged with a world-wide petition called the Stockholm Appeal, organized by the World Peace Council. The wording of the petition suggested that the spectre of the CPC still influenced the tactics of the "adult" group. It read, in part:

> The petition is not the result of any propagandist's work or any partisan
> cause organized by a few people, or by any group committed to any cause.

It was, they said, the "spontaneous expression" of people from every profession and from all across the country to be presented by a group of "distinguished Canadians."[87]

On 6 October 1961 a delegation from the CCND and CUCND presented the 142,000 name petition to Prime Minister Diefenbaker. Those present included the CCND's president, Dr. James N. Thompson, McGill university professor and former moderator of the United Church, William Smith, president of the Canadian Brotherhood of Railway Employees, Dr. H. G. Dion, dean of agriculture at McGill, and F.C. Hunnuis, executive secretary of the group. Thompson exemplified the conservative nature of the NCCRH when he told the media that they wanted the government to continue what they were doing. Outside the Prime Minister's East Bloc office "several hundred" members of the CUCND began a 72-hour Thanksgiving weekend vigil.[88]

Failure, Disillusion, Radicalization and a New Definition of Citizenship in the Nuclear Age

1963 was a watershed year in the CUCND's history. The inadequacy of their methods was placed in stark relief against the realities of parliamentary democracy. Since their modest beginning in 1959 with about 80 supporters they had been inspired by the British Campaign for Nuclear Disarmament. In the course of three years they had expanded their membership to the 1000s,[89] and in 1963 were starting to turn their attention to developments among American student activists in that country's civil rights campaign. The final push came with the failure of the peace movement to prevent the acquisition of the Bomarcs. The unsuccessful techniques of the petition, pickets, and publicity, coupled with their apocalyptic cause of nuclear disarmament, made them question not only the nature of their peace activism but the ability of governing elites to prevent the end of the world.

As lobbyists, the fate of the CCND/CUCND's campaign ultimately relied on the decisions of their political masters in Ottawa. The government was uncommitted on acquiring the missiles, a bizarre position in light of the construction of the Bomarc bases and the knowledge they could only be armed with nuclear warheads. Diefenbaker's ambiguity on the issue had resulted in the resignation of his Defence Minister, Douglas Harkness in early February 1963. Soon after on 5 February, the government fell on a vote-of-confidence. A month earlier, Pearson had, without consulting the Liberal party, chosen to reverse their position on the Bomarcs. He had announced that, if elected, he would accept the missiles and thereby honour the commitments made by the Conservatives.[90] During the following election campaign, *Sanity* produced a special edition on the nuclear question and distributed thousands of copies throughout the country; CCND pamphlets were distributed by the tens of thousands; "fact sheets" were sent to all members of parliament, provincial dailies and weeklies; meet the candidate nights were sponsored by local CCND groups; and candidates were privately lobbied.[91] In spite of their efforts, on 8 April 1963 the Pearson Liberals won a minority government.[92] Several months later on New Years Eve the warheads for 28 Bomarc missiles were delivered to North Bay.[93]

Pearson's electoral victory had important consequences for both the CCND and the CUCND. The loss of the anti-Bomarc campaign revealed their sharply contrasting natures. In the CUCND, the radical tradition of its origins expressed by the movement's journal, *Our Generation Against Nuclear War*, contributed to a redefinition of its peace activism. The creation of SUPA was, in part, facilitated by this tradition and by the crucible of their ban-the-bomb experience. The CCND, on the other hand, did not redefine itself in any significant way. Unlike the CUCND, the CCND had no tradition upon which to construct a new approach to their peace work.

The election was not interpreted as a mandate to acquire nuclear warheads; the division concerned the proper manner to proceed against their acceptance. The CCND continued to try to shape public opinion through the dissemination of information. A couple of months after the election, for example, the executive of the CCND issued a press release. It announced that in the judgment of eight nuclear physicists the Bomarc missiles would cause nuclear weapons intended for the United States to explode over Canada.[94] The CUCND, in contrast, embarked on a self-examination and exploration of the idea of non-violent methods of change and began to draw a link between peace and other issues. At a September public meeting of the group, Art Pape explained that in the nuclear age people should oppose war of any kind and consider the philosophy of non-violence. James Harding, a member from the university of Saskatchewan, related his experience in Washington weeks earlier in a civil rights march of 210,000. The Negro movement, Harding said, made the link between economic exploitation, physical abuse and the participation of youth. The lesson for the peace movement, he said, was that it must make the link between economic exploitation and war.[95] The third speaker, David Smith, spoke of his experiences at the non-violent training institute at the Quaker Grindstone Island facility.[96] At an August conference on the island, Carleton CUCND members discussed non-violence in relation to the civil rights and peace movements and Canadian foreign policy. President of the Carleton chapter, Cathie Rosenberg, showed the relationship being made between the methods of the civil rights movement and the Canadian peace movement. The civil rights movement fights the assertion of white supremacy, she wrote,

> In the peace movement, we are fighting a similar assertion of the right of a few military leaders to make decisions regarding the fate of humanity. We are struggling for the right of men to live; the Negro is struggling for the right of men to live decently, without which our victory would be meaningless.

The non-violent methods of change used by the civil rights movement are seen as a replacement of war as a method of social change. The only alternative, she writes, is "violence of nuclear war, and the balance of terror in which we are living now."[97]

At the September '63 Regina meeting, Pape advocated getting out of military alliances because they increased Cold War tension. We should, he said, become non-aligned and work through the United Nations.[98] A month later, this issue would divide students and the CCND at a general meeting in Montreal. Students wanted the country's withdrawal from all military alliances; the adults, in contrast, wanted to remain a part of NORAD and NATO.[99] The debate pointed to a fundamental difference between the CUCND and the CCND.

Reflecting their original concern with image, members of the CCND advocated the status quo, concerned for the group's legitimacy and its corollary ability to attract support from the public. The students insisted on a more radical critique of the country's foreign policy: in spite of the danger of damaging their legitimacy. Before the October meeting of the CCND/CUCND where the debate would come to a head, there was an internal preparatory discussion. Integral to the controversy was the discussion paper labelled the "Green Paper" that argued the neutralist option, proffered as a means of addressing the government's rationale for accepting nuclear weapons. If, as the government argued, it had an obligation to accept the Bomarcs under the terms of its membership in military alliances, the country should withdraw from these alliances. Further justification for neutralism was offered in the inefficacy of the alliance system to contain the spread of communism and its deleterious peace strategy based on the maintenance of comparative strength. As Pape had done, it argued that withdrawing from military alliances would mitigate Cold War tensions.[100]

For some, Canadian political culture rendered the proposal unviable and damaging to the group's credibility. Alarmed at the advocacy of neutralism, one adult member remarked on the practical limitations of a peace movement that hoped to influence government policy by attracting a significant amount of public support. "No matter how current intellectually its policy may be," he wrote,

> ...a Peace Movement (sic) can never be effective by isolating itself from the conditions of a Society (sic) but must work within the framework of that Society to be effective. If it does not appeal to and be supported by a large percentage of the population it has failed its purpose.

Idealistic policies, he warned, would result in the group's "self-destruction."[101] The British Columbia CCND branch also expressed concerns about damaging the effectiveness of the group. A radical position, they believed, would isolate them from the main currents of Canadian political life, and would weaken our ability to influence the Canadian government."[102] Students were apparently unconcerned, their belief in the rightness of the proposal outweighing its potential to de-legitimize their efforts. One of the neutralist advocates would implicitly denounce the organization's concern with respectability. The position of the CCND, he would write, was created out of a concern for "one's job, influence and reputation." He would advocate the formation of a new group capable of espousing a more radical position.[103]

In October 1963, months after Pearson's victory, eighty delegates attended a general meeting of the CCND in Montreal to discuss policy. On the agenda was the divisive proposal to advocate neutralism. Thorson, the president of the group, exemplified its opponents who argued the group had been influential with its current program. A student delegate to the meeting, John Lee, reiterated his neutralism and argued the peace movement needed to address the causes of war with a more radical critique. In contrast to Thorson, he argued the group had a negative influence: the effect of the group was to make governments "more subtle." In response, another delegate would remark that a policy that was out of touch with mainstream political thinking was "nothing but a heroic gesture."[104]

The CCND was fearful of losing its youth constituency but could not fully endorse the neutralist position. In an effort to assuage both sides they enlisted the help of University of Toronto political theorist C.B. Macpherson to broker a compromise. In the end, advocates of neutralism would have to be content with a new policy that renounced, in theory, all military alliances but would not advocate the withdrawal of the country from any military alliance.

Thorson was very much hostile to the prospect of withdrawing from NATO and NORAD. Though disappointed at Pearson's flip-flop, he saw no reason to seek structural changes in foreign policy. He saw hope instead in Pearson's talk of making the Canadian forces non-nuclear.[105] He represented an aspect of the group's thinking present from the beginning, that although it was necessary to work for disarmament in its absence the safety of the West was secured through strength. In his opposition, he invoked the weight of Cold War antagonism and tradition: "I certainly am not non-committed. I cannot accept that! Canada has always been a member of military alliances."[106] He could not accept the new policy no matter how diluted a neutralist position: he resigned the presidency and "cut all ties" with the group.[107]

Though preventing a split, the compromise did not eliminate the sharp division that it was intended to calm. The student group was becoming more radicalized and willing to consider the expansion of the student peace movement to other fronts. More than 50 delegates and observers attended the CUCND's Federal Conference in December 1963 in Montreal where it adopted neutralism two weeks after the General meeting of the CCND.[108] A speech given by Pape, the Chairman of the CUCND's Federal Council, described the university as one of the most powerful institutions in society. He concluded by saying that if members of the CUCND took their peace activism seriously they would use the university's resources on research for the peace movement. Thus, we see that for the first time, and notably a year before the Free Speech Movement in the United States, the university was coming to be perceived as an institution capable of being used for their political goals. This was significant because it pointed to a retrenchment in their fight for a society free from the threat of nuclear war. Having failed the first round, they were turning their attention to the university to marshall their resources and to prepare them for a protracted struggle for peace.

The nascent attention paid to the university indicated the CUCND's ability to assimilate areas they had not previously touched upon. This was also true of Quebec nationalism and this was the first conference that included the issue on the agenda. It was at once a teaching session on the nature of the phenomena and a time to determine their role, if any, in relation to it. Their guest speakers included M. Rodrigue Guitre, president of the Montreal branch of the Rassemblement pour l'indépendance Nationale; M. Guy Bertrand, editor of *Quartier Latin*, the student newspaper at the University of Montreal; and M. Jean David, the city editor of *La Presse*. They heard M.

Guitre's talk of the impending revolution, M. Bertrand's assertion that the "national question" was the primary one for French students, not the peace movement with which they all agreed, and M. David's contention that English Canada did not understand Quebec nationalism because of the irresponsible English press. In the end, they assimilated the issue into their project as peace activists. For them, world peace meant "the dynamic cooperation of peoples and societies and hence the dynamic cooperation of Quebec and the rest of the country." In the same year the Front de libération du Quebec was formed, they passed a resolution stating their obligation to research methods of conflict resolution that included non-violence as they might apply to the division between the "two nations."[109]

The inclusion of the Quebec question and Pape's critical look at the university pointed to a broadening out of the movement away from their previously more limited and exclusive concern with nuclear weapons policy. Also significant was their conclusion that all Canadians had a right and duty to make foreign policy decisions; they decided that questions of war and peace were too important to citizens to be left in the hands of government and so-called "experts." They were vague in their prescription. "This will require," the resolution reads,

> ... a fundamental reconstitution on the basis of the Canadian Confederation as a minimum and the changing of the constitution to allow people to have a more direct influence on these matters.[110]

They took their new criticism to Parliament Hill. The conference was followed by a lobbying session in Ottawa where they met Pearson, Cabinet Ministers, the NDP caucus and the deputy leader of the Social Credit Party, Mr. Réal Caouette. Every member was presented with a brief that asked not for specific changes, but for a "fundamental" questioning of the "assumptions which underlie public policy today." It revealed their discontent with a system that had failed, in their judgement, to adequately respond to the threat to human existence posed by nuclear weapons.

> For us, members of the COCND, the dilemma begins with the basic values which we hold—a society based on the worth and dignity of the individual, which recognizes equality and self-government as the rights and needs of all men.
>
> But we find that our society has not in fact developed ways to live and act according to those values...

Our public policies are filled with contradictions: in the name of protecting freedom, we threaten to destroy all freedom through nuclear destruction.[111]

In a seminar conducted by the CUCND at Queen's university in early 1964, Daniel Drache expressed the groups' increasing concern with deeper political criticism and the link they made between peace and form of government:

... peace work based on the removal of grotesque weapons aimed at mere survival was not attacking the root of our dilemma. Peace, rooted in man's dignity, respects the individual and the need for him to be involved in the determination of his own life and future.[112]

At the same conference, Pape spoke of the need for a new form of government to prevent the destruction of the world. Lobbying was ineffective. The success of the peace movement, he said, depended on the achievement of social systems and institutions predicated on the primacy of human life, dignity and freedom.[113] Thus, several months after Pearson's election, the CUCND enlarged the issues it thought were relevant to peace and had decided that representative democracy, that included citizens active as they had been as lobbyists, was no longer a sufficient means of preventing nuclear war. "Participatory democracy," had not yet been used to express the notion of a decentralization of power and a citizenry who were immediately involved in decisions on issues that effected their lives. But the prerequisite concepts were clearly in place, and they pointed once again to a change in the nature of citizenship they believed to be necessary in the atomic age. Importantly, it would not become a citizenship that was restricted to making decisions on foreign policy questions. To be sure, at their December 1963 conference it was foreign policy that they resolved be placed directly in the hands of the electorate. But their "Open Letter to Parliament" after that conference and speeches made at their February meeting in Kingston soon after indicated a disenchantment that went beyond the nuclear issue. If the failure of the Bomarc campaign was the spark, the prairie fire was the broad democratization of citizenship.

The implications of this line of thinking were not immediately apparent. It indicated, however, that the critical tradition exemplified by the movement journal, *Our Generation Against Nuclear War*, was being voiced outside of the journal and had an audience at CUCND seminars and federal meetings. A month after the Liberal's election victory, the CUCND Secretariat once again discussed an expansion of the organization's agenda to include social issues, but no official change in policy occurred.[114] In the short term, the failure of the old means of protest encouraged them to redefine their peace activism, sharpening the contrast between themselves and the CCND. Their Christmas 1963 march on Parliament Hill was their last. It marked an end to a tradition that had begun in 1959. The CCND was moribund. It lost members when the Bomarc campaign was lost and when the United States and the Soviet Union signed an above ground test ban treaty in 1963. In February 1965 it could no longer afford to finance *Sanity*, though the newspaper continued to publish independently. Its new head office in Ottawa was manned by a voluntary and part-time secretary. When it produced the first of its newsletters in May later that year it had only 150 "active members" to whom to send it.[115] Two years earlier, it claimed the support of 15,000 members.[116] By 1965, according to Gary Moffatt, most CCND branches were inactive or worked only with other organizations,[117] suggesting a paucity of resources. It appears to have operated only on a local level in the late sixties. There does not appear to have been a formal break with the students. The record seems to indicate, however, that the October meeting of the CUCND and CCND was their last.

The emerging ideas and tactics of the CUCND widened the difference between the two groups. The students' new methods of protest, for instance, contrasted sharply with the lobbying techniques of the CCND. Inspired by the activities of American student civil rights activists, members of the CUCND went to North Bay and La Macaza, the sites of the Bomarc missile bases, in actions that were significantly different from their march in North Bay in 1960. Where the British anti-nuclear campaign's protests were relatively brief, American students were staying in communities, at least for a time, and trying to mobilize citizens for long-term political action. Thus, the new techniques employed by the CUCND bespoke a change in influence—from the British to the Americans—and reflected the group's increasing concern with an active and effective citizenship.

The students themselves believed that the North Bay project was a fundamental break with the traditions of the CUCND. In preparing the project a document entitled, "Prospectus for North Bay '64," was sent to CUCND groups to find people interested in participating. "We have a long history of protests," it reads in part, "But time has shown that in many cases we represented only ourselves." Past methods, alone, they had come to realize, would not work. "We see more clearly than ever," they wrote, "the need to challenge and suggest alternatives to the fundamental policy assumptions of those whose business it is to decide and rule."[118]

The idea behind the project was consistent with their opposition to military alliances. "The purpose of North Bay '64 was to change a structural condition they thought was an obstacle to disarmament. The students argued that the economic importance of the bases in the city militated against an acceptance of disarmament because of its economic consequences. The project was meant to serve as a case study in converting the country from a war time to a peace time economy.[119] It was also intended to mobilize the community to promote disarmament. Pape described the effort this way: "All of this is related to preparing this community to be able to say to the government, disarm if you can—we will present no political obstacles."[120]

The CUCND was aware of the importance of the bases to the local economy. Their project prospectus included a brief economic history of the city that recognized the bases as the replacement for a declining train industry, the industry upon which the city was originally built. They knew that city hall had favourably embraced the new industry.[121] In 1964, the Mayor, Cecil Hewitt, described the air force as a "big part" of the lives of its citizens.[122] The city's Department of Industries used the bases in its publicity to attract secondary industry,[123] and a tourist booklet mentioned the base with a suggestion of civic pride:

> Recognizing the strategic importance of the city, the government has placed North Bay in the Atomic age. Construction is complete on the first Bomarc B Missile Base in Canada and the development of a SAGE communication centre is still under way.[124]

In spite of what appeared to be a formidable obstacle, the project renewed the spirits of at least some of the movement's members. In the wake of the failure of the Bomarc campaign, the CUCND Secretariat reported that the group suffered from a problem of low morale.[125] A committee of the CCND complained of the same problem. But being unable to again reinvent itself may have meant that it was unable to recover from the loss of the campaign.[126] In contrast, the CUCND's new activism gave students new hope. "It is hard to explain the spirit the group has generated," wrote participant Liora Proctor. "Everyone seems to feel that we will be doing the most radical thing of all, since we will be 'relevant' to the community while peace marches etc., often aren't."[127]

Twelve students were chosen for the project. They included Art Pape, Terry Shaw, Liora Proctor, Allan Berkely, Frank McEahy and Dan Roebuck from the University of Toronto, Cathy Moses and Peggy Morton from Queen's, Michelle Roshtyn from the University of Saskatchewan, Laura Mann from Sir George Williams, Tony Hyde from Carleton, and Don McKelvey, a staff member of the American group Students for a Democratic Society. They all lived in a four bedroom house with an office in a garage on the outskirts of the city with Jean Lee, a resident of North Bay who did their cooking, and her two young children.[128]

In preparing their proposal for conversion the students interviewed several relatively prominent members of the community. No one cared about the implications of the base for disarmament. Sam Jacks, the city's Director of Recreation, believed that it was very much appreciated for the money it brought the city. He warned them that to advocate getting rid of the base would jeopardize the success of their project.[129]

Generally, the interviews provided a pot-pourri of information about the city's poor, the economy and the connections between the pecuniary interests of the city's elite and the bases. Mr. Michaels of the Children's Aid Society complained—that North Bay had the lowest level of relief in the province affected further by a system that permitted the personal feelings of local bureaucrats to determine the amount given to applicants. He also reported that there was no impoverished area in North Bay, poor homes were found in otherwise nice areas.[130] T.S. Elliot of the District Health Unit reported that 8.3 percent of the homes in North Bay had outside toilets. The worst housing in the city, he continued, could not be heated in the winter and forced their occupants to leave. He did not know where they went. In addition, the moving of military personnel to the city had caused a housing shortage from which, he claimed, the motels benefitted. The shortage encouraged people to move in together precipitating charges of overcrowding. This led to a city by-law forbidding dwellings to have less then 600 square feet of space per occupant. In the opinion of Elliot, the law would only be enforced at the motels, thereby encouraging more rentals. The student who conducted the interview concluded the housing problem was an "opening for social action."[131]

New Democratic Party President, William Kowalchuck, told his interviewer of Ken Wallace, a prominent real estate developer in the city who, Kowalchuck claimed, owned most of the slum buildings in town by foreclosing on their mortgages. Kowalchuck alleged Wallace had benefitted from the construction of the SAGE and Bomarc bases by selling the land for both to the government. His student interviewer was further told that the former Mayor, Meryl Dickerson, owned the Voyager, Sands, and Ascot motels.[132] Hence, prominent members of the community, both business men and business men politicians, may have benefitted from the construction of the bases.

In addition to information gathered on their own, the students had at their disposal data provided by the RCAF that claimed to show the economic importance of the bases to the city. According to their information, the bases provided 13 percent of the total wages in the city; the base closings would result in the layoffs of 325 people in the city and a loss of 8.2 million dollars in wages.[133]

In the end, they suggested that to replace the economic benefits the bases provided there would have to be a program of "large-scale industrialization" and an educational institute for retraining that would serve the north eastern Ontario region.[134] To discuss the proposal Mayor Hewitt and the Reeves of adjacent Widdifield and West Ferris townships, Don King and Bill Forth convened a committee consisting primarily of local businessmen. The record is vague, but it appears as if the committee decided to ask the provincial government to help fund a conversion study that would be overseen by University of Toronto political economist, Meyer Brownstone, as suggested by the students. This was an early indication that the students had decided the university could be used as an intellectual base for their peace activism. It was not only to be a source for their membership, but was to be actively engaged in helping to bring about the change they desired. It was not, however, to be a base for elitist projects, as Levitt has suggested; it was to be used as a means of encouraging mass participation. In the North Bay project, for example, the students hoped that the community would participate in the making of the study. They suggested local people be enlisted to gather data and that the project include public forums to discuss the study and the plans for conversion.[135] As was so often the case, however, the ideal was far less than realized. The project does not appear to have been completed. As the students realized while conducting their preliminary study, community leaders did not have the will to act; the Mayor, for example, had expressed his hope that the bases would not leave. As Pape concluded, there was no concern about the bases, and the concern they did have was with its economic contribution to the city. Community leaders did not have the same perspective on the military as the students. For them, it was about business, not the Cold War, and as long as the Cold War showed no signs of ending there was no incentive to look for an economic alternative to the bases. In spite of their failure, Pape found something valuable in the experience:

> ... on the positive side, the students get some idea of the complexities of the problem and a few clues on how to link international issues with community problems.[136]

Students from the CUCND also participated in a short-term campaign in the town of La Macaza, 150 miles northeast of Montreal, the location of the second Bomarc base, another manifestation of the students new approach to peace activism. It also reflected their desire to politicize the community. The goal of the project was to have the whole community participate in the creation in the civil disobedience action. Again, like the North Bay project, the ultimate goal was to move the community to act for peace. They organized the action because they believed it was one way in which could have the power "to make decisions which crucially affect the way they live."[137] In the case of La Macaza this meant asking the federal government to close the base and provide an economic alternative.[138]

The use of civil disobedience (CD) at the base was another break with the tradition of activism in the CUCND. It was seen as a possibly more effective means to influence politicians and the military.[139] The choice of CD revealed the influence of the American civil rights movement. American Robert Gore, a Negro pacifist and fieldworker for the Congress of Racial Equality (CORE) was flown in from Atlanta, Georgia, to teach the techniques of CD. Before the action at the base, he conducted a training session instructing participants on how to sit down, how to go limp, and what to do if the police dragged them away.[140] Students practiced by dragging one another around in the dirt; they had decided during the training session to not cooperate if arrested.[141]

The students were welcomed into the community, gaining the support of the local council and individual townspeople. A beach was loaned by council for the students to camp on and a local restaurant donated space for the students to set up an office. They conducted their CD training camp and had their meals in a summer camp loaned by one of the town's citizens who had been a major in the Second World War.[142]

On 13 June, a twenty-four hour vigil began at the base; on weekends it was limited to ten hours permitting some of the students to work for support amongst the townspeople and encourage them to participate in the action. The mayor accepted a nuclear disarmament button; others were given to children in playgrounds and restaurants. Most of the people were reportedly sympathetic but felt powerless to effect change. The students hoped to attract huge numbers from the town, demonstrating the utility of civil disobedience. When planning the action in Montreal they entertained the idea of large numbers of supporters joining them in dismantling the Bomarcs. They hoped to turn the base into a children's summer camp to provide jobs for those displaced by the closing of the base.[143] During the CD townspeople indicated their support in a more modest way by delivering food and coffee to the students who participated; none were involved directly in the CD.

The vigil continued until the 21 June when about one hundred students stood on the roadside leading to the entrance of the base. Dan Daniels, a forty-two year old union organizer, and André Cardinal, a young French indépendantiste and member of the CUCND walked to the gate. A waist-high pole blocked the entrance and a line of air force police stood behind facing them as they approached. Daniels explained to the Sergeant what they were going to do:

> We're going to go down the road and ask permission to enter the base. If your answer is negative, we're going to sit down and block the road. If you try to remove us we won't resist because we believe in non-violence. We'll simply go limp. I want you to know that we're truly sorry for any inconvenience this may cause you. We respect your position—you have to carry out your orders—and I hope you will come to respect ours.[144]

Led by Daniels and Cardinal, 17 of the students and a United Church Minister walked to the entrance singing "We Shall Overcome." All but two sat down immediately when reaching the pole blocking the entrance. One sat down immediately on the other side. The other, Art Pape, shook hands with the sergeant in charge and said,

> You have skills and we think that if we all got together we could do something really constructive like what the UN and the Peace Corps are trying to do in Africa.[145]

He was told that he was arrested, and he sat down. The sergeant spoke to Daniels and claimed that they had lied to him about the protesters stopping at the pole. Daniels called a meeting of the protesters. They argued in front of the soldiers whether they had misled the sergeant or whether he had misunderstood their intentions. They decided that the two who had walked beyond the pole had violated the group's stated intentions; they asked that the two sit with the rest of the students.[146]

Not everyone stayed for the full time of the action. In the evening those who had to work Monday left La Macaza.

Those who stayed brought sleeping bags to the gate. They were awakened at 7:00 Monday morning when a bus arrived on its way out of the base. It was accompanied by a truck filled with air-force police. The pole was lifted and the police dragged the protesters into the ditch, the bus passed, the police moved back to the other side of the pole, and the students returned to their positions facing the police. Vehicles continued to make their way in and out of the base and the students were dragged into the ditch an additional thirty-one times.[147] At 9:30 the police began preventing the protesters from getting out of the ditch. As vehicles passed by the police lined the roadside and physically stopped anyone from getting onto the road.[148] In spite of the physical confrontation, the protest ended convivially. Forming a semi-circle on one side of a barb wire fence the students, led by the United Church minister, held a prayer meeting. The *Sermon on the Mount* was read followed by the *Lord's Prayer*. When ending the protest, the students once again sang "We Shall Overcome." The minister extended his hand over the fence to shake hands with one of the air-force policemen. The students followed him and went down the line of officers shaking hands.[149] Some of the soldiers joined the students in song and "eagerly" accepted copies of the CCND, publication, *Sanity*.[150]

The students returned in September over the Labour Day weekend; 58 people participated in the CD. This time the military was less tolerant of their presence at the entrance to the base. Intent on harassing and forcing sleep deprivation, the military shone a spotlight on the sleeping students and played loud music to keep them awake. *Sanity* reported that 90 soldiers "violently" removed the protesters from the road. Later, four students who attended the protest wrote Pearson and blamed the violence they experienced not on the military, but on a "state that accepts Bomarcs and RCAF training procedures."[151]

The Creation of the Student Union for Peace Action: The New Radicalism, and the Organization of a Disorganized Activism

La Macaza and North Bay were indications of a shift in strategy and a redefinition of their activism, the manifest consequence of failing to prevent the acquisition of nuclear weapons by focusing on a banner membership and lobbying government elites. The CUCND had already strayed from its tradition of protest marches and petitions by trying to politicize communities and encourage a participatory political culture. Both the North Bay and La Macaza projects indicated a willingness to go into communities and act as the initiators of change. It was in this, their expressed desire to go beyond the protest march and their recognition of the importance of changing Canadian society as a method of peace activism, which led to the creation of the Student Union for Peace Action (SUPA). SUPA marked a repudiation of the kind of society that led to the acquisition of the Bomarcs; it was also the organizational expression of the desire to change it.

SUPA was founded over Christmas 1964 in Regina. For the first time all members were invited to attend the conference. 150 students came from 18 universities and all of the provinces except the Maritimes. The conference included resource people from the American peace and civil rights movement. They made an immediate break with tradition in their method of decision-making. Previous meetings made decisions based on the outcome of a majority vote; the CCND continued to operate in this way. This was the first meeting of the CUCND that used consensus decision-making, already used by the American group, Students for Democratic Society (SDS) who had in turn adopted it from the Quaker community.[152] This was an important change that indicated two things: one, the organization was beginning to formalize the influence of the American movement that had previously been exhibited in their talks about non-violence, the use of civil disobedience, and their attempts at community organization in North Bay and La Macaza; two, it showed the group's increasing concern with giving individuals real power to participate and influence the decisions that would effect their lives, and it was symbolic of their desire to divest the elites—who had shown both their irresponsibility in accepting the weapons and the inefficacy of protest and petition citizenship—of their centralized power. In an early indication of the difficulty of making decisions by consensus with a diverse membership previously united by a few clearly articulated objectives but now considering a whole range of criticisms, debate lasted 60 hours over the five days of the meeting.[153]

A draft statement was created entitled "Students and Social Issues in the Nuclear Age." Its purpose was to focus argument in the discussion group's set-up to debate particular areas. A formal statement was to arise out of amendments made by these groups. The draft statement ranged over numerous topics drawing links between seemingly disparate subjects united in their relevance, the students believed to world peace and the prevention of nuclear war. Its introduction demonstrated a holistic concern:

> Mankind is today at an historic conjuncture which demands of us, at a global level, a fundamental reconstruction of institutions and attitudes. Technological revolutions—in the fields of mass communications, rapid transportation, nuclear technology, automated and now cybernated production processes—have brought forth an era in which problems of racial equality, economic and social order, and world peace are integrally related.[154]

It continued with a warning that the recent detente between the superpowers did not mean a less dangerous response to conflict. War was still the means by which nation-states addressed conflict, claimed its authors, and the conflicting interests of the U.S., the Soviet Union and China could lead to World War Three. They also contended that the detente helped focus attention on domestic problems, and that domestic problems shifted resources and attention away from global conflict.

It continued the criticism of military alliances, claiming that they "institutionalized and perpetuated" conflict by reinforcing fear and distrust and by encouraging a dictomous view of the world as friends or enemies. The bomb, they said, had made the system obsolete because warfare was no longer a practical alternative.

Domestic society was also blamed for perpetuating conflict between nations. Institutions and attitudes made war a "normalized part of Canadian society." Any institution that did not challenge the prospect of war needed, it said, to be changed. These included the educational system, the media, and any religious, voluntary, and political associations. The "key supports" of this war-inducing system, however, were the elites—economic, political/technological and military—who made the policies. "The implications of this," it reads,

> … is that it is to a *reconstruction of mainstream institutions and attitudes* which we must look if we are to create a warless world.[155]

It also talked about the role of the student in society and cited the "revival of iconoclasm and social action in North American universities," occurring largely in the U.S. The purpose of the university, it read, had been to produce workers for society as it exists. Therefore, the document concluded, it was a conservative institution. But this notion of the university, they wrote, was "dangerously out of date" because of the need for fundamental change.[156] It would not, however, go on to provide a "concrete definition of the society" that was wanted. Whatever its design, the document said it should reflect the values of "non-violence, cooperation, well-being and *universal participation and responsibility in public life.*"[157]

The presence of a critique of the university was significant for the direction a generalized student movement would take in working to democratize the schools. It was undoubtedly true, as both Westhues and Levitt have pointed out, that the Free Speech Movement (FSM) influenced the direction of the Canadian student movement. It was probably the case that Canadian students and perhaps activist students in particular, were aware of and paid close attention to the Berkeley students and their stand-off with the university's administration over whether or not students had the right to use the campus to promote political causes in general, and the civil rights campaign in particular. As "Students and Social Issues in the Nuclear Age" was being written and put together, there were protests and civil disobedience actions that had

involved as many as six thousand students on Berkeley' s campus. Only weeks before
the CUCND gathered in Regina, the FSM had won a dramatic victory when the faculty
of the university capitulated to the student's demands and voted in a solid majority
"that the content of speech or advocacy should not be restricted by the university."[158]
But it is significant that the critique of the university in the CUCND document
pointed to the American experience in only a cursory and indirect way when it mentioned the "revival of iconoclasm and social action in North American universities."[159]
What is particularly notable in this case is that this criticism grew from within the student peace movement; it was not a knee-jerk reaction to the FSM. As we have already
seen, the role of the university in Canadian society was being examined by the
CUCND at least as early as the December 1963 Federal Conference of the group.
Moreover, Canadian students in the CUCND had placed their critique of the university within the framework of their peace activism and the judgement that the institution's support of the status quo would not prevent a nuclear war.

The importance of the nuclear issue to the entire bundle of their criticisms was
obvious when the issues raised in "Students and Social Issues in the Nuclear Age"
were debated. It was the intention of those gathered to create a "Regina Statement"
outlining policy in detail. But discussion of the issues was often limited to the leaders
who prepared the discussion papers; most were unprepared to discuss the multiple
issues raised in the draft statement. They realized that they were incapable of substantive discussion and decided instead to create a general statement of purpose for
the new organization.[160] It was "widely" agreed that peace necessitated "fundamental social change,"[161] though there was no agreement about what that meant. The result of the conference was the Student Union for Peace Action Statement of Purpose.
They decided that it was to be an organization committed to working in many areas
to build in Canada a society consistent with, and leading to, the conditions of world
peace.

It continued:

To us, it is axiomatic that in the nuclear age man must create a warless
world. We recognize that to accomplish this, fundamental changes in institutions and attitudes throughout the world are necessary.[162]

If it was not as comprehensive a document as they had intended at the outset of the
conference, it included, nevertheless, a broad swathe of issues under the banner of
world peace. Non-alignment was restated as policy of the new organization; nation-states were repudiated and institutions based on effective international law

were prescribed. Behind the required changes was the student, defined as a "social catalyst and challenger of the institutions and attitudes of his nation-state." They would create, it said, "Unions" of people behind social issues related to peace. The student's role was also to challenge the conservative nature of the university, as they perceived it, and to create an institution that would be critical of all institutions and a base for their social activism. Non-violence was to be their method of change, reflecting the obsolescence of violence in the nuclear age. At the root of the statement of purpose, the CUCND's new philosophy, and a harbinger of the direction the movement would take was its definition of peace. It was defined as not merely the absence of war but "*a state in society where people participate in the decisions affecting their futures.*"[163] The belief in the importance of a participatory democracy in the atomic age, the reader will recall, had been given voice in a resolution passed at the December 1963 Federal conference, 8 months after the Bomarc campaign had failed, and only weeks before the missiles arrived in North Bay. They had called then for a restructuring of the political system that would permit citizens to make foreign policy decisions. The importance of foreign policy in the nuclear age meant that it had to be democratized and taken away from the elites who had made the decision to accept nuclear weapons. About a year later at the Regina Conference, this central idea of decentralizing power was still clearly present and was stated in vague terms that potentially broadened the areas that should be democratized to include all but the smallest of decisions. This was a significant change. While it was their experience in the Bomarc campaign that was largely responsible for bringing them to this point, their origins as an anti-nuclear organization would become increasingly less obvious. The value they placed on fostering a participatory democracy eventually took center stage; nuclear weapons became fifth business in the ongoing story of the Student Union for Peace Action.

The importance students attributed to the idea of participation in decision-making was reflected in the decision-making structure assumed by the new organization. SUPA would be highly decentralized and all decisions would continue to be made by consensus, another indication of their opposition to the centralized power of military institutions.[164] A National Council was set-up but its mandate was limited to discussion of national strategy and acting as a liaison between regions. It could not dictate policy to the regions, but if consensus was reached it could determine national programs in which all regions would participate. Membership was to consist of all regional chairman and members of regional staffs, all of the national staff and six members elected from yearly membership conferences. It was the regional councils that were to be responsible for strategy in their particular area, and they were to consist of one member from each university or "institute of learning."

The National Office became largely occupied with the production of a mimeographed newsletter that provided information on SUPA-related projects throughout the country. It also formed the Research and Information Publishing Project that published essays from SUPA members and others and distributed them for a fee. The list of available publications presumably indicated the myriad interests of its membership. They were divided into ten broad sections that included subjects on Canada, Vietnam, China, youth, education, Quebec, strategy, the United States, and pacifism. By selling the essays the National Office was reacting to the student's recognition of their lack of knowledge. It also provided them with a source of revenue since the student's antipathy for centralization extended to providing the National Office with a guaranteed source of money.[165]

The outcome of the conference was celebrated with heady optimism. In an article published in the NDP publication, *The Commonwealth*, the newly elected Federal chairman of SUPA, Jim Harding, described the creation of SUPA this way:

> The Canadian peace movement, which began as a threat to nuclear annihilation, has now matured to an extent where it potentially is one of the most important movements in our history…Historically, this founding conference may well prove to be as significant as the meeting which adopted the Regina Manifesto in 1933.[166]

"The new generation," he continues, "has to in fact build a new world," it has to see itself as a "revolutionary generation" if it is to prevent a nuclear war. Unlike political parties and voluntary organizations in the past, Harding confidently concluded his article; SUPA would not compromise its demands for radical change. Printed in the NDP publication, The Commonwealth, it was clearly intended as a rebuke of the political system in general and the NDP in particular.[167]

In the same month that Harding's article appeared, Roussopoulos published an article in *Sanity*. Written before the conference, it seemed to warn members not to lose sight of the centrality of their peace activism when working for "fundamental change." He hoped to see a new student peace movement emerge from the Regina Conference that would have "world peace as its central and first premise and relates all subsequent issues to this." Action should deliberately set out to raise the peace consciousness of others, he wrote, anything else would be "social work."[168] The article was indicative of a division at the conference. SUPA's vague and holistic criticism of society seemed to permit an activism that could occur in manifold areas. They were no longer united in an activism defined by a limited number of objectives and whose method seemed confined to marches, petitions, lobbying and the education of its members and the public. Everything needed reform, they said, and everything was connected. The division was between those who argued that the way to peace was through social issues and social action, and those who believed that the only way to combat social problems was by challenging the defence and military establishment. In both, peace and social change were interrelated; the difference lay in the focal point of action.[169]

The Canadian summer projects reflected the division. They were at least partly inspired by the work of the Students for a Democratic Society (SDS) which had begun working in community organization projects amongst the American poor in 1963. They took from the American movement the rather vague idea and hope that politicizing people on a local level made them aware of "the larger implications of their behaviour" and would lead to their working for radical change.[170] To become politicized was to be both responsible and disenchanted with the political system. This was a theory applied to others, but they could have been speaking of themselves and their own transition as an organization from lobbyists to advocates of wholesale change. The problem they were to encounter is that they tried to politicize those who, for the most part, did not want to be politicized.

Again they encountered the problem of relevancy to the community they tried to serve. In any case, the similarities between SDS and SUPA belied an important difference. SUPA was still primarily a peace activist organization. Their emulation of SDS work was not the same as copying the meaning of SDS work; issues like poverty and community action that they were now concerned with were ideationally integrated into a "peace action approach."[171] Perhaps owing to the division discussed above, this was not always obvious in the work they performed. Two of the summer actions, the Kingston Community project (KCP) and the Neestow project in Saskatchewan, placed peace activism much in the background. The second La Macaza project, in contrast, placed both social issues and global peace in the foreground.

The purpose of the KCP was to mobilize the poor in any way the poor themselves determined. Its long-term purpose was to create an organization whose goal it would be to abolish poverty. They worked in the area of the city encompassing 80 blocks from the St. Lawrence to the Cataraqui ward north to Joseph Street. They discovered that over half the people living in the area had an annual income of less than $3000 a year, the poverty line that had been established by the Ontario Federation of

Labour. 12.5 percent earned less than a thousand, 69 percent were renters, and a quarter of the accommodations were considered overcrowded.[172]

Their project report shows that the short-term goal was almost entirely unrealized. It is clear that the students wanted to mobilize a large number of tenants. But divisions between tenants and the lack of an over-all sense of community prevented this from happening. Some of the people on Rideau Street, for example, had housing problems like the ones of which a "Mrs. B." complained. Unable to find an affordable and better place, she, her seven kids, and a dog and a cat, lived in a three room basement apartment with a leaky roof, dangerous wiring and had a landlord who was slow to make repairs. But others did not have housing problems, and in any case they did not have the same landlord. Still, some action was taken. After "several" accidents in the area, their one common concern was the safety of their children. They asked the students to draw up a petition and they collected the signatures. They demanded that a fence be constructed to encircle the park in which their children played and that signs be erected reading, "Watch for Children." It was given to their local aldermen to present to council.[173] There was another petition action on Ontario Street that resulted in the conversion of a parking lot to a playground, and still another on Bay Street that asked council to forbid parking on the street.

The only action that involved an allegedly negligent landlord was also the case that received the most media attention. John Hewitt owned four homes on Bay Street, and had tenants on Miller's Lane and Montreal Street. A list of complaints was prepared at a meeting of disgruntled tenants presided over by the students. They wanted their backyards fenced to provide for the safety of their children, the repair of their leaky roofs and their apartments painted. Hewitt refused to speak with them. Fearing the tenants would lose their resolve, the students placed an ad in a local newspaper asking him to meet with them. Having been placed in the public spotlight, Hewitt agreed to a meeting but asked to be paid five dollars an hour, a demand that was reported in the media nation-wide. He thought he was wasting time on "bad tenants" who he believed were the ones at fault for the condition of their apartments. He was paid, but the attention this brought the case brought the media to the meeting. The students did all of the talking, tenants were intimidated into silence in the presence of Hewitt. In the end, he agreed to paint and wallpaper the apartments provided the tenants supplied some of the paper and paint. He also agreed to insulate the hot water tank, and make any repairs outlined in an impending Building Report by the city.[174]

The students successfully started, facilitated and largely led ad hoc groups of the poor for limited goals. If by success we mean the meeting of their own objectives, however, then they surely failed. The purpose was to politicize and by doing this radicalize the poor. But if there was a politicization at all it was ephemeral and appeared to last as long as, or even shorter than, the time required for their projects.

If by one standard the KCP was successful one may not be able to say the same for the Neestow project. It involved SUPA members in a similar exercise but with natives in Saskatchewan on reserves and in urban areas. KCP workers were outsiders who were introduced to the poor through intermediaries. Some of the poor, however, were insulted by their offer of help and would not participate in any effort to organize them.[175] For students in the Neestow project, being an outsider appears to have resulted in no tangible achievements. From the beginning, Neestow workers acknowledged their ignorance of the native communities in which they would be working. The project had no clear purpose beyond learning about the native communities. If issues for mobilization did arise, they were to come from the natives. Fieldworkers reported feeling alienated from the community. They had no intermediaries to introduce them, and Natives would not respond to attempts to initiate conversations on potential issues. Some were suspicious of the student's motives thinking they may have been sent by the Department of Indian Affairs, a welfare agency, or the provincial Department of Fisheries. Working in Prince Albert, participant Pat Uhl expressed the chasm between the lives of the students and the Natives:

> Probably the hardest thing about this summer has been the loneliness of being a university student in the midst of people most of whom have never heard of Bach or Baez or never read Salinger or Camus or (heard) of a teach-in or often even of the war in Vietnam, yet in the face of rats and fleas and hunger, and dirt and annual pneumonia, it's absurd to mention it.[176]

Of all the summer projects, only the one in La Macaza made an explicit connection between community organization and peace and nuclear weapons. The purpose was to involve the community in a study of their rural economy that drew a link between it, the Bomarc base, the devotion of public resources to the military, and the perpetuation of the Cold War. It does not appear as if they were at all successful. This as the third time in two years the students had come proselytizing; unlike the first time, community support appears to have been absent. City officials were not enthusiastic about their presence. The Mayor was reportedly glad that there would not be another demonstration and told them to get involved in something other than the peace movement. The municipal secretary answered their questions politely but was "not very useful." More than the object of the project, townspeople seemed more interested and perturbed about two male project workers living with one female worker, without supervision![177]

At the end of the summer, 150 members met for a postmortem discussion of the projects at Saint-Calixte, Quebec. At this point SUPA was said to have 450 members, though a sympathetic Peter Gzowski covering the event for *Maclean's* claimed they probably represented twice that much. To him, they reiterated their definition of peace which was not just the absence of war but the removal of its causes. To them, this meant bringing about a participatory democracy, defined only as a state in which people make the decisions that affect their lives. It was a means of divesting the politicians and the military, the war makers, of their power to make war. But SUPA's origins as a ban-the-bomb organization were becoming less obvious. At Saint-Calixte, the largest SUPA conference since its founding nine months earlier, the discussion was less about war, and not all about nuclear weapons, than it was about the necessity of living participatory democracy and encouraging its reception by others. The key concept, minutes of the meeting would say, is "participatory democracy."[178] The threat of nuclear, so prevalent at other times, was not mentioned. Where they once described themselves as an "expanding pressure group" they now referred to themselves as a "movement," thereby describing, they believed, a widely decentralized political activism.[179]

For the Canadian New Left, as they were now called, there was no centre.[180] The Federal Council was by the end of its first year almost inoperative.[181] Projects were autonomous and linked by the *SUPA Newsletter*, the contents of which indicated a Babel of student activity. A year after the SUPA's formation, for example, the newsletter contained a report from the University of Alberta where students were fighting the administration to distribute anti-Vietnam war literature; Joan Newman, a KCP project worker, reported on the visit of 7 SDS members from Buffalo; and the Carleton chapter announced it had run several candidates in a recent student election on issues that included student representation on the Senate and the Board of Governors of the university.[182] Several members became involved in the Liberal government's youth program called the Company of Young Canadians (CYC). By 1967, the CYC had absorbed many of its community workers and had linked up with most of the remaining SUPA projects.[183]

Thus, SUPA represented a change from a peace organization with limited and well-defined objectives and methods for convincing the government to refuse nuclear weapons on Canadian soil. It became a weak organization that was an expression of a movement under the vague, and therefore inclusive, banner of "participatory democracy" seeking change everywhere and in no place in particular. The polymorphic nature of the organization called for an amorphous definition. In the same year that SUPA folded, Edmontonian and member Ted Folkman described it this way:

> SUPA is an anarchist-oriented peace movement; SUPA is a left-wing liberal youth movement; SUPA is a conglomeration of peaceniks, beatniks, peace creeps, idealists, committed kids, utopian socialists, the avant-garde of the new generation.[184]

The *SUPA Newsletter* stopped publishing in late 1967. In its place rose the *New Left Committee Bulletin*; its first headline read, "SUPA is Dead. Long Live the Revolution." Fragmentation, a continual loss of membership in the two years of its existence and a lack of interest in maintaining a national organization were among the contributors of SUPA's demise. In its place there stood a small band of Marxists that assumed SUPA's $5,000 debt. They set out to create a new organization with a clear statement of ideology, complaining of SUPA's "ill-defined SDS notions of 'participatory democracy'," and that it was "ideologically confused" and "uncritically eclectic."[185] The attempt to recreate a national organization by adopting a clear ideological statement failed for lack of interest. This was the definitive end. The Committee announced its solution in early 1968,[186] and the papers of the CUCND, SUPA and the NLC were sold to McMaster University archives to pay off the remaining debt.[187]

Conclusion: A Changing Concept of Citizenship in the Nuclear Age

The separate beginnings of the Combined Universities Campaign for Nuclear Disarmament (CUCND) and the Canadian Campaign for Nuclear Disarmament (CCND) were traced to the late 1950s. They emerged in a political context that may have discouraged political activism and one in which, as S.D Clark contends, the new suburban communities were uninterested in the important issues of the world.[188] Universities appear to have reflected this relative lack of political dissent. Activism was present in the peace movement. Represented primarily by the Canadian Peace Congress (CPC), however, the peace movement appears to have been a largely illegitimate forum in which dissent could be expressed. It was vilified by the press and politicians as a subversive organization, "a trap so cunningly baited by the Communists and their sympathizers," in the words of Lester Pearson in 1950.

The National Committee for the Control Radiation Hazards began its conservative activism in this context in 1958. It did not build on the organizational foundation of the CPC; it distanced itself from their methods and insulated itself from the group's opprobrious legacy. Its objectives included regulations governing the safe use of radioactive technology and a prohibition on the atmospheric testing of nuclear weapons. It did not begin as a ban-the-bomb group, but as an organization seeking regulations to live with the bomb and its technological cousins. Its methods reflected the desire to be respectable. Like its American inspiration, SANE, it used a membership of distinguished Canadians to make itself legitimate. It repudiated methods used by the CPC and the British campaign for Nuclear Disarmament like protest marches and petitions. The group saw its role as an educator, a quiet mobilizer of public opinion to bring about change.

The CUCND emerged from the ban-the-bomb campaign in Britain and the domestic politics of the Bomarc question. They adopted the symbols of the British campaign: the name of the British student disarmament group and the black and white peace sign. The literature on the British CUCND, though poor for our purposes, suggests it was characterized by a rejection of old Left communists and a critique of the society that produced the bomb. The movement journal, *Our Generation Against Nuclear War*, expressed from its inception in 1960 the connection between social issues and the bomb. But the policy of the CUCND remained restricted to the Bomarc and its link to disarmament. It advocated that a non-aligned Canada assume the leadership of nations outside of the major blocs of the United States and the Soviet Union. This suggested to us the existence of two currents of thought: the one willing to make a more radical critique of the problem, the other content with limited objectives.

The NCCRH expanded its agenda to include opposition to the Bomarcs only after others had declared their opposition. Indeed, they justified the change in policy on the grounds the opposition liberals and others were against the acquisition of the weapon. They accepted the notion of petitioning the government and worked with the CUCND on a country-wide campaign to collect signatures. When the campaign was lost no significant changes were made to the organization's ideas and tactics remained the same.

In contrast, the loss of the campaign facilitated important changes in the CUCND. The students began discussing a redefined peace activism and interpreted the technique of non-violence, exemplified by the American civil rights movement, within the context of their own experiences. In North Bay and La Macaza, they tried politicizing the communities to reject the Bomarc bases. They used new methods indicating their frustration with the failure of the protest march and the petition. In both cases, they hoped they might be the catalysts to a participatory political culture that challenged the power of the governing elite. And in both cases, they failed to mobilize the community. But like in the wake of the failed Bomarc campaign, a redefinition of their activism followed. The creation of the Student Union for Peace Action was the distillation of their experience in the Bomarc campaign and their subsequent discussions of the required changes in attitudes and structures to prevent a nuclear war. The radical tradition suggested in *Our Generation Against Nuclear War*, combined with the failure of the Bomarc, along with the influence of the American student movement, to facilitate a change in the policy of the new organization. It went from a limited to a holistic critique, its methods changed from a relatively restricted repertoire of marches, lobbying and education, to a plethora of actions in a very decentralized and heterogeneous student movement.

This last stage reflected a significant transition. The students began as anti-nuclear lobbyists in 1959 who were content with their relatively limited objectives and who believed in the ability of their political culture to respond correctly to the threat of nuclear war. Its failure to do so precipitated a redefinition of the kind of citizenship necessary in the atomic age. To prevent a nuclear holocaust it was necessary, they came to believe, to effect radical changes that would allow citizens to participate in decision making. The seminal importance of the students' early peace work became obscured in their later activism and desire for a "participatory democracy," the crucible remained in the experience of the CUCND. It was, in sum, the story of a progressive unfolding of their disenchantment with centralized rule and of the importance of personal responsibility in modern government under the shadow of nuclear weapon.

Notes

1 L. Feuer, *The Conflict of Generations: The Character and Significance of Student Movements* (New York, 1969), 378, 385.

2 Henceforth, it will be referred to as the Bomarc.

3 Bothwell, R., Ian Drummond, John English, *Canada Since 1945: Power, Politics and Provincialism* (Toronto, 1981), pp. 255-257.

4 Levitt, *Children of Privilege* (Toronto, 1984). See Chapter Two "The Crucible of the Student Revolt," pp.19-39.

5 Levitt, *Children of Privilege*, p. 42.

6 K. Westhues, "Intergenerational Conflict in the Sixties," in S.D. Clark et al., *Prophecy and Protest* (Toronto, 1975), pp. 388-389.

7 Westhues, p. 402.

8 Westhues, p. 400. He draws from the research of Richard Flacks, an American sociologist who worked with data derived from American students. For a more comprehensive discussion of Flack's ideas see his *Youth and Social Change* (Chicago: Markham, 1971).

9 Westhues, p.390.

10 Kostash, *Long Way From Home* (Toronto, 1980), p. xiii.

11 Ibid., pp. 72-75.

12 Ibid., pp. 75-76.

13 K. Nossal, *The Politics of Canadian Foreign Policy*, (Scarborough, 1952), pp. 57-58.

14 D. Munton, "Public Opinion and the Media in Canada," in *International Journal* Vol. XXXIX, No.1, Winter 1983-84, p. 189.

15 R. Whitaker and G. Marcuse, *Cold War Canada: The Making of a National Insecurity State*, 1945-1957, (Toronto, 1994), pp. 332-33.

16 See, for example, Leo Zakuta's "The Radical Political Movement in Canada" in *Urbanism and the Changing Canadian Society* (Toronto, 1961), pp. 149-50. In explaining the lack in the 1950s of a radical CCF platform he writes: "Although the world has been hard on the party, it has been much kinder to its individual members and to the public at large." In other words, the strong economy of the 1950s removed the appeal from a radical restructuring of the economy as advocated in the Regina Manifesto.

17 S.D. Clark, *The Suburban Society* (Toronto, 1968), p. 194.

18 P. Axelrod and J. Reid (eds.), *Youth, University and Society* (Kingston, 1989). Lipset has described the quiet decade for American students in "Historical Background: The Twenties Through the Fifties," *Rebellion in the University*, pp. 159-170.

19 M. Hayden, *Seeking a Balance: The University of Saskatchewan 1907-82* (Vancouver, 1983), p. 216.

20 C. Stone and F. Gannett, *Brandon College* (Manitoba, 1969), pp. 181-82. See also C. Bissell's *Halfway up Parnassus: A Personal Account of the History of the University of Toronto* (Toronto, 1974). He de-

votes an entire chapter to "Student Power" in the 1960s while the 1950s are almost bereft of students.

21 Alan Bairava, "With Concern for Young Idealists," *Saturday Night* Sept. 1965, p. 22. Bairava, when writing of the Queen's University professor who was not permitted entry into the United States, is probably referring to Professor Shortcliffe. For a short account of his troubles see R. Whitaker and G. Marcuse, pp. 273-274.

22 Lucille Marr, "If you want peace, prepare for peace: Hanna Newcombe, Peace Researcher and Peace Activist," in *Ontario History* Volume LXXXIV No. 4, 1992, p. 269.

23 J. Nogee and R. Donaldson, *Soviet Foreign Policy Since World War Two* (New York, 1988), p. 339.

24 *Monthly Bulletin of the Department of External Affairs*, December 1949 Vo1.1, No. 12.

25 J. Nogee and R. Donaldson, p. 98.

26 Whitaker and Marcuse, p. 364.

27 Socknat, p. 289.

28 Socknat, p. 291.

29 Whitaker and Marcuse, p. xvii.

30 Socknat, p. 290; Whitaker and Marcuse, p. 366.

31 Socknat, p. 290.

32 G. Moffat, *A History of the Peace Movement in Canada* (Ottawa, n.d.), p. 17.

33 Moffat, p. 20.

34 Moffat, p. 19.

35 Whitaker and Marcuse, p. 375.

36 Whitaker and Marcuse, p. 373.

37 Whitaker and Marcuse, p. 373.

38 Whitaker and Marcuse, p. 375.

39 NAC M.G. C130 (Endicott papers) vol. 81, file 1660 Clippings 1959, Roderich Goodman, "From Alberta a sane fight to ban the bomb," *Globe and Mail Magazine* 15 August 1959, p. 10.

40 *Monthly Bulletin of the Department of External Affairs* December, 1955, Vol. 7, No. 12, pp. 327, 336.

41 *Maclean's*, "How Serious is the Threat of Radiation," December 8, 1956, p. 118.

42 Ibid., p. 116. X-rays determined whether or not the shoe fit.

43 NAC RG 18 (Records of the RCMP) Request number 95-A-00134, Vol. 738, Case History-CCND. This report is dated a few months after the group presented Diefenbaker with a 142,000 petition against the Bomarc missiles.

44 NAC M.G. 31 F9 (Feinberg Papers) Vol. 3, File NCCRH, Mary Van Stolk, "Report of the National Executive Secretary, Pro Tem," 20 March 1961.

45 NAC RG 18 (Records of the RCMP) Request number 95-A-00134, Vol. 738, Case History-CCND, p. 14.

46 NAC M.G. C130 (Endicott papers) Vol. 81, file 1660 Clippings 1959, Roderich Goodman, "From Alberta a sane fight to ban the bomb," *Globe and Mail Magazine* 15 August 1959, p. 27.

47 Feinberg was a prominent peace activist in Toronto. The Toronto Committee for Disarmament became an affiliate of the NCCRB.

48 NAC M.G. 31 F9 (Feinberg Papers) Vol. 4, file TCD Correspondence with NCCRB Groups, memo, minutes and meetings 1959-61, M. Stolk to A. Feinberg, 23 July, 1959.

49 Ibid.

50 "March on Ottawa," *Globe and Mail* December 28, 1959.

51 Interview with D. Roussopoulos, 1 June 1996, p. 2.

52 Canadian University Press, "McMaster CUCND," *The Carleton*, October 30, 1962, p. l.

53 Canadian University Press, "CUCND Ratified," *The Carleton*, October 30, January 16, 1962, p. 4.

54 Canadian University Press, "CUCND Policies Rejected," *The Carleton*, November 3, 1961, p. l.

55 Frank Marzari, "CUCND Ousted at St. Mikes," *The Carleton*, February 2 1962, p.3.

56 Canadian University Press, "CUCND Ousted at St. Mikes," *The Carleton*, February 2 1962, p.3.

57 "Ban the Bombers Not Carletoner," *The Carleton*, October 26, 1962, p. l.

58 Canadian University Press, "Goldstick Expelled from CUCND," *The Carleton*. December 1, 1961, p. 3.

59 National Archives of Canada, RG 18 (Records of the RCMP) Request number 95-A-00134, Vol. 738, Case History-CCND, p. 14.

60 Moffat, p.3.

61 NAC M.G. 31 F9 (Feinberg papers) Vol. 3, File TCD CUCND 1960, Combined Universities Campaign for Nuclear Disarmament, "Provisional Policy Statement."

62 P. Duff, *Left, Left, Left* (London, 1971), p.160.

63 NAC M.G. 31 F9 (Feinberg papers) Vol. 3, File TCD CUCND 1960, Combined Universities Campaign for Nuclear Disarmament, "Provisional Policy Statement.ö

64 C. Driver, *The Disarmers: A Study in Protest* (London, 1964), p. 74.

65 Stephen Hatch, "From CND to Newest Left," David Martin ed., *Anarchy and Culture: The Problem of the Contemporary University* (London, 1969), p. 123.

66 Duff, p. 132.

67 NAC M.G. 31 F9 (Feinberg papers) Vol. 3, File TCD CUCND 1960, Combined Universities Campaign for Nuclear Disarmament, "Provisional Policy Statement."

68 Williams Ready Division of the Mill's Library (Henceforth WRDML), McMaster University, (CUCND/SUPA Papers) Box 1, CUCND-Executive Meeting 1961 January.

69 "Statement of Purpose" *Our Generation Against Nuclear War*, Winter 1962, Vol. 1, No. 2, p. 1.

70 Autumn 1961, Vol. 1, No. 1, p. 3.

71 Winter 1961, vol.1, No. 2, p. 3.

72 Greg Connolley, "National CD Test Nov. 13," *Ottawa Citizen*, 17 October 1961, p. 1.

73 M. Barnes, *Gateway City: The North Bay Story* (North Bay, 1982), p. 102.

74 NAC M.G. 31 F9 (Feinberg papers) Vol. 3, File CUCND n.d. and 1961, CUCND pamphlet, "Motorcade to North Bay."

75 *North Bay Nugget*, 9 May, 1960, pp.3-4.

76 "Legion Protests Use of Park for Peace Rally," *North Bay Nugget*, 7 May, 1960, p. 1.

77 Starr Cote, "Students in Orderly Picket at Missile Sites in North Bay," *North Bay Nugget* 10 May 1960, p. 3.

78 (untitled) 12 May 1960, p. 2.

79 Orma McNaughton, 11 May 1960, p. l7.

80 NAC M.G. 31 F9 (Feinberg Papers) Vol. 4, file TCD Correspondence with NCCRH Groups, memo, minutes and meetings 1959-61, NCCRH Inter-committee memo 17 January, 1961.

81 NAC M.G. 31 F9 (Feinberg Papers) Vol. 4, file TCD Correspondence with NCCRH Groups, memo, minutes and meetings 1959-61, NCCRH Press Release, Toronto, 30 January, 1961.

82 NAC M.G. 31 F9 (Feinberg Papers) Vol. 4, file TCD Correspondence with NCCRH Groups, memo, minutes and meetings 1959-61, Dr. Keenleyside's Speech, 20 March 1961.

83 Interview with D. Roussopoulos, 1 June 1996, p. 2.

84 Roussopoulos, D., *The Coming of World War Three* (Montreal, 1986), p. 128.

85 NAC RG 18 (Records of the RCMP) Request number 95-A-00134, Vol. 738, Case History-CCND, p. 6.

86 Roussopoulos, *The Coming of World War Three*, pp.127-128.

87 NAC M.G. l 389 (Canadian Campaign for Nuclear Disarmament papers) Vol. l, file News releases 1961, News release Oct. 6, 1961.

88 Norman Campbell, "Petition on Hill For Nuclear Ban," *North Bay Nugget*, 6 October 1961, p. 1.

89 This is Roussopoulos' vague estimate. Interview with D. Roussopoulos, 1 June 1996, p. 27.

90 N. Hillmer and J. L. Granastein. *Empire to Umpire: Canada and the World to the 1990s* (Toronto, 1994), p. 261. There seems to be some disagreement on the reasons for Pearson's decision, though the reasons that have been proffered are not necessarily incompatible with one another. Historians Norman Hillmer and Jack Granatstein write that he was "avid for power," suggesting he believed that public opinion was behind him. Historians Robert Bothwell, Ian Drummond and John English, in contrast, say that he was "distressed both by the Cuban crisis and by the American military revelations that had revealed the full weakness and dishonesty of the Canadian position." See Bothwell et al., p. 248.

91 NAC M.G. 31 E38 (Thorson Papers) Vol. 23, f. Board of Directors, "Board of Director's Meeting —Ottawa, April 20-21, 1963."

92 When Pearson announced the new Liberal policy members of the University of Toronto CUCND picketed the Toronto Liberal office. They also collected 10,000 names on a petition in a week protesting the change. See *Sanity* Vol. 1, No. 3, (March 1963) p. 4.

93 P. J. Wilson, "The night the warheads arrived one of secrecy, security," *North Bay Nugget* 21 September, 1996, p. B-1.

94 NAC M.G. 31 E38 (Thorson Papers) vol. 21, File 8, Press Release, Wednesday July 10, 1963.

95 NAC M.G. 30 c130 (Endicott Papers) Vol. 82, File 1669, "Anti-war policy Considered by CND," *The Commonwealth* Sept. 25, 1963.

96 NAC RG 18 (Records of the RCMP) Request number D950-243-1, Vol. 534, No. 3286, Carleton CUCND Newsletter, Vol. 2, No. 1, Oct. 8, 1963.

97 NAC RG 18 (Records of the RCMP) Request number D950-243-1, Vol. 534, No. 3286, C. Rosenberg, "Shades of Grey," Carleton CUCND Newsletter, Vol. l, No. 5, Aug. 1963, pp. 3-4.

98 NAC M.G. 30 c130 (Endicott Papers) Vol. 82, File 1669, "Anti-War Policy Considered by CND," *The Commonwealth* Sept. 25, 1963.

99 Interview with D. Roussopoulos, 1 June 1996, p. 2. Also see J. Allock, pp. 75-76.

100 NAC, M.G. l 389 (Canadian Campaign for Nuclear Disarmament papers) Vol. 1, "Green Paper."

101 NAC M.G. 31 E38 (Thorson Papers) Vol. 21, File 8, Arnold Simoni's response to working paper, 1963.

102 NAC M.G. 31 E38 (Thorson Papers) vol. 21, File 8, Policy Proposals from B.C. Branch, 1963.

103 NAC M.G. l 389 (Canadian Campaign for Nuclear Disarmament Papers) Vol. l, Open letter to Members by John A. Lee, Oct. 18, 1963.

104 NAC M.G. 1389 (Canadian Campaign for Nuclear Disarmament Papers) Vol. 1, Minutes CCND Meeting Oct. 25 1963.

105 NAC M.G. 28 1389 (Canadian Campaign for Nuclear Disarmament Papers), Vol. 1, Minutes, Board of Directors, CCND, Oct. 25 1963.

106 J. Allock, p. 76.

107 NAC M.G. l 389 (Canadian Campaign for Nuclear Disarmament Papers) Vol. 1, Minutes CCND Meeting Oct. 25 1963.

108 *Sanity*, December 1963 Vol. 1, No. 9, p. 1.

109 "CUCND and French Canada," *Sanity*, December, 1963, Vol. 1, No.9, 5.

110 Ibid.

111 "Open Letter to Parliament," quoted in C. Levitt, "Canada," in P. Altbach (ed.), *Student Political Activism: An International Reference Handbook* (New York, 1989), p. 421.

112 *Sanity*, March 1964, Vol. 1, No. 11

113 WRDML CUCND/SUPA collection, Box 10, File Queen's, Art Pape, "The Future of the Peace Movement," in The Alliance System publication for the Feb. 1964 CUCND Seminar at Queen's University, Kingston.

114 WRDML CUCND/SUPA Collection, Box 1, File Executive Minutes, May 29, 1963 Secretariat Minutes.

115 "CCND national office moves to Ottawa," *Sanity*, June 1965, Vol. 2, No. 9., P. 8.

116 "The CCND," *Sanity*, January 1963, Vol. 1, No. 1, p. 2.

117 Moffat, p. 30.

118 WRDML CUCND/SUPA Collection Box B, File North Bay '64, The North Bay Project Prospectus

119 Ibid.

120 WRDML CUCND/SUPA Collection Box 8, File North Bay '64, Art Pape to Mr. and Mrs. Cadbury, 11 August, 1964.

121 WRDML CUCND/SUPA Collection Box 8, File North Bay '64, The North Bay Project Prospectus.

122 WRDML CUCND/SUPA Collection Box 8, File North Bay '64, *Globe and Mail*, January 11, 1964.

123 North Bay Public Library, North Bay Material Collection, Department of Industries, "Facts About the North Bay, Widdifield, West Ferris Area," 1962.

124 North Bay Public Library, North Bay Material Collection, Wilford D. Reeves, "Your Key to the Gateway of the North," 1963-64, p. 27.

125 WRDML CUCND/SUPA Collection Box 1, File CUCND Executive Meetings, Minutes of Secretariat Meeting January 28, 1964.

126 Roussopoulos, *The Coming of World War Three*, p. 128.

127 WRDML CUCND/SUPA Collection Box 8, File CUCND North Bay '64, Liora Proctor to Lynn McCann, June 2 1964.

128 WRDML CUCND/SUPA Collection Box 8, File CUCND North Bay '64, 1964. Newsletter North Bay '64, p. l.

129 WRDML CUCND/SUPA Collection Box 8, File CUCND North Bay '64, Terry Shaw's interview with Sam Jacks May 29, 1964.

130 WRDML CUCND/SUPA Collection Box 8, File CUCND North Bay '64, Liora Proctor's interview of Mr. Michaels, Children's Aid Society, n.d.

131 WRDML CUCND/SUPA Collection Box 8, File CUCND North Bay '64, Liora Proctor's interview with T.S. Elliot of the District Health Unit, May 29, 1964.

132 WRDML CUCND/SUPA Collection Box 8, File CUCND North Bay '64, Interview (the name of the interviewer is not provided) with Sam Jacks May 29, 1964.

133 "North Bay '64," *Sanity*, December 1964, Vol.2, No. 5, p. 3.

134 Ibid.

135 WRDML COCND/SUPA Collection Box 8, File CUCND North Bay '64, Suggested Approach, North Bay Conversion Study, November 15, 1964.

136 Ken Drushka, "Peace project at North Bay mixed success," *Globe Magazine* March 6, 1965, p. 3.

137 "La Macaza Project," *Sanity*, Vol. 2, No.2, p. 5.

138 "A Break-through at La Macaza," Sanity, July 1964, Vol. 2, No. 3, p. 2.

139 "They deliberately set out to break the law...because they believed this was the only way to make any impressions on politicians and the military." David Lewis Stein, "The peaceniks go to La Macaza," *Maclean's*, August 8, 1964, p. 11.

140 Interview with D. Roussopoulos, 1 June 1996, p. 13.

141 Stein, "The peaceniks go to La Macaza," p. 36.

142 Interview with D. Roussopoulos, 1 June 1996, p. 13.

143 Stein, "The peaceniks go to La Macaza," p. 36.

144 Stein, "The peaceniks go to La Macaza," p. 11.

145 Stein, "The peaceniks go to La Macaza," p. 36.

146 Stein, "The peaceniks go to La Macaza," p. 36.

147 Stein, "The peaceniks go to La Macaza," p. 36; *Sanity* July 1964, Vol. 2, No. 3.

148 Stein, "The Peaceniks go to La Macaza," p. 37.

149 Stein, "The Peaceniks go to La Macaza," p. 37.

150 *Sanity*, July 1964, Vol. 2, No. 3.

151 *Sanity*, October 1964, Vol.2, No. 6.

152 Interview with Roussopoulos, p. 17.

153 NAC M.G. 31 F9 (Feinberg papers) Vol. 3, File Clippings 1963-1965, Jim Harding, "Student Union for Peace Action Founded at Regina Conference," *The Commonwealth* January 13, 1965, p. 3.

154 WRDML CUCND/SUPA Collection Box 7, File Regina Conference, Matt Cohen, Art Pape and Liora Proctor "Students and Social Issues in the Nuclear Age—Draft Statement—CUCND Regina Conference—December 1964."

155 Ibid., p. 4. Italics are mine.

156 Ibid., p. 12.

157 Ibid., p. 14. Italics are mine.

158 Feuer, p. 452.

159 See footnote no. 154.

160 "A New Policy," *Sanity*, February 1965, Vol.2, No. 7, p. 7.

161 Ibid., p. 7.

162 Student Union for Peace Action, "Statement of Purpose," December-January, Regina Conference 1964-65.

163 NAC M.G. 31 F9 (Feinberg papers) vol. 3, File Clippings 1963-1965, Jim Harding, "Student Union for Peace Action Founded at Regina Conference," *The Commonwealth* January 13, 1965, p.3. Italics are mine.

164 Ibid.

165 Harvey Feit, "A Report on the New SUPA-structure," *Sanity*, February 1965, Vol.2, No.2, p. 7.

166 NAC M.G. 31 F9 (Feinberg papers) Vol. 3, File Clippings 1963-1965, Jim Harding, "Student Union for Peace Action Founded at Regina Conference," *The Commonwealth* January 13, 1965, p.3.

167 NAC M.G. 31 F9 (Feinberg papers) Vol. 3, File Clippings 1963-1965, Jim Harding, "Student Union for Peace Action Founded at Regina Conference," *The Commonwealth* January 13, 1965, p. 3.

168 "CUCND and Social Issues," *Sanity*, January 1965, Vol. 2, No. 6, 2.

169 "A New Policy," *Sanity*, February 1965, Vol.2, No.7, 1965, p. 7.

170 WRDML, CUCND/SUPA Collection, Box 8, File Kingston Community Project, Kingston Community Project Prospectus, 2.

171 Ibid.

172 Ibid., p. 5.

173 WRDML CUCND/SUPA Collection, Box 8, File Kingston Community Project, Kingston Community Project Report., p. 6.

174 Ibid., p. 8.

175 WRDML CUCND/SUPA Collection, Box 2, File Kingston Community Project, 8. Shepherd, A Report on Community Organizing Projects Summer '65, prepared for the Company of Young Canadians, p. 2.

176 WRDML, CUCND/SUPA Collection, Box ID, File Neestow project, "Report of the Neestow Project, May 12-September 2, 1965."

177 WRDML CUCND/SUPA Collection, Box 10, File La Macaza Project, Project La Macaza '65, 2.

178 WRDML, CUCND/SUPA Collection, Box 10, File Saint Calixte, SUPA Minutes of the Meeting of the Federal Council at Saint-Calixte, Sept. 912, 1965.

179 Ibid.

180 Gzowski, "Crusaders of the New Left," *Maclean's* Nov. 15, Vol. 78, No. 22, p. 18.

181 Matt Cohen, "A proposal for a change in SUPA structure," *SUPA Newsletter*, Dec. 21, 1965, Vol. 1, No. 13, p. 8.

182 *SUPA Newsletter*, Dec. 21, 1965, Vol. 1, No. 13.

183 L. Pal, *Interests of State: The Politics of Language, Multiculturalism and Feminism in Canada* (Montreal and Kingston, 1993), p. 47.

184 *SUPA Newsletter* Feb. 10, 1967, Vol. 3, No. 4, p. 18.

185 *New Left Committee Bulletin*, Oct. '67, Vol. l, No. l, p. 6a.

186 *New Left Committee Bulletin* Feb-Mar.1968, Vol. 1 No. 3.

187 Interview with D. Roussopoulos, 1 June 1996, p. 27.

188 Clark, p. 194.

Bibliography

Primary Sources: Documentary Collections

National Archives of Canada

Manuscript Collections

The Canadian Campaign for Nuclear Disarmament Papers

John Endicott Papers

Abraham Feinberg Papers

J.T. Thorson papers

Government Records

The Royal Canadian Mounted Police, RG18

North Bay Public Library

The North Bay Material Collection

William Readys Division of Mills Library, McMaster University
The Combined Universities Campaign for Nuclear Disarmament/Student Union for Peace Action Collection

Printed Primary Sources

Allock, J., "The Canadian Campaign for Nuclear Disarmament: A Study in the Dynamics of a Social Movement" (Ottawa: Carleton University: Master Thesis, Department of Sociology, 1968)

Altbach, P. (ed.), *Student Political Activism: An International Reference Book*(New York: Greenwood Press, 1989)

Author unknown, "March on Ottawa," *Globe and Mail* December 28, 1959

Axelrod, P. and J Reid (eds.) *Youth, University and Society* (Kingston: McGill-Queen's Press, 1989)

Barnes, M., *Gateway City: The North Bay Story* (North Bay: North Bay and District Chamber of Commerce, 1982)

Bissell, C., *Halfway Up Parnassus: A Personal Account of the University of Toronto 1932-71* (Toronto: University of Toronto Press, 1974)

Bairava, A., "With Concern for Young Idealists," *Saturday Night* (Sept. 1965), 22

Bothwell, R., et al. *Canada Since 1945: Power, Politics, and Provincialism* (Toronto: University of Toronto Press, 1984)

Clark, S.D. *The Suburban Society* (Toronto: University of Toronto Press, 1968)

Cote, S., "Students in Orderly Picket at Missile Sites in North Bay," *North Bay Nugget* (May 10, 1960) 3

Driver, C., *The Disarmers: A Study in Protest* (London: Hodder and Stoughton, 1964)

Drushka, K., "Peace Project at North Bay mixed success," *Globe and Mail Magazine* (March 6, 1965) 3

Duff, P., *Left, Left, Left London: Allison and Busby, 1971*

Feit, H., "A Report on the New SUPA-structure," *Sanity* 2 (February, 1965) 7

Feurer, L., *The Conflict of Generations: The Character and Significance of Student Movements* (New York: Basic Books, 1969)

Gzowski, P., "Crusaders of the New Left," *Maclean's* 78 (November 15, 1965), 18-19

Hatch, S., "From CND to newest Left," David Martin ed., *Anarchy and Culture: The Problem of the Contemporary University* (London Routledge and Kegan Paul, 1969)

Hayden, M. *Seeking a Balance: The University of Saskatchewan 1907-82* (Vancouver: University of British Columbia Press, 1983)

Hillmer, N., and J. Granatstein *Empire To Umpire: Canada and the World to the 1990s* (Toronto: Copp Clark Longman, 1994)

Kostash, M., *Long Way From Home: The Story of the Sixties Generation in Canada* (Toronto: James Lorimer and Company, 1980)

Levitt, C., *Children of Privilege: A Study of Student Movements in Canada, the United States and Germany* (Toronto: University of Toronto Press, 1984)

Maclean's "How Serious is the Threat of Radiation" (December 8, 1956), p.118

Marr, L., "If you want peace, prepare for peace: Hanna Newcombe, Peace Researcher and Peace Activist" *Ontario History* LXXXIV, (December, 1992) 263-281

Marzari, F., "CUCND Ousted at St. Mikes," *The Carleton* (February 2, 1962), 3

McNaughton, O., "Northgate Centre Gets off with a (Bomarc) Bang!" *North Bay Nugget* (May 11, 1960), 17

Moffat, G., *A History of the Peace Movement in Canada*, (Ottawa: Grape Vine Press, n.d.)

Monthly Bulletin of the Department of External Affairs Vol. l, No. 12, Dec. 1949

Munton, D., "Public Opinion and the Media in Canada," *International Journal* XXXIX, (Winter 1983-84), 171-213

New Left Committee Bulletin 1 (October, 1967) 6a

———. (February-March, 1968)

Nogee J., and R. Donaldson, *Soviet Foreign Policy Since World War Two* (New York: Pergamon press, 1988)

North Bay Nugget "Legion Protests Use of Park for Peace Rally," (May 7, 1960) 1

North Bay Nugget Untitled, (May 12, 1960) 2

Nossal, K., *The Politics of Canadian Foreign Policy* (Scarborough: Prentice-Hall, 1985)

Our Generation Against Nuclear War 1 "Statement of Purpose" (Winter 1962), 1

Pal, L., *Interests of State: The Politics of Language, Multiculturalism and Feminism in Canada* (Montreal: McGill-Queen's Press, 1993)

Priestly, J. B., "Preface to the Second Issue," *Our Generation Against Nuclear War* 1 (Winter 1961), 3

Roussopoulos, D., *The Coming of World War Three* (Montreal: Black Rose Books, 1986)

Russell, B., "Preface to the First Issue," *Our Generation Against Nuclear War* 1 (Autumn, 1961) 3

Sanity 1 "The CCND," (January, 1963) 2

———. (December, 1963), 1

———. "CUCND and French Canada," (December, 1963) 6

———. (March, 1964), 11

Sanity 2 "La Macaza project," (October 1964), 5

——. "A Breakthrough at La Macaza," (July1964), 2

——. "North Bay '64," (December 1964), 3

——. "CUCND and Social Issues," (January 1965), 2

——. "A New Policy," (February 1965)

——. "CCND National Office Moves to Ottawa," (June, 1965) 8

Socknat, T., *Witness Against War* (Toronto: University of Toronto Press, 1987)

Stein, D. L., "The peaceniks go to La Macaza," *Maclean's* (August 8, 1964) 11

Stone, C., and F. Gannett, *Brandon College* Manitoba: Brandon University, 1969

Student Union for Peace Action, *Statement of Purpose* Regina Conference, December /January 1964-65

SUPA Newsletter 1 "A proposal for a change in SUPA structure," Cohen, M., (December 21, 1965), 8

SUPA Newsletter 3 (February 10, 1967) 18

The Carleton "CUCND policies Rejected," (November 3, 1961) 1

——. "CUCND Ousted at University of Manitoba," (February 2, 1962), 3

——. "Ban the Bombers Not Carletoners." (October 26, 1962) 1

——. "Goldstick Expelled from CUCND," (December 1, 1962) 3

Westhues, K., "Intergenerational Conflict in the Sixties," S.D. Clark et al. *Prophecy and Protest: Social Movements in Twentieth Century Canada* (Toronto: Gage Educational Publishing, 1975)

Whitaker, R. and G. Marcuse, *Cold War Canada* (Toronto: university of Toronto Press, 1994)

Wilson, P. J., "The night warheads arrived one of secrecy, security," *North Bay Nugget* (21 September, 1996), B-1

Zakuta, L., "The Radical Movement in Canada," S.D. Clark ed. *Urbanism and the Changing Canadian Society* (Toronto: University of Toronto Press, 1961)

Bryan D. Palmer

| Chapter **3** | New Left Liberations: The Poetics, Praxis and Politics of Youth Radicalism[1] |

Canada's "most forgettable generation" was the subject of a carping September 1969 *Saturday Night* article. It wrote finis to a phenomenon. A Montreal associate editor of the popular magazine, Peter Desbarats, had apparently come back from an evening stroll around McGill University where, in a bowl-like depression at the north end of the campus, he had seen an ape-like gathering of what he took to be the "exhausted new wave of revolutionary youth." Hair obscuring their faces, reminding Desbarats of nothing so much as "the herd," the students undoubtedly talked among themselves, but all that the reporter could discern was "a few guttural noises." The journalist, obviously offended by the scene, took solace in the view that "this is the end of it."

> The easy poetry and trite melodies have palled. Pot has settled into its humdrum place and even the strong drugs are hardly worth a television programme any longer. The only thing that seems to remain, for those who have been spoiled by the whole game is…The hair. The sandals. The uniform. The liturgical slang and loose simian gestures.

Desbarats, like many others ensconced in a complacent repugnance, considered 1960s youth rebels little more than, "Cases of arrested individual development." He concluded that, "It will be a long time before the actual veterans of the movement, now moving into their twenties, will be able to evaluate their own mutilation." Content to forget what the 1960s had symbolized, Desbarats closed the book on the "silent, simian shapes squatting on the McGill campus," and in thousands of other locales across the country, as "a parody of the universe envisioned by McLuhan." He wished this generational blight on individual creativity good riddance, if not good luck.[2]

There was no denying, by late 1969, that something of the taste of the 1960s had soured. Locales like Toronto's Yorkville, the site of demonstrations and street occupations in August 1967, were sorry shadows of their former selves.[3] The influence of the lost generation of the 1950s, captured in Jack Kerouac's frenzied mobility of *On the Road*, seemed now confirmed in the poetic despair of Allen Ginsberg's *Howl*. An archetypal 1956 statement of the Beats, its lines of freewheeling, hard-bop verse appeared, at the close of the 1960s, eerily prophetic:

> *I saw the best minds of my generation destroyed by madness, starving*
> *hysterical naked,*
> *dragging themselves through the negro streets at dawn looking for an angry*
> *fix,*
> *angelheaded hipsters burning for the ancient connection to the*
> *starry dynamo in the machinery of night,*
> *who poverty and tatters and hollow-eyed and high sat up smoking in the*
> *supernatural darkness of cold-water flats floating across the tops of*
> *cities contemplating jazz,*
> *...*
> *who passed through universities with radiant cool eyes hallucinating Arkansas*
> *and Blake-light tragedy among the scholars of war,*
> *who were expelled from the academies for crazy and publishing obscene odes*
> *on the windows of the skull ...* [4]

Too many radical youth burned out.

Old Left ideas seem to creep back into the widening fissures of New Left thought. "The revolutionary process cannot be set in motion merely by the ardor of our convictions," lectured Irwin Silber in the pages of *Canadian Dimension,* "It is still true that only a revolution based in the working class is capable of destroying capitalism and developing socialism." There was a backing away from the nihilism of the new, as articulated by Jim Morrison of *The Doors*: "we're interested in anything about revolt, disorder, chaos, and activity that appears to have no meaning." Too often this seemed just a reproduction of old patterns of cultural and commercial ugliness: the *Rolling Stones* hired Hell's Angels to protect them from a crowd of love only to have that sea of emotion part in blood, with bikers swinging pool cues viciously, the almost scripted black male drawing his gun, the end a mournful, savage beating and deadly stabbing. Woodstock had taken a deep dive into a very bad Altamont trip. When the *Globe and Mail* featured a page one image of a 14-year old runaway girl, Mary Ann Vecchio, kneeling in anguish beside a dead Kent State student, Jeffrey Miller, on 5 May 1970, the headlines bold in their proclamation that, "Guardsmen kill 4 in Ohio protest," the 1960s were, for many, spiraling downward. If the decade was not over that spring, it surely crashed sometime between September 1970 and July 1971, with Janis Joplin, Jimi Hendrix, and Morrison all dead of drug overdoses.[5]

Desbarats was not, then, so much wrong in his dating of a 1960s post-mortem, as he was mean-spiritedly dismissive of its contribution when it had been in full flower. One of the movement's most sensitive Canadian commentators, Myrna Kostash, every bit a Desbarats' veteran, for instance, does not consider herself scarred and deformed by the experience of the 1960s. Her book, *Long Way From Home: The Story of the Sixties Generation in Canada* (1980), confirms that at the end of the decade much was in disarray. By 1970, she wrote, after what seemed an eternity of police harassment, physical beatings at demonstrations, the state's endless parade of repression, and the disillusionment of so many campaigns turning into something other than their original expansive and visionary intentions, "the hardest thing to bear was the nightmare that behind one's stumbling, fatigued and frightened stride came no one at all." Kostash nevertheless refuses the victimhood Desbarats imposed upon her and so many others. "While all about us insist that we failed and were absorbed into the consensus,"she wrote in recognition of the curtain of commentary that has descended on the 1960s and the New Left, it was nevertheless critical "to remember that there was a moment, an hour, a day when we were successful, when the system could not … proceed with impunity." Indeed, Kostash remains grateful for having lived during a unique moment: "What is special about growing up in the Sixties," she writes, "is how close our learning came to being revolutionary. You can't get much luckier than that."[6]

Desbarats, then, seemed to have missed at least something of the march of the 1960s, including its purchase on many of its activists. Ellie Kirzner of Toronto's *Now Magazine* declared of her involvements in the decade that they constituted "a delicious addiction."[7] Milton Acorn, a Canadian "People's Poet," put it slightly differently in his commemorative verse,"Ho Chi Minh": "We shall never have this sword again:/We will always need it;/even when, instead of 'sword'/we may say 'flower'."[8] *Canadian Dimension*, founded in 1963 and arguably one of the strongest and most sustained voices of the legacies of the 1960s, declared with more confidence in a 1988 commemoration of "The Explosive 60s": "We were brazen and brave and we shook them badly despite our mistakes. We'll do it again."[9]

The 1960s: A *New* Left

Few decades brand themselves with a political shift to the left. The 1960s did so. If the surge of oppositional thought and action was international, the left turn registering in metropolitan centers such as Paris, Berlin, London, New York, Warsaw, Tokoyo, Prague, Chicago, Mexico City, Rome, Sydney, Karachi and elsewhere,[10] Canada could hardly be exempt.[11]

Kostash presents the Canadian New Left as "seemingly overwhelmed by the American example yet fighting for its native life." A New Left participant told her: "We thought like Europeans and acted like Americans." Few could deny that in Canada's burgeoning and youthful New Left, the 1960s were a cauldron of British and French ideas and the proximate practices of the United States, with echoes of black struggles (from "We Shall Overcome" to "Burn, Baby, Burn") ringing in militant ears. Aldermaston peace marches and the idea of unilateral nuclear disarmament, Fabian socialism and the British Labour Party, the existentialism, Marxism, and anti-colonialism of Albert Camus, Jean-Paul Sartre, and Frantz Fanon jostled with the iconic personages, places, and powder kegs of the United States movement: Selma and Newark, Tom Hayden and Malcolm X, Students for a Democratic Society and the League of Revolutionary Black Workers, Eldridge Cleaver and Stokely Carmichael.

New Left news outlets like the New York-based "independent radical newsweekly," the *Guardian*, were especially influential. Originating in the non-communist Old Left of the 1948 Henry Wallace campaign, and founded as the *New York Guardian*, the paper shed much of its traditional leftism in the mid-to-late 1960s. After a 1968 clash between owner and co-founder, James Aronson, and his increasingly New Left staff and columnists, the paper changed hands, shortening its name and broadening its influence. Affiliated with no particular political organization, the *Guardian* was nonetheless resolutely New Left, a guide to what was happening in the movement as well as a publication venue for a wide array of writers staunch in their antagonism to imperialism, racism, and the exploitation of the working class. For many young Canadian leftists, searching for alternative reporting of the events of the 1960s and a radical perspective in which to situate them, the *Guardian* was their preferred source of information. It was supplemented by access to the offerings of the Liberation News Service or the glossy monthly, *Ramparts*. The latter publication, edited by Robert Scheer, rode the explosive growth of the New Left to massive subscription and newsstand sales approaching 250,000 each issue by the end of the 1960s. Compared to such venues of New Left thought, more mainstream left-of-centre publications like *The Nation* or *Canadian Forum* seemed oddly out-of-step with the 'movement' scene, far too staid and limp in their willingness to break moulds and rock boats.

Marxism did not initiate the decade's radicalism, but it did, eventually, come to influence it mightily, even if many would, in turn, reject it forcefully. It was not, however, the *old* Marx of political economy, long days of pouring over Blue Books in the British Museum, *Das Kapital*, and carbuncles. Rather, it was the *young* Marx of the yet-to-be widely published *Economic and Philosophic Manuscripts of 1844*, the rebel Hegelian, theorist of alienation, and beer-downing author of a sheaf of love poems. And, surprising in its influence, Mao Tse Tung thought found its way from study groups through party formations and into street protests, no texts being more widely read in the late 1960s than the cream-coloured and embossed-covered pocket volumes of Peking's Foreign Language Press. The slogans of the time were a uniquely dualistic mix of Mao's materialism and the anarcho-surrealist graffiti of a metaphorical Parisian Left Bank. How could an era embrace simultaneously the maxims that "Political Power Grows Out of the Barrel of a Gun" and "Grasp Revolution, Promote Production!" with "Workers of the world, have fun!" "Boredom is counterrevolutionary," "Be realistic, demand the impossible!" and "Those who take their desires for reality are those who believe in the reality of their desires." Yet it was done.

When Parisian students scrawled "Down with the Stalinist carcass. Run, comrade, the old world is behind you," on the walls of the Sorbonne, moreover, they were separating themselves out from a past left. Its rigidities and ossifications were so entirely foreign to them that they had trouble grasping what the long march of revolutionary degeneration associated with the Soviet Union was really all about. They wanted not so much the program of revolution, as its adventure. The inspiration of the Cuban Revolution was seen in this way, elevating Che Guevara in the eyes of millions. This and much else forced the significance of decolonization movements and anti-racist struggles to the forefront of New Left appreciation. At few historical junctures was the trade in the theory and practice of revolution more exhilaratingly wild and seemingly pregnant with promise than in the 1960s.[12]

The promise dawned with a rejection of politics as it had been known. As Carl Ogelsby wrote in the introduction to a collection of essays on the radicalism of the 1960s, "The New Left is properly so called because in order to exist it had to overcome the memories, the certitudes, and the promises of the Old Left."[13] C. Wright Mills, drawn to the newness of the first New Left in Britain, penned his transatlantic comrades a 1960 letter in response to their publication of a book of essays, *Out of Apathy*. Wright Mills situated himself in opposition to the twinned ideological pillars of Vulgar Marxism and Liberal Rhetoric. They were joined at the stiff hip by a bureaucratic denunciation of "radical criticisms of their respective societies," the socialist realist Soviet Union and the end of ideology United States. These power blocs in an oppositional global order governed by the arms race and complacency were what needed to be rejected. Their very connectedness conditioned outmoded, hierarchical, thinking. Wright Mills wanted to shed the "labour metaphysic," that Old Left *faith* in the working class "as *the* historic agency of social change," as little more than the legacy of an unrealistic Victorian Marxism. He was equally insistent on the need to dump the disillusionment "with any real commitment to socialism in any recognizable form" that was the foundational structure of the raging ideologies of non-ideology in western capitalism. In their place, Wright Mills offered the relentless utopian drive of criticism, rigorous analysis of the agencies of historical change, and a moral commitment to act. When he looked at who, trapped in the ossified structures of both the East and the West, was waging war against "all the old crap" (he was quoting Marx), Wright Mills saw only "the young intelligentsia." Content to let the old men ask sourly, "Out of Apathy—into what?" Wright Mills reveled in the rise of the New Left. "We are beginning to move again," he concluded confidently.[14]

When the Port Huron Statement was drafted by Tom Hayden two years later as the manifesto of Students for a Democratic Society (SDS), it contained a number of C. Wright Mills-like formulations. Tragically, the rebellious New Left sociologist had died of a heart attack shortly before the first 20,000 mimeographed copies of the Statement found their way across America as university classes commenced in 1962, hawked for 35 cents. Attacking communism as anathema to American democracy, Hayden's Statement also rejected the mirror image of anti-communism. These global power polarizations, configured as they were around colonizations of the world's resources and the menace of nuclear arms, threatened humanity. They made inevitable revolutionary movements of opposition. In the United States, SDS targeted racist discrimination as *the* decisive oppression disfiguring democracy. It was also inseparable from poverty, alienation, and the stalled historic New Deal drive of American workers to secure justice and just compensation. What was new in the Port Huron Statement was that in Wright Mills's call for identification of agents of change, it drew less on Old Left understandings of the laws of motion of capitalist accumulation than on a "movement spirit." The eclectic document promoted less of a program than it set an agenda for a generation, seeing the University and its students as a decisive agency of social change, arguably the first time such a perspective had been put forward seriously and with passionate political conviction. In the end, the echoes of Wright Mills's brief for utopianism and his assault on apathy were perhaps the final loud endnote of a reverberating call to espouse values and struggle for change. "A new left must start controversy across the land, if national policies and national apathy are to be reversed," the Statement insisted, its refusals as well as its righteousness ringing in the last sentence of the 63-page manifesto: "If we appear to seek the unattainable, as it has been said, then let it be known that we do so to avoid the unimaginable."[15]

One of the New Left's most esteemed theoreticians, Herbert Marcuse, framed the radical project in philosophical terms in his *Essay on Liberation* (1969):

> The new sensibility has become, by this very token, *praxis*: it emerges in the struggle against violence and exploitation where this struggle is waged for essentially new ways and forms of life: negation of the entire Establishment, its morality, culture; affirmation of the right to build a society in which the abolition of property and toil terminates in a universe where the sensuous, the playful, the calm, and the beautiful become forms of existence and thereby the form of the society itself.

This philosophy of praxis thus fused theory and practical activity, in an aesthetic and politics of the deed that promised a possibility of true social transformation and the ultimate realization of freedom, both individual and collective:

> If now, in the rebellion of the young intelligentsia, the right and the truth of the imagination become the demands of political action, if surrealist forms of protest and refusal spread throughout the movement, this apparently insignificant development may indicate a fundamental change in the situation ... The political action which insists on a new morality and a new sensibility as preconditions and results of social change occurs at a point at which the repressive rationality that has brought about the achievements of industrial society becomes utterly regressive—rational only in its efficiency to 'contain' liberation.

Praxis, in the New Left sense, entailed the freedom to think about what the movement was going to do with new sensibilities, especially those cognizant of the extent to which, "Revolutionary forces emerge in the process of change itself; the translation of the potential into the actual is the work of political practice." In struggling to make history, New Leftists were engaged, in their view, in an unprecedented undertaking. The forms that such struggles took were as decisive in determining outcomes as any theoretical laws of social motion, specific predetermined agencies of transformation, or programmatic maxims.[16]

What was strikingly new about all of this was that 1960s radicals were in actuality well ahead of their times in locating "an end to history" malaise that later writers —on the right and in the center-left—would make much of with the collapse of the Soviet Union in 1989.[17] Understanding that both the Soviet Union and the United States, as bureaucratic societies curbing democratic initiative and the movement of progress, had stopped history in an end that silenced the soul and numbed the mind, prompted 1960s radicals to showcase the need to kickstart historical process anew. As Mario Savio, catalyst of the Berkeley Free Speech Movement, argued at a December 1964 sit-in of an Administration building, "Here is the real contradiction: the bureaucrats hold history as ended. As a result significant parts of the population on campus and off are dispossessed, and these dispossessed are not about to accept this a-historical point of view." In Savio's conclusion he voiced the New Left insistence that history had not ended, and that its promise demanded struggle and sacrifice:

> The most exciting things going on in America today are movements to change America. America is becoming ever more the utopia of sterilized, automated contentment. The 'futures' and 'careers' for which American students now prepare are for the most part intellectual and moral wastelands. This chrome-plated consumers' paradise would have us grow up to be well-behaved children. But an important minority of men and women coming to the front today have shown that they will die rather than be standardized, replaceable and irrelevant.[18]

Savio's interventions were not decisively severed from Old Left connection. His wife at the time was a member of the Communist Party and Berkeley's Free Speech Movement had a part of its origins in defending the right of a Communist Party figure, the historian of African American experience Herbert Aptheker, to speak on campus. Yet they were new in the nature of their argument. The accent was less on the class struggle than on the refusal to succumb to bureaucracy. Automation, alienation, and segregation were Savio's crucial problems and, indeed, the Old Left had much to say about them as well. Savio, however, said what he had to say in New Left ways, using words, examples, inflections, and tones that were different than those employed by an older communist or social democratic left, let alone men and women from the Democratic Party.

In Canada, this newness of the New Left was evident from the beginnings of the movement. Born underneath the cloud of Hiroshima and Nagasaki, chilled by the deforming iciness of the Cold War, Canada's New Left distanced itself from "centralized undemocratic decision-making," which it claimed was "inexorably related to the growth of the war-fare state." Electoral politics was conceived as a dead-end: "Despite all our glorification of democracy in Canada the real centres of power remain far out of reach of the electors and remain intact and totally undisturbed by elections no matter who is elected." The New Left wanted a "new and self-directing order."[19]

As these tendencies crystallized over time, in actions, debates, and struggles over the political direction of diverse movements and groups, an increasingly fragmented New Left actually hardened in its distinctive separation from Old Left political formations. Many New Left figures had their origins in social-democratic youth movements and, even as late as 1965, almost half of the 150 founding members of the Student Union for Peace Action were affiliates of the New Democratic Party. Nevertheless, over time a deep suspicion of the parliamentary reformism of the Cooperative Commonwealth Federation-New Democratic Party (CCF/NDP) tradition developed. The NDP was quite often seen as little more than centralized state planning of the kind that merited the derisive dismissal of "liberals in a hurry." Some New Left leaders, to be sure, chastised their movement for its isolation from important, established centres of social democratic politics, including the New Democratic Youth (NDY) movement. Most New Leftists, however, regarded the NDP as but one of many houses on which they would cast a plague of rather jaundiced disdain.[20]

Communist parties, whether of the staid Stalinist sort or of the ultra-left, usually fared no better although, again, a number of Canadian New Leftists were red-diaper babies, and certainly had connections to, if not direct membership in, the Communist Party of Canada.[21] Marcuse, widely read in Canadian New Left circles, nonetheless offered a widely-accepted critique of Soviet Marxism. Communist organization was often judged little more than an appendage to bureaucracy and oppression, "a party of order."[22] As Peter Gzowski noted in *Maclean's*, the New Left, unlike the Old, was not interested in 'isms', which it regarded as a hangover from the 1930s. "The Communists, they're empty man," a New Leftist was quoted as saying, "They've got the same stale ideas, the same bureaucracy. When he gets mixed up with us, a Commie dies, and a person develops." Not even sure they were right, Canadian New Leftists were capable of making a virtue of their necessary programmatic uncertainty. "Lots of us have doubts," one young radical told Gzowski in 1965, "But maybe that's exactly why all the radical movements of the 1930s went wrong. When they found out they *couldn't* save the world they just felt defeated. Well none of us are sure we can save the world. I suppose we don't even *think* we can. But we know we have to try. And we're trying to find new ways to work for it."[23]

Radical activities within university departments and classrooms, spreading to and growing out of communes, high schools, day-care centres, and community organizations, were understood to be "stepping stones towards a larger revolutionary movement, yet to be constituted."[24] A major figure in the western Canadian New Left and a President of the Saskatchewan NDY, James Harding, held to the preeminent importance of "confrontation with the authoritarian bureaucracies." Sounding very much like Mario Savio, Harding often put forward views remarkably similar to those in the Port Huron Statement, although he might also understate the connection, insisting that SDS's influence was regionally rooted in Ontario. By 1969 he widened the net the New Left would cast:

> An extra-parliamentary opposition will have to struggle against liberal democratic bureaucracies at all levels in society: on campus, in trade unions, in all the institutions of the corporate society. This strategy must be explicit, to work; because the institutions of neo-capitalism are so all-encompassing, radical politics can not be abstracted from the people (as is, for example, the case with party politics or any form of bureaucratic politics). Our struggle must be at the base of society, where the people are, not among the elites and those who yearn to become part of the elites. This means, ultimately, organizing in mental hospitals, prisons, offices and the military in addition to schools and factories.[25]

Within the segments of the New Left drawn to anarchism, the assault on "bureaucratic manipulation," the proclaimed virtues of civil disobedience, and embrace of the boldest concepts of a realizable utopia were perhaps most vehement. Such statements co-joined the attack on capitalist centralization, state authoritarianism, *and* the ideas and practices of the Old Left. Class discontent was valuable only in as much as it disgorged the young from the repressions of the work ethnic, Puritanism, consumerism, and obedience to authority. Thus, a prominent Montreal New Leftist, Dimitrios I. Roussopoulos, borrowed the words of Murray Bookchin, arguing that "the most promising development in the factories today is the emergence of young workers who smoke pot, fuck-off on their jobs, drift into and out of factories, grow long hair, demand more leisure time rather than more pay, steal, harass all authority figures, go on wildcats, and turn on their fellow workers." Small wonder, given this rather indiscriminate list, that Roussopoulos also pilloried capitalist institutions and the entirety of Old Left experience in one stunning paragraph of repudiation:

At a time when hierarchy as such is being brought into question, we hear the hollow echoes of 'vanguards', and 'trained cadres under our discipline'. At a time when centralization and the State have been brought to the most explosive point of historical negativity, we hear the hollow echoes of a 'centralised movement' and a 'proletarian dictatorship'. This search for security in the past, this attempt to find a haven in a fixed dogma and an organizational hierarchy—all as substitutes for creative thought and praxis—is bitter evidence of how many little 'revolutionaries' are capable of 'revolutionising themselves and things', much less revolutionising society as a whole. And as to those conservatives who in the midst of a technological society wave the 'little red book' to rephrase Trotsky's juicy description of Stalinism, they are the syphilis of the radical youth movement today. And for syphilis there is only one treatment—an antibiotic not argument.[26]

That a statement such as this could appear in the first Canadian collection of articles on the New Left written by New Leftists themselves, was an indication of the capacity of the new radicalism to define itself in opposition to older revolutionary claims, organizational forms, and histories. It was also an articulation of the implosion of the New Left by the end of the 1960s, as contending forces fed off the body of a movement struggling to keep its energy and momentum. In a sense this strident statement proved something of a eulogy for a New Left organizational initiative that had already passed into a long night of fractious encounter, its demise missed in the clash of perspective.[27] For its embittered and extreme tone was *not* characteristic of the radical decade's entirety of struggle, a contest carried on over years of challenging adversity, to be sure, but one that also rang with joy. In the many and myriad makings and mobilizations of Canada's 1960s New Left lay encounters in which glimpses of the origins of this ultimate angry sectarianism can certainly be seen. Yet a more insightful vision would reveal histories of comradeship and solidarity far more tender and affectionate, in which Roussopoulos and countless others participated. Brief as it was, this New Left experience encompassed an eternity of meaning, and it helped to remake understandings of Canada in the years to come.

Peace or Cease: The Unilateralist Origins of the Canadian New Left

We are strangers in a strange land
Of flesh and tissue and dead moving
Under naked trees burnt in the holocaust
Of passion that feeds on itself.
Not from distances of land and water,
We come from dwellings in the zenith of time
Blind with gunpowder in the circle of the eye;
This is the difference—no other.
                    —*Ruth Lisa Schechter*[28]

Cold War stasis and the race to nuclear annihilation prodded the New Left into being. Canadians worried by the prospects of nuclear war—writers, scientists, liberals, clergymen, unaligned radicals, socialists, and a smattering of students—formed the Canadian Committee for the Control of Radiation Hazards (CCCRH). Based in Edmonton, the CCCRH was promoted by the energetic Mary Van Stolk, whose cross-country lectures, meetings with a wide array of concerned citizens, and testing of baby teeth to ascertain concentrations of Strontium 90 drew increasing attention to the atmospheric dangers of testing nuclear weapons. This soon led to the founding of the Canadian Campaign for Nuclear Disarmament in 1959 (CCND). A small but committed group of students and faculty pioneered the Montreal and Toronto chapters of the Combined Universities Campaign for Nuclear Disarmament (CUCND) in October/November of the same year. Montreal's Sir George Williams hosted the new organization's first public event, where two of the featured speakers were former Canadian Army Major W.H. Pope and the city's titular head of social democracy, Frank Scott. Irving Layton, poet laureate of the discontented, declined an invitation to address the anti-nuclear activists, denouncing them as "Reds." On Christmas Day, 1959, 80 of these opponents of nuclear weapons trekked through the cold, unwelcoming streets of Ottawa to lay a wreath at the base of the National War Memorial and present a petition signed by 1500 Canadians to the Governor-General. It was said to be the country's first student political demonstration since the end of World War II. With a federal secretariat in Montreal (later moving to Toronto in 1963), CUCND soon boasted locals from Memorial University in the east to the University of British Columbia in the west. Quebec's Anglophone and francophone CUCNDers were particularly active, with chapters established at the universities of Laval, Sherbrooke, and Montreal, as well as McGill and Sir George. Presided over initially by Dimitri Roussopoulos, and then by Toronto's Art Pape, CUCND stimulated the growth of CCND, which published a monthly newspaper, *Sanity*.[29]

A coalition of radicals and liberals, 'red diaper babies' and more moderate idealists, CUCND was a highly complex and somewhat differentiated political pastiche. It brought together, according to Dimitri Roussopoulos, distinct streams of political youth in the making. A contingent of young Pearsonites, many of whom were reared in the youth section of the Liberal Party and were destined for disillusionment after their leader's acceptance of U.S. nuclear warheads for Canada's Bomarc missiles, complemented a collection of left-of-centre small-l liberal youth. According to Roussopoulos, this originally liberal cohort, many of whom would gravitate towards more radical politics as the decade wore on, included Clayton Ruby, Stewart Goodings, Arthur Pape, Joan Newman, and Peter Boothroyd. To the left of this contingent were regionally-rooted enclaves of social democratic sympathizers, where connection to the CCF-NDP tradition was strongest in the west and weaker the further one moved east. Saskatchewan's James Harding was at one end of this spectrum, while Montrealers such as Lucia Kowaluk were at another. There was also a Communist Party (CP) connection to CUCND, operative on two levels. In the first stages of the campaign, for instance, active members of the CP such as Danny Goldstick were involved, but as the position hardened against Soviet nuclear weapon testing Goldsick and other communists took their leave. A number of 'red diaper babies' remained active, however, among them Danny Drache, Stan Gray, Liora Proctor, and an especially strong group of Montreal women: Elka Cohen, Dorothy Leibensaun, Judy Labow, and Dorothy Fraid. Montreal was, indeed, an especially strong centre of early CUCND support, and it was there, perhaps, that the specific influence of the British Campaign for Nuclear Disarmament, the post-1956 British New Left and the publication the *New Reasoner*, European anti-nuclear weapons mobilizations, and American anti-war movements registered most decisively. Roussopolous, Gerry Hunnius, Hélène Senecal-David, Louise Trois-Maison, and others were central in this 'internationalizing' tendency within CUCND, which functioned as a conduit to SDS in the United States and figured forcefully in the founding of the journal, *Our Generation Against Nuclear War*. Finally, particular types of religiously-inspired youth were also drawn to the anti-nuclear weapons cause. The Student Christian Movement (SCM) had been a formative experience for many. Echoes of the early twentieth-century social gospel could still be heard in CUCND meetings, just as a radical Catholicism, associated with Dorothy Day's Catholic Worker Movement, could well be discerned.[30]

Early CUCNDers struggled to comprehend the contradictory character of Canadian public policy, animated by commitments to decency, equality, fairness, and peace. How could Canada claim to be a peacekeeper in the global community, wearing its benevolence proudly in international forums such as the United Nations, and even consider bringing atomic weapons on to Canadian soil to arm Bomarc missiles? Always aware of other social issues, CUCND presented a brief to Parliament in November 1960 that extolled "the worth and dignity of the individual" and embraced "equality and self-government as the rights and needs of all men." CUCND youth were perplexed that Canadian society paid lip-service to such values, but failed to develop ways to live and act according to them. "In the name of a decent standard of living," CUCNDers pointed out, "we destroy food surpluses while millions starve."[31]

Soon CUCND students were attending workshops on non-violent disobedience run by Quakers on Grindstone Island, Ontario; sitting in meetings with Voice of Women journalists, professors, and authors like Lotta Dempsey and Ursula Franklin; even rubbing shoulders with hardened trade union radicals or soft-spoken communist-sympathizing clergymen in the Canadian Peace Congress. From people like these, experienced in organizing campaigns and raising a consciousness of opposition, CUCNDers learned much. They circulated petitions, held vigils, and picked up guitars as they sang for peace. Hanging out in Saskatoon's Humanity House, putting out an issue of the strikingly impressive Montreal theoretical journal, *Our Generation Against Nuclear War,* mobilizing a pan-Canadian opposition to atomic weaponry, CUCND members were becoming a movement. The NDP was pressured to adopt variants of CUCND's "positive neutralism" and unilateralist disarmament positions. These had developed out of discussions about Canada's role in the U.S.-dominated North Atlantic Treaty Organization (NATO) and the extent to which this contributed to the arms race, exacerbating the possibilities of nuclear war. Inroads were made in the labour movement.[32]

At a federal conference in Toronto in late February 1963, CUCND moved in tandem with its past and with the future of student radicalism, as outlined months before in the Port Huron Statement. It opposed the "Cold War military and political policies of both nuclear blocs," insisting that students had a special role to play in resisting the drive to war, suggesting that the university needed to take the lead "in the mobilization of social forces internationally for the achievement of world peace." There were signs that the anti-nuclear arms movement was having an impact: daily newspapers like the *Toronto Star,* and mass magazines such as *Saturday Night,* embraced the politics of refusing nuclear arms in Canada; tens of thousands signed petitions of protest; demonstrations outside the House of Commons voiced growing popular fears of arms proliferation. And then Lester Pearson and the Liberals cut the ground out from underneath CUCND, signing a clandestine 1963 accord with the

United States that committed Canada to accept U.S. nuclear warheads. With the euphemistically named "special ammunition" secretly delivered to the La Macaza, Quebec and North Bay, Ontario, missile silos in 1964 Canada became the fourth country in the world to embrace nuclear arms. Those who sported CUCND buttons on campuses across the land never recovered from this blow. For years they had faced ugly Cold War attacks as 'commie' sympathizers or worse, but they had the rightness of their cause behind them. Now they had lost.

The radicals among them, a minority of those CUCND forces still willing to continue the fight, led the way forward. They marshaled energies in a new organization founded in December 1964 in Regina, named the Student Union for Peace Action, or SUPA. No ideological conformity characterized this first New Left formation, but it had moved beyond the seeming fixation on a single cause that many associated, however wrongly, with CUCND. Many, to the extent that they were turned on by intellectual concepts, were captivated by the imaginative SDS formulation of 'the Triple Revolution'. Activism was seemingly ordered by the issues flowing out of revolutions designated as cybernetics (computerization, automation, and the transformation of human labour), nuclear weaponry (the ongoing struggle for peace in the atomic age), and civil/human rights (struggles of minorities such as African Americans, but also those linked to organized labour, the unemployed, and the poor).[33] A Canadian New Left had emerged, one animated by the possibility of participatory democracy.[34]

SUPA's Sixties, 1965–1967

SUPA, like the New Left as a whole, defied easy categorization. SUPA's raison d'etre was in actuality a fusion of forms and contents, in which non-violence, participatory democracy, equality, non-hierarchical structures, and open-ended objectives that valued consensus became both means and end. Talk tended to trump reading, writing, and seriously reflective thought; to the extent that a national organization existed, it was premised on a regionally-ordered decentralization. There were always acute differences separating SUPA's strong western Canadian contingents, its cosmopolitan Montreal dissidents, and the 'centre', defined broadly as Ontario, but often casually and dismissively telescoped into 'Hogtown'. A central figure such as Dimitri Roussopoulos is actually insistent that there were three SUPAs. That said, there was common ground forged in this pioneer New Left movement. Meetings happened, and structures evolved, with a growing recognition that decision-making had to involve SUPA members across the country, and not just in the seemingly privileged—if often quite competitive and different—secretariats of Montreal and Toronto. Tensions certainly existed. The theory of how SUPA was supposed to work often foundered on personalities and the ways in which different leaderships emerged, counter to one another with respect to place, imposing their will on others within a specific locale.[35] As James Harding, one of western Canada's leading New Leftists in 1966 noted, SUPA managed quite early in its brief history to crystallize the meaning of the movement in five interrelated features.[36]

First, SUPA acknowledged that it needed to undertake an analysis of power in Canada in order to challenge the systematic inequality that was foundational to the nation state. This nation-state system was central to the global crisis of a world order threatened with annihilation by competing communist and anti-communist blocs. It was also the primary context in which alienating technologies of governance and repression were unleashed on exploited workers, colonized peoples, students, the unemployed, and minorities of all kinds. Second, SUPA, like CUCND before it, was committed to non-alignment in a highly polarized world.[37] This refusal to place itself on one side or another in the Cold War was the only path to world peace. Third, SUPA took up the idea of student syndicalism, in which it was understood, as it was in SDS, that students had to foment controversy, organize campaigns, and take a lead in confronting social problems by bringing various possible agents of historic change together in "people's unions." Fourth, it was absolutely necessary that SUPA extend its theory and its practice to encompass the notion of a totalizing order of oppression in which the linkages of war, peace, and suffering on an everyday level were made visible and connected in ways that they had not been in the past. Fifth, the political ends that SUPA sought to achieve were to be consistent with the means it utilized to secure them, which related to the organization's ideas and training in non-violent direct action: "Please don't believe/The use of force/Is how we change the social course/The use of force/You surely know/Is how we keep the status quo."[38]

The notion of student syndicalism was particularly important because it launched SUPA on a series of initiatives, direct actions, and struggles to empower oppressed groups in Canada. Likening their educational experience to the routinized production of the assembly line, student syndicalists demanded something more than a business unionism content with wage increases and company paternalism. In its origins student syndicalism imagined a union of students battling university bosses to create a decentralized student control of their entire learning environment. SDS Vice-President Carl Davidson promoted a student syndicalist movement that would "sabotage the knowledge factory machinery" by promoting a countercurriculum guided by Paul Goodman and A.S. Neil; challenge professors by demanding student participation in shaping the structure, format, and content of courses; denounce, strike against, and picket excessively large classes; and hold mock trials of Deans of Men and Women for their "crimes against humanity." Women students in particular, it was suggested, might take the lead in forming dormitory councils or soviets that could rewrite the 'rules' or eliminate them altogether. As Barbara Godard has recently suggested, in the earliest stages of student syndicalism at major universities in Toronto and Montreal over the course of 1963-1964, the practical activities of university youth might be far less challenging of established norms. Indeed, student activists might well have embraced syndicalism less as Wobblies and more as liberal reformers, regarding their political mission as becoming "intellectual workers" or serving an apprenticeship in citizenship. By the time SUPA was founded, however, radical student syndicalists were turning decisively toward the politics of community involvement. Most student syndicalist efforts in the crucial 1965-1967 years were conceived as attempts to intersect with the poor and powerless in Canadian society, so that students could both learn from direct experience with the dispossessed and, possibly, provide guidance as to how such people could overcome their subordination. Student syndicalism, in this undertaking, meshed with the movement's fundamental commitment to participatory democracy.[39]

The participatory democracy initiatives that SUPA undertook in the first year of its existence were almost all *ad hoc* undertakings growing out of local affinity groups of activists. There may well have been larger, national discussions, and funds were raised across the country, to be sure, but for the most part it was the field workers themselves who came together and decided the direction their work would take. Among SUPA collectives different strategic understandings contended. Some wanted to "enable" the poor and the dispossessed, others to offer a more traditional "leadership." If one SUPA member might stress the need to "confront capitalism," another would be as likely to locate their contribution in the group effort as "equalizing opportunity," or even merely "helping" those who were disadvantaged by poverty or race or lack of education.[40] Yet at the base of community organizing projects, undertaken as summer initiatives, was perhaps a common, if unexamined, assumption that they would "radicalize the student," or at the very least broaden horizons and bring into view "the basic contradictions within … society."

André Cardinal, affiliated with the ongoing La Macaza research and civil disobedience project at Quebec's nuclear arms base,[41] was convinced that "Social action will develop in the student a social conscience, provided that the project has a revolutionary ideology and that the leadership of the project applies that ideology to the situations it has to face."[42] Reflecting on the experience of the La Macaza undertaking, which embraced anti-militarism, non-violent direct action, an ongoing mobilization of young recruits and seasoned veterans, and a creative and original attempt to bring the emerging left nationalist movement in Quebec into contact with those active in the pan-Canadian New Left, Dimitri Roussoppoulos is insistent that SUPA's Montreal Peace Centre was the "radical crucible" of this first phase of the New Left. At a time when civil disobedience was shunned by much of the broader peace movement and social democratic and communist inclination was that non-violent direct action was dangerously radical, the LaMacaza activists drew on their ties to United States New Leftists such as Congress of Racial Equality staffer, Robert Gore; Igal Rudenko from the War Resister's League; and Chicago Student Peace Union's Bob Creasley. Figures such as these came to Montreal to offer advice, guidance, organizational and support work, and training in the techniques of civil disobedience. Roussopoulos and Cardinal clearly thought that the LaMacaza protests could springboard into a wider radicalization, encompassing the Quebec labour movement and the Canadian New Left. In the end, the achievements were more modest, although perhaps more noteworthy than has generally been recognized. A few years later, in the Trudeau era, LaMacaza was finally shut down, becoming an educational and training centre for Aboriginal people, a demand first put forward by SUPA in the mid-1960s. Elsewhere, SUPA's first summer of field work led to less illustrious achievements.[43]

One of SUPA's early 1965 endeavours, illustrating well the ways in which the group worked, the influences it drew upon, and its limitations, was the Kingston Community Project (KCP). Community organizing had been embraced by SDS and its Economic Research and Action Project (ERAP) as a means of encouraging the dispossessed to voice their discontents; about 100 student radicals lived and worked in slums in the northern United States over the summer of 1964. Eight organizing projects, the most well-known of which were the Newark Community Union Project and Chicago's Jobs or Income Now Community Union, identified housing, urban renewal, welfare, police brutality, and the limitations of state-sponsored 'wars on poverty' as fundamental issues animating black and white inner-city discontent. Led by national SDS spokesmen such as Tom Hayden and Todd Gitlin, with whom SUPA had direct connections, these projects conceived the poor to be "the main thrust behind any broader movement for radical change—partly because their needs are more crude and insistent, and partly because they seem most insulated from some of the more deadening shibboleths of 'the American dream'."[44]

Prodded by one of the last position papers of CUCND, co-authored by the organization's chairman, Art Pape, Kingston SUPA members struggled to bring the movement against war into the social conditions that nurtured violence. They cajoled student societies at Queen's University into giving them $3,000; Liberal Finance Minister, Walter Gordon, and NDP leader, Tommy Douglas, wrote the young radicals modest cheques; a letter of commendation from John G. Diefenbaker came their way. The dozen or so Limestone City student activists then imported future United Automobile Worker and Canadian Labour Congress leader, Dennis McDermott, at the time a young organizer with "slum experience," into the eastern Ontario city to direct their work. McDermott, two Queen's professors, and Tom Hathaway, Ontario regional head of SUPA, chose ten organizers, sent two of them off to a Toronto training session with Hayden and Pape, and then turned the neophyte organizers loose after they had written their final exams in May. It wasn't hard to find the poor in a city divided into Town and Gown. Segregated in the North End, Kingston's dispossessed lived on the wrong side of the city's main thoroughfare, Princess Street. It was relatively easy for SUPA organizers, all of whom eventually resided in two old ramshackle houses among those they wanted to interact with, to go out every day in groups of two or three, knock on doors, talk to people over cups of coffee and domestic chores, listen to accounts of hardship and resentment, and offer suggestive prods as to how things might be improved. Week by week the "on the block" organizing proceeded. In the words of one KCP field worker, Bill Martin, this "ordered procedure" carried with it the "stench of unions or social workers." Nonetheless, "amid the piles of tedium, from around the edges of the clouds of everyday door to door conversations with housewives who are too busy to listen and husbands who are too busy listening to their spouses to give a guild edge damn, arises or glows the odd ray of light."[45]

There was a sense of accomplishment in the KCP, then, but as it wound down for the summer in August 1965 the ironies of the activist season dawned on SUPA members. Journalists gave SUPA's confrontations with slumlords coverage, but at the expense of actually talking to the tenants, who were intimidated and retreated into the background. Landlords seemed to be organizing faster than the poor renters, placing ads in the local newspaper suggesting the value of "exchanging information about tenants." One SUPA field worker reported caustically, "Perhaps a landlord's cooperative is in the making." One of the hardest blows to accept, however, was hearing a hated North End housing magnate, his cash-clucking tongue well in cheek, praise "the Queen's students" for stirring up his tenants to clean up their property and take pride in their living spaces. Joan Newman summed up the growing realization that SUPA's Kingston work seemed bogged down: "We didn't know what made us different from ordinary social workers. We were supposed to be intellectuals activating the masses, but where do you begin?"[46]

In retrospect, many of the SUPA organizers of the summer 1965 initiative found themselves disillusioned and dispirited. Kingston was not Newark, and it did not have the explosive potential that a community dominated by racial poverty inevitably exhibited. Rent strikes were difficult to organize among tenants who did not inhabit ghetto high-rise apartments, and the rage that would explode in the 1967 Newark race riots was never simmering to quite the extent in Kingston that it obviously was in Hayden's New Jersey stomping grounds. The collective spirit of the enterprise left many wondering if the KCP's accent on trust, friendship, and community was enough. Women, the most adept at balancing the daily grind of domestic labour, part-time paid work, and connecting with poor working-class people (especially housewives), began to experience and then appreciate the gendered inequalities of SUPA's mission. Inherent assumptions about women's roles surfaced in a report from KCP 'leader', Dennis McDermott. He reported in June 1965 that, "The five boys will live in a combined office-house on the periphery of the project area, and commute for meals to the girls' apartment." Students with romanticized misconceptions of poor people's innate radicalism, instead found them often conservative and cautious. They could even be unwilling, as the intelligent dispossessed often are, to risk what little they had on a throw of the dice prompted by those who had many more tosses in their riskless pockets. Depression, self-deprecation, guilt, bewilderment, exhaustion, anger, resentment, and an unease with the emerging 'heavies' of the SUPA leadership, who were never centrally involved in the mundane "block organizing," set in.

All of this jostled uneasily with the exhilaration of having done something to develop change, of struggling to transform oneself as well as the social conditions of others, of learning from people quite different than themselves. The bottom line was not easily reduced to a single figure, for the balance sheet of SUPA's Kingston work was never merely a ledger like set of plus/minus columns. Moreover, it laid the groundwork for further community organizing in 1966, paced by two SUPA women, Joan Newman and Myrna Wood. Their apartment became a place for local youth to gather, a coffee house was started, welfare recipients were given much-needed assistance, and Newman ended up elected to municipal office. Women such as Peggy Morton, Bronwen Wallace, and Sarah Spinks, who first cut their political teeth on the KCP, some little more than eighteen years of age, went on to contribute mightily to the New Left.

Spinks was later involved in the Toronto Community Project at Trefann Court and was a mainstay, with George Martel, of the influential youth publication, *This Magazine is About Schools*. Edited by Bob Davis, the imaginative small-format collection of articles, poetry, and communications relating to education was a sounding board for alienations bred in the bone of the public school system. It made its way from its base in Toronto to the SDS stronghold of Ann Arbor Michigan, where it was touted by Weatherman-to-be Bill Ayers; soon radical educational theorists such as John Holt or Berkeley's Herbert Kohl were singing its praises. Pre-university youth, especially in south-central Ontario and metropolitan centres across Canada, turned its pages avidly. They found in them a rising crescendo of criticism of 'the school', increasingly perceived as little more than a vehicle of indoctrinating students with the values of conformity and the ethos of the marketplace. Few Canadian voices of the New Left reached high school students with the same ease and vigour as *This Magazine*.[47]

There were other ventures in student syndicalism. Ten SUPA radicals spent the summer living with status Indian and Métis families in Saskatchewan. Having raised $3000 (the going rate in 1965, it seemed, for a SUPA group of 10-12 to make it through the summer), largely from the Student Council at the University of Toronto, a small group met in Saskatchewan. It then launched the Student Neestow Partnership Project, '*neestow*' being a Cree word for brother-in-law (although there was, subsequently, embarassed recognition that in some northern Aboriginal communities it also translated loosely as cuckold). The Neestow initiative had its origins in a February 1965 Canadian Union of Students-sponsored conference on "The Status of the Indian and Métis in Canada." Held at the University of Saskatchewan, the gathering solidified ties that had developed between western SUPA figures such as Harding and socialist Métis organizer Malcolm Norris. Norris was the first person Harding encountered in Saskatchewan "who could blend Marxism and libertarian politics … [talking about] the importance of a racial analysis of class society … about the colonization of the Indian and Métis." Norris's dynamism, oratory, and analytic acumen galvanized the student conference, stimulating the young radicals to launch an American civil-rights-like summer of encounter with Aboriginal peoples. Guided by Indigenous and Métis activists such as Don Nielson, Jim Brady, and Norris, the students contacted Native bands, reserves, and Métis communities before fanning out across the province with their seemingly relatively simple goal. They merely wanted to make contact, observe, live with Native peoples, and help them in the work of everyday life, achieving something of an education in the process. No doubt SUPA had a sense that social actions against the Indian agents of the federal government would take place.[48]

Instead they found that while they learned of the subtle ways in which colonial dependency was cultivated on the reserves, they had little political possibility of making inroads into communities which were sensibly suspicious of white students and kept their silence among 'visitors' they knew too little about. Struggling to break down images of whites as incapable of the kinds of everyday work that Native peoples do to survive, an American radical studying at the University of Toronto, Pat Uhl, washed clothes, baked bannock, weeded gardens, hayed, milked cows, chopped wood, beaded costumes, made butter, even laid a cement foundation for a house. As their skins browned in the sun, with hands blistered and necks ravaged by mosquitoes, backs stiff from sleeping on the bug-infested floor or in a tent on the ground, SUPA figures like Uhl felt they had proven their commitment. It was not quite enough to transcend the barriers separating them from those who would not be leaving the reserves in August to return to the Universities of Toronto or Saskatchewan. Naïve field workers, innocent in their enthusiasms to learn and to help and to politicize, were pained to find out that Native peoples were not what they had imagined them to be. Too often their Aboriginal friends seemed passive and submissive. It did not help to hear, via the rumour mill, that some on the reserve looked on radical students as undercover agents for the Department of Indian Affairs, or spies for welfare agencies. Even more troubling was to be wrapped up in the complex problem of erotically-charged competitions among young Native men, some of whom considered it a status boost to be hanging out with white women student radicals. Adding insult to injury, mainstream elements in the Canadian Union of Students denounced the SUPA leftists for ostensibly high-jacking the Project and making it "political"; some of the sponsors, including Don Nielson, withdrew their support and denounced the students.[49]

As the project stumbled into a second summer, things did not improve. At the Métis settlement of Green Lake, where two SUPA *neestowers* had wintered, protests developed around issues of land and logging payments. The Liberal provincial government was outraged that student radicals seemed to be fomenting discord, forcing the state to *ante* up with cash payments and property rights acknowledgements. "Until the people of Green Lake ... kick out these communist interlopers ... we can do little for [the residents]," thundered one Member of Parliament in the Legislature. The Green Lake Métis were threatened with material deprivations if they continued to harbour student radicals in their midst. SUPA's *neestowers* were soon an unwanted element, and it was not long before they packed their bags, coming to the conclusion that "native people must organize their own liberation."[50] Liora Proctor, who spent some time in the Métis community of Green Lake in the winter of 1965-1966, wrote a critical assessment later in the autumn. She noted that Native people had no under-standing of why white students had come into their midst and, indeed, they had a right to feel resentful of the intrusion. Interviewed by Krista Maeots, Proctor later re-alized that SUPA's idealized "picture of the Indian" as "someone whose whole culture rejects what is hollow about Middle Class America" was a problematic foundation on which to build the Neestow initiative. Sadly, after three years, SUPA had come to be regarded in a number of Native communities as "just white men who came and dab-bled and went away again." In a related commentary, Proctor's comrade and a sum-mer Neestow field worker, Clayton Ruby, suggested that SUPA had undertaken its entry into the Saskatchewan reserves in order to help Native people assert power over their lives. Paraphrasing Stokely Carmichael of the Student Non-Violent Coordi-nating Committee [SNCC], Ruby concluded that power was 'white' and the 'white-ness' of SUPA fieldworkers was never really addressed. This meant that SUPA had to confront the extent to which its entire understanding of participatory democracy and struggling for power through such vehicles as education was a racialized dead-end from its very beginnings: "it may be that the road to education is power, but certainly not Indian power, because by the time you're successful all the Indians are white men—or as close as makes no difference."[51]

It was one thing to conclude that race mattered on an Indian reserve, a 'discov-ery' difficult enough but also natural and inevitable. Among the Doukhobor commu-nities of Castelgar, Krestova, and Ootoshenie, British Columbia, where another eight SUPA field workers set up the Kootenays Project in the summer of 1965, neophyte ac-tivists faced a rude jolt to their assumptions about youth and radicalization. Doukhobor pacifism drew the New Leftists. They wanted to connect with the Union of Doukhobor Youth, and they expected that "the older folk," who spoke only Rus-sian, would be less than receptive to their message. In understanding its project as persuading Doukhobors that they were agents of an unfolding social revolution, aligned with "the poor, native peoples, radical students, the labour movement, and intellectuals," SUPA discovered that not all youth were captivated by the prospects of social transformation, especially in the interior of British Columbia. Young Doukhobors, the Kottenays Project field workers discovered, were actually less in tune with SUPA than the Old World elders. They had been educated in the Canadian public schools, worked in the region's pulp and paper mills, spent their money on car loans, and drank their evenings away in boisterous bars. The spiritual inner life of Doukhobor pacifism and the rejection of capitalist materialism that SUPA had seen from a distance was, up close among the assimilated youth, an illusive organizational straw to grasp in the modernizing winds of the immigrant milieu. Oddly enough, perhaps the most lasting lesson learned in the SUPA experiment in crossing cultural lines in British Columbia was that old was not necessarily inferior to young and new. As Lynne Butts wrote in a SUPA report for the Kootenays entitled, "The Beauty that is Age," one of the Doukhobor women elders was a "symbol of old age and what it could be, if we stopped fearing it."[52]

SUPA's sole African Canadian field worker, Rocky Jones, found his head so "full of ideas" that he thought he could "create a Utopia" within Halifax's black community. He ended up isolated, lonely, and desperate for help. Not a student, Jones, who grew up in Truro, Nova Scotia, had been motivated by Carmichael's SNCC work in the American South and Tom Hayden's Newark community organizing project. SUPA was the only connection he could establish in Canada, and he gave up a good government job in Toronto to return to the Maritimes and work with Halifax blacks, then suffering through the urban renewal dislocations of the assault on Africville. His dreams shattered, he concluded that "Superman does not exist and I can't play the role he supposedly played." SUPA reinforcements did arrive, sustaining the Nova Scotia Project for two years. But by January 1967 it was on its last legs. A SUPA activist summoned up a recollection of the events years later, "We sent [Rocky Jones] down without any money. I think he must have eventually given up on us."[53] Other SUPA activists, such as Montreal-based Stan Gray, who toured the country to raise money for non-violent protest, and a contingent of civil disobedience practitioners in Comox and Courtney, British Columbia, kept the CUCND tradition of protesting Canada's nuclear arms and warfare state bases alive. Research on peace and the professions, for which many SUPA activists no doubt (and not wrongly) considered themselves destined, was undertaken. Yet regional discontents and differences chaffed, even as commitment to non-alignment in the Cold War and the need to convert war industries to peaceful economic production deepened.[54]

The Toronto-based School for Social Theory revealed how things could fall apart rather quickly. Of all the 1965 SUPA projects, the School probably involved more activists than any other undertaking, with a dozen full-time participants, including a Director, Matt Cohen, and upwards of fifty people drifting in and out of two on-going, part-time seminars. Discussions could turn on how to sabotage the Bell Telephone Company, later reported on under the title, "Hegel and the New Left." An organizer from the Communist Party of India might drop in for an afternoon talk.[55]

It all seemed relatively straight-forward in the beginning. SUPA activists were keen to learn about social change, hone their theoretical expertise, and discuss how it could be applied to specific areas. Among the subjects that seemed to suit SUPA's needs were Marxism, the New Left, and psychoanalysis. From the first day, however, Cohen indicated he would not lead. It was up to the participants to determine how the school would work, what would be taught within it, and how that pedagogical exercise would be structured. Faced with no structure, SUPA members immediately constructed a fairly rigid one, with daily written papers and oral presentations. But "pressured by assignments, bugged by non-directed discussion, unsure of their own place in the school, and frustrated by lack of communication," the students rebelled and decided instead to prepare what they thought useful to discuss the next day. This led nowhere: "we really had no idea how to learn from each other. What seemed a disintegration of the school was blamed on the fact that we met too early in the morning, intellectual levels were different, other people weren't reading, there was no motivation." After a week at which an average of three people a day attended classes, Cohen stepped in, assuming more authority, lecturing, assigning papers. Expectations adjusted, people began to work on their own, and "the school picked up again." In the end, the lessons learned were negative ones, but no less significant for being so:

> The school was an experiment to provide an experience through which people can learn freely from each other, unhampered and unaided by limits and structures such as deadlines, exams, curriculum, systems of organization. I think we underestimated the frustration and confusion that occurs when accustomed structures are removed and people are forced to confront themselves and each other. We failed to provide support for each other during this upheaval.

In its failures, SUPA's School for Social Theory was typical of all of the undertakings of the summer of 1965. It never became a "nerve centre for the movement." As with most of SUPA's intense summer work, the School confirmed among participants that two months was an insufficient time frame in which to accomplish what they had set out to do.[56]

Throughout all of this, SUPA was intimately connected to SDS in the United States. Few of those truly active in the Canadian New Left could, in 1965, discern that much separated Canadians and Americans in the student syndicalist movement. These were revolutionaries who knew no country, at least at this point in their youthful lives. As one of them told Cyril Levitt, "the people that I knew didn't feel the profound sense that we were part of the same country that the powerful were part of."[57] Asked to comment on how the movement differed in Canada and the United States, SUPA leader Peter Boothroyd replied bluntly, "I don't think there is a difference."[58] From ERAP literature sold on SUPA tables, to Tom Hayden coming to Toronto to chill out from the pressures of Newark and national SDS commitments, to the voter-registration drives in Mississippi, and SNCC support work, the Canadian and American New Lefts at mid-decade shared much that mattered.[59]

Indeed, prior to the summer 1965 projects, perhaps the single most important *action* in both galvanizing SUPA and bringing fresh forces of radicalizing youth into its midst, was a March 1965 series of protests outside the United States Consulate on University Avenue. Called in support of a civil rights march from Selma, Alabama to the state capital in Montgomery which aimed at securing black voting rights in the violently segregated American south, the SUPA demos propagandized about the ways in which state troopers and racist vigilantes had unleashed a torrent of deadly abuse on the student activists, a handful of whom were Canadians. As the small, daily sit-ins at the Consulate gained press attention, publicizing racist atrocity and the growing opposition to it, the crowds gathering on the sidewalk outside of the U.S. consular grounds grew. Signatures on petitions mounted, and SUPA's numbers mushroomed. From this date on, SUPA retained close ties to SNCC through joint endeavors, a linked Committee in which the key figures were Anne Cohen and Harvey L. Shepherd, and a May 1965 Conference.[60]

It was of course the war in Vietnam that ultimately linked Canadians and Americans in the mid-1960s New Left. Indo-China had been an outpost of European (particularly French) colonization for decades. Having defeated France in the 1950s, Viet Minh guerillas found themselves confronted with an oppressive, United States-backed Saigon regime headed by Ngo Dinh Diem. By 1960 a resistance movement was calling on the country to rise up and overthrow the Diem dictatorship; the National Liberation Front, and its military wing, the Viet Cong, mounted a guerrilla war that threatened to take power. The United States moved to pacify the region. It quietly sent almost 20,000 military personnel, euphemistically designated 'advisors', into Vietnam by 1963. It was not enough. Soon the United States was embroiled in an all-out war effort, one that necessitated drafting American youth to fight in a country half way around the world, against an enemy few combatants understood. As of 1968, almost 500,000 American troops were stationed in Vietnam. The United States death toll had climbed to approximately 20,000. Roughly 150,000 Vietnamese were being slaughtered annually, many of them civilians with no actual involvement in armed resistance. With the United States detonating 700,000 tons of explosives a month and spending billions on an undeclared war against communism, American society fractured down the middle. An anti-war movement emerged and dominated politics of the mid-to-late 1960s, eventually defeating President Lyndon B. Johnson. Millions of protesters marched on Washington and in every major metropolitan city of the country. Students for a Democratic Society, one of a number of anti-war organizations, exploded in growth to the point that it could claim 100,000 members in 1968. War, long the business of the nation, was now its decisive divide, and the New Left stood on one side of what was increasingly looking like a barricade-strewn society. Democracy took to the streets, youthful protests proclaiming at first, "Bring the Boys Home," and, as radicalism escalated, "We Are All Viet Cong" and "Ho, Ho, Ho Chi Minh, The NLF Is Going to Win." An anti-war movement had become an anti-imperialist mobilization. Soon there would be those who would champion the need to "Bring the War Home."[61]

Vietnam registered with Canadian radicals, to be sure, but even as late as 1964 opposition to the war was posed rather mildly. *Canadian Dimension* offered an understated liberal editorial that opened with the weakly posed question, "How much longer can the war in Vietnam go on?" as late as spring 1965. But from that point on the New Left grew increasingly concerned, and prolific in its publications and criticisms of the Canadian state's complicity in imperialist atrocity. *Dimension's* Cy Gonick offered a lengthy three-part article entitled "What Every Canadian Should Know About Vietnam" that ran from mid-1965 into the last published issue of the year, and many others also bent their pens in opposition to the United States' military intervention in Indo-China. By 1968 there were few New Leftists in the country who had not read and researched the imperialist imbroglio and its Canadian connections.[62]

SUPA's anti-war activities followed a similar course. A protest vigil at the University of Toronto in the spring of 1965 formed a silent ring of students and faculty, staring down the American liberal apologist for Vietnam, Adlai Stevenson, as he bowed and scraped his way to an honourary degree. A passive media plug-in to a mid-May 1965 Washington Teach-In on the Vietnam war was promoted by SUPA, but it proved disappointing. The audience of 400-500 was smaller than anticipated, and the broadcast discussions rather staid. More robust protests, which involved defiance of the University Administration's ban on political book tables, took place at the University of Alberta, forcing the censors to back down.[63] SUPA participated in a Vietnam Conference organized by the Canadian Friends and Service Committee (Quakers) at

Carleton University in mid-June 1965.[64] These and other demonstrative anti-war undertakings, however, were soon overshadowed by the officially-sanctioned International Teach-In on "Revolution and Response," organized at the University of Toronto in October 1965, in which SUPA figures Liora Proctor, Matt Cohen and Henry Tarvainen had been early organizational contacts.[65]

The International Teach-In at Toronto quickly became top-heavy in its institutionalization, and to radical students it appeared conformist and Ivory Towerish. SUPA figures such as Art Pape, while drawn to some of what could be accomplished in such settings, nevertheless rebelled at the extent to which, "People were talked *to* about personal issues, not talked *with*." Governed by liberal premises—such as dropping from the platform a Berkeley graduate student who had visited Hanoi when another non-radical participant refused to share the front table with him—the University of Toronto Teach-In was an *academic* and hierarchical undertaking, orchestrated by faculty and sanctioned by University President Claude Bissell. At a cost of $35,000, it hardly seemed a model of mobilizing and participatory democracy. The liberal trajectory of the Toronto International Teach-Ins was evident in the post-1965 drift away from the concern with war and revolution: future Teach-Ins would address "China: Co-Existence or Containment," "Religion and International Affairs," and "Exploding Humanity: The Crisis of Numbers." Yet the first International Teach-In, undoubtedly the most radical, drew 4,000 students and 120 journalists, the proceedings transmitted by radio to an audience reported to top one million. It undoubtedly fired enthusiasm for more anti-war activity.[66] It was followed, for instance, by SUPA buses chartered to attend Washington anti-war rallies, open letters to Parliament, another Teach-In at the University of Ottawa (featuring *Our Generation* editors and SUPA leaders Tony Hyde, Art Pape, and Dimitri Roussopoulos), and civil disobedience aimed at disrupting the business-as-usual attitude of the Canadian state. In the latter March 1966 event 61 SUPA activists were arrested, many of whom were found guilty on charges of obstruction.[67]

By 1966, SUPA was playing an increasingly important role in aiding American draft resisters who wanted to come to Canada in order to avoid being forced into the armed forces and sent to Vietnam. Clayton Ruby and others set up an office next to a SUPA house; established a telephone roster and a counseling service; found temporary housing for draft dodgers, putting them up with sympathetic families; and even helped smuggle young war resisters into the country. Over the course of the last half of the 1960s thousands of such legal and illegal draft evaders came to Canada, materially aided by SUPA and well-informed about the nature of the country and their prospects by reading a text that the Toronto radicals had inspired. A SUPA associate, Martin Satin, edited *A Manual for Draft-Age Immigrants to Canada*, building on an earlier New Left pamphlet that had been produced to ease the war resister's entry into a new country. The tremendously successful *Manual* sold 65,000 copies in the latter half of the 1960s. Draft dodgers were a mixed lot. Many simply wanted to avoid military service and settle into comfortable lives. Others, however, were committed leftists who would have an important immediate impact on the small Canadian New Left, as well as in decades to come.[68]

There were nevertheless signs of trouble on SUPA's anti-Vietnam War horizon. The Ottawa Vietnam Week had been characterized by a growing divisiveness, with some claiming decisions were being made in bureaucratic ways by an elitist cohort of Toronto leaders. Resentments grew over 'power plays' and 'oligarchies'. George Grant, who was supposed to address the Teach-In withdrew because of conflicts with SUPA leaders. Attendance never really reached much past 100.[69]

Subsequent anti-war activities in Canada from 1966-1968 revealed how an increasingly sluggish SUPA was being left behind by a growing anti-war mobilization. The University of British Columbia's Vietnam Day Committee led the way, and was quickly followed by the formation of some 22 pan-Canadian campus Committees to End the War in Vietnam. In Montreal anti-war mobilizations culminated in a large mid-November 1967 protest at the U.S. Consulate. Organized by the Quebec Union of Students, the demonstrators were militant and vocal in their condemnations, shouting "Johnson, napalm, murderer." They linked the wars of resistance abroad with those at home: "Vietnam for the Vietnamese/Québec for the Québécois." Thousands strong, the Montreal marchers arrived at the American embassy and showered it with missiles, precipitating a police attack that left twenty people injured and 46 arrested. SUPA, while involved in such actions, was now clearly a waning force. Students, pacifists, and a rising anti-imperialist movement, a part of which was composed of Marxist organizations with Trotskyist or Maoist programs, was supplemented by the Old Left ranks of the Communist Party, which retained a presence of importance in locales such as Vancouver and Winnipeg. Committees of such united fronts mobilized Vietnam protests across the country, militant expressions of a rising crescendo of opposition, much of it youth oriented. But SUPA was less and less visible, its role increasingly marginal.[70]

In 1965, after a "Fall Institute" gathering of 80 field workers and SUPA leaders in St. Calixte, Quebec, Peter Gzowski had seen the roughly 1,000 students and youth radicals comprising the Union as the best and the brightest of a new generation of thinking, doing, dissident youth, "the heart of the new left."[71] Yet as Kostash records, "It was downhill from St. Calixte." SUPA conferences in Saskatoon (December 1965), Waterloo (December 1966), and, finally, Goderich (September 1967), were wracked by increasingly pessimistic reflections on the summer projects. The numbers of committed cadre took a nosedive: from 200 to 40. As a vehicle of revolutionary advance, SUPA was stuck in reverse. More and more activists were asking themselves just what it was that was guiding them in their field work. They didn't have answers. And as they questioned, the distinctiveness of the New Left, with its accent on community organizing, faith in the dispossessed, and deeply engrained opposition to all structures and hierarchies, seemed to drift into spaces occupied by the Old Left.

Where do you do revolutionary work and why? If power oppresses, how can power be mobilized to counter this? Who, or what, has the power to challenge the state? Can the trade unions, the Communist Party, the NDP—all be written off as irrelevant? Was not Marxism something more than merely a relic of antiquated Victorianism? Paul Goodman, invited by SUPA to facilitate a session at its Waterloo conference, found his audience impatient with his subjective orientation, with its understanding of alternative as a project of self-education. The old libertarian departed the conference muttering that in Canada, of all places, there seemed to be a lot of Marxism. Certainly more than Goodman was used to in the United States, and a tad in excess of what he perhaps would have liked.

How *could* SUPA transcend a materialist analysis when it ran questions like this in its newsletter: "Your father wants you to go back to University in September and to graduate next May, but you want to stay out a year to work for SUPA. So your father says, 'OK, but if you go back this year, I'll not only pay your fees, but I'll give SUPA a post-dated cheque for one thousand dollars ($1000.00) which they may cash in May of next year provided you graduate." SUPA polled individual members as to what they would do if they found themselves in this "true to life actual problem." 'Just say No' was not, apparently, in the vocabulary of SUPA's 1960s.[72]

SUPA's Slip Slidin' Away

> *Slip slidin' away*
> *Slip slidin' away*
> *You know the nearer your destination*
> *The more you're slip slidin' away*
>   —*Paul Simon*

As facetious as it may sound, the individual dilemma of a father bribing his son or daughter to stay in school while he bankrolled the New Left captured the reality of a larger threat to SUPA. The biggest of daddies, with the blankest of cheques, was the state. At the same point that SUPA began to charter the political territory of community organizing the Prime Minister's Office of Lester B. Pearson was promoting citizen participation through a series of well-funded government programs. One of these was the Company of Young Canadians (CYC). In April 1965 Parliament was asked to approve a project "through which the energies and talents of youth can be elicited in projects for economic and social development both in Canada and abroad." Enticing one of SUPA's leading figures, Toronto's Art Pape, on to the CYC governing council proved an early state coup, and one that fostered divisions and animosities within the nascent New Left. CYC funded SUPA's 'Fall Institute' at St. Calixite to the tune of $4000. It sent observers to cultivate the notion that CYC and SUPA shared an approach to community organizing that should bring the bodies together. Key CYC figure and former Canadian Union of Students activist, Stewart Goodings, promoted close relations between the Company and SUPA, visiting with KCP field workers, addressing members through contributions to the newsletter, and developing connections with a number of New Left figures.[73]

There were many in SUPA, understandably, who wanted nothing to do with state bureaucracy. They cautioned that there was much to be lost if the hand-outs of state grants and incorporation into elite structures came to define the New Left. *Our Generation's* editor, Dimitrios Roussopoulos, was quick to denounce anyone who snuggled up to the state.[74] Pape seemed, to some, to have succumbed to the lure of office and its largesse as he argued that, "Man, there's four hundred million dollars on the table. If we don't pick it up somebody else is going to."[75] It didn't help that in January 1967 a SUPA anti-Vietnam war rally in which two CYC volunteers—David DePoe and Lynn Curtis—were organizers brought the wrath of the Prime Minister's Office down on the head of the Company.[76] There were, it was now clear, limits to what the paymasters in Ottawa were willing to put up with.

Furthermore, rumours abounded that the CYC was a nest of corruption. There had supposedly been an automobile buying spree, netting eight Volvos for the use of Quebec volunteers. Pape's trips to left-wing think-tanks in Santa Barbara or civil-rights training camps in New Orleans were bankrolled, replete with $25 helicopter trips from the California airport. It mattered little that this may well have been an economical means of transport. When it was bandied about in Parliament at the end of 1968 that Pape had drawn $17,000 as a CYCer over the course of a year, the damage in some New Left quarters was irreversible. An *Our Generation* editorial closed the CYC book bitterly, drawing on Marcusian notions of repressive tolerance to condemn the "seasoned radicals" and "intellectual eunuchs" who "turned a tender day-dream into a nightmare" and, in the process, aborted "a movement of youth that was *feeling* its way towards an effective opposition." The moral of this sad tale of state intervention and attractive accommodation was that "more activists should take horror films seriously."[77]

Kostash concludes that after the disappointingly small and politically acrimonious September 1967 Goderich conference, SUPA simply disintegrated. There were, of course, many lesser SUPA lights than Art Pape. Over the course of 1966-1967, they quietly took the CYC bait rather than struggle in uncertainty and confusion. There seemed so little difference between being a SUPA field worker or a CYC volunteer, except the level of poverty one was expected to endure. As SUPA's ranks thinned dramatically in 1967, the CYC recruitment of youth volunteers picked up. By the end of 1967, the CYC "had absorbed most of SUPA's Toronto-based leadership in staff or consultant jobs, had hired half of its project workers into its own volunteer groups, and had linked up with most of SUPA's extant projects." The eulogy was definitively blunt: "SUPA was dead and the chance to mature politically was forfeited."

SUPA stalwarts charged those who went over to the CYC with careerism, compromise, and complicity, the three C's of co-optation's cash-induced 'sell-out'. "I can remember when CYC came out to Saskatchewan to court us," recalled one New Leftist disdainfully. "They picked us up in their big, beautiful van, took us to the hotel, fed us filet mignon and wine and asked us, would you like to work for us, we pay well, blah, blah. We said no, this is an attempt to co-opt us, its crap, it's bullshit." But the bullshit traveled far, wide, and with considerable effect. At its highwater mark in 1967-1968, the Company of Young Canadians had 228 volunteers working in dozens of projects, many of them in the politically volatile environment of Quebec. New Leftists Art Pape and a non-SUPA former University of Buffalo SDS high-flyer, Rick Salter, were now centrally involved in the CYC, trying to push it in a "harder left" direction and gaining some ground. But their plans would soon be scuttled, resisted by the bureaucracy in Ottawa as well as by critics who remained wedded to New Left principles, what Salter would later refer to as "all the old, clichéd radical reasons." As 1968 closed, Pape and Salter had made their exit from CYC, and its last years, before being incorporated directly into the state bureaucracy in 1970, were a winding down of any New Left impulses that remained within the government-affiliated organization. With the passing of the 1960s, the Company of Young Canadians was both "idealistically and for all practical purposes, dead." Its volunteers in May 1970 numbered barely one-third of those who criss-crossed the country in 1968 and, while it lived on until 1977, the CYC was but a pale and inconsequential reflection of the radical purpose and commitment that it had fed off of from its founding in 1965-1966.[78]

The irony was an old one. SUPA's destination, the building of a revolutionary youth opposition that could truly live up to the promise of a New Left, seemed so close in 1967-1968. The loose affinity groups of the organization and their commitment to a radical *praxis* that cojoined critical thought and socially transformative action had nonetheless slipped away. There is no denying the role of the CYC, as a state agency, in not only coopting SUPA's leaders and ranks but, more importantly, in culturally disrupting the solidarity and collective experience of the nascent New Left formation. This happened, in part, because SUPA lacked a clarity of perspective and anything approximating a programmatic orientation to the illusive revolutionary change it embraced with such fervour. But as the CYC held out the carrot of officialdom's call—access to state power, funds to pay for meals, books, and good works, and, seemingly, a structure that could carry on beyond the summer—there were those wielding the stick of what was increasingly called 'ideology'.

As early as the end of 1966, *Canadian Dimension's* Cy Gonick had penned an incisive and widely-read critique of SUPA. A radical born and bred in Winnipeg, a city rich in the multicultural diversity of the Old Left, Gonick had gravitated to the rather wilder Berkeley-based California New Left. There, as a graduate student, he connected with many figures prominent in 1960s mobilizations. Somewhat harsh in his characterization of SUPA as made up of "part-time radicals" and "coffee-house revolutionaries," Gonick claimed that notwithstanding "a few outstanding exceptions" northern student syndicalists couldn't hold a militantly-activist candle to SDS, SNCC, and the Berkeley Viet Nam Day Committee. He thought the Canadian New Left "more of a myth than a reality."

Aside from this jaundiced judgmentalism, however, Gonick's more serious qualms about SUPA were that it had failed to move beyond a nebulous, if evocatively promoted, assault on bureaucratism. This led inevitably to a concentration on the means by which power elites ruled rather than the substance and content of that dominance. In the New Left reification of participatory democracy, Gonick claimed, lay the seeds of political indifference to the actual content of power. There was, he discerned, a problematic willingness to concentrate the struggle for social transformation on forms that were undemocratic and hierarchical. Thus, Gonick suggested that the logic of SUPA's New Leftism was that, if "an inhumane, illiberal programme was arrived at at the 'grass roots' level and represented a 'consensus,' and provided it were implemented by the 'grass roots,' then it would be acceptable to the New Left." Rejecting all "traditional agencies of protest," from the NDP to the trade unions, the New Left, according to Gonick, embraced the alienated and the powerless and, in the process, elevated understandings of "counter communities" to a place of prominence in revolutionary social change that such marginalized people could never fulfill. Questioning the notion that the poorest and most dispossessed in any society have no stake in the status quo, the *Dimension* editor suggested that their utter helplessness and dependency on the state made them dubious material to lead the revolutionary struggle for overthrowing contemporary capitalist society. Isolated in ghettoized communities of their own mind, as well as those of capitalist inequality's making, SUPA New Leftists, Gonick suggested, had been irresponsible in placing all of their revolutionary eggs in the one basket of "a national network of community organizing." The need of the hour, in Gonick's view, was not avoidance of established venues of already-established organization, but the absolute necessity of penetrating "the major institutions where people are—trade unions, churches, teachers' societies, student organizations, the NDP, to create within them constituencies which can be harnessed to a political movement aimed at national independence and socialism, to guard against elitism, and to insist, in all of these activities, on member participation in decision-making." To do this, the New Left needed what, according to Gonick, it lacked: "a political programme."[79]

Gonick spoke out of two sides of the radical mouth, which was not necessarily a bad thing. As a New Leftist attentive to the message and meaning of Old Leftism, he was looking for bridges to build between the young and those who were, in their oppositional commitments, young at heart. In Canada, Gonick argued, this resonated with historical practice. The formation of dissident third party movements, the possibilities of realizable socialism, and the viability of Marxism as a theoretical and analytic guide were less awkwardly posed in Canada than they were in the United States. There, the hegemony of anti-communism and the inviolate sanctities of individualism and private property were weighty ideological anchors that sank the appropriation of Marxist sensibilities deeper in conservative waters than was the case in Canada. Indeed, as SUPA faltered and then fell by the wayside in 1967-1968, a new New Left emerged, one that could never quite, ironically, manage to be as centered as was the admittedly decentered SUPA, but one that rode out what remained of the revolutionary wave of the 1960s. In this discontinuous continuity, the New Left shifted gears, accelerating its growth but doing so in ways that moved people into different political and interpretive lanes. No easy pigeon-holing of these emerging post-1967 tendencies could ever capture either the diversity or the commonality of the New Left's brief, but powerfully creative, last Canadian gasp. Yet within the pattern of a broad, common political development, three complicatingly related, albeit often eventually divided, radical trajectories emerged: Marxism, Left Nationalism, and Feminism.

Political Reproduction: New Left Expropriations of Marxism and Campus Revolts

As SUPA quietly imploded at the end of 1967's summer,[80] its failures and its successes led its more reflective members to seek out a more rigorous analytic *praxis*. The limitations and frustrations of community organizing, as well as grappling with why America was in Vietnam, all pushed activists in the direction of theory. In January 1967 one SUPA activist had declared:

> Things are pretty grim at the moment. Can anything be done about this? The Left on campus has been failing for one fundamental reason—it has always reacted to specific crises … rather than educating the campus, and in this way, establishing a base of support upon which to draw … . By educating the campus, I mean the setting up of a broadly-based organization of the Left which would conduct seminars, invite speakers, hold conferences, and possibly even publish a periodical of some kind. This is necessary to combat the widely-accepted 'non-political' quasi-ideology which asserts the irrelevance of the student in society.

It was difficult to avoid the obvious analytic authority of a body of writing that placed the accent on the structured class inequalities and imperatives of accumulation evident in capitalism or the ways in which that same economic order, blocked by its inner contradictions, turned to colonialism, making imperialism its highest stage. Student radicals could see that the weak links of the global chain of oppression and exploitation were exposed in revolutionary struggles that might actually *defeat* capitalism in Third World movements of guerilla warfare or colonial liberation. The New Left began the process of congealing different strands of revolutionary thought, from Marx and Lenin, on the one hand, through Che Guevara, Regis Debray, Frantz Fanon, and Kwame Nkrumah on the other, into a mix in which Mao often percolated to the surface. His ideas were championed by groups like The Internationalists, led by former University of British Columbia student radical leader, Hardial Bains. This had the ironic impact of moving the *praxis* of the New Left away from field work projects and more and more into what was increasingly called "ideological communication." For a brief moment in 1967 this effort was concentrated in a New Left Committee of a dozen ex-SUPA figures who put out a *Bulletin* that aimed to draw student radicals across the country together: "O we can't organize, it's a pity/In country or campus or city./We need an analysis/To stop our paralysis/So we'll set up another committee."[81]

The New Left Committee wrote and thought and spoke in an idiom different than had SUPA. When it looked back on the brief history of the Canadian New Left, it was clear to some where predecessors had faltered:

> Key to SUPA's failure was its inability to develop a coherent strategy of the structure of modern capitalism and of its specific characteristics in Canada. Instead SUPA remained ideologically confused, uncritically eclectic. It drew on various elements of the pacifist-direct action approach and ill-defined SDS notions of 'participatory democracy'. But the war in Vietnam, the powerlessness of the poor, the authoritarian governing of the universities were never traced to their structural roots in the political economy of modern capitalism, and the constituencies essential to revolutionary change were vaguely defined and analysed.

In this short paragraph of judgment lay the approach that would define the New Left's engagement with what remained of the 1960s.[82] The road of simultaneously interpreting *and* changing the world, however, would not be an easy one.

To the extent that SUPA had failed, it was apparent in 1967 that there were those prepared to resist the growing tide of Marxist theory that seemed to be crashing the New Left shorelines of *praxis*. Some continued to base an understanding of the revolutionary possibilities of the youth movement on the counterculture. "Politics in the widest sense," insisted one student activist, "must be made as interesting as pot." For another, protest needed to be inspired, as it was throughout the world, by avant-gardes and those who refused all incorporation in the Establishment's machineries of governance. Among the exalted were the Provos of Amsterdam, Timothy Leary, Bob Dylan, Dadaists, Surrealists, and civil rights marchers; tactics championed included "chalk drawing on the sidewalk, Black Masses, public 15-minute semi-spontaneous orgies, a poet on every corner, the right of spontaneous spectacle —enthusiasm, participation, IMAGINATION AND BEAUTY: spontaneous solidarity and creativity." Some thought the vanguard was destined to be those who refused all complicity in capitalism's drudgery and addictive consumerism—the hoboes, tramps, and permanently unemployed.[83]

This anarchistic intransigence to the fundamental program of Marxism certainly characterized a segment of Canada's New Left. It was, however, countered in the growth of new organizations that championed the energy and activism of 1960s youth radicalism at the same time that they engaged with a range of issues posed in the decidedly Old Left accent on party structure, political program, and proletarian orientation. The history of the proliferation of revolutionary organization in the 1967-1977 years has yet to be written.[84] This breathtaking explosion of Trotskyist, Maoist, and revolutionary direct action groups lay in the late 1960s encounter of the New Left and Marxism. Out of this would emerge the New Left Caucus, Red Morning, Rising Up Angry!, Canadian Party of Labour, Progressive Worker, Communist Party of Canada/Marxist-Leninist (formerly The Internationalists), League for Socialist Action (an older body, but we can enter it on the list), Socialist League/Forward Group, Spartacist League (later Trotskyist League of Canada), Revolutionary Marxist Group, Revolutionary Workers League, En Lutte/In Struggle, and Workers Communist Party.[85] To have lived in the intense cross-fire of this late 1960s/1970s cauldron of revolutionary thought, activity, and organizational commitment was an experience of endless and sharpening debate, argument, and exchange over the tactics and strategy of a new kind of left practice. Some would recognize the contribution that this made to deepening and developing the project of dissent, opposition, and socialism in Canada. Thus, Mel Watkins was generous in his understanding of how the left push in the New Democratic Party was accelerated by what he termed "the sectarian groups in Canada," naming the Trotskyists in particular as playing an important role in building the "anti-war movement in Canada."[86] Yet there were also those who saw in all of this an ongoing fragmentation and acrimony deserving of censure. "There were a whole lot of splits then," one SUPA leader told Myrna Kostash, "The Trots were getting heavy and there were the Hegelian phenomenologists and the hard-line Marxists. I remember one night at the NDY house when people were screaming, roaring, practically having fist fights over the issues of where we were politically. This was supposed to be a party."[87]

A party, or *the* Party? The word had different connotations, according to accents and capitalization. Increasingly this was the issue posed, and with it came, inevitably, questions of affiliation. Marxist or not-Marxist further divided along axes of distinguishable Marxisms, in the plural. Veteran Canadian New Left liberationist, James Harding, penned a decisive 1970 rebuke of an intellectual and political opponent, labeling him "a reductionist, mechanist, vulgar maoist Marxist, and anything else I can say with tongue in cheek. He wants to stay outside humanity and its struggles for freedom with his grand, deterministic theory of revolution." Harding's mindset spoke to "the poles on the left in Canada" that were widening in these 1967-1970 years.[88]

One pole within SUPA's political contestation was represented by Stan Gray, who in the spring of 1967 was working on a dissertation in England. His view was that a turn to Marxist understandings of class struggle was precisely the direction demanded. Gray, who had grown up in a Communist family, was for the first half of the 1960s a quintessential New Leftist. Later in the decade he began to reflect on where youth radicals had been going and whether they were not missing something. "If there is one thing that the new left, at least in Canada, has consistently sought to avoid," thought Gray after his years in CUCND and SUPA, "it is the radicalizing experiences and organizational importance of the productive process, and thereby of the working class as a class." Gray wrote to Don McKelvey, a member of SDS who had left the United States to work with SUPA and who advocated the writing of a Canadian equivalent of the Port Huron Statement, in the summer of 1967. He expressed opposition to the drift into what he judged the excessive subjectivity of middle-class students. In contrast, Gray championed "Marxist emphasis on class and workers control."[89] A year later, Gray was adamant that, "Marxism is coming more and more to be the common denominator of all student movements in North America and Western Europe."[90]

The New Left, born of the campus but separated somewhat from it in the mid-1960s engagement with 'community', would ironically make its prodigal return via a commitment to working-class analysis and Marxism. A first phase of the Canadian New Left gave way to a second, in which former SUPA activists figured prominently, but were supplemented by a younger wave of disaffected youth. Marxism was to be a necessary component of their radical, growingly anti-capitalist, arsenal. To be sure, *some* veterans of the New Left were now well placed to lead the emerging student movement, and of those males who survived the demise of SUPA, many embraced Marxism and class analysis in one way or another. But few joined the Trotskyist and Maoist organizations that, by 1968-1969, were a force to reckon with on the left in general, and within student radical politics in particular. 'Student syndicalism', undertaken in particular ways in the mid-1960s, came increasingly to mean a worker-student alliance orchestrated by a party formation which understood its ultimate aim as the creation of a revolutionary vanguard organization.[91] Even if such bodies did not lead, they were ubiquitously present. Moreover, the ethos of the New Left in this period meant that "participatory democracy" and "community organization," evident in 1969-1970 in the anti-poverty agitations of Toronto's Just Society Movement and its links to a contingent of radical social workers, academics, and urban rebels who took the eminently New Left name, Praxis,[92] was overtaken by more boisterous protests. Increasingly, these aimed to disrupt the university and its pretence of civility or organize picket line militance in support of striking workers.[93]

This, then, was an intellectual movement of radicalization that affected many university youth, often those affiliated with the Canadian Union of Students (CUS). It was an oddly uneven development, characterized by what one participant/commentator, Andrew Wernick, dubbed "a quasi-Marxism" in which "much talk of movement-building" was sobered by "an acute suspicion of leadership and organization." As much as all seemed to agree that "theory lagged far behind practice," the importance of acting on one's radical beliefs was nevertheless paramount. The New Left lived on in the accent on spontaneity and the significance of "the grass roots." Centralization was to be avoided, used only when formal structures were necessary for fulfilling the objectives of local activism. The enthusiasm of a loosely Marxist, theoretically-inclined student left in 1968 was summed up in Wernick's account of a CUS gathering in Winnipeg: "the history of those ten days seemed to suggest that mainstream middle-class Canadian students placed in the intense hot-house of a 'free' community and prodded a little by radical ideas and experiences, are but ten days from revolutionary consciousness."[94] Sometimes, of course, this "revolutionary consciousness" required nurturing, and this often came in the form of specific local developments.

A case in point was the Toronto Student Movement (TSM), organized in the summer of 1968. TSM largely leapfrogged over its immediate student radical predecessors, CUCND, SNCC, SUPA, and the anti-Vietnam war coalitions that, by 1966-1967 were being pieced together by Trotskyist organizations such as the League for Socialist Action.[95] Its eyes at first set on radicalizing university life TSM soon found itself supporting striking newspaper guild members in Peterborough, pursuing Marxist analyses of power that connected the obscure dots of corporate profit and research, the state and higher education, and capitalist culture and the ideological pacification of the oppressed and exploited. Along with the Canadian Union of Students, TSM adapted to the militancy of the moment, evident in student revolts in France, Italy, Germany, the United States and elsewhere. Marxist classics and anti-colonialist writers were now supplemented by attention to the speeches and positions of European student leaders such as Red Rudi Dutschke, Karl Dietrich Wolff, and Dany Cohn-Bendit. The latter's 1969 *Obsolete Communism: The Left-Wing Alternative,* soon became a New Left best-seller. Campus revolt was now front-page news. Tom Hayden, his New Jersey community organizing terminated by the 1967 Newark riots, saw SDS's revitalization in linking campus upheaval to the anti-war drive. When students occupied Columbia University in April 1968, Hayden called for "Two, Three, Many Columbias." The SDS leader's formulation suggested that in the heart of the imperialist Empire, student radicals could draw state repression and its material resources to them, thereby directly aiding the Vietnamese and other Third World revolutionaries.

University of Toronto never quite managed to rise to the 1968 occasion. But there were plenty of rallies and disruptive actions. TSM gave way to the New Left Caucus (NLC), broadly Marxist in its approach, but uninterested in direct alliance with any party formation. Toronto student radicals prevented University of California President and industrial relations authority Clark Kerr from speaking at the Royal Ontario Museum, 150 of them piling on to the stage, pantomiming Kerr's suppression of Mario Savio's freedom of speech. They protested the University's connection with Dow Chemical, a corporation whose products and profits were widely, if rather loosely, seen as fuelling the imperialist war drive. Classrooms became challenging stand-offs between dissident students and professors as the NLC refined its tactic of "spectacular radicalism." The ideology of higher education was assailed by a "theatre of revolt," exposing its sham hypocrisy and empty platitudes. Commencement ceremonies were heckled and unaligned students treated to an extemporaneous NLC lecture on youth's sexual oppression. As the meaning of the female orgasm became a hot topic of political discussion, button-wearing radicals popped up at the multiversity's various colleges sporting a slogan that immediately generated a playful mass appeal: "Bring University of Toronto to a Climax."[96]

At the University of Toronto, the New Left Caucus broke the back of a draconian disciplinary code. In Montreal, Sir George Williams University had a rougher student radical ride. There, protesters almost cracked the university's bank, trashing and torching the room where computers, tapes, and punch cards were kept. The damages were reported to have reached from $2 to $5 million. Race ignited the explosive protest, a special committee convening at the end of January 1969 to hear student testimony on allegations of a Biology professor's racism and incompetence.

> They designate institutions
> we disintegrate in infernoes.
> They consumate animals
> that abort us.
> Nursing grounds for dysgenic beasts.
> Developing ghettoes/employing social workers
> to create negroes.
> Man-trap, I know your name, your face.

Montreal in the mid-1960s had been a magnet attracting black student activists and radicals, many of whom had origins and interests in the Caribbean. Robert and Anthony Hill, Ann Cools, Roosevelt (Rosie) Douglas, Alfie Roberts and others formed a Conference Committee on West Indian Affairs. They drew deeply on the presence of C.L.R. James, who was sojourning in Canada over the course of late 1966 and into 1967. With James as a stimulus, this group of Montreal blacks organized a number of conferences, workshops and talks. These culminated in a 1968 Sir George Williams symposium that addressed black grievances in Canada, as well as a major Black Writers conference held at McGill University in mid-October 1968, at approximately the same time that West Indian student resentments were rising at Sir George Williams University. Speakers at the influential McGill forum included the charismatic James; Black Power advocate Stokely Carmichael, then at the height of his legendary status as the movement's most powerful orator; Guyana's Marxist historian, Walter Rodney; Olympian athlete and protester, Harry Edwards; and Halifax's Rocky Jones.[97]

The atmosphere approaching the Sir George Williams hearing was tense and untrusting. Administrators and most faculty had done little to convince black students that their complaints of professorial racism, classroom inadequacies, and dissatisfaction with how students were treated by instructors were going to be addressed sensitively. Grievances had been launched as early as April 1968, but they were largely swept under the University's bureaucratic rugs. There they gathered resentments over the summer and fall. A number of the Caribbean students were older and more experienced than their Canadian counterparts; many had considerable education under their belts, and were training to work in the medical profession. They were not about to be put off. As the fall of 1968 gave way to the winter of 1969, the January hearing to finally address the matter was shaping up to be an explosive event. The black students were rightfully incensed with the University's prevarications, and the consciousness of Black Power that had been raised and emboldened by the almost life-transforming oratory of dazzling speakers like James and Carmichael was not to be denied.

With the meeting about to begin, demonstrators overtook the stage, disrupted the proceedings, shut the hearing down, and 200 students occupied a number of rooms and gathering places, including the faculty club and the computer centre in the multi-storied Hall Building. The sit-in dragged on for two weeks. On 11 February 1969, however, there was every indication of an agreement that would have seen the occupation end. But the faculty vetoed it being signed, and a first entry of municipal police inspected the computer room and withdrew. Things took an ugly and destructive turn as those occupying university space heard on radio that the riot police were about to descend on them. Uncertain of their role and purpose, apparently, this second wave of police entered the rooms taken over by the students, departed, and then barricaded the building, their behaviour menacing in its threatened violence. When they returned and broke in a glass door, the protesters ransacked a cafeteria and the computer room was torched.

As the smoke cleared, 87 Sir George Williams students were arrested: 38 of them were black, the majority from the Caribbean. Many of those taken into police custody were badly beaten, racist taunts ringing in their ears as they were roughly escorted from the building. Douglas, a future Prime Minister of Dominica, and Cools, later appointed by Trudeau to the Senate, were among those who landed in jail. The University ostensibly spent hundreds of thousands of dollars to lay a total of 1044 criminal charges of which, one year after the event, only 50 had been heard, a mere nine upheld, with 22 dropped. Singled out as *the* leader, Kennedy Frederick, a West Indian from Grenada, endured a 25-day hearing, during which time he was held without bail (later granted), and was on occasion brought to court in a cage-like vehicle, has hands shackled behind his back. Frederick faced 12 charges, six involving conspiracy and six relating to arson and damage to and prevention of lawful use of property. Most such charges, blanketing the scores arrested, were later dropped for "lack of proof." Across Canada, the media denounced the "gang of hooligans," "rampaging criminals," "anarchists," and "thugs" responsible for the destruction of property. In Ottawa federal politicians pointed the finger of blame at Caribbean students and the lax immigration laws that allowed them access to Canadian higher education. They were soon demanding that more restrictive practices govern the entry of foreigners to universities.[98]

There were those quick to claim that there was little that was overtly Marxist that could be discerned as the rubble was cleaned up and the bruises healed in the Sir George Williams University affair. There had undoubtedly been more left rumblings of dissidence in the complicated making of the upheaval than many were willing to acknowledge. One western conservative did claim that the occupation had featured much chanting of slogans and direction quotation from "copies of Mao Tse Tung's Little Red Book." This did little to impress some older Marxist critics who saw nothing more than "obscurantism, egocentric pseudo-existentialism, and abstract moralizing" as the computer cards fluttered from atop Sir George Williams on to McKay Street below. Some grew increasingly hostile in their refusal to countenance "the romantic incendiarism and apocalyptic messianism of many segments of the new left." One professor at Sir George Williams, an associate editor of *Canadian Dimension*, condemned the nihilism that was "always at war with the idea of civilization—socialist civilization as well as bourgeois civilization." Charles Taylor, whose experience in the British New Left commenced in the *Universities and Left Review* of the late 1950s, and reached into Canada and Quebec in the 1960s, translated the growing unease with the practice of youth radicalism into a theoretical interrogation of one of the movement's analytic pillars, Herbert Marcuse. Taylor questioned the New Left theorist's "blithe unconcern with what rebellion is *for*, as long as its stridently enough against." He also deplored Marcuse's ruling out "the possibility that a paroxysm of rebellion could destroy the discipline and character-form of one civilization without building those of another, higher one." The result could only be "disillusionment and despair: a binge of agitation followed by a prolonged hang-over."[99]

Down the road from Sir George Williams, McGill University had been a centre of agitation since November 1967. With Stan Gray as its President of the local Students for a Democratic University (SDU) chapter, calls went out for a campus-wide General Strike. The galvanizing event proved to be the disciplining of some *McGill Daily* staff. They had published a satirical extract from Paul Krassner's *The Realist* that higher education officials considered "obscene libel." In retaliation, students occupied all six floors of the Administration Building. It took a brigade of policemen, and liberal use of nightsticks to clear the occupiers off McGill property; Stan Gray was knocked unconscious and arrested; and many students suffered injuries. A year and a half later, Gray, anything but subdued, headed a 15,000-strong 28 March 1969 demonstration outside of the gates of the Anglophone university, chanting, "McGill francais! McGill aux Québécois! McGill aux Travailleurs!" Police barricaded the University, helicopters hovered overhead, while some diehard Tory teenagers circled the wagons of retrenchment, standing strong for nineteenth-century values. Proud to protect McGill from the radical hoards, they planted themselves firmly on University property and sang "God Save the Queen." A coalition of trade unionists, students, socialists, and independence advocates, the McGill Francais movement cost Gray his teaching job at the prestigious bastion of English-speaking Montreal, catapulting him into prominence in the increasingly militant milieu of the Quebec revolutionary left. He soon headed an agitational mass movement of extra-parliamentary opposition, the *Front de libération populaire*, playing a prominent role in the establishment of a Quebec Committee for Solidaritiy with the Black Panthers. As the repressive atmosphere worsened, the provincial Legislature passed anti-demonstration laws. *Front de Libération du Québec* (FLQ) kidnappings of British High Commission staffer James Richard Cross and Quebec Minister of Labour and Immigration, Pierre Laporte, provoked the declaration of the War Measures Act, and the October Crisis. Gray was eventually swept up in the Black Friday arrest and detention of 500 leftists. McGill's SDU, for its part, denounced the University in 1969 as responsible for "more than two hundred years of economic exploitation and national oppression."[100]

From east to west, SDU chapters at Canadian universities agitated in 1968-1969, their demands paralyzing campuses. Libraries were locked down, buildings occupied, faculty clubs invaded by squealing pigs and gas-masked students screaming, "Thought police! Thought police!" Teach-ins, boycotts of classes, marches on department chairs, challenges to traditional behaviours and curriculum, and students petitioning for and rallying around a small but significant number of victimized Marxist professors were commonplace.[101]

The conflict peaked at Simon Fraser University (SFU), where a longstanding battle involved not only radical students and teaching assistants, but New Left Marxist faculty and some committed liberal colleagues. It confronted the class power of the University, demanding open admissions for working-class students. Student researchers uncovered the not terribly well-hidden story of corporate capital's dominance of Simon Fraser, how its Senate was ruled by presidents and directors of major enterprises. Labour unions and Native, welfare, tenant, and teacher organizations, however, had nary a voice in the corridors of power. Former SUPA activists James Harding and Sharon Yandle were among the shit-disturbers. When hundreds of students occupied the Administration buildings in November 1968, rifling through files as they lunched on peanut butter sandwiches, they discovered that RCMP dossiers had been compiled on 600 students, including a number of American war resisters. At 2:15 AM on the fourth day of the occupation, the Mounties broke in on the sit-in, arresting 114 students as a public address system blared, "The Party's Over." Cries of 'police state' echoed on Burnaby Mountain. During the course of the next summer, the experimental Red center of SFU radicalism, its Political Science, Sociology, and Anthropology Department, was moved on by the Administration. It disbanded the program's elected committees of students and faculty, removed its Chairman, imposed a trusteeship, and refused a number of faculty, including senior professors, tenure or renewal of existing contracts. A strike was declared on 24 September 1969. After six weeks the academic walkout, which had the support of thousands of students, and gave rise to arrests and injunctions, was broken. The largely New Left-Marxist faculty was locked out and subsequently purged. SFU President Kenneth Strand could not countenance the bold and utopian exercise in critical thinking and radical democracy that his political science, sociology, and anthropology professors, students, and staff pioneered. He told them: "the society and economy is capitalist and the university serves that system." Strand wanted the 1960s to end, and at SFU he brought it all to an abrupt halt.[102]

Canada: The Wealthiest Colony[103]

> *And what's good for GENERAL MOTORS*
> *obvious benefits the kingdom of*
> *heaven not to mention certain suburbs and*
> *the dominion of*
> *Canada*
> *tho some*
> *(communists!)*
> *might disagree.*
>   *—A.W. Purdy[104]*

The New Left was born talking about liberation, independence, even socialism. This was the discourse of its being. It did not, prior to the mid-1960s, voice much concern about how all of this related to Canadian identity. Indeed, in the general political context of the early 1960s, national identity was hardly a raging concern north of the 49th parallel. Where there were rumblings, they came from the left.[105] As Philip Resnick has suggested, the 1955-1965 years were ones in which nationalism in Canada was largely a dead letter. In the latter half of the 1960s, however, nationalisms of many kinds floated in and out of a variety of politics. They structured much of the economic agenda of the Liberal Party, influenced greatly cultural policy and priorities, and, as well, permeated the organizations and arguments of the Canadian left, old as well as new.

Central to the emergence of an effervescent nationalism was a rising anti-Americanism, evident in a poem, "1966," published in *Canadian Dimension*:

America America
the burnt seed lies by the side
of your turnpikes
auto graveyards
motel cities
military camps
the heaped-up contempt of every dream of paradise on earth
stinking your greens
the burnt seed
shines darkly
blasting out
the sun.[106]

The politico-intellectual trend that words such as these articulated, lapsing into essentialist condemnation, could not but shake New Left thought to its foundations, aligned as it was with developments in the United States.[107]

There were many reasons for the late 1960s birth of left nationalism in Canada. The most serious conservative thinker who sustained a critical and supportive engagement with the SUPA-style New Leftists, George Grant, did so unashamedly as a nationalist. He ended what was, in effect, a 1966 Open Letter to the New Left, with the conviction that "our greatest obligation as Canadians is to work for a country which is not simply a satellite of any empire." This resonated with the Canadian New Left in the mid-1960s, searching as it was for a direction unambiguously differentiated from imperialist aggression and the brutal practice of power. Gad Horowitz, for instance, was voicing the need for "Canada to be something other than a collection of disintegrated particularisms of the American Mind." He and Grant would carry on something of a dialogue as the 1960s gave way to the 1970s. With Grant willing to voice his challenging opposition to the war in Vietnam in a language of imperialism, many New Leftists seemed equally amenable to opposing warmongering with words championing a distinct Canadian nationhood. Horowitz summed up the emerging argument for a popular front of all Canadian socialists and nationalists to turn back the tide of Americanization in ways that appealed directly to Grant: "The Canadian tory might want to stay out of a society in which the masses are given to excesses of violence and intolerance, noblesse oblige nowhere to be found, tradition is a dirty word and individual greed rides roughshod over all feelings of community." Only socialism, Horowitz suggested, could in the long run preserve Canadian independence, because it would require the class forces of a mobilized revolution to decisively defeat the coordinated, massive power of continental capitalism in Canada. But "this dream may never be realized," and in the interval much could be done to insure that Canadians would not "be stuck with Americanism."[108]

By the early 1970s, confronting just how overwhelming a left nationalist Anti-Americanism could become, even Horowitz moved toward acknowledgement that the socialist/nationalist dilemma was not quite as easily bridged as he had suggested a few years before.[109] But as the New Left emerged out of its "community organizing" phase to embrace a more Marxist analytic accent on the political economy of Canada, the exploration of foreign ownership of the country's resources and industries and understanding of its role in supplying the United States war machine with much-needed materials pushed many to embrace left nationalism and espouse an independent socialist Canada.[110] In nascent party formations, especially those with a Maoist tinge, such as the Progressive Worker movement in British Columbia, independence and socialism were twinned. More and more classroom discussion turned on the political economy of dependency and the struggle for an autonomous Canada.[111]

As the left went, so went the nation. (Would that it were so!) In a *Toronto Star* poll published in *Canadian Dimension* (something of a rarity!), the magazine's left-wing readership was treated to a progressive variant of 'meet the Ugly American'. The survey indicated a woeful ignorance on the part of a U.S. citizenry that clearly wanted no controls placed on its imperialist reach into Canada. In contrast, Canadians polled seemed worried about their country's independence. With the Liberal newspaper declaring that "most Canadians believe that in our relationship with the U.S. we are trading our soul for the American way of life," *Canadian Dimension* applauded the bourgeois publication as "one of the leading nationalist forces in Canada today, strengthening the will to resist further Americanization." *Dimension's* next cover was adorned with a Red Maple Leaf, over which was superimposed a red and black bold-printed "Open Letter to Canadian Nationalists." Segments of the New Left were clearly going new nationalist.[112]

As this happened the debate that might have taken place over the political economy of *formal* dependency within a United States-dominated continental capitalism versus the *substantive content* of domestic capitalist exploitation and the autonomous role of the Canadian bourgeoisie in its own imperialist penetration of the developing world was largely postponed until the 1970s.[113] Instead, the Pandora's Box of nationalism, however much it was draped in socialist intent, once opened proved a difficult politics to keep within Marxist bounds. Left nationalists soon embraced a plethora of essentialist positions.

Writing out of the denouement of SUPA, James Laxer utilized a newly-found nationalism to tar the entire New Left with the brush of American domination. He explained the failure of youth dissent to light the spark of mass resistance as a result of relying on the inappropriate guide of United States New Left radicalism. Laxer thought Canada's 1960s ideas of dissent had been "conceived out of the conditions of the heart of the empire rather than the conditions of a dependent country ... ." If Laxer's critique contained insight—like Gray he was dubious of New Left disdain for organized labour and working-class struggle, as well as raising important questions about the ways in which SUPA and others isolated themselves from Canadian traditions of resistance—it nevertheless retreated too easily into a hectoring insistence that the national question, in and of itself, was "the most powerful force for combating the American empire that exists in Canada."[114] Ironically, this New Left assault on Empire often proved a substitute for more sustained inquiry, drifting in the direction of moral condemnation. John W. Warnock, for instance, entitled one assault on American liberal individualism, "Why I Am Anti-American," opposing the United States as a "Sick Society." America's justification of inequality, worship of property and profit, and cultivation and dependence on violence relegated it to ethical condemnation. Warnock managed to avoid discussion of just how different Canada was in being similarly diseased.[115] Robin Mathews and James Steele launched a broad-ranging crusade to revive Canadian culture in the throes of its incessant Americanization, the most effective component of which was their pressuring of universities to hire Canadians. Few subjects proved more divisive to a New Left that leaned intellectually on contributions from the United States. The problem was exacerbated by the significant contribution genuinely radical and often Marxist expatriots had made to the growing sophistication of critical, oppositional thought in Canadian universities, especially with respect to anti-imperialism. The pages of both mainstream and left publications bristled with debate as the relentless Mathews pursued his course of opposition to Americanization, drawing other left nationalists such as Mel

Watkins into his cause.[116] Mathews could push the envelope too far. In an article on "Draft Dodging and U.S. Imperialism in Canada," he argued that war resisters, while worthy of Canadian compassion, carried Americanization with them as they fled induction into the U.S. Army and refused the patriot's cry to wage war on the communist Vietnamese. For Mathews, these exiles were little more than agents of the colonial Empire, and he found himself "past the sentimental outpourings about Morality and the tender souls of U.S. draft dodgers." It seemed that Mathews would have preferred that the American war resisters return home. Barring that, he thought they might write a letter of thanks to the Federal Minister of Manpower and Immigration, an Ottawa "representative closest to the fact that they" had been able to secure sanctuary in Canada. Such a request, posed in a magazine of the Canadian left, was a long way from the spirit of SUPA's pioneering projects of smuggling draft evaders across the border at Niagara Falls.[117]

Mathews thought that draft dodgers might also want to write an appreciative cheque to the Waffle Manifesto Group. The ardent nationalist claimed that this body was the only serious force fighting U.S. imperialism in Canada. Originating as a youthful dissident caucus within the New Democratic Party, the Waffle was part of a 1968-1969 ferment over left nationalism that spilled out of the fragmentation of the initial SUPA New Left and the turn to Marxist-inspired political-economic analysis of Canada. It was built by a 1960s radical who had close connections with both the Old and New Lefts, Jim Laxer, and former liberal economist, Mel Watkins, in motion to the left over the course of a decade that saw him increasingly committed to taking up 'the dismal science' cudgels against foreign ownership of Canadian industry.[118] Laxer and Watkins quickly rallied to their cause figures such as *Canadian Dimension* editor and Manitoba NDP MLA, Cy Gonick; Nova Scotia NDP leader, Jeremy Akerman; and a half dozen prominent British Columbia NDPers. Their support grew among a younger, New Left-inspired cohort of activists. An NDP-Waffle Labour Committee was formed. Although it never attracted mainstream union support, being anathema to the leading layer of officialdom within the hegemonic international unions, it did promote militant struggles for workers' control, rank-and-file administration of trade unions, women's rights in the labour movement, and the organization and support of immigrant, unemployed, and non-unionized workers. It also raised the obligatory demand to increase Canadian autonomy and authority within the institutions of the working class.[119]

With its main strength in Ontario the Waffe also garnered support on the prairies and in British Columbia.[120] It promoted its left-nationalist message within the

NDP through publication of a 1969 Manifesto, which carried its barbed politics of challenge in a combined New Left rhetoric and a strong assault on the Americanization of Canada. Six of the twelve authors of the document for an independent socialist Canada were graduate students in the Queen's University History Department and their spouses: Laxer and Krista Maeots; Pat and John Smart; and the Saskatchewan radicals, Caroline and Lorne Brown.[121] The Manifesto first surfaced with a bang at a Winnipeg Convention, and before long NDP votes on policy matters were being posed as a left-right party division, with Wafflers leaning decidedly left. Carrying as its banner of preference the linked demands of national independence *and* socialism, Wafflers threw the more cautious and bureaucratized reform-minded NDP leadership—ensconced in the Lewis family and buttressed by the trade union tops—into quite a tizzy in the 1969-1972 years. Then, able to take it no longer, Stephen and David Lewis, the lapsed New Leftist, Dennis McDermott, now a heavy in the United Automobile Workers, and a triumvirate of United Steel Workers of America officialdom—William Mahoney, Lynn Williams, and Bob Mackenzie—forced the Waffle out of the Party at an Orilla, Ontario gathering of the NDP provincial council. This was not before the Waffle had challenged the hegemony of the international unions' leaders in the trade union movement, questioning their commitment to labour militancy; spread the radical left-nationalist position throughout social democratic circles, claiming the support of 3,000 of the country's 50,000 NDPers; and managed to run Laxer against David Lewis for the federal leadership of the Party, it taking four ballots for the elder Lewis to defeat his Waffle opponent, 1046 to 612 at the Party's Sixth Convention in Winnipeg in 1971. In pressing what many felt was a strident anti-Americanism, the Waffle did nonetheless expose the vulnerabilities to the left of Canada's mainstream social democratic tradition. It promoted a vigorous anti-imperialist Canadian nationalism that differentiated itself from both staid social democrats and the rising, narrowly economistic bourgeois nationalism of the Liberal Party's Walter Gordon.[122] As New Leftists struggling to make common cause with Old Leftists found themselves finally referred to in the 1970s as "social misfits," as "a cancer" that needed to be cut out of the New Democrats, or warned that they were about to receive "a lesson in gutsmanship today," they knew, deep in their heart of liberation theory, that something of the Sixties had definitely passed.[123] When the Waffle was wound down by its NDP opponents, Cy Gonick editorialized in *Canadian Dimension*. His New Left lament for a socialist nationalism lost was cynically downbeat in its repudiation of a moderate electoralism: "The Liberals have coopted the nationalist issue because it has been shorn of its socialist content. David Lewis sounds like an an-

gry Trudeau or a petulant Stanfield. Maybe his driving fist and his outraged indigna-
tion will be enough to win a few more seats for the NDP in the upcoming federal
election. Somehow it doesn't seem to matter."[124] The wealthiest colony, understandably enough given a materialist analysis, could not quite sustain an anti-imperialist
mobilization within a core constituency of the Old, albeit moderate, Left. The ironies
of the situation could only go so far politically. When the Saskatchewan Waffle finally
exited the NDP after a 6-8 October 1973 Moose Jaw Conference decided that it was
time to break from social democracy and "establish a socialist party," the movement
for an independent socialist Canada seemed to some to be growing. In actuality it
would fragment and prove still-born.[125]

Further complicating the situation was an irrepressible demand, developing
within the Waffle, but also generalized throughout New Left circles, that women now
be heard. Largely male led, the Waffle harboured a contingent of vocal and authoritative feminists who widened the discussion of what an independent socialist Canada
would look like. Among them Krista Maeots, Kelly Crichton, and Varda [Burstyn] Kidd
were powerful advocates of creating a new politics in which women's place would
not be one of subordination and silence. As Burstyn recalled in 1990, early women's
liberation registered strongly in the Waffle and, through it, exercised a considerable
impact on the NDP: "Prior to the onslaught on the Party's program led by Waffle
women at constituency associations, provincial conferences and national conventions, NDP policy on women's issues was bland and unobjectionable, shaped by a
mild (not to say gutless) fifties-style social democratic rhetoric of equality which had
little substance or meaning. Waffle women, with Waffle men supporting them often
enough to register their presence as different from many mainstream NDP men, tack-
led the big issues: childcare (universal, for the first time); abortion rights (fireworks
that still explode on a predictable basis); equal pay; quotas for women on party bodies; the right to caucus." NDP loyalist, Douglas Fisher, noted that the Waffle had
"used brilliantly ... the women's liberation movement. The women cry outrage over
under-representation on councils, committees, etc. of the party. This unsettles, di-
verts, and gives the Wafflers a popular support which swells over into other areas."

Wafflers and New Democrats clashed repeatedly in the 1969-1972 years over issues associated with Quebec self-determination, the influence and seeming conser-
vatism of a powerful layer of trade union officialdom, nationalization of key resource
industries, and promotion of the NDP as a *socialist* party. Yet it was resolutions on the
women's question that provoked an initial, and embittered, rupture at the Party's
1971 Winnipeg Convention. The social-democratic establishment defeated two con-

stitutional amendments designed to increase women's representation. On the last day of the gathering, those in control adopted a tepid policy statement on women that infuriated Waffle feminists and many other women in the NDP as well. With delegate hostility rising, the Convention Chair, Eamon Park, a United Steel Workers' of America official and well-connected NDP-insider, ran the proceedings with a dictatorial procedurialism that outraged left-leaning feminists. Park ruled out of order a referral motion calling on the NDP to convene a Women's Conference within a year to redraft Party policies relating to women. Stung by this contemptuous silencing, women implored the NDP to make amends, only to find their pleas drowned out as union-affiliated delegates broke into a deafening chorus of 'Solidarity Forever'. Cries of 'Seig Heil' were directed venomously at the podium. Gender politics such as these have tended to be lost sight of in the titanic clash of male leaders (Laxer vs. Lewis) and the seemingly gender-neutral politics of a period dominated by discussions of Americanization, Quebec independence, and nationalization, but they were nonetheless quite important at the time. In the end much kept Burstyn and other Waffle feminists separate from conventional social democratic men and women in the NDP, as well as from those hardened left nationalists who would, upon being forced out of the NDP, go on to form the Movement for an Independent Socialist Canada in 1972. Burstyn nevertheless remembers the positive impact that women's liberation exercised in radical political circles at the end of the 1960s.[126]

Something of this would characterize the New Left as a whole, but like the Waffle it was not destined to survive the post-1960s political traumas of the early 1970s, at least not on the gendered terms it had set for itself from 1967-1970. A feminist challenge both extended and enriched the New Left experience and, ultimately, fragmented and divided it. This was all the more evident as the relatively coherent first phase of late 1960s women's liberation itself soon fractured into various 1970s camps.

'Typers of Letters and Distributors of Leaflets No Longer'

As Simon Fraser University's Political Science, Anthropology, and Sociology Department erupted in September 1969, the venerable New York-based independent socialist magazine, *Monthly Review*, published a 14-page article entitled, "The Political Economy of Women's Liberation." Its author was an unlikely pioneer of a Marxist analysis of women's oppression, a feminist critique of orthodox historical materialism's blindness to the fundamental importance of unpaid household work as "socially necessary production." Few would have expected such an article to be written by a member of a university Chemistry Department, unschooled, by all accounts, in the workings of Old or New Left throughout her period of formative intellectual development in the 1950s and 1960s. Of working-class background, and trained in the United States as a scientist, Margaret Benston had no deep connection to left or Marxist *praxis* until 1966, when she came to Simon Fraser and was immediately caught up in the intellectual turmoil of a campus enlivened by revolutionary thought. Benston was transformed by the atmosphere of the later 1960s, her identical twin sister, Marian Lowe, later describing what amounted to a political conversion experience:

> She used to credit the dancing of the 60s and its freedom of movement with allowing her to hear what the radicals were saying. Freedom of the body helped to free the mind. Marxism as a framework made sense, something that for the first time offered the possibility that social forces could be understood and then changed. It was a revelation, and her life and work began to be informed by political ideas.

Drawing on largely male Marxist theoretical writing, including unpublished papers that had been delivered at SFU by the Trotskyist economist, Ernest Mandel, as well as the influential 1966 Juliet Mitchell *New Left Review* essay, "Women: The Longest Revolution," Benston insisted on the necessity of revolutionary social transformation, one that would in fact "end women's oppression."

"The Political Economy of Women's Liberation" fused Marxism and feminism and, in a few pages, crystallized understandings that had been circulating in a nascent New Left women's movement in Canada and the United States, reverberating around the world. Traveling across Canada in mimeographed, samizdat-like versions, the essay's before-publication impact registered in the women's consciousness raising groups that were springing up in the post-1967 implosion of the first New Left. Soon Benston's short article was grinding its analysis into male-dominated theoretical discussions in bodies like the New Left Caucus, where feminism now registered as a potent challenge to a rekindled interest in Marxist theory. It left a lasting impression on a peculiarly and insightfully rich Canadian theoretical debate about housework and its meanings within the capitalist mode of production, resonating internationally in the writings of Mariarosa Della Costa and Selma James. Translated into Spanish, French, Italian, German, Swedish, and Japanese, "The Political Economy of Women's Liberation" affected the developing global women's movement as an interpretive statement unlike almost any other. In Italy segments of the women's movement called themselves Benstonistas. German feminists considered Benston's article "one of the first to analyze women's housework from a new left perspective." Soon copies of Benston's article were coming out of every radical movement pamphlet-producing plant: the United Front, the Radical Education Project (Detroit or Ann Arbor), the Eugene, Oregon SDS chapter, Boston's New England Free Press, the San Francisco Bay Area Radical Education Project. It would later be anthologized in countless collections of the pivotal writings of so-called 'second wave' feminism. Benston's argument anchored a particular materialist feminist approach rooted in the briefly happy marriage of Marxism, women's liberation, and the New Left in the last years of the 1960s. Many young women considered Benston's article "one of the milestones of passage into women's liberation," among them Adrienne Rich.

Benston had many sides to her wonderfully engaged and influential life: a chemist who jumped ship from her discipline to find a home in Computer Science, she also helped create SFU's Women's Studies Program. Benston was as well a founding member of the Euphoniously Feminist Non-Performing Quintet. In her commitment to community organizing, her love of people, and her important feminist labours, she made possible a part of the rising of the women that grew out of the New Left and transformed it in the 1967-1970 years. The Vancouver Women's Caucus and its publication, *The Pedestal*, would have been unimaginable without women like Maggie Benston, as would like bodies and forums throughout the country.[127]

"The Political Economy of Women's Liberation" began as a 1967 draft and found its way into print two years later. This chronology marks the birth of New Left feminism in Canada, a major statement appearing in the fall of 1967.[128] Judy Bernstein, Peggy Morton, Linda Seese, and Myrna Wood, four SUPA women, wrote a position paper for the ill-fated Goderich Conference. Entitled "Sisters, Brothers, Lovers … Listen," it quickly became the founding document of the Toronto Women's Liberation Movement. SUPA women had read Betty Friedan's *The Feminine Mystique* (1963) early on their road to activism, but it was the movement itself that registered with them the experience of being female in a male-dominated world. When women began to talk in SUPA about their discontents—in and of itself perhaps a sign that the first phase of student radicalism was about to implode—their male comrades responded with jokes and gendered put-downs. "We talked about how it was men who did the writing and women the Gestetnering, about how our political influence in the group was directly related to how 'heavy' the guy was that we were coupled with," one budding feminist told Myrna Kostash years later. Word spread of women's caucuses sprouting up throughout North American radical student circles. Even the Canadian government was recognizing that the "status of women" was a legitimate topic of inquiry, striking a Royal Commission to investigate and "ensure for women equal opportunities with men in all aspects of Canadian society."

Unlike Benston's analysis, the SUPA women's document was more quintessentially New Left in its accent on liberation and love, alienation and anger, conformism and creativity. They drew as well on early feminist anthropology and their direct experience in African American struggles for freedom, where the gendered differentiation of race in the deep South led them to acknowledge how black men and women lived through systemic racism and came out of it formed in contradictory ways. Mourning "the loss of manhood of Negro men," these early New Left feminists regretted that so few cared about the "loss of humanity of the exploited half of the human species—the women."

Anything but radical separatists, the SUPA women recognized that it was necessary to "attempt the most humane interaction," insisting that men and women in the New Left must "act as though the revolution had occurred by our relationships with one another." They drew attention, for the first time, to the reality of those relationships, and the extent to which the New Left suffered "the same hang-ups, frustrations, and neuroses as the rest of society." SUPA had, for many women, been a quest to transcend their Marcusian one-dimensionality by developing ego identity through attachment to the New Left itself. But this project of substitutionism had failed: "We created father figures or allowed them to be created. … we never gained the principles of participatory democracy. A few people were allowed to lead. Many people were excluded from leadership. The largest excluded group was women. SUPA, in respect to women, totally accepted the mores of the dominant society." In what was undoubtedly a series of barbs that brought painfully home to male leftists the seriousness of feminist discontent, "Sisters, Brothers, Lovers … Listen" pointed to black power advocate Stokely Carmichael's claim that, "The only position for a woman in SNCC is prone." Such a statement had never been publicly proclaimed by SUPA men, they noted. It was bad enough, however, that they might well have been thinking it. Old Leftists often seemed astounded with the level of male chauvinism in the New Left these SUPA feminists reported with regret. They went so far as to suggest that SUPA women sometimes felt that they were in a "civil rights organization with a leadership of southern racists." Confronting "masculine intellectualism" and "feminine emotionalism," the SUPA position paper addressed issues that would ring loudly in feminist writing for decades. Seeing first hand that to be accepted by men as theoretical and political equals was often to sacrifice their emotional lives as lovers and partners, Bernstein, Morton, Seese, and Wood refused the either/or dichotomization. Instead they realized that in their struggle for equality lay "a feeling of beauty and power." They closed their manifesto-like document with the simple assertion that, "We are going to be the typers of letter and distributors of leaflets … *no longer*."[129] A phase of the New Left had definitely ended.

Women ended this phase when they spoke out against their own oppression. Their voices unleashed, the meaning of their words expanded. Soon a perspective, drawing women, pushing them to act to develop it, and stimulating deep attraction to basic rights of equality, provided a sense of social movement. Women's liberation as a loose structure of discussion groups, as a mobilizing possibility, and as a demand for new theoretical clarity on a range of orthodox Marxist questions became, in 1967-1970, an increasingly vocal presence in the renewed but fragmenting New Left. Feminist consciousness raising groups emerged in Regina and Saskatoon, Winnipeg and Halifax, Sudbury and Thunder Bay, Kingston, Ottawa, Galt, Guelph, and Edmonton, as well, of course, as in Vancouver, Toronto, and Montreal. As Nancy Lubka noted in an early assessment of this development, women were claiming "their share of the freedom which this decade has wrested from history." They did so, not as some new social formation on the left, however, but as part of 1960s radicalism. As such, early Canadian women's liberation was a challenge to the decade's New Left as well as something that grew organically out of it. One part of its making was the oppressive, confining, and maddeningly traditional repression of women's capacities, initiatives, and needs, in the wider society as well as in circles of the radical left. Another component was "the thought-expanding perspectives offered by the new left." It was no accident that when Women's Liberation surfaced in Montreal it grew out of the repression of the Québécois struggle for national liberation as well as the mobilizations at McGill and Sir George Williams.[130]

New Left women's liberation advocates, like their male counterparts, read Marx, and read him through standard 1960s sources such as Marcuse.[131] Increasingly they also read Betty Friedan, Simone de Beauvoir, and Juliet Mitchell.[132] As Naomi Black remarks, they brought with them from the student movement "a significant commitment to a Marxist or at least an economic, class-oriented analysis of women's situation; they were to identify themselves as Marxists or socialist feminists."[133] This was where Benston's "The Political Economy of Women's Liberation" had come from. At McGill University, a young Marxist sociologist, Marlene Dixon, who had just published an important article entitled, "Why Women's Liberation?" in the American radical magazine, *Ramparts*, gathered around her a group that would later be described as "certainly one of the first self-consciously feminist women's groups in Montreal." In 1969 an uneasy alliance of Anglophone and francophone feminists had been forged, their commitment to liberation simultaneously demanding women's rights and the rights of the oppressed *Québécois*. Soon connections were being made among various left socialist organizations and young women's liberationists. Debates unfolded as to how women were not all of the same class and race, and their oppression, while universal to some degree, also needed to be viewed in light of other aspects of their identity. When Black Panthers promoted insulting views of women's role in radical movements, referring in public meetings to women using their "pussy power" to support revolutionary men, bodies such as the Maoist Canadian Party of Labour might walk out in protest, chanting opposition to such blatant male chauvinism.[134] Many left women struggled to maintain their Marxist perspective alongside of their realization that male domination of the left and of society was deforming them as women and as human beings.[135]

In this, the women's liberationists of the late 1960s differentiated themselves from the liberal state's project of promoting gender equality through agencies such as the Royal Commission on the Status of Women.[136] Their consciousness-raising, however, also often attacked frontally the seemingly *private* dimensions of women's oppression, thus marking women's concerns as different from an older New Left's focus on *public* issues, such as poverty and dispossession. Hidden from history, the meanings of women's sexual objectification or the particular experience of grappling with pregnancy and childbirth in an age when abortion was illegal and inaccessible, were brought to the forefront of women's liberation thought and practice.

Women's liberationists thus translated their growing refusal to accept subordination into performative attacks on beauty contests that included staging denunciations of the proceedings from the podium.[137] Judy Darcy, a member of Toronto Women's Liberation Movement (TWLM), entered the 1969 Miss Canada University Pageant, having talked the student government into letting her be Miss York University. "Okay, but don't tell us what you are going to do," the lefty student politicos said with a wink and nod. Then, with Darcy one of the seven semi-finalists, she awaited an attack on the event, being televised live. One of her TWLM comrades burst into the room, approached the podium chanting and began a public argument with the Master of Ceremonies. Darcy marched off the stage into the audience, proclaiming, "It's a meat market, and they do exploit women," singing "Solidarity Forever" as she exited the pageant.[138]

Advocates of women's liberation also played roles in the widespread dissemination of birth control information, which at the time was technically illegal. The McGill Student Society's 1968 *Birth Control Handbook*, arguably the most widely-circulated pamphlet in Canada in the late 1960s and early 1970s, was distributed in massive quantities at the time. Fifty thousand made their way throughout the country in the first eight months of its publication. Within a few years three million of the newsprint booklet had been distributed. Often, university women's caucuses spearheaded mobilizations for day-care, as they did at Simon Fraser in the spring of 1968. Supported by the New Left Caucus, Toronto women's liberationists occupied a vacant house on the outskirts of the University of Toronto, converting the dilapidated domicile to a cooperative nursery. Blocked by bureaucracies, the day-care struggle moved directly into the University Senate Chamber, 200 New Leftists sitting-in. They extracted concessions from the Administration, which agreed to renovate the seized building so that it would meet standards. Across the country the gaining of day-care facilities was proclaimed a victory of the Women's Liberation Movement.

Above all, the early women's liberation movement began, in 1969, the impetus that would sustain a national campaign against the liberalized, but still inadequate, federal abortion law of that year. Within Trotskyist organizations such as the League for Socialist Action and its youth wing, the Young Socialists, ideas of women's liberation were debated and discussed, gaining ground and adherents, and forcing shifts in understanding that translated into active commitments. Such bodies participated with women's groups across the country in the Vancouver Women's Caucus April 1970 call for an Abortion Caravan to make its way from the West Coast to Ottawa to demand "Free Abortion on Demand" and "Every Child a Wanted Child." As the women's automobile convoy picked up people, cars and vans en route, it gathered petitions signed by thousands upon thousands of women, demanding the repeal of all abortion legislation, and the right to truly choose the freedom to give birth. Eventually hundreds of women and their supporters, whom Trudeau had no taste for meeting having locked horns with women's liberationists before, descended on Parliament Hill, 24 Sussex Drive, and even into the House of Commons. They chained themselves in the gallery, closing down the seat of Canadian government for the first time in history. Behind them they left a coffin, symbolic of the women who had died seeking unsafe and illegal abortions. It overflowed with women's petitions and the tools of the trade of back-room abortionists: knives, coat hangers, cans of Lysol.[139]

As women New Leftists of the 1967-1970 years battled their oppression inside the left and in the mainstream society, they also built links with women who worked for wages and were part of the trade union movement. A slogan of the Abortion Caravan had been "Just Society Just for the Rich." Women's liberationists were well aware of the class inequalities that affected women's, children's, and men's lives. Much of this would bear fruit in campaigns of the 1970s, when Canadian feminists inside and outside of trade unions would be actively involved in making the pre-Spring International Women's Day marches major local and national events. In Vancouver, bodies such as Working Women's Association grew out of the New Left. Feminist activists often saw as their goal the development of liberationist ideas among trade union women and the convincing of all radicals, male and female, that organizing women in the workplace was an essential activity, one that would enhance fundamental collective strengths. As the women's movement in Quebec emerged out of the national liberation struggle, it grappled with the ways in which women had been sidelined in both the left and in the labour movement. By the early 1970s, such feminists were, like their SUPA counterparts of 1967, defiant in their refusal to countenance any longer their relegation to a place of inferiority in the movement: "We have typed their papers, painted their placards, listened to their speeches, marched in their demonstrations, marked the measure of their slogans, 'Power to the Workers!'."[140]

There were, of course, also developing divergences *within* the women's liberation camp, evident in the TWLM, which experienced a number of splits and breakaways in the 1969-1970 years. One of these, the New Feminists, saw the course of radical politics determined by exclusion of women from power. "Trudeau and Trotsky are just another pair of men," they declared. They were not prepared to grant "impartial credence to the gospel according to Mark, to Marx or Marcuse, to Mohammed or to Malcolm X." For such women the New Left project, and with it a good part of the 1960s, had ended with their realization that, "The total society is based on the discrimination of sex roles, and the total society must be changed." They would align with anyone—"whether these friends are found on the left, the right or the center"—supporting their goals; they would consider enemies, "whatever their other political persuasions," those who threatened "the realization of their radical feminist goals."[141] This kind of movement, along with other fissures in the New Left, spelled the end of an era, just as the rise of post-Royal Commission on the Status of Women contingents of liberal and socialist feminists marked a departure from the youth radicalism of the 1960s.[142]

The Sixties and Radical Social Change

As the decade of the 1960s closed chronologically, then, the ethos of the Sixties was fracturing in some quarters, fading in others. The contagious exuberance of a seemingly generational revolt could no longer be maintained as the first wave of radical youth aged and found itself arguing over the direction the revolutionary movement should take. Into the unions, against Americanization, for Marxism (and which Marxism!), against the state (or utilizing the state in some form), back to the NDP, or, alternatively, into a widening range of new party formations, Maoist and Trotskyist, in which the woman's question would invariably be discussed, leading to new organizational possibilities. The university campus, which had for so many radical youth been a nursery of oppositional thought and organization, seemed, moreover, no longer *the* place to be: with the lock-down of radicalism at McGill, Sir George Williams, and Simon Fraser, the classrooms of higher education in the 1970s were less promising venues of dissent than they had seemed to be in 1968. Experimental forms of living, be they communes in rural regions or urban endeavours such as the University of Toronto's Rochdale College, had apparently run their course. Quebec, a powderkeg of radicalism was on the verge of the explosion that would trigger the counterrevolution of October 1970, unleashing a wave of reaction which highlighted how, within Canada, there were two distinct societies of the political left, which no organizations, movements, or mobilizations had ever quite been able to either transcend or integrate. The Canadian Union of Students, after a brief but intense effort to become "a national liberation front for Canada," explicitly anti-imperialist, socialist, and militantly activist, was buried in an avalanche of local resistance. Its ostensibly strident agenda apparently failed to address the mundane, material needs of its student constituency. In October 1969, in what was a decisive blow, students at the large and centrally powerful University of Toronto voted in a referendum to withdraw from CUS, as other student bodies across the country had done before and would do in the immediate future. Its financial support evaporating, a national centre of the Canadian student left folded up its once revolutionary tent, disbanding in the spring of 1970.[143]

The disruptions and destabilizations of these years were of course pressured by varied repressive onslaughts, including infiltrations and extensive surveillance orchestrated by the Royal Canadian Mounted Police and its security state forces.[144] Nevertheless, as Howard Adelman noted in a *Canadian Forum* "coroner's report," the death of these institutions and movements of the Sixties also resulted from a fundamental paradox, one that the New Left never proved able to address.[145] Its poetics, *praxis*, and politics of liberation were, deep into the radical root of New Left thought, unable to grasp that structure and agency, institution and movement, direction and freedom, were not, in actuality, ever counterposed as merely and simply bureaucracy vs. participatory democracy. Rather, such orga-nized structures of resistance, from parties, programs, and perspectives, were (as they have always been and remain today) simultaneously threats to freedom and social transformation as well as the only vehicle capable of their realization. They need to be built and guarded in particular ways, rather than rejected out of hand. The New Left, inspired and insightful as it was, had one-half of the *praxis* that could have secured a political shift to the left. Strong on poetics—an activism of will and a rhetoric of radicalism—it was weaker on the politics of program; born with the aspirations of agency already formed on its young lips, it needed to learn the language of structure. It struggled to do this, in part via a revived, late 1960s English Canadian encounter with Marxism as analysis and as political program. In Montreal, in particular, an anarcho-communist wing of the New Left tried val-iantly to keep the principles of extra-parliamentary opposition alive in a rich blend of publishing activity, advocacy of participatory democracy, and engage-ment with the potentially transformative terrain of resistance as it applied to the politics of urban locale. Tragically, the Quebec/English Canada divide was squeezed between the hard place of cooptation and the rock of repression be-tween 1967-1970, as the seductively coercive liberal state turned, in the changed atmosphere of these charged times, from the enticements of patronage and the incorporating impulse of the Company of Young Canadians under Pearson to Tru-deau's tough stance of the War Measures Act. In the resulting failure of English Canada and Quebec to revive a common New Left stand, the demise of radical-ism's unified voice strengthened a poetics of anti-program, evident, for instance, in the renewal of antagonism to Marxism that began to appear in certain circles by 1970. If, in the early 1960s, the New Left knew little of Marxism and had much to gain by an encounter with the theory and history of revolutionary communism, it had at least grasped that the crude ideology of anti-Marxism was a part of the Cold War conventionality that all radicals were required to shed. By 1970, a changed context and a revived hostility to Marx that would gain momentum throughout the remaining years of the century meant the New Left's point of de-parture had a freshness to it that had to be resuscitated.

Irving Layton's poem, "Marxist," appearing in the social-democratic *Canadian Forum*, articulated this sad development:

out of certitude
or terror a Marxist
will knock out your teeth
break your jaw
with a crowbar
hang you from
your feet your head
in scalding water
crush
your balls before
your wife and children
and make you
spit
on friends and convictions
he will flay you
while still alive rip-
pling the skin
in neat strips of
three: thesis, etcetera…
when you are nothing
he'll wipe you out with
machine-gun executions:
negation of the negation
he will my sons
do this and more
if you let him
look for no pity
in this highest product
of evolution: dialectical
of course[146]

This poetics would have been unlikely in much of the New Left, even as it was spawned in some of its select enclaves. The irony of 1960s radicalism was that as it so fruitfully challenged the dream of capitalist affluence and equality that had done so much to stamp its particular being, it also nurtured a part of that deep sleep of traditional prejudice that inhibited conscious human agents of liberation from the realization of their ends. But seeing those ends, in and of itself, was an advance of monumental significance. The Sixties had, in part, been very much about this vision.

To speak of Canada and the generation of the 1960s is, of course, to over-generalize. For every radical SUPA fieldworker, for every militant anti-Vietnam War protester, for every women's liberationist, there were countless Canadian youth who followed no rebel road. Minorities nevertheless sometimes make history, and they are certainly capable of putting a strong stamp on it, as elites have always understood. In the 1960s, the impact of youth revolt was unmistakably evident on the pages of the decade, and it remains there to this day. For those who lived the radicalism of the decade, and even for people who merely walked softly and often silently in its shadows, the Canada of their times had been changed. Future generations would be unable to think complacently and quietly after experiencing a sit-in, a protest march, a reading of Marx, Marcuse, or Mitchell. From the ashes of Sir George Williams Computer Center, to turning the pages of the *Birth Control Handbook*, to protesting imperialist war—the times they were indeed 'a changing, and there was no going back. Women's liberation, if it did not transform gender relations in its 1960s praxis, nevertheless laid the foundation for unanticipated advances for women, a movement that changed forever the *politics* of sexual being and our appreciation of essential *human* rights. As ideas of justice, equality, entitlements, and freedoms—to choose this path and designate that necessity—permeated the consciousness of an era, nothing would, in the future, look quite the same. Gays and lesbians, for instance, were neither very visible in the New Left of the 1960s, nor were they accorded much sensitive treatment in the movement, either theoretically or practically. Even the New Feminists that emerged out of the TWLM, and that contained lesbian members, did not handle the issue adequately in their public presentation of the group's concerns and purposes. Yet in spite of this less than admirable history, new doors would open in the aftermath of the 1960s because of what had taken place within that decade of altercation and change. When, eventually, a gay and lesbian liberation movement did emerge in Canada it would surface, in part, in circles originating in the late 1960s. Its relationship to Marxism was fractious, but undeniable.[147]

Nowhere was this general process more evident than in Quebec, where the New Left actually threatened to achieve a serious destabilization of the social order.[148] In the New Left struggle for liberation in Quebec, the intensity of the drive for emancipation had many of the same impulses, innovations, and intentions, but it was placed on an entirely different level by the realization, for the first time historically (at least in a revolutionary sense), that the national question was not just the Canada question, but it was also the Quebec question. In its insistence that Quebec could only be understood as an ongoing *history* of exploitation, oppression, misery, *and* consequent nationalist aspiration, the 1960s and the specific lefts that it spawned, broke the ossified *old* moulds of oppositional politics. At the same time, the decade's experiences called forth the need to resolve, not only a plethora of new challenges, but a body of long-entrenched, seemingly antiquated, ones, with which an older series of lefts had long grappled: class exploitation, state power, and the issue of how alternatives can be realized. All of these central questions raised issues of organization and program, of the means required to achieve specific ends. And as the Canadian state, in turn, crushed Quebec's New Left liberationists, turning to a ruthless repression, it ironically secured its continuity at the cost of its long-standing, socially constructed identity. Some part of the1960s ended, for all Canadians, in the October Crisis of 1970. So too did a significant part of the mythology of 'the peaceable Kingdom'. This meant, of course, that the ongoing struggle to reconfigure Canadian civil society would continue, but that it would do so in different ways.

Notes

1 An earlier version of this essay appears in Bryan D. Palmer, *Canada's 1960s: The Ironies of Identity in a Rebellious Era* (Toronto: University of Toronto Press, 2009), 245-310.

2 Peter Desbarats, "The most forgettable generation: A sad glance at the exhausted new wave of revolutionary youth," *Saturday Night,* 84 (September 1969), 35-36. For a general statement on the generational clash of the 1960s see Kenneth Westhues, "Inter-Generational Conflict in the Sixties," in S.D. Clark, J. Paul Grayson, and Linda M. Grayson, eds., *Prophecy and Protest: Social Movements in Twentieth-Century Canada* (Toronto: Gage, 1975), 387-408. More positive is Evelyn Latowsky and Merrijoy Kelner, "Youth: The New Tribal Group," in D.I. Davies and Kathleen Herman, eds., *Social Space: Canadian Perspectives* (Toronto: New Press, 1971), 240-243; Marcel Rioux, "Youth in the Contemporary World and Quebec," in W.E. Mann, ed., *Social and Cultural Change in Canada*, Volume I (Toronto: Copp Clark, 1970), 302-315; "CEGEPS, Charlebois, Chartrand: The Quebec Revolution Now—An Interview with Dimitri Roussopoulos," in W.E. Mann, ed., *Social and Cultural Change in Canada,* Volume II (Toronto: Copp Clark, 1970), 200-210.

3 June Callwood, "Digger House," in W.E. Mann, ed., *The Underside of Toronto* (Toronto: McClelland and Stewart, 1970), 123-128; "Yorkville Revisited," *Toronto Telegram,* 22 July 1969, quoted in Stuart Henderson, "Toronto's Hippie Disease: the Yorkville Hepititis Epidemic, August 1968," Paper presented to the Canadian Historical Association, York University, May 2006, published as "Toronto's Hippie Disease: End Days in the Yorkville Scene, August 1968," *Journal of the Canadian Historical Association*, New Series, 17 (2006), 205-234.

4 Allen Ginsberg, "Howl," in Ginsberg, *Collected Poems, 1947-1980* (New York: Harper & Row, 1984), 126. "Howl's" significance is alluded to in Judith Clavir Albert and Stewart Edward Albert, eds., *The Sixties Papers: Documents of a Rebellious Decade* (New York: Praeger, 1984), 68. On the Beats see, for an introduction only, Bryan D. Palmer, *Cultures of Darkness: Night Travels in the Histories of Transgression* (New York: Monthly Review, 2000), 370-386. The influence of jazz on the 1960s and its relationship to the New Left is brilliantly evoked in Scott Saul, *Freedom Is, Freedom Ain't: Jazz and the Making of the Sixties* (Cambridge, Massachusetts: Harvard University Press, 2003).

5 For accounts signaling the demise of aspects of 1960s New Leftism see, among many possible statements, the cluster of articles headed "Cultural Revolution" in *Canadian Dimension*, 7 (August-September 1970), 15-27: David Lewis Stein, "Yippies/Defining a Revolutionary Life Style"; Alvin Finkel, "Wither Commune—ism"; and Irwin Silber, "Living the Revolution—and Living Off It," quote from 26, or for more detail, Silber, *The Cultural Revolution: A Marxist Analysis* (New York: Times Change, 1970). Note as well Jonah Raskin, *For the Hell of It: The Life and Times of Abbie Hoffman* (Berkeley: University of California Press, 1996), and the books of Hoffman and Rubin: Abbie Hoffman, *Revolution for the Hell of It* (New York: Dial, 1968); *Woodstock Nation: A Talk-Rock Album* (New York: Random House, 1969); *Steal This Book* (New York: Pirate Editions, 1971); Jerry Rubin, *Do It! Scenarios of the Revolution* (New York: Simon and Schuster, 1970); *We Are Everywhere* (New York: Harper and Row, 1971). See for the countercultural denouement, Myrna Kostash, *Long Way From Home: The Story of the Sixties Generation in Canada* (Toronto: Lorimer, 1980), 107-144, which sites an account of a unruly rock festival in Toronto more subdued than Altamont, but not markedly different in its hucksterish façade. Note as well Larry Haiven, "Festival Scene II," *The Varsity*, 26 September 1969. Kent State headlined in *Globe and Mail*, 5 May 1970. See also Martin Loney, "Canada's New Left Still Needs a Biography," *Canadian Dimension*, 7 (December 1970), 75-76.

6 Myrna Kostash, *Long Way From Home: The Story of the Sixties Generation in Canada* (Toronto: Lorimer, 1980), xiii, 135, 260, 276. Kostash was perhaps less subdued than a number of her counterparts, who were profiled in a journalistic account two years after her book appeared. But if these 1960s veterans were not loud in voicing the continuity of their radicalism, few, if any, were outright repenters. See Olivia Ward, "The Sixties: Ideals have quietly survived," *Toronto Sunday Star,* 28 March 1982.

7 Thomas Walkom, "1968: It was spring and it was a time. And the whole world exploded," *Toronto Star*, 7 June 1998. See also Kristin Ross, *May '68 and Its Afterlives* (Chicago: University of Chicago Press, 2002).

8 Milton Acorn, *More Poems for People* (Toronto: NC Press, 1973), 86.

9 "Editorial: Sanitizing the Sixties," *Canadian Dimension*, 22 (November-December 1988), 3. For discussion and evidence of the Canadian New Left's collective commitment to a politics of revolutionary transformation see John W. Cleveland, "New Left, not New Liberal: 1960s Movements in English Canada and Quebec," *Canadian Review of Sociology and Anthropology*, 41 (February 2004), 67-84.

10 For broad international studies see, as a sampling only, Arthur Marwick, *The Sixties: Cultural Revolution in Britain, France, Italy, and the United States, c. 1958-1974* (Oxford: Oxford University Press,

1998); David Caute, *The Year of the Barricades: A Journey Through 1968* (New York: Harper and Row, 1988); Ronald Fraser, et al., *1968: A Student Generation in Revolt* (New York: Knopf, 1988); Donald Sassoon, *One Hundred Years of Socialism: The West European Left in the Twentieth Century* (New York: New Press, 1996), 275-440; Geoff Eley, *Forging Democracy: The History of the Left in Europe, 1850-2000* (Oxford: Oxford University Press, 2002), 341-404. Most New Lefts had more complex origins in the Old Left than commentators have recognized. This was most obvious in Britain, and is evident in intellectual histories such as Lin Chun, *The British New Left* (Edinburgh: Edinburgh University Press, 1993); Michael Kenny, *The First New Left: British Intellectuals After Stalin* (London: Lawrence and Wishart, 1995). But for the Old/New Left connections see as well Maurice Isserman, *If I Had a Hammer: The Death of the Old Left and the Birth of the New Left* (New York: Basic, 1987), a useful study if one does not take its title's termination of old left organizations and ideas too seriously; and Paul Buhle, *History and the New Left: Madison, Wisconsin, 1950-1970* (Philadelphia: Temple University Press, 1990. Two British reminiscent treatments are Sheila Rowbotham, *Promise of a Dream: Remembering the Sixties* (London: Penguin, 2000); Tariq Ali, *Street Fighting Years: An Autobiography of the Sixties* (Glasgow: William Collins, 1987). The Unites States literature is immense and growing, but useful starting points are Todd Gitlin, *The Sixties: Years of Hope, Days of Rage* (New York: Bantam, 1987); Richard Flacks, *Making History: The American Left and the American Mind* (New York: Columbia University Press, 1988); David Farber, *Chicago '68* (Chicago: University of Chicago Press, 1988); Farber, ed., *The Sixties: From Memory to History* (Chapel Hill: University of North Carolina Press, 1994); James Miller, *Democracy in the Streets: From Port Huron to the Siege of Chicago* (Toronto: Simon and Schuster, 1987); Paul Buhle, *Marxism in the United States: Remapping the History of the American Left* (New York: Verso, 1991), 228-257. Seymour Martin Lipset and Sheldon S. Wolin, eds., *The Berkeley Student Revolt: Facts and Interpretations* (Garden City, New York: Doubleday, 1965); Seymour Martin Lipset, *Rebellion in the University* (Boston: Little, Brown, 1971), were indications of early sociological interest in the student uprisings of the decade. For the right-wing assault on the New Left in the United States see Phillip Abbott Luce, *The New Left Today: America's Trojan Horse* (Washington: Capitol Hill Press, 1971). For documents of the rebellious 1960s that would have been read in Canada see Priscilla Long, *The New Left: A Collection of Essays* (Boston: Porter Sargeant Publisher, 1969); Mitchell Goodman, ed., *The Movement Toward a New America: The Beginning of a Long Revolution (A Collage) A What?* (Philadelphia: Pilgrim Press, 1970); Massimo Teodori, *The New Left: A Documentary History* (New York: Bobbs-Merrill, 1969); Judith Clavir Albert and Stewart Edward Albert, eds., *The Sixties Papers: Documents of a Rebellious Decade* (New York: Praeger, 1984). Particularly repressive was the killing of Mexico City protesters in 1968. See Elaine Carey, *Plaza of Sacrifices: Gender, Power, and Terror in 1968 Mexico* (Albuquerque: University of New Mexico Press, 2005).

11 Canada's New Left student movement is presented in international context in Cyril Levitt, *Children of Privilege: Student Revolt in the Sixties—A Study of Student Movements in Canada, the United States, and West Germany* (Toronto: University of Toronto Press, 1984). See also, Doug Owram, *Born at the Right Time: A History of the Baby Boom Generation* (Toronto: University of Toronto Press, 1996), 159-316; Ron Verzuh, *Underground Times: Canada's Flower-Child Revolutionaries* (Toronto: Deneau, 1989); Kostash, *Long Way from Home*; Ian McKay, *Rebels, Reds, and Radicals: Rethinking Can-*

ada's Left History (Toronto: Between the Lines, 2005), 183-210; Bryan D. Palmer, ed., *A Communist Life: Jack Scott and the Canadian Workers Movement, 1927-1985* (St. John's, Newfoundland: CCLH, 1988), 158-203; and the important early collection, Dimitrios J. Roussopoulos, ed., *The New Left in Canada* (Montreal: Black Rose, 1970). An unpublished study that I read after completing the writing of this book is an important contribution, detailing the particularity of developments in Montreal and providing a useful larger perspective as well. See Sean William Mills, "The Empire Within: Montreal, the Sixties, and the Forging of a Radical Imagination," PhD thesis, Queen's University, Kingston, 2007.

12 The above paragraphs draw on many sources, but see especially, Kostash, *Long Way from Home*, 251-252; Max Elbaum, *Revolution in the Air: Sixties Radicals Turn to Lenin, Mao, and Che* (New York and London: Verso, 2002); Stokely Carmichael with Ekwueme Michael Thelwell, *Ready for Revolution: The Life and Struggles of Stokely Carmichael [Kwame Ture]* (New York: Scribner, 2003); Robin D. G. Kelley, *Freedom Dreams: The Black Radical Imagination* (Boston: Beacon Press, 2002); Jeremy Varon, *Bringing the War Home: The Weather Underground, the Red Army Faction, and Revolutionary Violence in the Sixties and Seventies* (Berkeley: University of California Press, 2004). The *Guardian* was of course but one of many news outlets which came out as underground publications. For a sense of this contentious world of the U.S. alternative press in the 1960s see, for instance, Ray Mungo, *Famous Long Ago: My Life and Times with Liberation News Service* (Boston: Beacon Press, 1970); Ken Wachsberger, ed., *Voices from the Underground: A Directory of Resources and Sources on the Vietnam Era Underground Press* (Ann Arbor, Michigan: Azephony Press, 1993); Abe Peck, *Uncovering the Sixties: The Life and Times of the Underground Press* (New York: Pantheon, 1985).

13 Carl Ogesby, "The Idea of the New Left," in Obelsby, ed., *The New Left Reader* (New York: Grove Press, 1969), 13.

14 C.Wright Mills, "Letter to the New Left," *New Left Review*, 5 (September-October 1960), 18-23. As the prod to Wright Mills's letter see E.P. Thompson, ed., *Out of Apathy* (London: Stevens and Sons, 1960). For a New Left reading of Mills see Tom Hayden, *Radical Nomad: C. Wright Mills and His Times* (Boulder and London: Paradigm Publishers, 2006).

15 Tom Hayden has recently provided an evocative introduction to the republication of *The Port Huron Statement: The Visionary Call of the 1960s Revolution* (New York: Thunder's Mouth Press, 2005), upon which this paragraph draws. See, for the fullest statement on the importance of the document, Miller, *Democracy in the Streets*.

16 See Herbert Marcuse, *An Essay on Liberation* (Harmondsworth, England: Penguin Books, 1969), esp. 33, 37, 82. Note as well the mimeographed radical student bulletin, published at the University of Waterloo by the Federation of Students in 1968-1969, *Praxis*. It struggled with questions that remain with the left today, as in Philip Resnick, "Repressive Liberalism," *Praxis*, 2 (March 1969), 2-5. Callwood, "Digger House," 124 linked 'the Movement' of the 1960s with Marcuse, associating the 1966 hippies with "the great refusal."

17 See Lutz Niethammer, *Posthistoire: Has History Come to an End?* (New York and London: Verso, 1992); Francis Fukuyama, "The End of History?" *The National Interest* (Summer 1989), 3-18; *The End of History and the Last Man* (New York: Maxwell Macmillan, 1992); and the impressive essay by

Perry Anderson, "The Ends of History," in Anderson, *A Zone of Engagement* (New York and London: Verso, 1992), 279-375.

18 Mario Savio, "An End to History," *Humanity: An Arena of Critique and Commitment*, 2 (December 1964), reprinted in Lipset and Wolin, eds., *The Berkeley Student Revolt*, 216-219.

19 Quotes from original New Left documents, cited in Kostash, *Long Way from Home*, 13-14.

20 See, for instance, Stanley Gray, "The New Democratic Youth Convention," *Canadian* Dimension, 2 (September-October 1965), 23; Gray, "New Left, Old Left," *Canadian* Dimension, 3 (November-December 1965), 11-13; James Harding, "The NDP, the Regina Manifesto, and the New Left," *Canadian Dimension*, 4 (November-December 1966), 18-19; Gary Teeple, "'Liberals in a Hurry': Socialism and the CCF-NDP," in Teeple, ed., *Capitalism and the National Question in Canada*, (Toronto: University of Toronto Press, 1972) 229-250; Kostash, *Long Way From Home*, 249-250; Cy Gonick "Students and Peace," *Canadian Dimension*, 2 (January-February 1965), 12; James Laxer and Arthur Pape, "The New Left ... As it Sees Itself," *Canadian Dimension*, 3 (September-October 1966), 14-15. For a social democratic critical response to the New Left see Lloyd Stinson, "Reply to the New Left," *Canadian Dimension*, 3 (March-April/May-June 1966), 56-57.

21 Gonick, "Students and Peace," 12; Kostash, *Long Way from Home*, 6.

22 Herbert Marcuse, "On the New Left," in Teodori, ed., *New Left*, 473.

23 Peter Gzowski, "The righteous crusaders of the New Left," *Maclean's* (15 November 1965), 18-19, 39-42. See also, Murray Bookchin, *Listen Marxist!* (New York: Times Change, 1971), reprinted in Bookchin, *Post-Scarcity Anarchism* (Berkeley: Ramparts Press, 1971), 173-220.

24 Philip Resnick, "The New Left in Ontario," in Roussopoulos, ed., *New Left in Canada*, 100.

25 James Harding, "The New Left in British Columbia," in Roussopoulos, ed., *New Left in Canada*, 39. For a later Harding statement see "Still Thinking Globally Since the Sixties," *Canadian Dimension*, 22 (November-December 1988), 16.

26 Dimitrios I. Roussopoulos, "Towards a Revolutionary Youth Movement and an Extra-Parliamentary Opposition," in Roussopoulos, ed., *New Left in Canada*, esp. 135-136, 141, 138. Roussopoulos borrowed a great deal from Bookchin's *Listen Marxist!*

27 For a contemporary critique of the Roussopoulos edited *New Left in Canada* see Martin Loney, "Canada's New Left Still Needs a Biography," 75-76.

28 Ruth Lisa Schechter, "Translations of the Exile," *Our Generation Against Nuclear War*, 3 (June 1964), 73.

29 Levitt, *Children of Privilege*, 40; Owram, *Born at the Right Time*, 218; Roussopoulos, ed., *New Left in Canada*, 8; Kostash, *Long Way from Home*, xxii; Catherine Gidney, "Poisoning the Student Mind? The Student Christian Movement on the University of Toronto Campus, 1920-1965," *Journal of the Canadian Historical Association*, New Series, 8 (1997), 147-163; Personal communication, Dimitri Roussopoulos to Bryan Palmer, 4 September 2008 [hereafter Roussopoulos to Palmer.].

30 Roussopoulos to Palmer. On the religious motivation of CUCND see Levitt, *Children of Privilege*, 41-42; Owram, *Born at the Right Time*, 219.

31 The 3 November 1960 CUCND brief is quoted in Roussopoulos, ed., *New Left in Canada*, 9.

32 Roussopoulos, ed., *New Left in Canada*, 8-9; Kostash, *Long Way from Home*, xxii-xxiii; Owram, *Born at the Right Time*, 165; Judy Rebick, *Ten Thousand Roses: The Making of a Feminist Revolution* (Toronto: Penguin, 2005), 3-5; Kay Macpherson and Meg Sears, "The Voice of Women," in Gwen Matheson, ed., *Women in the Canadian Mosaic* (Toronto: Peter Martin, 1976), 71-89; Kay Macpherson, "The Seeds of the 70s," *Canadian Dimension*, 10 (June 1975), 39-41. Early issues of *Our Generation Against Nuclear War* were edited by a large collective that included an impressive array of New Left and anti-disarmament figures from the United States, Great Britain, and Canada. With Dimitrios I. Roussopoulos a mainstay in Montreal, the quarterly journal was a considerable accomplishment and made many academic faculty sit up and take notice of the fledgling movement. For extensive discussion of unilateralism see the special issue of *Our Generation Against Nuclear War*, 3 (April 1965). On the influence on the NDP see "New Party Declaration," in Michael S. Cross, ed., *The Decline and Fall of a Good Idea: CCF-NDP Manifestoes, 1932 to 1969* (Toronto: New Hogtown Press, 1974), 41-42; *Policies of the New Democratic Party, 1961-1973* (Ottawa: NDP, 1974), 79-81.

33 The above paragraphs draw on Levitt, *Children of Privilege*, 159; Gonick, "Students and Peace," 12; Kostash, *Long Way from Home*, 5; Owram, *Born at the Right Time*, 220; Roussopoulos to Palmer. On the Triple Revolution see W.H. Ferry et al., *The Triple Revolution* (Santa Barbara: The Ad Hoc Committee on the Triple Revolution, 1964), excerpts of which appear in Albert and Albert, eds., *Sixties Papers*, 197-208. The labour component of this Triple Revolution would, in the later 1960s, mesh well with a Gorzian strategy for labour that drew on much New Left theorizing, especially that of Marcuse, as well as Old Left concerns of the 1950s that accented proletarian discontents (Harvey Swados), to insist that workers were being assailed by technology, deskilling, and immiseration. Gorz thus laid great stress on alienation, consumption, and the remaking of a working class order dominated by marginalization and poverty. This 'new working class' thus coexisted with students rather well, precisely because university youth faced situations remarkably parallel to that of advanced capitalism's workers. See André Gorz, *Strategy for Labor: A Radical Proposal* (Boston: Beacon Press, 1967); Gorz, "The Way Forward," *New Left Review*, 52 (November-December 1968), 47-66; Gorz, *Réforme et Révolution* (Paris: Editions du Seuil, 1969).

34 See C. George Benello and Dimitrios Roussopoulos, eds., *The Case for Participatory Democracy: Some Prospects for a Radical Society* (New York: Viking, 1971). For a critical questioning of participatory democracy as an American New Left initiative trapped in the cul-de-sac of a liberal tradition that could not "perceive the necessity of evolving a political program that could engage the working class as a whole in revolutionary change" see Krista Maeots, "Some Problems in the Redefinition of Activism: The Rise and Fall of SUPA," in D.I. Davies and Kathleen Herman, *Social Space: Canadian Perspectives* (Toronto: New Press, 1971), 230-233.

35 Rousoppoulos to Palmer. That there were leaders whose ideas were known to the members, and were seen as carrying more weight, is indicated in some SUPA lines of verse referring to two key figures: Toronto's Art Pape and Montreal's Dimitri Roussopoulos. SUPA member Harvey L. Shepherd wrote: "I know of all the problems of peasants and metropolis;/I know all that you need to know to organize the populace:/I know how to go limp so the policeman has to stop you less:/I

know all the opinions of Art Pape and of Roussopoulos." HLS, "The Modern Radical," *SUPA Newsletter,* 1, #3, June 1965.

36 James Harding, "An Ethical Movement in Search of An Analysis: The Student Union for Peace Action in Canada," *Our Generation*, 3 and 4 (May 1966), 20-29; Kostash, *Long Way from Home*, 5-9. For one early suggestion of problems in SUPA, which emphasized the need to transcend moralism, raised questions about non-violence, advocated building a larger mass organization, and pointed to the need for firmer lines of connection between systematic capitalist exploitation and war, see Andre Beckerman, "A Critical View of SUPA," *SUPA Newsletter*, 1, #4, 23 June 1965. On decentralization, debates over it, and problems of SUPA's structure see S. Howard Gray, "SUPA Federal Staff—Some Questions," *SUPA Newsletter*, 1, #6, 21 July 1965; Ken Drushka, "Proposed Changes of the SUPA Structure," 1, #7, 10 August 1965.

37 See Stanley Gray, "Nationalism and Non-Alignment," *Canadian Dimension*, 3 (March-April / May-June 1966), 48-49.

38 Harding, "Ethical Movement in Search of an Analysis," 22; Dan Daniels, "The Philosophy of Non-Violence," *Canadian Dimension*, 1 (September-October 1964), 14-15; John K. Rooke, "The Use of Force," *SUPA Newsletter*, 1, #4, 23 June 1965.

39 On student syndicalism and its development in the New Left from 1965-1968 see Serge Joyal, *Student Syndicalism in Quebec* (Toronto: SUPA, 1965); Serge Joyal, "Student Syndicalism in Quebec," *Canadian Dimension,* 2 (March-April 1965), 20-22; Carl Davidson, "Student Syndicalism," *Our Generation*, 5 (May 1967), 102-111; Levitt, *Children of Privilege*, 171-176. On poverty and powerlessness see, for instance, *Our Generation*, 4 (March 1967), which contains an editorial statement by Lucia Kowaluk, "The Dimensions of Powerlessness," (5-7); Bryan M. Knight, "On Poverty in Canada," (8-22); Todd Gitlin, "Organizing the Poor in America," (22-29); and Nicholas Van Hoffman, "Organizing the Ghetto," (30-40). On the earlier more moderate understandings of 1963-1964 I benefited from hearing the presentation of Barbara Godard, "Quebec, The National Question, and English-Canadian Student Activism in the 1960s," presented the conference, "New World Coming: The Sixties and the Shaping of Global Consciousness," Queen's University, Kingston, Ontario, 13-16 June 2007 [hereaftes "New World"], a talk that accented the relations of student activists in Montreal and Toronto around questions of Quebec and Canada.

40 Kostash, *Long Way from Home*, 15.

41 See Dan Daniels, "Why Civil Disobedience at La Macaza," *Canadian Dimension*, 1 (July-August 1964), 16.

42 Andre Cardinal, "SUPA's Summer Projects," 1, #6, 21 July 1965.

43 Roussopoulos to Palmer. Echoes of the Montreal SUPA leadership's accent on Quebec as a radical crucible can be discerned in the collection of essays published ten years later: Dimitri Roussopoulos, ed., *Québec and Radical Social Change* (Montreal: Black Rose Books, 1974).

44 Gitlin, "Organizing the Poor in America"; Richard Rothstein, "A Short History of ERAP," *Our Generation*, 3 /4 (May 1966), 40-45; Eric Mann, "New School for the Ghetto," *Our Generation*, 5 (September 1967), 67-73; Richard Rothstein, "Evolution of the ERAP Organizers," *Radical America,* 2 (March-April 1968), reprinted in Priscilla Long, ed., *The New Left: A Collection of Essays* (Boston: Por-

ter Sargeant, 1969), 272-288; Miller, *Democracy in the Streets*, 192-215, 262-264, 270-271; and the excellent collection of material in Teodori, ed., *New Left*, 128-149. As an endnote to Hayden's Newark project, see Tom Hayden, *Rebellion in Newark: Official Violence and Ghetto Response* (New York: Random House, 1967).

45 Levitt, *Children of Privilege*, 162-164; Kostash, *Long Way from Home*, 17-19; "Students Win Where Others Lost," *Toronto Star*, 17 August 1965; Peggy Morton, "Kingston Community Project," *SUPA Newsletter*, 1, #4, 23 June 1965; Don Carmichael, "Kingston Community Project," *SUPA Newsletter*, 1, #6, 21 July 1965; Olivia Howell, "Kingston Community Project," *SUPA Newsletter* 1, #5, 7 July 1965; Tony Tugwell, "Kingston Report," and "Letter from Kingston," *SUPA Newsletter*, 1, #7, 10 August 1965.

46 Tugwell, "Kingston Report"; Richard Harris, *Democracy in Kingston: A Social Movement in Urban Politics, 1965-1970* (Kingston and Montreal: McGill-Queen's University Press, 1988), 68-70; Maeots, "The Rise and Fall of SUPA," 230-231.

47 The above paragraphs draw on Kostash, *Long Way from Home*, 17-20; Dennis McDermott, "Kingston Community Project," *SUPA Newsletter*, 1, #3, June 1965; McDermott, "Graplo Spasms on a Poverty Project," *SUPA Newsletter*, 1, #6, 21 July 1965; Harris, *Democracy in Kingston*, contains much on Newman and Kingston activities, as does Margaret Daly, *The Revolution Game: The Short, Unhappy Life of the Company of Young Canadians* (Toronto: New Press, 1970), 15-25. For Spinks and the Trefann Court project see Graham Fraser, *Fighting Back: Urban Renewal in Trefann Court* (Toronto: Hakkert, 1972); Sarah Spinks, "Urban Renewal: Toronto Community Union Project," *Our Generation*, 5 (September 1967), 102-105; Spinks, "Trefann Court," *SUPA Newsletter*, 3, #3, January 1967; Spinks, "Participatory Bureaucracy and the Hall-Dennis Report," *This Magazine is about Schools*, 2 (Autumn 1968), 137-149. For *This Magazine* see the extremely useful collection of articles from its 1966-1969 issues in Satu Repo, ed., *This Book Is About Schools* (New York: Pantheon, 1970), which contains a Marshall McLuhan contribution to Volume 1, Number 1, "Electronics and the Psychic Drop-Out," (383-389).

48 George Bain, "The SUPA Affair," *Globe and Mail*, no date, reprinted in *SUPA Newsletter*, 1, #6, 21 July 1965, claimed that "the student Neestow project will place 25 students among the Indians of Saskatchewan with a view to (among other things) instructing the Indians in how to use the weapon of public protest to secure their rights as citizens." See also Levitt, *Children of Privilege*, 71-72. A useful discussion of the origins of the Neewstow Project, and the place of Malcolm Norris, appears in Murray Dobbin, *The One-And-A-Half Men: The Story of Jim Brady and Malcolm Norris, Metis Patriots of the Twentieth Century* (Vancouver: New Star, 1981), 224-230, in which interviews with Harding and other SUPA figures are quoted.

49 Kostash, *Long Way from Home*, 15-16; Gzowski, "The Righteous Crusaders of the New Left," 40-41; Jill Annweiler, "Student Neestow Partnership Project," *SUPA Newsletter*, 1, #3, June 1965; Dobbin, *One-And-A-Half Men*, esp. 228. Uhl's later disillusionment is chronicled in "No Hope for Indians," *Pro-tem: The Student Weekly of York University*, 3 December 1965.

50 The most accessible brief account of the Green Lake difficulties is in Dobbin, *One-And-A-Half Men*, 228-229. A four part series in the Saskatoon *Star Phoenix* by the journalist Volkmar Richter outlined the government machinations as well as Malcolm Norris's militant rejoinders.

51 Liora Proctor, "The Student Neestow Project," and Clayton Ruby, "Comments," *Our Generation*, 4 (November 1966), 40-48; Maeots, "The Rise and Fall of SUPA," 231, and for more on Proctor, Dobbin, *One-And-A-Half Men*, 234-235.

52 Kotash, *Long Way from Home*, 16-17; Lynne Butts, "The Kootenay Project,"SUPA Nwslatter, 1, #4, 23 June 1965; Butts, "The Beauty That is Age," *SUPA Newsletter*, 1, #6, July 1965; Peter Boothroyd, "Kootenays Project Report," *SUPA Newsletter*, 1, #8 , 30 August 1965; Gzowski, "The Righteous Crusaders of the New Left," 41. Interest in the Doukhobors had been stimulated by Sima Holt's, *Terror in the Name of God* (1964), which condemned the pacifist Sons of Freedom as fanatics and zealots. Among the New Left Holt's book was regarded as a variant of 'hate literature'. See Kouozma J. Tarasoff, "Zealots and Doukhobors," *Canadian Dimension*, 2 (March-April 1965), 23-24. For the reification of youth see John and Margaret Rowntree, "Youth as a Class," *Our Generation*, 6 (May-July 1968), 155-189; James Laxer and Arthur Pape, "Youth and Canadian Politics," *Our Generation*, 4 (November 1966), 15-21, which concluded: "It is the Canadians under thirty years of age, who did not live through a period of accommodation to the 'Great Society', and who have few vested interests in it, who will form the basis for an opposition movement." Note, finally, the discussion of Doukhobors and the New Left in British Columbia in Benjamin Isitt,, "Working-Class Agency, the Cold War, and the Rise of a New Left: Political Change in British Columbia, 1948-1972," preliminary draft of PhD dissertation, presented to the University of New Brunswick, 2007, Chapter 7, 302-307.

53 Gzowski, "The Righteous Crusaders of the New Left," 41; Rocky Jones, "Letter from Nova Scotia," *SUPA Newsletter*, 1, #8, 30 August 1965; Kostash, *Long Way from Home*, 12; Lynne Burrows, "The Nova Scotia Project," *SUPA Newsletter*, 3, #1, January 1967. For more on Rocky Jones and Halifax see James Walker, "Black Confrontation in 1960s Halifax," paper in the "Debating Dissent: Canada and the Sixties," Workshop, University of New Brunswick, Fredericton, New Brunswick, 21-22 August 2008. On Africville see David Lewis Stein, "The Counterattack on Diehard Racism," *Maclean's*, 20 October 1962; Sylvia Fraser, "The slow and welcome death of Africville," *Star Weekly* (1 January 1966), 1-7; Donald H. Clairmont and Dennis William Magill, *Africville: The Life and Death of a Canadian Black Community* (Toronto: Canadian Scholar's Press, 1997).

54 Stan Gray, "LaMacaza," *SUPA Newsletter*, 1, #3, June 1965; "Project La Macaza," 1 #6, 21 July 1965; "National Fund-Raising Trip for Project La Macaza," 1 #8, 30 August 1965; Nancy Hannum, "Peace and the Professions," *SUPA Newsletter*, 1 #3, June 1965; 1 #8, 30 August 1965. The Comox Project seemed in perpetual conflict with SUPA's Toronto office. See Linda Light, "Letter from Comox," 1 #4, 23 June 1965; "Comox Project '65: The Comox Project Bulletin—A Review," 1 #7, 10 August 1965; Peter Light, "Comox Project '65—The Report," 1, #8, 30 August 1965; Light, "An Answer to Tony Hyde," 1, #8, 30 August 1965.

55 "School for Social Theory," *SUPA Newsletter*, 1 #6, 21 July 1965; 1 #8, 30 August 1965; Matt Cohen, "Hegel and the New Left: Report of a Meeting of Seminar of the School for Social Theory," 1 #7, 10 August 1965; Miles Murray, "An Afternoon with Darshan Singh: Report from the School for Social Theory," 1, #7, 10 August 1965.

56 "School for Social Theory," *SUPA Newsletter*, 1, #8, 30 August 1965.

57 Levitt, *Children of Privilege*, 36.

58 Quoted in Owram, *Born at the Right Time*, 170.

59 Levitt, *Children of Privilege*, esp. 48, 209; George Clark, "Students for a Democratic Society," *Our Generation*, 3 (May 1966), 30-39. For a somewhat mechanical nationalist critique of SUPA and the Canadian New Left as Americanized see James Laxer, "The Americanization of the Canadian Student Movement," in Ian Lumsden, ed., *Close the 49th Parallel: The Americanization of Canada* (Toronto: University of Toronto Press, 1970), 275-286. Cy Gonick thought the Canadian New Left an imitation of its U.S. counterpart, little more than "a pale reflection." See Gonick, "Strategies for Social Change," *Canadian Dimension*, 4 (November-December 1966), 7. Hayden's connection to Toronto's SUPA leadership was close, and he both offered advice, instruction, and inspiration, but he also used his Canadian connections as an escape from pressures in the United States. Thus one SUPA member told Myrna Kostash: "SDS people used to come up to Toronto to rest. Tom Hayden came up and Carl Ogelsby. Tom stayed with Clay (Ruby) a week and didn't say a word. He was overdosed, burned out; he came up to rest and never said one word to us." Kostash, *Long Way from Home*, 26. See also, for Hayden's influence on the highly dissimilar SUPA leaders, Pape and Roussopolous, James Laxer, "The Student Movement and Canadian Independence," *Canadian Dimension*, 6 (August-September 1969), 32.

60 Kostash, *Long Way from Home*, 9-10; "The Sitdowners," *Toronto Star*, 20 March 1965; Harvey Shepherd, "Men Must Speak," *The Varsity*, 10 March 1965; "A Guide to Forming a Friends of SNCC Group in Canada," (Toronto: Friends of SNCC, no date, c. 1964-1965); Shepherd, "SNCC Conference May 8-10: A Step Towards a Movement in Canada," *SUPA Newsletter*, 1, #3, June 1965; Shepherd, "Mission to Mississippi," *SUPA Newsletter*, 1, #7, 10 August 1965; Shepherd, "SNCC in Canada," *SUPA Newsletter*, 1, #8, 30 August 1965.

61 Writing on radical opposition to the Vietnam War is extensive. See, for only an introduction to the subject: Miller, *Democracy in the Streets;* Varon, *Bringing the War Home*; and the extremely useful gathering of relevant material in Teodori, ed., *New Left*, 240-270; Albert and Albert, ed., *Sixties Papers*, 271-400. For the view of a Canadian New Leftist, Kostash, *Long Way from Home*, 31-54.

62 "Ending the War," *Canadian Dimension*, 2 (March-April 1965), 3; Cy Gonick, "What Every Canadian Should Know About Vietnam," and J.W. Warnock, "Canadian Policy in Vietnam," in *Canadian Dimension*, 2 (May-June 1965), 3-7, 19-22; Gonick, "What Every Canadian Should Know About Vietnam, Part II," "Debate on Vietnam: Douglas vs. Martin," "The Ugly Canadian," and "Open Letter," *Canadian Dimension*, 2 (July-August 1965), 3-5, 8-11, 29; Gonick, "What Every Canadian Should Know About Vietnam, Part III," and "Norman Mailer on LBJ and Vietnam," *Canadian Dimension*, 2 (September-October 1965), 7-9, 10-12; W.E. Wilmott, "Dominoes," *Canadian Dimension*, 3 (November-December 1965), 26-27; James Steele, "Ottawa/Saigon Complicity," *Our Generation*, 4 (July 1966), 71-83; Philip Resnick, "Canada, Vietnam, and the War Industries," *Our Generation*, 5 (November-December 1967), 16-30.

63 Richard Price, "The New Left in Alberta," in Roussopoulos, ed., *New Left in Canada*, 43.

64 "Conference on Vietnam, Carleton University, 12-13 June 1965," *SUPA Newsletter*, 1 #3, June 1965.

65 Liora Proctor, "Teach-In," *SUPA Newsletter*, 1 #3, June 1965; Henry Tarvainen, "International Teach-In for Toronto this Fall," 1, #4, 23 June 1965.

66 On the International Teach-Ins see Charles Hanly, *Revolution and Response* (Toronto: McClelland and Stewart, 1966); and Jeffrey Rose and Michael Ignatieff, eds., *Religion and International Affairs: International Teach-In* (Toronto: Anansi, 1968). Extensive discussion/debate in *Canadian Forum* occurred around the "Revolution and Response" Teach-In. See Charles Hanly, "The Toronto Teach-In," *Canadian Forum*, 45 (September 1965), 130-131; and "Symposium on the Teach-In," *Canadian Forum*, 45 (November 1965), 172-179, especially Art Pape's contribution, "Teach-In as Institution," 178. See also "That Was a Teach-In that Was—Or was it?" *Maclean's*, 15 November 1965.

67 "Open Letter to the 27th Parliament and the Government of Canada," *Our Generation*, 3 (May 1966), 90-95.

68 See Kostash, *Long Way from Home*, 44-62; Renee Goldsmith Kasinsky, *Refugees from Militarism* (New Brunswick, New Jersey: Transaction Books, 1976); Martin Satin, ed., *Manual for Draft-Age Immigrants to Canada* (Toronto: Anansi, 1970); Roger N. Williams, *The New Exiles: American War Resisters in Canada* (New York: Liveright, 1971); Kenneth Fred Emerick, *War Resisters in Canada: the World of the American Military-Political Refugees* (Knox, Pennsylvania: Free Press, 1972); Jack Colhoun, "The Exiles' Role in War Resistance," *Monthly Review*, 30 (March 1979), 27-43; John Hagan, *Northern Passage: American Vietnam War Resisters in Canada* (Cambridge, Massachusetts: Harvard University Press, 2001); Frank Kusch, *All American Boys: Draft Dodgers in Canada from the Vietnam War* (Westport, Connecticut: Praeger, 2002); Pierre Berton, *1967: The Last Good Year* (Toronto: Doubleday, 1997), 197-203; David Churchill, "An Ambiguous Welcome: Vietnam Draft Resistance, the Canadian State, and Cold War Containment," *Histoire Sociale/Social History*, 37 (mai-May 2004), 1-26.

69 Maeots, "The Rise and Fall of SUPA," 231.

70 John S. Wagner, Secretary, University of Toronto CEWV, "Draft Statement: Purposes and Structure," Student Anti-War Conference Working Paper, no date, in possession of the author; Louis Fournier, *F.L.Q. The Anatomy of an Underground Movement* (Toronto: NC Press, 1984), 119.

71 Gzowski, "The righteous crusaders of the New Left," 19. See also, for an equally enthusiastic insider report, Stanley Gray, "New Left, Old Left," *Canadian Dimension*, 3 (November-December 1965), 11-13.

72 The above paragraphs draw on Kostash, *Long Way from Home*, 21-24; Maeots, "The Rise and Fall of SUPA," 231; "Question of the Issue," *SUPA Newsletter*, 1, #4, 23 June 1965.

73 The two standard works on the Company of Young Canadians are Margaret Daly, *The Revolution Game: The Short, Unhappy Life of the Company of Young Canadians* (Toronto: New Press, 1970); Ian Hamilton, *The Children's Crusade: The Story of the Company of Young Canadians* (Toronto: Peter Martin, 1970). I draw as well on the brief discussion in Kostash, *Long Way from Home*, 19-28; Gzowski, "The righteous crusaders of the New Left," which contained an insert "Why activists are anti-Peace Corps," 41, that maintained that most SUPA activists "distrust the idea of the Company of Young Canadians." See as well Martin Loney, "A Political Economy of Citizen Participation," in Leo Panitch, ed., *The Canadian State: Political Economy and Political Power* (Toronto: University of Toronto Press, 1977), 446-472; Levitt, *Children of Privilege*, 98; Berton, *1967: Last*

Good Year, 172-186. On Goodings see Stewart Goodings, "The Company of Young Canadians," *SUPA Newsletter*, 1, #8, 30 August 1965; Hamilton, *Children's Crusade*, 132-152.

74 Note Kostash, *Long Way from Home*, 21; Daly, *Revolution Game*, 132; "CYC: The Bird That Cannot Even Fly," *Our Generation*, 6 (May-July 1968), 13-14.

75 Daly, *Revolution Game*, 31.

76 Hamilton, *Children's Crusade*, 46-58. For a SUPA statement on the anti-war rally see Donald McKelvey, "That Vietnam Demonstration," *SUPA Newsletter*, 3, #3, January 1967, with the same issue containing a statement on "THE CYC and Social Change," with a letter from Art Pape and Anthony Hyde of SUPA's Federal Council to Alan Clarke, Director of CYC.

77 Daly, *Revolution Game*, 101-133; "CYC: The Bird That Cannot Even Fly," 13-14; and comments in James Laxer, "The Student Movement and Canadian Independence," *Canadian Dimension*, 6 (August-September 1969), 33-34; and in Maeots, "The Rise and Fall of SUPA," 232-233.

78 The above two paragraphs draw on Kostash, *Long Way from Home*, 20-28; Hamilton, *Children's Crusade*; Daly, *Revolution Game*, esp 238; Loney, "Citizen Participation," 465-466; Jeremy Ashton, CYC Volunteer, "Organizing Alberta Indians," *SUPA Newsletter*, 3 #3, January 1967; Melville Watkins, "CYC," *Canadian Dimension*, 6 (February-March 1970), 5-6. For a representation of CYC in Quebec see Louis Fournier, *FLQ: The Anatomy of an Underground Movement* (Toronto: NC Press, 1984), 145-146, while a social democratic critique of CYC is Douglas Fisher, "The New Left ... As Others See It," *Canadian Dimension*, 3 (September-October 1966), 15.

79 Cy Gonick, "Strategies for Social Change," *Canadian Dimension*, 4 (November-December 1966), 8, 39-40. See also Maeots, "The Rise and Fall of SUPA," 233, which concludes: "As the Canadian radical youth movement became increasingly socialist and anti-imperialist, it began to face up to the problems of corporate control of Canada and the challenges of the Canadian left tradition. The difficulties created by attempts to organize around the left liberalism of American populism were replaced by a new set of problems concerning the relationship of the socialist left with Canadian social democracy and with the country's social democratic labour tradition."

80 For the final statement of denouement see Sue Helwig, "SUPA Disbands," *The Varsity*, 24 September 1967.

81 Kostash, *Long Way from Home*, 25; George Haggar, "Wretched of the Earth (Frantz Fanon)," *Canadian Dimension*, 3 (July-August 1966), 33-36; Roger O'Toole, *The Precipitous Path: Studies in Political Sects* (Toronto: Peter Martin, 1977), 33-56; "The Role of the Left," SUPA Newsletter, 3, #4, January 1967; Harvey Shepherd, "Poetry," SUPA Newsletter, 3, #3, January 1967; Levitt, *Children of Privilege*. 102-103.

82 This New Left Committee statement is quoted in James Laxer, "The Student Movement and Canadian Independence," *Canadian Dimension*, 4 (August-September 1969), 33. While the push to analyze Canadian society and its particular structure of modern capitalism often entailed utilizing the Marxist categories of political economy, such interpretive probes could also take anarchist directions, particularly if the subject was the state. See Dimitrios I. Roussopoulos, ed., *The Political Economy of the State* (Montreal: Black Rose, 1973).

83 Note the quotes and arguments developed in Owram, *Born at the Right Time*, 232; Levitt, *Children of Privilege*, 176; Roussopoulos, "Towards a Revolutionary Youth Movement," in *New Left in Canada*, 143; Roussopoulos, "What is the New Radicalism?" *Our Generation*, 6 (May-July 1968), 15-26; Roussopoulos, "The Provos: Dutch Political Beatniks," *Our Generation*, 4 (July 1966), 67-70; Gerald Heard, "LSD—The Way to Nirvana," *Canadian Dimension*, 1 (July-August 1964), 11-13; Abraham Hoffer, "The Confrontation Between the Psychedelic Experience and Society," *Canadian Dimension*, 4 (July-August 1967), 5-7. Note, as well, the debate over the article C. George Benello, "Wasteland Culture: Notes on Structure, Restructuring and Strategies for Social Change," *Our Generation*, 5 (September 1967), 19-47, continued in "The New Movement and Its Organizational Theory," by various authors and Benello's rejoinder, "Politics, Resistence, and Marxism," *Our Generation*, 5 (March-April 1968), 53-87; Christian Sivrel, "The Big Fuss about Marihuana," *SUPA Newsletter*, 3, #3, January 1967.

84 For a regional account of developments in British Columbia see Isitt, "Working-Class Agency, the Cold War, and the Rise of a New Left," Chapter 8, 313-341.

85 See as one contemporary survey, Andy Wernick, "A Guide to the Student Left," *Varsity*, 24 September 1969, and for Wernick's rejection of vanguard organizations, Wernick, "The Theory of the Vanguard Party and the Notion of Contradiction," *Praxis*, 1 (August 1968), 1-14 (pagination anew each article). Note as well, Varda Burstyn, "Remember the Old Mole?" *Canadian Dimension*, 22 (November-December 1988), 13.

86 Mel Watkins in *This Magazine* (November-December 1979), 42, quoted in Robert Hackett, "Pie in the Sky: A History of the Ontario Waffle," *Canadian Dimension*, 15 (October-November 1980), 4. See from the socialist-feminist perspective the brief comment of Meg Luxton, "Feminism as a Class Act: Working-Class Feminism and the Women's Movement in Canada," *Labour/Le Travail*, 48 (Fall 2001), 83-86.

87 Kostash, *Long Way from Home*, 25.

88 Jim Harding to Dear Cy, *Canadian Dimension*, 7 (December 1970), 62.

89 Gray quoted in Levitt, *Children of Privilege*, 176; *SUPA Newsletter*, 3, #7, 9 May 1967; Stan Gray, "The Greatest Canadian Shit Disturber," *Canadian Dimension*, 38 (November-December 2004), 13.

90 Stanley Gray, "The New Student Radicalism: Is It An American Import?" *Praxis*, 1 (August 1968), 6-7.

91 On student syndicalism in this period, and the controversy surrounding the strategic orientation, see John Cleveland, *Student Syndicalism: A Program of Action* (Edmonton: Confrontations mimeograph, 1969); Andrew Wernick, "The Student Government Left, Syndicalism, and the Search for Strategy," *Praxis*, 2 (March 1969), 17-21.

92 On the Just Society Movement see Howard Buchbinder, "The Just Society Movement," in Brian Wharf, ed., *Community Work in Canada* (Toronto: McClelland and Stewart, 1979), 129-152; George Ford and Steven Langdon, "Just Society Movement: Toronto's Poor Organize," *Canadian Dimension*, 7 (June-July 1970), 19-23. The Howard Buchbinder-led Praxis group struggled to keep alive the community-focused participatory democracy of SUPA, but its relations to bodies like the Just Society Movement, founded by single welfare mothers, were anything but smooth. See Margaret

Hillyard Little, "Militant Mothers Fight Poverty: The Just Society Movement, 1968-1971," *Labour /Le Travail*, 59 (Spring 2007). On the bridging of community and class struggle via the fusion of participatory democracy and workers' control see Gerry Hunnius, ed., *Participatory Democracy for Canada: Workers' Control and Community Control* (Montreal: Black Rose Press, 1971). Praxis had connections to the League for Social Reform, and included figures such as Stephen Clarkson, Jane Jacobs, and Peter Russell. See Howard Buchbinder, "Guaranteed Annual Income: The Answer to Poverty for All But the Poor," *Canadian Dimension*, 7 (October-November 1970), 27-32; Buchbinder, "Participation, Control, and the EPO: A Consideration of Strategies," *Our Generation*, 7 (September 1971), 9-22; Buchbinder, "Social Planning or Social Control: An Account of a Confrontation with the Social Welfare Establishment," in Alan T. R. Powell, ed., *The City: Attacking Modern Myths* (Toronto: McClelland and Stewart, 1972), 131-160; Buchbinder, "The Toronto Social Planning Council and the United Community Fund," in D.I. Davies and Kathleen Herman, eds., *Social Space: Canadian Perspectives* (Toronto: New Press, 1971), 196-205. For New Left discussions of urban poverty and planning issues see James Lorimer and Myfanwy Phillips, *Working People: Life in a Downtown City Neighbourhood* (Toronto: J. Lewis and Samuel, 1971); Graham Fraser, *Fighting Back: Urban Renewal in Trefann Court* (Toronto: Hackett, 1972); and for the general context of state initiatives and popular mobilizations surrounding the period's 'war on poverty' see James Struthers, *The Limits of Affluence: Welfare in Ontario, 1920-1970* (Toronto: University of Toronto Press, 1994), 211-230; Lawrence Felt, "Militant Poor People and the Canadian State," in Daniel Gleanday, Hubert Guidon, and Allan Turowetz, eds., *Modernization and the Canadian State* (Toronto: Macmillan, 1978), 417-441.

93 Note Peter Warrian, "The State of the Union, or Brothers and Sisters This is Our Thing So Let It All Hang Out," *Canadian Dimension*, 5 (September-October 1968), 10-11.

94 Wernick, "Blowin' in the Wind: CUS in Winnipeg," *Canadian Forum*, 48 (September 1968), 132-33.

95 On the League for Socialist Action see O'Toole, *Precipitous Path*, 12-32.

96 The above paragraphs draw on Resnick, "The New Left in Ontario," in Roussopoulos, ed., *New Left in Canada* , 98-103; Owram, *Born at the Right Time*, 289, 295-296; Melville H. Watkins, "When the Kissing Had to Stop," *Canadian* Forum, 48 (September 1968), 134; Danny Drache, "Canadian Students: Revolt and Apathy," *Canadian Dimension,* 5 (December-January 1967-1968), 24-25; James Laxer, "The Student Movement and Canadian Independence," *Canadian* Dimension, 6 (August-September 1969), 31; Caroline Brown, "Student Protest in Canada," in D.I. Davies and Kathleen Herman, eds., *Social Space*, 234-239; John Cleveland, *Radical Youth and Alternatives for Action* (Edmonton: Confrontations mimeograph, 1969); Howard Zinn, *Dow Shall Not Kill* (Nashville, Tennessee: Southern Student Organizing Committee, 1967); Stanley Aronowitz, "Columbia: Turning Point for Radical Strategy," *Guardian*, 1 June 1968; Tom Hayden, "Two, Three, Many Columbias," *Ramparts*, 15 June 1968, reprinted in *Our Generation*, 6 (May-July 1968), 151-152; Eric Mann, "The Columbia University Insurrection," *Our Generation*, 6 (May-July 1968), 101-120; Peter Lust, "Red Rudi: The Dutschke Phenomenon," *Canadian Dimension*, 5 (April-May 1968), 10-11; Daniel Cohn-Bendit, *Obsolete Communism: The Left-Wing Alternative* (Harmondsworth: Penguin, 1969); "Interview with Daniel Cohn-Bendit," *Our Generation*, 6 (May-July 1968), 95-100.

97 The best introduction to the Sir George Williams events is Dennis Forsythe, ed., *Let the Niggers Burn! The Sir George Williams University Affair and its Caribbean Aftermath* (Montreal: Black Rose Books, 1971), which contains the poem, Rawle R. Frederick, "Man Trap," 75, quoted in this paragraph. For useful discussion of West Indian radicalism in Montreal in the mid-1960s, especially as it relates to the specific conferences organized in the 1966-1968 years, see David Austin, "All Roads Led to Montreal: Black Power, the Caribbean, and the Black Radical Tradition in Canada," *Journal of African American History*, 92 (Fall 2007), 516-539; Alfie Roberts, *A View For Freedom: Alfie Roberts Speaks on the Caribbean, Cricket, Montreal, and C.L.R. James* (Montreal: Alfie Roberts Institute, 2005), esp. 65-88; and there is brief mention of the conferences organized in this period in Carmichael [Kwame Ture], *Ready for Revolution*, 544, 581. Sean Mills has uncovered much on black Montreal in the 1960s. See Mills, "The Empire Within," 174-227.

98 The above paragraphs draw on a number of sources. As a journalistic description, Dorothy Eber's *The Computer Centre Party: Canada Meets Black Power* (Montreal: Tundra, 1969) is a reasonable, albeit depoliticized, account. For a more radical statement see the articles in Forsythe, ed., *Let the Niggers Burn!* See as well Owram, *Born at the Right Time*, 286-287; and for a discussion of newspaper reporting of the Sir George Williams events, Marcel Martel, "'Riots' at Sir George Williams: Construction of a Social Conflict in the Sixties," Paper presented to the Canadian Historical Association, York University, May 2006. The prosecutorial zeal and overkill is addressed in "SGWU Blacks get a taste of just society," *Last Post*, 1 (April 1970), 5-7. Douglas and Cools, as well as the Sir George Williams events and other developments, are discussed in Roberts, *View for Freedom*, 65-88. Douglas would later, in 1971, be targeted by the RCMP, which had an *agent provocateur* function as his bodyguard and chauffeur. Allegations were made that Douglas was involved in a plot to bomb Sir George Williams University and he was arrested and eventually deported. See Fournier, *FLQ*, 318. Cools headed Toronto's Women in Transition counseling centre and was appointed to the Federal Parole Board in 1982, later to be a Trudeau appointment to the Canadian Senate. See Olivia Ward, "The Sixties: Ideals have quietly survived," *Toronto Star*, 28 March 1982; Walkhom, "1968: It was spring…"

99 *Montreal Star*, 15 February 1969, quoted in Forsythe, ed., *Let the Niggers Burn!* 9. There was consistently hostile comment from segments of the left with respect to the nihilism of the Sir George Williams destruction. See, for instance, G. David Sheps, "The Apocalyptic Fires at Sir George Williams University," *Canadian Dimension*, 5 (February 1969), 6-7, 52; Eugene D. Genovese, "War on Two Fronts," *Canadian Dimension*, 6 (April-May 1969), 25-29; Charles Taylor, "Marcuse's Authoritarian Utopia," *Canadian Dimension*, 7 (August-September 1970), 49-53. Neil Compton's, "Sir George Williams Loses its Innocence," *Canadian Forum*, 49 (April 1969), 2-4 struggled to be balanced. For a decidedly more upbeat presentation of student revolt and its radical possibilities see the discussion of the 40,000-strong CEGEPS protest strikes in Quebec in October 1968 in "CEGEPS, Charlebois, Chartrand: The Quebec Revolution Now: An Interview with Dimitri Roussopoulos," in Mann, ed., *Social and Cultural Change*, Volume II, 200-210.

100 Kostash, *Long Way from Home*, 84, 95; Philip Rosen, "The McGill Daily Incident," *SUPA Newsletter*, 3, #3, January 1967; Marlene Dixon, *Things Which Are Done In Secret* (Montreal: Black Rose Books, 1976), 28-55; "Stan Gray: Greatest Canadian Shit Disturber"; Stanley Gray, "The Troubles at

McGill," *Canadian Dimension*, 5 (January-March 1968), 35-39; and for Gray's movement into non-university struggles in Quebec, Gray, "The Struggle for Quebec," *Canadian Dimension*, 6 (December-January 1969-1970), 23-26; Louis Fournier, *FLQ: The Anatomy of an Underground Movement* (Toronto: NC Press, 1984). For a harsh critique of Gray from a student political figure see Julius Grey, "The Paradox of Stanley Gray," *Canadian Dimension*, 6 (October-November 1969), 6-9.

101 See, for instance, John Braddock, "Strife on Campus," in julyan Reid and Tim Reid, eds., *Student Power and the Canadian Campus* (Toronto: Peter Martin, 1969), 115-125; Kostash, *Long Way from Home*, 83-101; Alan Walker, "The Revolt on Campus," *Star Weekly Magazine*, 13 January 1968; Richard Wilbur, "Go Away—the Strax Affair," *Canadian Dimension*, 6 (April-May 1970), 9-10, 54; James Pitsula, "Cicero versus Socrates: The Liberal Arts Debate at the University of Saskatchewan, Reginal Campus," *Historical Studies in Education*, 15 (Spring 2003), 101-129; Pitsula, "Competing Ideals: Athletics and Student Radicalism at the University of Saskatachewan, Regina Campus, in the 1960s and 1970s," *Sport History Review*, 34 (May 2003); Dennis Lee, "Getting to Rochdale," in Repo, ed., *This Book is About Schools*, 354-380.

102 Kostash, *Long Way from Home*, 83-84, 93-94, 99-102; James Harding, "What's Happening at Simon Fraser University," *Our Generation*, 6 (December-January 1969), 52-67; Kathleen Gough, "The Struggle at Simon Fraser University," *Monthly Review*, 22 (May 1970), 31-45; Isitt, "Working-Class Agency, the Cold War, and the Rise of a New Left," Chapter 9, 358-366; Owram, *Born at the Right Time*, 242-247; "Is Universal Accessibility Henceforth Only for the Rich?" *Peak*, 4 May 1966; Sharon Yandle, "Post-Mortem on Strike Action," *Peak*, 5 April 1967; Yandle, "The End of PSA at Simon Fraser," *Canadian Dimension*, 6 (February-March 1970), 16-19; Mordecai Briemberg, "Radical Campus—or Haunted House on the Hill?" *Canadian Dimension*, 40 (March-April 2006), 57-58, a review of Hugh Johnson, *Radical Campus: Making Simon Fraser University* (Vancouver: Douglas and McIntyre, 2005). For the benevolent critique see Northrop Frye, "Student Protest Has Shallow Roots," *Toronto Star*, 19 September 1968.

103 The term is borrowed from Glen Williams, "Canada—The Case of the Wealthiest Colony," *This Magazine*, 10 (February-March 1976).

104 A.W. Purdy, "syllogism for theologians," *Canadian Dimension*, 5 (June-July 1968), 35.

105 See, for instance, Scott Gordon, "Foreign Investment in Canada," *Canadian Dimension*, 1 (Nos. 1-2, 1963), 18-20; H.C. Pentland, "Is Canada Possible? A Plan for a Canadian Owned Economy," *Canadian Dimension*, 1 (September-October 1964), 5-8.

106 C.J. Newman, "1966," *Canadian Dimension*, 3 (September-October 1966), 19.

107 Philip Resnick, *The Land of Cain: Class and Nationalism in English Canada, 1945-1975* (Vancouver: New Star, 1977); Stephen Azzi, *Walter Gordon and the Rise of Canadian Nationalism* (Montreal and Kingston: McGill-Queen's University Press, 1999). Indicative of the rising anti-Americanism of the period was Ian Lumsden, ed., *Close the 49th Parallel: The Americanization of Canada* (Toronto: University of Toronto Press, 1970). More subtle, but reflective of the nationalist impulses of the late 1960s, was Gary Teeple, ed., *Capitalism and the National Question in Canada* (Toronto: University of Toronto Press, 1972).

108 George Grant, "Critique of the New Left," *Our Generation*, 3 (May 1966), 46-51; Grant, "Tories, Socialists, and the Demise of Canada," *Canadian Dimension*, 3 (May-June 1965), 12-15; Grant, "Canadian Fate and Imperialism," *Canadian Dimension*, 4 (March-April 1967), 21-25; Grant, *Lament for a Nation: The Defeat of Canadian Nationalism*, 40th Anniversary Edition (Montreal and Kingston: McGill-Queen's University Press, 2005); Gad Horowitz, "Mosaics and Identity," *Canadian Dimension*, 3 (January-February 1966), 19; Horowitz, "On the Fear of Nationalism—Nationalism and Socialism—A Sermon to the Moderates," *Canadian Dimension*, 4 (May-June 1967), 7-9; "Horowitz and Grant Talk," *Canadian Dimension*, 6 (December-January 1969-1970), 18-20.

109 See the review of Lumsden, ed., *Close the 49th Parallel* by Horowitz, "Pigs and Cops: Reflections on Closing the 49th Parallel, Etc.," *Canadian Dimension*, 6 (April-May 1970), 34-35.

110 See, for instance, J.M. Freeman, "Economic Continentalism," *Our Generation*, 4 (March 1967), 43-73; Frank W. Park, "The Price of Independence," *Canadian Dimension*, 4 (March-April 1967), 26-28; Cy Gonick, "The Political Economy of Canadian Independence," *Canadian Dimension*, 4 (May-June 1967), 12-19; "The Task Force Report on Foreign Ownership," *Canadian Dimension*, 5 (April-May 1968), 15-20; Melville H. Watkins, *Foreign Ownership and the Structure of Canadian Industry: Report of the Task Force on the Structure of Canadian Industry* (Ottawa: Queen's Printer, 1968).The full fruit of this argumentation would appear in the early 1970s. See, for example, Kari Levitt, *Silent Surrender: The Multinational Corporation in Canada* (Toronto: Macmillan, 1970); Dave Godfrey, ed., *Gordon to Watkins to You: The Battle for Control of Our Economy* (Toronto: New Press, 1970); Frank and Libbie Park, *Anatomy of Big Business* (Toronto: James Lewis and Samuel, 1973); Robert M. Laxer, ed., *Canada, Ltd.: The Political Economy of Dependency* (Toronto: McClelland and Stewart, 1973).

111 Resnick, *Land of Cain*, 187-188; Bryan D. Palmer, ed., *A Communist Life: Jack Scott and the Canadian Workers Movement, 1927-1985* (St. John's: CCLH, 1988), 167-168; Kostash, *Long Way from Home*, 28-30; Owram, *Born at the Right Time*, 300-301; Levitt, *Children of Privilege*, 84, 162.

112 "Do Canadians Really Want Independence? Yes! Toronto Star Poll," *Canadian Dimension*, 4 (March-April 1967), 18-19; "An Open Letter to Canadian Nationalists," *Canadian Dimension*, 4 (May-June 1967), front cover.

113 Steve Moore and Debi Wells, *Imperialism and the National Question in Canada* (Toronto: Better Read Grapics, 1975).

114 James Laxer, "The Student Movement and Canadian Independence," *Canadian Dimension*, 6 (August-September 1969), 27-34, 69. The positions taken in the Laxer article had in part been responded to in Stanley Gray, "The New Student Radicalism: Is This An American Import Too?" *Praxis*, 1 (August 1968), 1-8 (pagination anew each article).

115 John W. Warnock, "Why I Am Anti-American," *Canadian Dimension*, 5 (November-December 1967), 11-12.

116 For a rather uncritical account of the Mathews-Steele endeavours see Jeffrey Cormier, *The Canadianization Movement: Emergence, Survival, and Success* (Toronto: University of Toronto Press, 2004). Note, as introductions only, James Steele and Robin Mathews, "The Universities: Takeover of the Mind," in Lumsden, ed., *Close the 49th Parallel*, 169-178; Mathews, "Canadian Culture and

the Liberal Ideology," in Laxer, ed., *Canada, Ltd.*, 213-231; Melville H. Watkins, "Education in the Branch Plant Economy," *Canadian Dimension*, 6 (October-November 1969), 37-39.

117 Robin Mathews, "Opinion: On Draft Dodging and U.S. Imperialism in Canada," *Canadian Dimension*, 6 (February-March 1970), 10-11. Critical responses to Mathews' views appeared in later issues of *Canadian Dimension*.

118 For an evocative statement of Watkins's development see Mel Watkins, "Learning to Move Left," *This Magazine is About Schools*, 6 (Spring 1972), 68-92, which also contains much on the history of the Waffle prior to its expulsion by the NDP. Also, Mel Watkins, "A Personal Dimension," *Canadian Dimension* 40 (November-December 2006), 51-55.

119 Much of this would be evident in early 1970s labour struggles in Ontario such as strikes buttressed by Waffle and other left-wing picket support. As RCMP files for the autumn of 1971 reveal, battles such as those unfolding at the Brantford Texpack plant indicated how critical Waffle support was for militant labour, which also gained endorsement from various Maoist and Trotskyist groups. See National Archives of Canada, Royal Canadian Mounted Police Files, Volume 113, Waffle File, 2000/000182, with thanks to Joan Sangster for giving me her notes on these files. See also Joan Sangster, "Remembering Texpack: Nationalism, Internationalism, and Militancy in Canadian Unions in the 1970s," *Studies in Political Economy,* 78 (Autumn 2006), 41-66.

120 For a discussion of the Waffle in BC, where future NDP premier David Barrett was an early, if uneasy, associate, see Benjamin Isitt, "Working-Class Agency, the Cold War, and the Rise of a New Left," Chapter 5, 224-235.

121 Pat Smart recently offered a personal memoir in her presentation at the "New World" conference: "For an Independent Socialist Canada: Queen's University History Department and the Birth of the Waffle."

122 One reflection of the differentiation of anti-imperialist, socialist, left nationalism from that of a rising economic nationalism in the ranks of the Liberal Party and mainstream New Democrats was the initiative taken by Gordon, economist Abraham Rotstein, and *Toronto Star* editor Peter Newman, who formed the more middle-of-the-road Committee for an Independent Canada in September 1970 to counter the possibility that the Waffle would be seen as the voice of Canadian nationalist ideas. See Cy Gonick, "Liberal-izing Continentalism," *Canadian Dimension*, 7 (October-November 1970), 4-5; Christina Newman, "Growing Up Reluctantly," *Maclean's*, August 1972, 58; Dave Godfrey, ed., *Gordon to Watkins to You: The Battle for Control of Our Economy* (Toronto: New Press, 1970).

123 The above two paragraphs on the Waffle draw on John Bullen, "The Ontario Waffle and the Struggle for an Independent Socialist Canada: Conflict within the NDP," *Canadian Historical Review*, 64 (June 1983), 188-215; Robert Hackett, "Pie in the Sky: A History of the Ontario Waffle," *Canadian Dimension*, 15 (October-November 1980), 1-72; a symposium on "The 20th Anniversary of the Waffle," appeared in two issues of *Studies in Political Economy*, 32 (Summer 1990), 167-201; 33 (Autumn 1990), 161-192; Owram, *Born at the Right Time*, 301-303; Cy Gonick, "The 'Waffle' Manifesto," *Canadian Dimension*, 6 (October-November 1969), 4; Cy Gonick, "The Lewises versus the Waffle," *Canadian Dimension*, 8 (June 1972), 4-6, 46-47; "Wither Waffle," *Canadian Dimension*, 7

(April 1971), 24-26; "Stephen Lewis's War with the Waffle: Double, double, toil and trouble," *Last Post*, 2 (July 1972), 32-33. On labour and the Waffle see especially Varda Burstyn, "The Waffle and the Women's Movement," and Gil Levine, "The Waffle and the Labour Movement," *Studies in Political Economy*, 33 (Autumn 1990), 180, 185-192. The Waffle Manifesto appears in Cross, ed., *The Decline and Fall of a Good Idea,* and for an account of the Waffle from an NDP mainstream loyalist see Desmond Morton, *NDP: The Dream of Power* (Toronto: Hakkert, 1974).

124 Cy Gonick, "DeaD-en-Ded," *Canadian Dimension*, 8 (March-April 1972), 5.

125 "Saskatchewan Waffle Leaves NDP," *Ontario Waffle News*, 1 (November 1973), 1. Evidence of the Waffle stalling in lack of organization and programmatic coherence can be gleaned from reading various statements in a 1974 Ontario internal discussion bulletin, among them Treat Hull, "Comment on the Waffle Election Programme," Boyd Neil, "Report on the CLC Convention," and Corileen North, "Fiscal Reform in the Waffle: An Opinion," all in *Advance: For Independence and Socialism—Internal Discussion Journal of the Ontario Waffle*, 2 (17 July 1974), 6-14.

126 See Burstyn, "The Age of Women's Liberation," *Canadian Dimension*, 18 (October-November 1984), 21-26; Burstyn "The Waffle and the Women's Movement," 175-184 for suggestive opening statements, as well as Burstyn, "Remember the Old Mole?" *Canadian Dimension*, 22 (November-December 1988), 13; and, most tellingly, Varda Kidd, "Sexism Prevailed at the NDP Convention," *Canadian Dimension*, 8 (June 1971), 7-9. Fischer is quoted in what remains perhaps the best overall treatment of the Waffle, Hackett, "Pie in the Sky," 42. On the 1971 Winnipeg convention and women's issues see as well, Hackett, "Pie in the Sky," 42-42; Michael S. Cross, "Third Class on the Titanic: The NDP Convention," *Canadian Forum* (April-May 1971), 5. For an early materialist-feminist statement associated with the Waffle and published in the Movement for an Independent Socialist Canada's 'coming-out' statement see Christina Maria Hill, "Women in the Canadian Economy," in Robert M. Laxer, ed., *Canada, Ltd.: The Political Economy of Dependency* (Toronto: McClelland and Stewart, 1973), 84-106. Note as well Krista Maeots, "Organizing Woman," in *Towards a Movement for an Independent Socialist Canada: A Proposal for the Ontario Waffle Conference, 19-20 August 1972*, a 5 page statement in a mimeographed collection of short 'position papers' prepared as the Waffle faced the prospect of being drummed out of the NDP; and the important later contribution of the Kingston Waffle, "Marxism, Feminism, and the Waffle," *Advance: For Independence and Socialism—Internal Discussion Journal of the Ontario Waffle*, 2 (17 July 1974), 1-5.

127 The above paragraphs draw on Margaret Benston, "The Political Economy of Women's Liberation," *Monthly Review*, 21 (September 1969), 13-27; Margaret Benston and Pat Davitt, "Women Invent Society," *Canadian Dimension*, 10 (June 1975), 69-79; Meg Luxton and Pat Armstrong, "Margaret Lowe Benston, 1937-1991," *Studies in Political Economy,* 35 (Summer 1991), 6-11; "Margaret Benston: A Tribute," *Canadian Women Studies*, 13 (Winter 1993), 6-36, which contains seven separate articles, including one by Marion Lowe. Benston's article was almost immediately responded to by Mickey and John Rowntree, "More on the Political Economy of Women's Liberation," *Monthly Review* 21 (January 1970), 26-32. For the Canadian research and writing of the 1970s and 1980s that grew out of Benston's discussion see, as examples only, Peggy Morton, "Women's Work is Never Done," in *Women Unite! An Anthology of the Canadian Women's* Movement (Toronto:

Canadian Women's Educational Press, 1972), 46-68; Dorothy Smith, "Women, the Family, and Corporate Capitalism," and Marylee Stephenson, "Housewives in Women's Liberation," in Stephenson, ed., *Women in Canada* (Don Mills, Ontario: General Publishing, 1977), 14-48, 109-125; Meg Luxton, *More Than a Labour of Love: Three Generations of Women's Work in the Home* (Toronto: Women's Educational Press, 1980); Bonnie Fox, ed., *Hidden in the Household: Women's Domestic Labour Under Capitalism* (Toronto: Women's Educational Press, 1980); Roberta Hamilton and Michelle Barrett, eds., *The Politics of Diversity: Feminism, Marxism, and Nationalism* (London: Verso, 1986). For a fuller survey see Heather Jon Maroney and Meg Luxton, eds., *Feminism and Political Economy: Women's Work, Women's Struggles* (Toronto: Methuen, 1987), 17-19. Mariarosa Dall Costa and Selma James, *The Power of Women and the Subversion of the Community* (Bristol: Falling Wall Press, 1972); Juliet Mitchell, *Women: The Longest Revolution* (New York: Pantheon, 1984). Among the long list of women's movement anthologies that republished Benston's article were *Liberation Now?*, *Roles Women Play*, *Women in a Man-Made World*, and *Feminist Frameworks*. For a recent collection that accents the historical importance of "The Political Economy of Women's Liberation," see Rosemary Hennessy and Chrys Ingraham, *Materialist Feminism: A Reader in Class, Difference, and Women's Lives* (New York: Routledge, 1997).

128 This was remarkably *early* in the history of New Left feminism. In Britain, for instance, the first major conference of New Left feminism was not conceived and organized until 1969-1970.

129 On the context of the SUPA women's statement see Kostash, *Long Way from Home*, 166-171; Owram, *Born at the Right Time*, 272-279. The major document is Judy Bernstein, Peggy Morton, Linda Seese, Myrna Wood, "Sisters, Brothers, Lovers ... Listen," in *Women Unite! An Anthology of the Canadian Women's Movement* (Toronto: Women's Educational Press, 1972), 31-39, which originally appeared as a New England Free Press pamphlet, but see as well Betty Burcher, "'Blue Meanies', Wheelies, Feelies, and Personalist Bullshit," *Praxis*, 2 (March 1969), 15-16, 21. On the Royal Commission on the Status of Women see Barbara M. Freeman, *The Satellite Sex: The Media and Women's Issues in English Canada, 1966-1971* (Waterloo: Wilfrid Laurier University Press, 2001); Cerise Morris, "'Determination and Thoroughness': The Movement for a Royal Commission on the Status of Women," *Atlantis*, 5 (Spring 1980), 1-21. For the New Left/early women's movement critique of the Royal Commission see Jackie Larkin, "Status of Women Report: Fundamental Questions Remain Unanswered," *Canadian Dimension*, 7 (January-February 1971), 6-8.

130 Quoting Nancy Lubka, "The Ins and Outs of Women's Liberation," *Canadian Dimension*, 7 (June-July 1970), 24-29, quoted 25. Lubka drew heavily on Margaret Benston's 1969 essay. For brief accounts of the development of a New Left Women's Liberation Movement see Owram, *Born at the Right Time*, 277-279; Naiomi Black, "The Canadian Women's Movement: The Second Wave," in Sandra Burt, Lorraine Code, and Lindsay Dorney, eds., *Changing Patterns: Women in Canada* (Toronto: McClelland and Stewart, 1993), 154, 164-165, 172; Nancy Adamson, Linda Briskin, and Margaret McPhail, *Feminist Organizing for Change: The Contemporary Women's Movement in Canada* (Toronto: Oxford University Press, 1988), 42-44, 70; and Ian McKay, *Rebels, Reds, Radicals: Rethinking Canada's Left History* (Toronto: Between the Lines, 2005), 192-199.

131 As one woman involved in the McGill Student Movement and women's liberation recalled: "When I entered university in 1966 I rapidly discovered a whole world of rebels and radicals. I

early became interested in Marxism; in particular the 1844 manuscripts, the most humanist writings of Marx, had a profound effect on me." Quoted in Adamson, Briskin, McPhail, *Feminist Organizing for Change*, 41.

132 See, especially, Laurel Limpus, "Liberation of Women," *This Magazine is About Schools,* 3 (Winter 1969), 61-74.

133 Naoimi Black, "Canadian Women's Movement," 154. See also the very helpful overview by Nancy Adamson, "Feminists, Libbers, Lefties, and Radicals: The Emergence of the Women's Liberation Movement," in Joy Parr, ed., *A Diversity of Women: Ontario, 1945-1980* (Toronto: University of Toronto Press, 1995), 252-280.

134 Marlene Dixon, "Why Women's Liberation?" *Ramparts*, November 1969; Dixon, *Things That Are Done in Secret*, 101; Adamson, Briskin, McPhail, *Feminist Organizing for Change*, 43, 49; Chandler Davis, "Hemisfair at Montreal," *Canadian Forum*, 48 (January 1969), 219-220; Mark Rudd, "The Death of SDS," in Dimitri Roussopoulos, ed., *The New Left: Legacy and Continuity* (Montreal: Black Rose, 2007), 84; Kostash, *Long Way from Home*, 184. A useful discussion of women's liberation in Montreal in the 1960s is Mills, "The Empire Within," 228-274.

135 Adamson, "Feminists, Libbers, Lefties, and Radicals," 257.

136 See, for instance, "Pie in the Sky: Royal Commission Recipe," and "Brief to the House of Commons," *Women Unite!* 40-42, 114-120. Much is written on the Royal Commission on the Status of Women (RCSW), which was initiated in 1967, and finally reported in 1970. Conventional understandings of the divergence of liberal and socialist feminists in their perspective on the RCSW have recently been problematized by Mary-Jo Nadeau, "The Making and Unmaking of a 'Parliament of Women': Nation, Race, and the Politics of the National Action Committee on the Status of Women (1972-1992), PhD dissertation, York University, 2005.

137 Such actions in Toronto and Kingston are described in Adamson, "Feminists, Libbers, Lefties, and Radicals," 262-263.

138 Judy Rebick, *Ten Thousand Roses: The Making of a Feminist Revolution* (Toronto: Penguin, 2005), 10-11.

139 The above paragraphs draw on Rebick, *Ten Thousand Roses*, 7-13, 35-46; Adamson, "Feminists, Libbers, Lefties, and Radicals," 263-264; Owram, *Born at the Right Time*, 278; Kostash, *Long Way from Home*, 171-174; Women's Liberation News Services, "University of Toronto Women Win Daycare," *The* Pedestal, April 1970; Donna Cherniak and Allan Feingold, "Birth Control Handbook," in *Women Unite!* 109-113; Adamson, Briskin, McPhail, *Feminist Organizing for Change*, 45-47, 201-202; Frances Wasserlein, "'An Arrow Aimed at the Heart': The Vancouver Women's Caucus and the Abortion Campaign, 1969-1971," MA thesis, Simon Fraser University, 1990; "Abortion March Only a Start," *Last Post*, 1 (April 1970), 4-5. For an early statement on abortion and choice see Myrna Wood, "Abortion and the Liberation of Women," *Canadian Dimension, 5* (June-July 1967), 2. Two recent discussions are Ann Thompson, *Winning Choice on Abortion: How British Columbian and Canadian Feminists Won the Battles of the 1970s and 1980s* (Victoria: Trafford, 2004); and Christabel Sethna and Steve Hewitt, "Staging Protest: The Abortion Caravan, Feminist Guerrilla Theatre and RCMP Spying on Women's Groups," presented at "New World."

140 Kostash, *Long Way from Home*, 179-184; much of the material reprinted in *Women Unite!*; Luxton, "Feminism as a Class Act"; Z. Farid and J. Kuyek, "Who Speaks for Working-Class Women?" *Canadian Dimension*, 10 (June 1975), 80-82; Myrna Wood, "Whatever happened to the women's movement?" *Canadian Dimension*, 37 (September-October 2003), 23-24; Isitt, "Working-Class Agency, the Cold War, and the Rise of a New Left," Chapter 6, 273-279.

141 Adamson, Briskin, McPhail, *Feminist Organizing for Change*, 264-265; Kostash, *Long Way from Home*, 179; Bonnie Kreps, "Radical Feminism," *Women Unite!* 71-75.

142 See, for instance, Marlene Dixon, "Women's Liberation: Opening Chapter Two," *Canadian Dimension*, 10 (June 1975), 56-68; Nadeau, "The Making and Unmaking of a 'Parliament of Women' "; Wood, "Whatever happened to the women's movement?"

143 Kostash, *Long Way from Home*, 101-102; Owram, *Born at the Right Time*, 233-235, 297-298; Ralph Osborne, *From Someplace Else: A Memoir* (Toronto: ECW Press, 2003); Finkel, "Wither Commune—ism,"; Steve Langdon, "C.U.S.," *Canadian Dimension*, 6 (February-March 1970), 6-8.

144 See, for instance, Steve Hewitt, *Spying 101: The RCMP's Secret Activities at Canadian Universities, 1917-1997* (Toronto: University of Toronto Press, 2002), 119-170.

145 Howard Adelman, "A Decade of Protest: Coroner's Report," *Canadian Forum*, 49 (February 1970), 258-260.

146 Irving Layton, "Marxist," *Canadian Forum*, 49 (January 1970), 234.

147 On the limitations and development of gay and lesbian liberation in the 1960s and early 1970s see as introductions only Donald W. McLeod, *Lesbian and Gay Liberation in Canada: A Selected Annotated Chronology, 1964-1975* (Toronto: ECW Press, 1996); Becki L. Ross, *The House That Jill Built: A Lesbian Nation in Formation* (Toronto: University of Toronto Press, 1995); Adamson, Briskin, McPhail, *Feminist Organizing for Change*, 58-74; Gary Kinsman, *The Regulation of Desire: Homo and Hetero Sexualities* (Montreal: Black Rose Books, 1996), 288-293; Deborah Brock, "'Workers of the World Caress': An Interview with Gary Kinsman on Gay and Lesbian Organizing in the 1970s," *Left History Online*, accessed 21 May 2006.

148 I have offered an extended statement on developments in Quebec in Bryan D. Palmer, *Canada's 1960s: The Ironies of Identity in a Rebellious Era* (Toronto: University of Toronto Press, 2009), 311-366. See also Sean Mills, "The Empire Within," which is surprisingly reticent to address the Front de Libération du Québec (FLQ); and Louis Fournier, *FLQ: The Anatomy of an Underground Movement* (Toronto: NC Press, 1984).

Sean Mills

Chapter **4**

Democracy, Dissent, and the City:
Cross-Cultural Encounters in Sixties
Montreal

Neither accident nor coincidence dictated that Montreal become the scene of one of
the most profound, far-reaching, and lasting political revolts in North America during
the 1960s. For in many ways the revolt grew out of specific conditions prevailing in
the city. On various occasions, crowds denounced unequal power relations between
French and English, women and men, Blacks and Whites. A multitude of groups began applying various strands of international theory to their local environment, and
by the second half of the 1960s thousands of artists, intellectuals, union militants
and community activists worked to place their struggles within the larger trajectories of worldwide movements. Propelling much of the political activity of the 1960s
was a complex and often contradictory grappling with the meaning and legacy of empire in Quebec. While the various movements of Sixties Montreal imagined themselves as operating in a larger international sphere, they were also profoundly
shaped by their local environments.

   In this essay, I want to explore how our understanding of Sixties protests in
Montreal changes if we alter our angle of vision, seeing them from the angle of both
the international and the local. Throughout the decade, critiques of global injustice
converged with new understandings of local power relations, and activists opposed
the Vietnam War while others fought for greater control over their communities. After first outlining the meaning of anti-colonial ideas in Quebec in the 1960s, I will discuss three movements that are not generally included in discussions of the 'Sixties' in
Montreal: community organizing in Montreal's working-class neighbourhoods, Black
political organizing, and the women's liberation movement. All three movements, I
will argue, were profoundly shaped both by conceptions of empire and by the spatial
configurations and complex interactions of life in the city.

   It was the idea of Quebec decolonization—first articulated by the Right in the
late 1950s before becoming predominantly associated with the Left by the mid-1960s

—which captured the imagination of a wide array of activists and intellectuals in Montreal.[1] As a political project, decolonization came to mean more than merely achieving political independence; it symbolized a rejection of a habit of passive submission to society's dictates, demanded a democratization of market forces, mobilized poetry and cinema, liberated sexuality, and led to a search for an entirely new way of living and thinking. Yet because of the contradictions inherent in attempting to 'decolonize' the descendents of European colonizers, Quebec's status as a colony was always contested both within the province and by potential sympathizers abroad.

It was in the years following the Second World War that the term 'Third World' first entered popular language, coined by French economist Alfred Sauvy in 1952 with specific reference to the 'Third Estate' of the French Revolution. Like the Third Estate, the Third World seemed poised to take its rightful place in the world.[2] The idea of the "Third World," as Vijay Prashad reminds us, originally referred not to a geographical place, but to a political project of emancipation.[3] Of all the various writers involved in Third World liberation, intellectuals in Montreal looked above all to Albert Memmi, Jacques Berque, Aimé Césaire, Frantz Fanon, and Jean-Paul Sartre. Drawing on these works, many authors sought to understand the power relations which shaped their own society, and they sought to outline the possibilities of deepening democracy.

The dissident energies of the period were fed not only by a wide range of theoretical influences, but also by activists coming from many of the city's different social milieus. For the emerging francophone intelligentsia, the 1960s represented an artistic and cultural renaissance, and poets, filmmakers, artists and writers began creating a new culture of resistance. In *La Revue socialiste*, *Révolution québécoise*, *Socialisme 64...*, and other journals of the kind, intellectuals sought to apply the insights of Fanon, Memmi, Malcolm X, Sartre, and others to the realities of Quebec society. Although many groups and individuals worked to define ideas of Quebec decolonization, *Parti Pris* had the greatest impact on the formation of a larger language of dissent, becoming the epicentre of the bourgeoning attempts to outline the meaning of Quebec liberation. The journal combined literature and poetry with politics and philosophy, and, within its first year of existence, it had expanded to become a publishing house, and, shortly afterwards, a political movement. In its attempt to portray the harsh reality of poverty and cultural degradation in Quebec, it published works written in *joual*, the urban French of east Montreal, and sought to build a literature of struggle. Throughout the decade, many political organizations were formed, from the Rassemblement pour l'indépendance nationale (RIN) to the Mouvement de libération populaire (MLP), and tactics varied from the electoral politics of the Parti socialiste du Quebec (PSQ) to the politically and morally destructive violence of the Front de libération du Québec (FLQ).

For political activists of the Sixties, Montreal was not merely the site of their activism. In the lived and imagined geographies of everyday life, the city, divided into two distinct halves, became a physical manifestation of the colonial relationship which Montreal's radical thinkers attempted to transform. With the largely French-speaking working class living in the neighbourhoods to the east, and the English-speaking middle and upper classes living in the wealthy neighbourhoods to the west, radical francophone theorists began to map linguistic and ethnic identity onto social class, seeing Montreal as a classic colonial city. Yet just as the theorists of national liberation were portraying Montreal as a city of ethnic and linguistic absolutes, these strict divisions were continually being disrupted by the complexities of the interactions of daily life. Montreal is a complicated city and, while power relations between the dominant linguistic groups were (and, to a lesser degree, remain) both real and powerful, the histories of its many different groups and individuals intersect and overlap. If many radicals felt alienated by the segregated nature of the city, they also constructed alternative spaces where debate and artistic creativity could thrive. And in these avant-garde cafés and meeting places Leftists of different political tendencies and linguistic backgrounds interacted, learning from one another in the process.

By the late 1950s a group of important cafés clustered around Stanley, Victoria, and Clark Streets, along with jazz nightclubs on Saint-Antoine, and the Librairie Tranquille, provided spaces where culturally marginalized and anti-conformist thinkers and artists could congregate. In the very early 1960s, many of the city's young francophone bohemian poets, artists, and *chansonniers* began meeting at Le Mas, a third-floor loft on Saint-Dominique St., just above Sherbrooke. In the late-night atmosphere, amidst poetry and music and art, discussion topics increasingly drifted towards the new climate of political rebellion. Situated at the crossroads of different worlds—just one street east of Saint-Laurent, the traditional dividing line between the French-speaking east and the English-speaking west, and in a neighbourhood composed largely of European immigrants and working-class francophones—Le Mas maintained a vibrant dynamism. Politicized francophone artists interacted with the jazz musicians who played throughout the night, and two different expressions of rebellion collided. Although Le Mas closed its doors in the spring of 1962, the political and cultural mixing which occurred in the venue would take place in other cafés, meeting places, and protests in the years to come.[4]

Other cafés—La Paloma on Clark St., just below Sherbrooke—or the Swiss Hut and the Asociación Española on Sherbrooke near Bleury, became meeting spaces for many of the diverse elements of the Montreal Left, including Spanish anarchists who had fled Spain in the aftermath of the Spanish Civil War, anglophone radicals from McGill, and francophone activists. Many of the young radicals gravitating to avant-garde cafés were not only English-speaking, but were also people who emerged from a milieu which was culturally and materially far-removed from francophone Quebec. Yet the world of English-speaking youth radicalism interacted with elements of the progressive francophone community since the beginning of the decade.[5] As the decade progressed, a combination of shared theoretical sensibilities, social preoccupations, and daily interactions of city life ensured that anglophone radicals would become increasingly affected by the political events taking place all around them. By the mid-1960s, *Our Generation Against Nuclear War*, a radical journal based in Montreal, changed its name to *Our Generation* and began focusing on "the total implications of pursuing peace and freedom."[6] Only a few months later it announced an important change in orientation by claiming that, from that moment forward, social developments in Quebec were going to become "a permanent feature of the journal."[7] The following year the journal's editors proclaimed that their most important task was "the fight against continentalism in Canada as well as colonialism in Québec."[8]

If the concept of decolonization inspired hopes and kindled dreams, it was not without its own inner contradictions and ambiguities. For those who had developed their ideas of decolonization in the context of French settler-colonialism in North Africa, seeing White descendents of French settlers claiming to be 'colonized' immediately raised questions. Albert Memmi spoke of being a "bit frightened" by the influence that *The Colonizer and the Colonized* was having on those who were not "well-defined colonized people," like "South Americans, Japanese, Black Americans, and French Canadians." And he "looked with astonishment on all this, much as a father, with a mixture of pride and apprehension, watches his son achieve a scandalous and applauded fame."[9] After taking the time to learn of the situation in Quebec, Memmi did come to accept the legitimacy of the Quebec liberation struggle, although he managed to avoid stating categorically that Quebec formed a colony.[10] Another well-known decolonization theorist who supported the struggle for autonomy and self-determination in Quebec, Islamic scholar Jacques Berque, wrote that Quebeckers, as the "colonized among the colonizers," were entangled in their exceptions and were no longer understood by anyone.[11] Jean-Paul Sartre, for his part, refused throughout the 1960s to believe that Quebec formed a colony, but suddenly changed his mind during the October Crisis of

1970.[12] And Aimé Césaire, Martiniquan intellectual, activist, and poet, recalls his confusion and surprise when he first learned that radical francophone Quebeckers were employing the insights of *négritude* to understand their own identity as the 'colonized.'[13] Because of the ambiguities, challenges, and questions that surrounded Quebec's status in the colonial world, interpretations of decolonization in Quebec were constantly in flux, never settling into a stable interpretation, continuously melting away before they could ossify.

Another problem loomed on the horizon for those who attempted to portray Quebec, and francophone Quebec in particular, as a colonized society. If for the majority of activists in Montreal, 'decolonization' meant Quebec decolonization, this was far from being the only way to conceive either the present or a possible liberated future. Montreal was a city where various understandings of 'empire,' 'colonization' and 'decolonization' collided with one another, becoming the site for not one, but many different movements of resistance. Already in 1965, at the public hearings of the Royal Commission on Bilingualism and Biculturalism, Khan-Tineta Horn pointed out that, from an Aboriginal perspective, French Canadians were far from being Canada's colonized subjects. Rather, she argued, they should be considered "the first invading race."[14] Horn therefore indirectly articulated a critique of the Quebec liberation movement by turning its language back on itself, and by claiming that francophone Quebeckers themselves constituted a colonizing power. At roughly the same time that Horn was defending Aboriginal rights in Quebec, a more sustained alternative understanding of empire, imperialism, and decolonization was being developed by Black Montrealers of West Indian origin who came together to form their own political organizations.[15]

By the late 1960s, critics of the concept of Quebec decolonization abounded. Black and Aboriginal critics questioned its use of racial metaphors, and women began challenging the gendered terms in which it was expressed. Yet it remained that for those attempting to imagine a deeper and more meaningful democracy, it was necessary to engage with a politics of anti-imperialism. By the late 1960s the politicization of new groups and individuals proceeded at a staggering pace. Activists organized in their local communities, created daycares and medical clinics, formed organizations in defence of the rights of tenants and the unemployed. The student New Left became increasingly radicalized, staging a series of student strikes in the fall of 1968.[16] Women challenged the everyday dismissals and devaluation that they experienced in wider society and within organizations of the Left, Black activists challenged racism, and thousands demanded that the economic, cultural, political,

and educational structures be brought under democratic control. Many other movements and organizations emerged, all of which were shaped to at least some degree
by the anti-imperialist and anti-colonial politics of the period. In what remains of this
paper, I want to briefly explore three of these movements. All three were at once
shaped by international conceptions of empire and by specific geographies and locally shared meanings in Montreal.

Citizens' Committees

At roughly the same time that intellectuals and artists were challenging the status quo
prevailing in the province, political ferment was brewing in Montreal's working-class
neighbourhoods. The first citizens' committees emerged in the early 1960s in the
neighbourhoods of Saint-Henri and Pointe Saint-Charles, under the influence of 'social
animators' hired by the Conseil des oeuvres de Montreal. While dissident members of
the Catholic clergy were drawing on France's 'worker-priest' tradition, community activists drew inspiration from Saul Alinsky and his campaigns to organize the poor and
marginalized in American cities.[17] In community publications like Saint-Henri's *Voix
populaire* and, as of 1967, *L'Opinion ouvrière* —a publication read by roughly 20% of the
neighbourhood—the anger and hope of the population was palpable.[18] As the tears
progressed, a whole array of popular institutions began to emerge. In Pointe
Saint-Charles, citizens began organizing consumer co-ops and collective kitchens,
fought for greater community control over streets and schools, and formed organizations to fight landlords and welfare agents. In Saint-Henri, a citizens' bookstore was
opened, and, throughout the city, citizens began to understand not only the structural
roots of poverty, but also their own capacities to act and shape the world around
them.[19] As Mme Gareau of the Hochelaga-Maisonneuve citizens' committee put it,
through community activism, power and authority were not only being demystified,
but also challenged and contested.[20] According to women activists from Pointe
Saint-Charles, grassroots politics help break the isolation of daily life, allowing them to
develop skills and to "assert themselves as people and as women."[21]

All throughout the city, thousands of individuals were rethinking the meaning of
democracy from below. By 1968, radical professionals had joined with community activists to found a network of parallel health institutions, organized and run by citizens.[22] In the impoverished neighbourhood of Saint-Jacques—where thousands of
apartments were without hot water or proper bathing facilities—residents, with the
help of anglophone medical students from McGill, formed a people's clinic.[23] The
clinic's doctors had ideological backgrounds ranging from the CCF to the RIN. Ameri-

cans, anglophone Montrealers, and professionals of Jewish origin not only worked in French, but took directions from the largely impoverished French-speaking residents, and both groups learned from one another in the process.[24] The mixing of people and ideas which characterized the Saint-Jacques clinic were repeated in community groups throughout the city. In the bilingual neighbourhood of Pointe Saint-Charles, tensions between French- and English-speaking activists sometimes surfaced, but they did so in an atmosphere in which the two groups lived and struggled side-by-side.[25] In the downtown neighbourhood of Milton-Park, citizens from across the multiple worlds of political opposition came together to fight Concordia Estates, a real-estate developer that threatened to destroy old houses and put poor people out of their homes. According to Claire Helman, opposition to the project grew out of the neighbourhood, which was "the perfect cauldron for mixing people and their ideas."[26]

The proliferation of citizens' committees throughout the city took place at the same time that the Quebec labour movement was undergoing an important period of radicalization. CSN president Marcel Pepin announced a decisive move to the left with his 'moral report' of 1966, and two years later he launched his famous call to arms, calling on the CSN to open up a 'second front'. Labour activists, he argued, could not restrict their activity to the arena of collective bargaining alone (the 'first front'), as too many aspects of workers' lives could not be dealt with within the confines of collective agreements. Price increases, poor housing conditions, exploitation through credit, unemployment and inflation were all problems that called for the opening up of a new 'second front,' a front in which workers would organize outside of the workplace as consumers, renters, and parents.[27] The new sensibilities of the Quebec labour movement, which began to be articulated in their most radical form by the CSN's Montreal Central Council, converged with those of community activists.

By the late 1960s, the lines separating the many worlds of dissent in Montreal were beginning to blur. Theoretically, community activism drew not only upon Left Catholic traditions, but also on the militant secularism and anti-colonial politics of *Parti Pris*. Organizing in working-class neighbourhoods built upon international movements against imperialism, and activists began making links between the growing opposition to the Vietnam War and the necessity of ending poverty at home. Drawing on images of radicals burning draft cards in the United States, hundreds of Saint-Henri residents marched to a government building on Dorchester Street to burn their cards for unemployment insurance.[28] Léandre Bergeron, one of the most important theorists of Quebec decolonization, first outlined his radical reinterpretation of Quebec history—an interpretation which would later be published as *Le Petit manuel d'histoire du Québec*—at meetings of the Saint-Jacques citizens' committee. When tens of thousands of citizens took to the streets to defend the French language in 1969, among many of the protestors were those who had been organizing in their communities in the preceding years.[29] And when in 1969 a coalition of anglophone and francophone activists organized Operation McGill—an attempt to challenge the dominance of Anglophone capital in Quebec society—the Saint-Jacques clinic set up a temporary medical clinic to help injured protestors. The clinic would do so again at the protest in support of striking *La Presse* workers in 1971.[30]

The convergence of community groups with the larger world of political opposition had its most concrete form in attempts to challenge the entrenched power of Montreal's municipal government. In May 1968, citizens' committees from throughout the city met in Saint-Henri with the intention of exchanging information and developing a common program of action. And, two years later, in May 1970, community activists joined with student radicals, intellectuals, and representatives from Quebec's three main labour unions to found a radical municipal party, the Front d'action politique (FRAP).[31] Despite the eventual unravelling of the FRAP, the community activism which had begun in the 1960s would continue, albeit in different forms, throughout the 1970s and beyond, becoming a permanent feature of the Left and deeply changing the nature of Quebec society.

The Politics of Race

Historical accounts of the 1960s in Quebec have almost completely ignored the experiences of Black Montrealers. Yet, in the spring of 1969, few issues caused more controversy than the actions and thoughts of the city's Black activists and intellectuals. The English-speaking Black population of Montreal numbered somewhere between ten and fifteen thousand people in the mid 1960s,[32] and both a Black presence and a Black resistance to racism stretch back to the seventeenth century. But in the winter of 1968-1969, Montreal, partly through the influence of a small but dedicated group of students from the Caribbean, suddenly became a major centre of Black activism and thought, and Black activists began challenging both the established order and the efforts which had been devised to oppose that order.[33] Black activism in Montreal, moreover, took on unique characteristics by virtue of the specific local environment in which it developed.

The most frequently remembered episode of Black activism in Montreal is the 1969 occupation of the computer centre of Sir George Williams University in response to charges of racism, an occupation which ended with the blows of riot police, $2 million in damage, and 97 arrests. While the Sir George Williams Affair was an important part of the larger story, the entire history of Black activism cannot be reduced to this one event. Before the Sir George Affair, many of the most influential Black intellectuals and activists of the age—Michael X, Walter Rodney, Stokely Carmichael and C.L.R. James—spent time in the city, giving lectures and meeting with students. And after the Sir George Williams Affair, a cultural and political renaissance took place in Montreal's Black community. Many Black activists founded their own independent means of communication, *UHURU*, through which they articulated their own narratives of liberation, their own logic of victim and oppressor, and their own vocabulary of imperialism and decolonization.

Black activism in Montreal had ramifications that spread far beyond the Canadian border, initiating a whole series of political revolts throughout the Caribbean.[34] In Montreal, through the pages of *UHURU*, writers attempted to reclaim Black dignity, to decolonize the mind through a redefinition of 'Blackness,' and to work towards freeing the world's Black population from colonial oppression. For many, the ultimate logic of Black Power led to Pan-Africanism, the belief that the world's Black population should eventually aim to return to a united and socialist Africa.

Reading their local situation through the lens of empire, it did not take long for radical Black intellectuals in Montreal to recognize the plight of Aboriginal Canadians,[35] and, although it took somewhat longer, the legitimacy of the Quebec liberation movement.[36] When Black activists began presenting new narratives of colonization into Montreal's public sphere, their ideas collided with the language of Quebec decolonization already circulating throughout the city. Montreal differed from other North American cities in that radicals of the majority population claimed to be colonized by a foreign power. Unlike Black militants in the United States, Montreal's Black Power advocates were therefore faced with a situation in which many in the White population surrounding them had theorized themselves—drawing on the very same literature of Third World liberation and Black Power—as being culturally, economically, and psychologically dominated by an imperial system of power.

As late as 1968, many Black leaders had greatly resisted acknowledging the legitimacy of the Quebec liberation movement. It is not difficult to understand why. Black people had been enslaved by French colonists from the earliest days of French settlement. They had been subject to the discrimination and racism of French- and English-speaking Montrealers alike, and it is easy to see how the struggle for Quebec liberation, which up until the late 1960s had been predicated on the language of francophone victimization, could be seen to be of little concern to them.

The first opening towards mutual recognition came in 1969, during the lonely days of the aftermath of the Sir George Williams Affair. The Montreal Central Council of the CSN, a nerve centre of radical political activity in Montreal, publicly declared its support for the students, as did authors in the student newspaper at the Université de Montréal, *Le Quartier Latin*.[37]

Black activists in Montreal had always been aware of the local context in which they operated. In the late 1960s, with the political landscape shifting all around them as a result of mass popular upheavals over language rights, they developed an even greater sensitivity to political questions in the city. By 1970, many prominent Black activists were advocating that Blacks learn French, and they were openly supporting the Quebec decolonization movement.[38] Lines of collaboration were also opening up between Black radicals and the radical wing of the Quebec labour movement, which came to give both moral and material support to the city's Black community.[39] By the late 1960s and early 1970s, it was clear that Black activism in Montreal not only formed one part of a larger story of a worldwide diaspora attempting to come to terms with the legacy and present day ramifications of racism and oppression, and it not only formed part of a North American story of Black Power. Black militancy in Montreal had also become deeply rooted in the history of the city itself, and integral to the city's larger political developments.[40]

Women's Liberation

If the language of decolonization developed throughout the 1960s was liberatory in many ways, it remained profoundly circumscribed by the gendered nature of its discourse. Because the new 'subject of history' was by definition male, the new language of dissent had the paradoxical effect of constructing new boundaries of exclusion. By portraying revolution as a hyper-masculine activity, much of the New Left literature served to undermine the very ideals of universal emancipation that it had played such an important role in creating.

But women were involved in the movement from the beginning, and they were well aware of the contradictions of those who preached universal values of equality yet marginalized the women among them. And they began to take action. Ideas of women's liberation first arrived in Montreal on the fertile ground of the city's politically charged English-speaking university campuses. In 1968, the pages of the *McGill Daily*—a paper which was widely read and which acted as one of the most important voices of anglophone student activism—began publishing articles arguing that women's liberation must form part of the larger radical upheaval taking place throughout Montreal.[41] In the fall of 1969, a group of English-speaking university students founded the Montreal Women's Liberation Movement (MWLM).[42] The group's members were deeply shaped by American feminist theory, yet they were also keenly aware of the local political climate in which the English language was being associated with imperial domination. As an English-speaking group in the midst of a French-speaking society, and knowing that their language was associated with social and cultural privilege, members of the group began working to establish contacts with women in the increasingly radical Quebec labour movement. In the meetings and contacts which ensued, anglophone women began talking with francophone women about the possibility of holding an all-women's protest to denounce the city's increasingly repressive political climate.[43] On 28 November 1969, women from different backgrounds took to the streets to defend the right to protest in the city in opposition to a new municipal by-law banning political demonstrations.

The protest marked the first major public demonstration of the nascent women's liberation movement. Two hundred women, many wearing chains to symbolize their oppression, charged out of their meeting-place on Saint-Laurent Boulevard into the middle of the street, where they sat in a circle and waited to be arrested. The hundreds of riot police who were waiting outside proceeded to arrest 165 of the protesters, and, in less than an hour, Saint-Laurent was again open to its regular flow of traffic. In the aftermath of the protest, English- and French-speaking women, in roughly equal numbers, formed the Front de libération des femmes du Québec (FLF), a group which would become the public voice of women's liberation in Montreal.[44]

Montreal's first main voice of women's liberation was formed in a moment of cross-fertilization between English- and French-speaking activists. The mixing of anglophone and francophone women, this merging of different bodies of radical literature, ensured that the movement in Montreal, while forming part of a wider feminist revival that was sweeping cities across North America, remained, in many ways, distinct. From its beginnings, women's liberation in Montreal was a hybrid movement, one which combined the insights of the nascent women's liberation movement in the United States (and, somewhat later, France) with conceptions of decolonization that were being developed locally.

The concept of Quebec decolonization therefore acted as one of the central elements of the ideological foundations for the women's liberation movement. The group's main slogan: 'No liberation of Quebec without the liberation of women, no liberation of women without the liberation of Quebec,' highlighted its belief in the integrated nature of struggle. The group argued that Quebec women were marginalized both as women and as Quebeckers, and that, as a result, their fight needed to be framed in the broad terms of radical humanism and universal emancipation. Their fight was therefore never just about women, or just about Quebeckers for that matter; what was at stake, as one group put it, was "not only our liberation, but also the liberation of all our people, and of all the peoples of the world."[45] Through their activism and writing, women in Montreal worked not only to reconceptualize the place of women in society, but also to broaden Montreal's political imagination, an effort which had the ultimate effect of profoundly altering the city's vocabularies of dissent.

Conclusion

Throughout the late 1960s and early 1970s, Montreal experienced an unprecedented wave of political activism, and the revolts of this period profoundly altered the nature of Quebec society. While not completely disappearing, by the mid-1970s the idea of decolonization had lost its hegemonic ground on the Left. Ideas of decolonization lived on in Quebec throughout the 1970s, but these ideas never again commanded the influence that they did in the late 1960s and very early 1970s. Throughout the decade to come, political activism in Montreal thrived. Thousands of groups and individuals worked to deconstruct and oppose oppression based on gender, race, class, and—an issue which was largely absent from debates on decolonization—sexual orientation.[46] But very few still argued that Quebec was a colony. In 1975, Pierre Vallières, one of Quebec's better-known defenders of the idea of decolonization, was forced to concede to the new line of interpretation prevailing in the province: Quebec did not belong to the Third World, he argued, "but to the privileged West."[47]

The adaptation of anti-colonial ideas to Quebec society was ambiguous and fraught with contradiction. An absence of a reflection about Aboriginals in Quebec society and a reliance on a gendered language of hyper-masculinity significantly limited its scope. Yet the wide variety of social groups which built upon conceptions of decolonization is testament to their appeal and adaptability. All of the various movements that emerged in Montreal were shaped by the daily interactions which occurred in the city's streets and meeting places. Living and working in the same city, and drawing upon and adapting the same ideas, these various groups built on each other's insights, learning from and responding to each other's challenges. Exploring these interactions challenges a simplistic conflation of political ideas with linguistic and ethnic origin, reminding us of the complex ways in which new ideas are forged, challenged, and ultimately displaced.

Notes

1 For an important look at the Right of the Quiet Revolution, see Xavier Gélinas, *La droite intellectuelle québécoise et la Révolution tranquille* (Québec: Les Presses de l'Université Laval, 2007).

2 As Arif Dirlik explains, "Politically, the idea of the Third World pointed to the necessity of a common politics that derived from a common positioning in the system." Arif Dirlik, "Rethinking Colonialism: Globalization, Postcolonialism, and the Nation," *Interventions* 4, no. 3 (2002): 433.

3 Vijay Prashad, *The Darker Nations: A People's History of the Third World* (New York: The New Press, 2007), xv-xvi.

4 For a description of Le Mas and its role in the history of Jazz in Montreal, see John Gilmore, *Swinging in Paradise: The Story of Jazz in Montréal* (Montréal: Véhicule Press, 1988), 209-13.

5 See Simonne Monet-Chartrand, *Les Québécoises et le mouvement pacifiste (1939-1967)* (Montréal: Les Éditions Écosociété, 1993).

6 "Editorial Statement," *Our Generation* 3, 4, no. 4, 1 (1966): 3.

7 "Editorial Statement on Quebec," *Our Generation* 4, no. 2 (1966): 1-2.

8 "Towards a Peace and Freedom Movement," *Our Generation* 5, no. 1 (1967): 5.

9 1965 "Preface" Albert Memmi, *The Colonizer and the Colonized*, trans. Howard Greenfeld (Boston: Beacon Press, 1967), xi.

10 See ———, *Portrait du colonisé. Précédé du Portrait du colonisateur, et d'une préf. de Jean-Paul Sartre. Suivi de Les Canadiens français sont-ils des colonisés?*, Éd. rev. et corr. par l'auteur ed. (Montréal: L'Étincelle, 1972), 7, 144.

11 Jacques Berque, preface to *Les Québécois* (Paris: François Maspero, 1967).

12 During the October Crisis, Sartre argued that it was clear that "the Québécois are not part of Canada, because you are considered to be insurgents and warriors, and then prisoners of war." "Sartre applauds Québécois," *McGill Daily*, 21 January 1971.

13 He would later go on write that even if he still considered it a bit of an exaggeration, Quebec intellectuals had at least understood the concept at a profound level. Aimé Césaire, "Le discours sur la négritude, prononcé le jeudi 26 février 1987," in *Discours sur le colonialisme* (Paris: Présence Africaine, 2004), 81.

14 Canada, Royal Commission on Bilingualism and Biculturalism, "Submission of Miss Kahn-Tineta Horn" *Transcripts of Public Hearings*, 1 December 1965. 4321, 4322, 4323. Seen in Richard Gordon Kicksee, "'Scaled down to size': contested Liberal commonsense and the negotiation of 'Indian participation' in the Canadian Centennial celebrations and Expo '67, 1963-1967" (M.A., Queen's University, 1995), 56.

15 For important insights, see David Austin, "All Roads Led to Montreal: Black Power, the Caribbean, and the Black Radical Tradition in Canada," *Journal of African American History* 92, no. 4 (2007).

16 For an important look at the student movement during the period, see Jean-Philippe Warren, *Une douce anarchie: les années 68 au Québec* (Montréal: Boréal, 2008).

17 For a fascinating look at grassroots activism in Pointe Saint-Charles, see The CourtePointe Collective, *The Point Is... Grassroots Organizing Works: Women from Point St. Charles Sharing Stories of Solidarity* (Montreal: les éditions du remue-ménage, 2006). Also see Donald McGraw, *Le développement*

des groupes populaires à Montréal, 1963-1973 (Montréal: Editions coopératives A. Saint-Martin, 1978), Hélène Pilotte, "Quand les adultes aussi contestent la société: Les comités de citoyens," *Châtelaine*, octobre 1969.

18 See *Les gens du Québec 1, St-Henri*, (Montréal: Éditions québécoises, 1972), 61-6. For a study of one of the most important 'worker priests' of the period, see Martin Croteau, "L'implication sociale et politique de Jacques Couture à Montréal de 1963 à 1976" (M.A., Université du Québec à Montréal, 2008).

19 For the role of women in community activism, see Collective, *The Point Is... Grassroots Organizing Works: Women from Point St. Charles Sharing Stories of Solidarity*.

20 "Le rôle des femmes dans l'animation sociale," *Châtelaine*, juin 1970, 60.

21 ——, *The Point Is... Grassroots Organizing Works: Women from Point St. Charles Sharing Stories of Solidarity*, 161.

22 For a discussion on the development of the community clinic in Point St.-Charles, see Ibid., 91-3.

23 Robert Boivin, *Histoire de la Clinique des citoyens de Saint-Jacques (1968-1988). Des comités de citoyens au CLSC du plateau Mont-Royal* (Montréal: vlb éditeur, 1988), 17-18.

24 Ibid., 32, 53. Also see Bonnie Sherr Klein, "Citizens' Medicine," (Canada: NFB, 1970).

25 See Collective, *The Point Is... Grassroots Organizing Works: Women from Point St. Charles Sharing Stories of Solidarity*.

26 Claire Helman, *The Milton-Park Affair: Canada's Largest Citizen-Developer Confrontation* (Montréal: Véhicule Press, 1987), 30.

27 Marcel Pepin, "The Second Front: The Report of Marcel Pepin, National President, to the Convention of the CNTU, October 13, 1968," in *Quebec Labour: The Confederation of National Trade Unions Yesterday and Today*, ed. Black Rose Books editorial collective (Montreal: Black Rose, 1972).

28 *Les gens du Québec 1, St-Henri*, 76.

29 Ibid.

30 Boivin, *Histoire de la Clinique des citoyens de Saint-Jacques*, 51-60.

31 Ibid., 69-71. On the FRAP, see Marc Comby, "Mouvements sociaux, syndicats et action politique à Montréal: l'histoire du FRAP (1970-1974)" (M.A., Université de Montréal, 2005), Marc Comby, "L'expérience du FRAP à Montréal (1970-1974): La tentative de créer au Québec un parti d'extrême gauche," in *Contester dans un pays prospère. L'extrême gauche en Belgique et au Canada*, ed. Anne Morelli and José Gotovitch (Bruxelles: P.I.E. Peter Lang, 2007).

32 Dorothy W. Williams, *Blacks in Montreal, 1628-1986: an urban demography* (Cowansville, 1989). 65.

33 For the most important works on Black activism in Montreal, see Austin, "All Roads Led to Montreal: Black Power, the Caribbean, and the Black Radical Tradition in Canada.", David Austin, "Contemporary Montréal and the 1968 Congress of Black Writers," *Lost Histories* 1998, Dorothy W. Williams, *The Road to Now: A History of Blacks in Montreal* (Montreal: Véhicule Press, 1997), Dennis Forsythe, ed., *Let the Niggers Burn! The Sir George Williams University Affair and its Caribbean Aftermath* (Montréal: Black Rose Books/Our Generation Press, 1971). Alfie Roberts, *A View for Freedom: Alfie Roberts Speaks on the Caribbean, Cricket, Montreal, and C.L.R. James* (Montréal, 2005).

34 For important insights, see Dennis Forsythe, ed., *Let the Niggers Burn! The Sir George Williams University Affair and its Caribbean Aftermath* (Montréal, 1971).

35 See, for example, "Check Point: Montreal," *UHURU* 1 (12 January, 1970), Ainsley Mark, "Letter to the Editor," *UHURU* 1 (2 February, 1970), Edmund Michael, "'Red Power in Canada'," *UHURU* 1 (29 September, 1969), "Press Release - Project: Think Indian," *UHURU* 1 (8 December, 1969).

36 See, for example, "Editorial," *UHURU* 1 (11 May, 1970).

37 ACSN, CCSNM fonds, Congrès 1969, Fernand Foisy, "Rappord du sécrétaire – décisions du comité exécutif," 19. Roméo Bouchard, "Vous êtes des nègres," *Le Quartier Latin*, 11 février 1969, 2.

38 Rosie Douglas, "The Irrelevance of the Quebec Elections," *UHURU* 1 (27 April, 1970): 6.

39 See, for example, Fernand Foisy, "Rapport du secrétaire" Congrès CCSNM 1970, p. 33. Press release, "Sir George Williams et le cas de Charles Gagnon: les deux masques de la répression", 21 février 1969. ACSN, CCSNM, publications.

40 For an important work which places the struggle of Blacks in Montreal within the local context in which it emerged, see Dennis Forsythe, "By way of introduction: 'The Sir George Williams Affair'," in *Let the Niggers Burn! The Sir George Williams University Affair and its Caribbean Aftermath*, ed. Dennis Forsythe (Montréal, 1971).

41 For examples of radical women writing in the *McGill Daily* in 1968, see Myrna Wood and Marsha Taubenhaus, "The Doll House, revisited: Further notes on the condition of women in our society," *the Review (McGill Daily supplement)*, 22 November 1968, 7, Martine Eloy, "Woman: why is she?," *the Review (McGill Daily supplement)*, 6 December 1968, 5.

42 Martine Lanctôt, "La genèse et l'évolution du mouvement de libération des femmes à Montréal, 1969-1979" (M.A., UQAM, 1980), 52.

43 Ibid., 58. See, also, "F.L.F.Q. Historique" été 1970 *Québécoises deboutte!:* Tome I (Ville Saint-Laurent: les éditions du remue-ménage, 1982), 65.

44 For an important new work on the FLF, see Marjolaine Péloquin, *En prison pour la cause des femmes: la conquête du banc des jurés* (Montréal: Les éditions du remue-ménage, 2007).

45 ——, "Revolution in the Revolution: second manifesto by a collective of women in the Front de Liberation des Femmes Québecoises." Box 31, Montréal, September 1971. p. 1. The Canadian Women's Movement Archives, Ottawa.

46 Few, if any, of the various groups and individuals discussed in this paper had anything substantial to say (during the period) about discrimination against homosexuals. In the early 1970s, the first group defending homosexual rights, the Front de libération homosexual (FLH), emerged. By the time that the homosexual liberation movement achieved more concrete form, both theoretically and organizationally, it was situated in the Marxist language of class oppression. See Roger Noël, "Libération homosexuelle ou révolution socialiste?," in *Sortir de l'ombre: Histoires des communautés lesbienne et gaie de Montréal*, ed. Irène Demczuk and Frank W. Remiggi (Montréal: VLB éditeur, 1998), 189.

47 Pierre Vallières, "Memmi, le Québec, le Tiers-Monde et la sexualité" Reproduced in Pierre Vallières, *Paroles d'un nègre blanc* (Montréal: VLB, 2002), 173.

Marcel Martel

| Chapter 5 | "They Smell Bad, Have Diseases and are Lazy": RCMP Officers' Reporting on Hippies in the Late Sixties[1] |

In 1969, an undercover Royal Canadian Mounted Police (RCMP) officer concluded his report on the Saskatchewan drug scene by stating that "my experience and conclusion of the drug user is that he is slowly destroying [the] society that we have tried to develop and perfect."[2] After spending six months in Toronto's Yorkville neighbourhood and at Rochdale College, another officer wrote that he was "convinced these people do not contribute to the dignity of man and do try to destroy all they can through slothfulness, indolence and eventually violence though the use of drugs."[3] Were these two undercover RCMP officers the only ones to have a pessimistic assessment of the drug scene? Far from it. Their reports are but a small sample of those of the sixty-six officers who were asked by RCMP headquarters to describe the drug reality in Canada at the end of the sixties.

This paper is about RCMP undercover operations among drug users in general, but more specifically among hippies, since these two groups were often conflated in the minds of the RCMP officers who reported on them. It looks at why and how the RCMP conducted surveillance, assembled information on its targets and gave meaning to this social phenomenon. It will in part contribute to the growing literature on state repression. The field of domestic intelligence activities has been investigated by several scholars in the United States, partly because they had earlier access to FBI files through access to information legislation comparatively to Canada.[4] However, a growing body of literature in Canada on state security has analysed surveillance and undercover operations during the post-1945 era by assessing the extent of these activities. In particular, scholars have looked at which individuals, groups and organizations were targeted and how the RCMP Security Service used its expertise in gathering and disseminating information on those targets. Reg Whitaker examined the quality of the intelligence gathered, arguing that the RCMP was becoming better informed, especially in assessing the risks and potential threat posed by nationalist groups in Quebec and the *Front de libération du Québec*. For his part, historian Steve Hewitt has been very prolific. In addition to analyzing the creation of the Security Service and its relations within the RCMP and with the federal bureaucracy, his works have focused on groups targeted by the RCMP, such as university students and more recently women's groups, and depicted the federal law enforcement force as ill-prepared as well as ideologically shaped by Cold War ideas and the fear of communism.[5] By looking at the results of the RCMP's 1969-70 undercover operations among hippies and drug users, this paper sheds some light on how the state responded to the counterculture movement, the drug scene, youth and other social realities of the 1960s.

I argue that collecting information on hippies was a useful weapon in the battle against softening penalties for marijuana offences since the RCMP was among the strongest opponents of legalizing or decriminalizing marijuana for recreational purposes. The RCMP needed to establish an easily recognizable threat in order to rally other groups and individuals who had similar fears and concerns about marijuana use for recreational purpose. Through the process of collecting information on drug users, and then identifying "the hippie" as a drug user, the RCMP was able to successfully depict hippies as a threat, and argue against their cultural, social and political demands on the grounds that this was necessary to preserve society as it was. In the 1960s, the RCMP attempted to prove that deviance and dissent were confined to the small group known as hippies. Since many societal groups were unwilling to embrace the cultural changes proposed by hippies, the RCMP sought to produce evidence that would reinforce the fears of those who were uneasy and anxious about these young men and women with long hair, distinctive clothing and different values and ideals, and then link these fears to the culture of recreational marijuana use.

The first section of this paper provides an overview of the drug issue as defined by the RCMP. The second part looks at the officers who participated in undercover operations and the factors that prompted the RCMP to collect lengthy reports on these operations. I then analyze the main elements of the reports sent to the RCMP Criminal Investigation Branch and draw some conclusions about the objectives of these reports and the manner in which they were used to influence public debate.

Illegal Drug Use: An Ongoing Concern

The *Narcotic Control Act* and the *Food and Drugs Act* constitute the core of Canadian public policy on drugs. Since 1923, marijuana has been an illegal substance in Canada. Under the *Narcotic Control Act*, anyone charged with possession of marijuana faced a maximum penalty of seven years in jail.

Enforcement of Canada's drug laws has been the responsibility of the RCMP since the beginning of the 1920s. During the 1960s, the RCMP approached illegal drug use as a problem and a social threat, as it did in the past. The RCMP's understanding of the drug issue was based on data collected on offences committed under the *Narcotic Control Act* and the *Food and Drugs Act*. In 1969, every sign pointed to a worrisome trend: an increase in the number of individuals charged under federal drug laws. As demonstrated in table 1, offences related to the possession, trafficking and/or cultivation of illegal drugs under the *Narcotic Control Act* and the *Food and Drugs Act* actually remained much less numerous than traffic and property offences between 1968 and 1971. However, the rate of drug offences was increasing more than the rate of other offences.

Table 1 Crimes and Offences Committed in Canada, RCMP jurisdiction, 1968-1971

Years	Murders, Attempts, and Manslaughters	Narcotic Control Act and Food & Drugs Act Offences	Offences Against Property	Sex Offences	Traffic Offences	Other Offences	Total Offences
1968	146 (0.02%)	5,456 (0.75%)	92,838 (12.9%)	1,622 (0.23%)	340,014 (47.3%)	278,551 (38.8%)	718, 627
1969	135 (0.02%)	10,513 (1.29%)	102,605 (12.4%)	1,611 (0.20%)	383,578 (47%)	316,190 (38.9%)	814, 632
1970	183 (0.02%)	18,658 (2.1%)	117,661 (13.6%)	1,652 (0.19%)	402,039 (46%)	328,062 (37.8%)	868, 255
1971	194 (0.02%)	24,019 (2.58%)	125,875 (13.57%)	1,777 (0.19%)	419,215 (45.19%)	356,491 (38.43%)	927, 571

Source: Annual Reports, Solicitor General of Canada

The number of charges against Canadians under the *Narcotic Control Act* for marijuana-related offences such as possession, possession for trafficking, trafficking, cultivation, and importation/exportation, only began to increase in 1965-66.[6] In that year, 162 persons were charged. This figure rose to 398 the following year, and then to 1,678 in 1967-68. This trend continued well after 1968 as demonstrated in table 2. For the RCMP, these arrests represented only the tip of the iceberg. As a result of the force's lack of human resources, many Canadians were not arrested for using illegal drugs. The Commission of Inquiry into the Non-Medical Use of Drugs estimated that about 1.5 million Canadians had used marijuana at least once by the end of the sixties.

Table 2: Number of persons charged under the Narcotic Control Act (marijuana offences)

Years	Possession	Trafficking	Importation	Cultivation, Conspiracy, etc.	Total
1964/65	62	9	1	6	78
1965/66	138	23	1	0	162
1966/67	307	83	6	2	398
1967/68	1,305	362	4	7	1,678
1968/69	2,144	544	17	10	2,715
1969/70	3,539	852	31	28	4,450
1970/71	8,288	1,928	68	101	10,385
1971/72	9,963	1,721	66	135	11,885
1972/73	13,760	2,308	122	108	16,298
1973/74	20,179	2,713	102	177	23,171

Source: RCMP, Proposed Cannabis Legislation Bill S-19, n.d., LAC, MG 32 C 55, vol. 5, file 5/4

The RCMP also compiled data on drug seizures. Until 1966, heroin was the main focus of law enforcement officers. This began to change in 1967-68, starting with a major RCMP seizure of 123.06 kilos of marijuana (table 3).

Table 3: Amounts Seized (in kilograms)

Years	Marijuana
1964/65	1.59
1965/66	2.31
1966/67	24.00
1967/68	123.06
1968/69	388.30
1969/70	280.11
1970/71	1,220.95
1971/72	1,921.90
1972/73	3,967.59
1973/74	8,987.45

Source: RCMP, Proposed Cannabis Legislation Bill S-19, n.d., LAC, MG 32 C 55, vol. 5, file 5/4

Finally the RCMP gathered information on Canadians through its undercover operations and the use of informants. From these data, senior officers concluded that recreational marijuana use had become a major problem, if not an epidemic, in the country.

Having reached this conclusion, the RCMP's main task was to convince elected politicians that they should not make any changes that would weaken the current drug policy. At the same time as the RCMP observed these troubling statistics, a public debate about marijuana questioned whether the repressive approach was the best way to discourage Canadians, especially youth, from using the substance. In response to a call from various activists to decriminalize or legalize marijuana, the Minister of Health and Welfare John Munro and his department's officials entertained the idea of reducing penalties for marijuana offences.

Since marijuana use was a controversial social issue, the federal government appointed the Commission of Inquiry into the Non-Medical Use of Drugs (also known as the Le Dain Commission) in 1969. This signalled to the RCMP that a new battle was about to start, centred on the hearings of the commissioners who would tour the country and invite Canadians to express their views on marijuana and other drugs. The commissioners' conclusions would have the potential to radically alter federal government policy; a change that the RCMP was determined to prevent. In the battle to gain the commissioners' support and continue to have their views shape the policies of the federal government, the RCMP made it clear to the Le Dain Commission that law enforcement was a necessity. It asserted that the legalization or the decriminalization of marijuana had to be rejected outright. In pursuing its objectives, the RCMP paid close attention to the Commission's work.

Undercover Operations

The RCMP had a long history of dealings with drug traffickers and users, and had developed expertise through a combination of surveillance, data collection and information analysis. As Catherine Carstairs and Steve Hewitt note, the RCMP had used undercover agents, informants and other methods in its repression of drug use since the beginning of the 1920s.[7] The shifting profile of drug users in the 1960s posed new challenges for the force, as more and more Canadian youth, in particular university students and members of the middle class, took to using drugs for recreational purposes. The main challenge for the RCMP was to infiltrate these milieus using officers who were not too old and could blend into the drug scene. Any data collected would be handy when the RCMP submitted briefs and other documents to the Le Dain Commission.

The Commission proved unresponsive to early interventions from the RCMP. The RCMP's strategy of depicting marijuana use as a very dangerous practice on the basis of health-related facts proved ineffective with the Le Dain Commission. Moreover, the blunt language used in RCMP statements to the Commission reflected both a strong bias against drug users and negative value judgments of various aspects of the counterculture movement, which raised doubts in the minds of the commissioners. They were not convinced by the RCMP's depiction of the drug scene, the motives that led people to try illegal drugs, or the health and social effects of illegal drug use.

Following meetings with the commissioners in August, September and October 1969, the RCMP reached the conclusion that the only way to shape commissioners' views and prevent any fundamental change to Canada's drugs laws was to share the results of its recent undercover operations. It launched an important project of compiling information on drug users, especially users of marijuana. The federal police force ordered officers engaged in undercover operations to send reports on drug users, youth and hippies.

In conducting this surveillance, was the RCMP acting under strict orders, or did it undertake it at its own initiative? Documents alluding to direct orders from the Solicitor General about these undercover operations, because the RCMP reports to the Solicitor General since 1966, were not found. However, the Commission of Inquiry Concerning Certain Activities of the Royal Canadian Mounted Police (known as the McDonald Commission) offers a possible answer to this question. Despite the fact that undercover operations were of some concern to Canadians, the McDonald Commission stated that these activities constituted "one of the RCMP's most effective investigative techniques [because] undercover operatives can gather more important information than any technical or mechanical source."[8]

Although the RCMP Criminal Investigation Branch orchestrated several undercover operations in its ongoing battle against illegal drugs, why did the RCMP target the hippie milieus? As stated by Hewitt, the RCMP approached the sixties in the ideological context of the Cold War and the division of the world into two camps: communism vs. anti-communism. With the development of the counterculture movement, student activism, feminism, anti-Vietnam demonstrations and other protest groups, the RCMP did what the FBI did by broadening the scope of what it labelled as subversive groups by including any of the following: "black nationalist, student agitator, anarchist, red power advocate, or an associate of communists."[9]

In this context, were drug users a subversive group? Most drug users targeted by these undercover operations were not subversive in terms of planning to overthrow the government or associating themselves with leftist elements. Officers were looking for evidence of illegal drug use and were arresting those involved. However, the RCMP targeted a specific group among drug users: the hippie. Hippies constituted a threat because they challenged morality and established social values with their ideology, lifestyle and values.

Recent literature has shown that the term hippie encompassed a complex and broad social reality since it was used as a category in the sixties to label indistinctly people who wore particular attire, had long hair and in the case of men, had facial hair. Some of these people adopted this lifestyle on a full-time or part-time basis. As opposed to feminist organisations, the *Front de libération du Québec*, and organized student groups, hippies were a loose group of people with no formal structure and no identifiable leaders, although in Yorkville, Toronto, David Depoe was identified by some media as a leader. They gathered and met, often in an urban setting, with other individuals who were eager to "turn on, tune in, drop out."[10] Despite the fact that hippies represented a broad social category, RCMP targeted them in their reports sent to the Criminal Investigation Branch in order to support their battle against the legalization or decriminalization of marijuana. By gathering information on them, the RCMP created a negative public image of hippies. In this war against drugs, it was crucial to put a face on the enemy and hippies became that face through the targeting of their values, lifestyle, behaviour and ideology.

My analysis is based on sixty-six reports that were submitted in late 1969 and early 1970. It is difficult to assess the authors of these reports, since not much was revealed about their identity. Most reports were written by male officers because the RCMP was a male-dominated organization. Although women did work for the RCMP, most were assigned to clerical duties.[11] Only one of the RCMP officers mentioned that he worked with a female officer from the Vancouver city police department. As for ethnicity, only one of the officers noted that he was not Canadian-born (he was born in Britain). Nineteen of the officers who took part in undercover operations belonged to drug squads.

The RCMP reports indicate that undercover operations took place all across Canada. Although there were no reports from Newfoundland and Prince Edward Island, this does not necessarily mean that undercover operations did not take place in these two provinces. Despite the limits of my inquiry, it is interesting to consider a breakdown of these reports by province and city. As indicated in table 4, a breakdown by province reveals that most undercover operations took place in British Columbia, Ontario, Quebec and Saskatchewan. In terms of cities, most undercover operations were in Vancouver, Montreal and Toronto.

Table 4: Number of reports by provinces

Alberta	2
British Columbia	16
Manitoba	3
New Brunswick	2
Newfoundland	0
Nova Scotia	2
Ontario	18
Prince Edward Island	0
Quebec	12
Saskatchewan	11

The duration of the undercover operations varied. The McDonald Commission mentioned that officers in this kind of undercover operation knew that their activity would run for a short time period. Most operations were carried out in 1969, with a few between 1966 and 1968. The shortest undercover operation lasted a mere four and a half days because the undercover agent was discovered, while the longest lasted most than a year, from 1968 to 1969.

Most of the officers were given a similar assignment: to gather information on drug users, the hippie milieu and youth in general in order to collect evidence of the criminal activities of drug users and traffickers. The reports are vague about the specific details of the assignments. One officer worked at a small university in the Maritimes, probably St Francis Xavier; another worked near a "large university campus' in Montreal, a third was a waiter at a beer parlour in British Columbia, while a fourth worked at the Aldergrove Rock Festival in British Columbia.[12]

Some officers included observations on the difficulty of their task. An undercover agent who worked in Quebec City, Montreal and Ottawa stated that the most important challenge was to be accepted by hippies and other drug users. "Once you are accepted, they begin to trust you."[13] In a published account of their work, Constables Stewart Brown and Raymond Cardinal mentioned that they earned the nicknames of "Tonto" and "Lone Ranger," which they interpreted as a clear sign of acceptance from those who were under their scrutiny.[14] But not all officers succeeded; among them, an undercover officer who worked in a small university in Nova Scotia mentioned that hippies were "distant with strangers" and believed that "Narcotics Agents [were] everywhere." Consequently, they were "suspicious of strangers." His undercover operation in another city was unsuccessful since he was unable to infiltrate a hippie milieu.[15] Since not all undercover officers were accepted, it was clear that hippies and others had developed resistance strategies. Securing trust, mastering drug street jargon, and blending in were a challenge. Some officers met hippies while others were not welcome as the new "kids on the block" because of rumours of undercover police activities and informants.

Did these undercover officers commit unlawful acts in order to gain or maintain the trust of targeted groups? Not much was said in the reports about this. For some, it meant being under pressure to try drugs.[16] As revealed by the McDonald Commission, undercover officers who were asked to smoke marijuana or use other drugs were instructed "to simulate the act where possible or, if necessary, refuse the drug and pass it on."[17] For many, the most difficult part of their assignment was compromising their personal hygiene, which meant abandoning their strictly disciplined world. An officer who worked in Vancouver in 1969 wrote that "after spending a week without changing, I made a comment that I wouldn't mind a bath and a clean shirt. My friend's reply to this was, "I haven't had a bath, nor a clean shirt for six weeks."[18] Another officer who worked in Ottawa added that he "slept on the floor of a garage for two weeks without getting out of my clothes, or washing them, and the blankets which we used to sleep under were dusty and dirty."[19]

Were these assignments physically dangerous? In most reports, it seems that this was not the case, since no one wrote that they feared for their lives. Yet many had to deal with the fear that their cover would be blown and they would be subject to retributions such as beatings.[20] One agent talked about the psychological pressure that he dealt with. Reflecting on his experience and what his female partner went through, a Vancouver undercover officer stated that the "mental pressure' was great because "the world we were entering was so unreal and unbelievable." This pressure could be explained by the fact that he and his female partner had their cover blown. "We were called "Finks" (persons working for the police), and threats of bullets in our heads commenced."[21] Another officer mentioned that he was discovered and some wanted to kill him. "I later learned that they contemplated giving me a large overdose of LSD in my food or drink, but were talked out of it by an informant."[22]

Before undertaking their operations, did officers receive any specific training? The RCMP had courses on various aspects of drug enforcement, but most reports are silent on this aspect. One officer mentioned that he received two weeks of training and another trained for a month, but neither provided any details. If the formal training was limited, officers had to become familiar with the language of these milieus.

In their published account of undercover activities in Vancouver, constables Brown and Cardinal had to assimilate drug street jargon such as "speed" (methamphetamine), "narcs" (drug squad men), "nickel or dime bags" ($5 or $10 purchases of marijuana), "stuff" or "junk" (heroin), "up tight" (frightened), "fix," "score," hit" and so on.[23]

Updating the Drug Narrative: Hippies Are the New Threat

The RCMP had been collecting information on drug users since the 1920s. As revealed by Catherine Carstairs, police reports were used by prosecutors in courts or passed on to journalists or other parties interested in the repression of drug use. By doing so, the RCMP played "a critical role in constructing the 'image' of the drug user."[24] In the sixties, reports submitted by officers addressed specific aspects of the drug scene, but few officers made clear distinctions among drug users, hippies, youth in general, dropouts and other groups. American draft dodgers and deserters were not mentioned, except in one report. Although their comments referred to all these different groups, one group in particular was targeted: hippies.

RCMP officers targeted hippies because of the very nature of their assignments, which involved entering that subculture. Furthermore, they had to go through a physical and clothing transformation in order to look like hippies. It is not surprising that their reports contain so much information on this specific group. Finally, in the context of the battle against marijuana, opponents constructed their narrative of drug use around the image of the hippie. The RCMP officers targeted those who were identified with the counterculture movement, new lifestyles and new values—all issues that divided Canadians.

The officers were given specific guidelines on how to write these reports. Undercover officers were to report on the following aspects of their subjects: 1) "general appearance"; 2) "health and sanitation"; 3) "living habits"; 4) "criminal or violent tendencies as revealed by specific acts or conversations"; 5) "their aspiration in life"; 6) "their inclination toward physical efforts"; 7) "philosophy of their being"; 8) "their consideration for their fellow man, particularly whether they would induce other persons to their way of life"; 9) "their attitudes towards education, politics and religion"; 10) "their attitude towards the state"; 11) "their attitude to family and their attitude to sex"; and 12) "their inclination or otherwise to matters other than drugs."[25] These twelve items can be reduced to four categories: appearance, criminal behaviour, goals and values, and attractiveness to others. All these categories relate to aspects of hippie lifestyles.

Dirty and Smelly Hippies

The first three items in the reports deal with issues such as general appearance, health, and living habits. RCMP officers' descriptions of drug users focused on hippies. According to the officers, hippies had long hair and facial hair (beards, moustaches, sideburns). They wore blue jeans, shirts or t-shirts with bright or "flashy"[26] colours or floral prints, hats, cowboy boots or sandals, or were barefoot. Some wore military shirts, coats or jackets, "love beads" or medallions. Female hippies, the reports noted, wore clothes similar to those of their male counterparts and often did not wear bras.

Invariably, officers referred to personal hygiene, often emphasizing that hippies had "not taken a bath for several weeks."[27] An officer who worked in Yorkville in 1966 said that "most of these people wore the same clothing for the six months that I knew them."[28] Most officers could not restrain themselves from making value judgments in their descriptions of physical appearance and clothes. Words and expressions such as "dirty," "sloppiness," "unclean," "unkempt," "bad breath, teeth and body odour" and "clothes barely washed" were used by officers in their descriptions of drug users, hippies and other youths without making any clear distinction between these individuals. An officer learned (to his horror) that females used "newspapers for sanitary napkins."[29] An undercover officer who worked in Ottawa in 1968 concluded that hippies chose to be dirty because of their "laziness."[30]

This emphasis on cleanliness was likely part of a strategy of dehumanizing these individuals. As studies on poverty and the state response to the poor have demonstrated, civil servants would often investigate and comment on the lack of cleanliness as a way for justifying their policies of social control.[31] In the case of hippies, RCMP officers wanted to undermine their social appeal, particularly by revealing what the police considered the disturbing implications of the cultural changes that hippies wanted to introduce: being or becoming dirty. At the same time, this insistence on cleanliness played well into the anxiety expressed by elites and other Canadians towards youth and hippies. While some hippies and youth were dirty, the RCMP's general statements applying to everyone under investigation offered nothing reassuring about these dirty individuals.

In fact, hippies embodied the polar opposite of police officers' training and prescribed general appearance. Assuming that the investigating RCMP officers belonged to the same age group as most hippies, the latter constituted a cultural shock and also reinforced what RCMP officers were trained for: to maintain order, discipline, and clean-shaven appearance. For these officers, love of self required a clean appearance and physical fitness. Certainly the general appearance of hippies revealed a lot about them and RCMP officers wanted to emphasize it in order to counter any sympathy the public could have for hippies.

From time to time some officers would remind their superiors that not all hippies fit these descriptions. By pointing to differences among hippies, the few RCMP officers who did so indicated the flaws in the questionnaire, since they had been sent to observe, infiltrate and interact with young people, drug users, hippies and others. In reminding their senior officers that they were differences among hippies, they highlighted the fact that they had been asked to construct a general "portrait" of what was in fact a heterogeneous group. Some drug users did not have long hair. They were clean and they did not wear old and sloppy clothes. Others were only part-time drug users, known also as "weekenders," who kept their hair long enough to be welcomed by hippies, but at the same time not too long to risk their jobs. "A lot of them take pride in their cleanliness, especially of their hair."[32] Senior RCMP officers used the reports to reinforce the narrative about "dirty hippies" and the voices that insisted on the heterogeneity of the group under scrutiny were mostly ignored.

Many officers went beyond commenting on cleanliness to detail the hippies' poor health and malnourishment. They argued that hippies chose malnourishment in order to satisfy their appetite for drugs. Except for a few cases, most officers did not distinguish between individuals who were addicted to hard drugs such as heroin and suffered from malnourishment because of their addiction, and regular or occasional users of soft drugs who did not suffer this fate. Some officers even speculated about their subjects' mental health. For instance, an undercover officer who worked on weekends for six months in the Niagara Falls area wrote about addicts and narcotic users, and argued that the mental "ability is virtually non-existent" in marijuana and LSD users.[33]

The section in the report about health provided an opportunity to raise serious concerns about hepatitis, venereal diseases and suicides. Living habits were deemed responsible for the propagation of hepatitis since hippies and other youths lived in close proximity, sometimes in communes, and shared many possessions.[34] As for venereal diseases, the lifestyle embraced by hippies and their followers was again blamed since free love and promiscuity meant picking up sexually transmitted disease.[35] Finally, drug use was blamed for suicides, although no data were provided to support this assertion.[36]

When RCMP officers used this section of their reports to raise awareness about illnesses, it played well into fears that unfolded in Toronto in August 1968 and received a great deal of publicity. At one point, authorities encouraged people to avoid the infected area. As revealed by Henderson's study, the 1968 hepatitis scare in Yorkville contributed to the fall of the area as a center of hippie life, while at the same time comforting those who were uneasy about this group. Rumours of illnesses spread by hippies in Yorkville confirmed that repression was in order.[37]

It was the same fear of death that was attached to illegal drug use, notably LSD. Likewise, suicide as a sensationalist way of dying also captured media attention since people were debating the health consequences of illegal drug use.

The physical description of the places inhabited by drug users, and especially hippies, revealed the revulsion felt by officers. In addition to their comments on the lack of furniture and the few mattresses used as beds, the reports focussed on the lack of cleanliness in these places. Terms such as "filthy" and "slums" were used to describe apartments or houses where hippies and their friends lived. Among the details provided by officers were descriptions of these places as slums, full of domestic garbage and populated by rodents, dogs and cats. Pet excrement was often all over the place. Dishes were unwashed, beds were not made, and floors were not swept. Bathrooms were often the most disgusting room in the house or apartment. Two undercover officers who worked in Calgary summarized the hippies' living habits by stating that they "live in houses and apartments resembling "pig pens" with an accumulation of garbage and rubble throughout. In one particular house there was a toilet which had overflowed and it appeared there had been no effort to rectify the situation."[38]

Assuming that the descriptions were accurate, few officers took the time to wonder why hippies (and other young people, since they were, after all, a heterogeneous group) would choose to live in such abject conditions. For many officers, dirty houses and apartments went hand in hand with sloppy hippies. Since hippies were dirty individuals, their living quarters reflected their general appearance. In fact, most officers had neither the skills nor the training to conduct sociological inquiries. They were sent to observe, look for criminal behaviours, and report on them. All the non-criminal comments about these people revealed more about the values and judgments of RCMP officers than inquisitive minds trying to understand these groups and capture the nuances among those they were sent to observe. However, one undercover officer who worked in Winnipeg challenged the narrative that slums were the normal living conditions of hippies, observing that they often had no choice but to live in rundown places because of their limited financial resources.[39]

Criminal Behaviour

One might reasonably assume that the inclusion of a section about crime and violence was intended to demonstrate that criminality extended beyond drug use in these communities. However, this criterion created some difficulties. Most reports stated that hippies did not have violent tendencies, although two undercover officers noted that possession of illegal drugs was a criminal offence in and of itself.[40] Consequently, it was difficult to establish a link between hippies and violence.

Even without direct evidence of violent acts committed by hippies, undercover officers insisted that they had witnessed violence anyway. They did it by broadening their definition of hippies to include individuals such as drug users, drug traffickers, and other youths. It allowed them to state that there were criminal activities going on such as shoplifting, breaking-and-entering and other thefts, such as leaving a restaurant without paying. An officer who worked for two months in Kamloops wrote that he did not witness any crimes but he "was told on a number of occasions of persons named to [him] who committed such offences as assault and various sexual offences, under the influence of drugs."[41] Why were these crimes committed? According to these officers, drug users needed money to satisfy their drug needs. Others claimed that violence and criminal behaviour could occur among drug traffickers and hard drug users, although reports were often short on supporting evidence.[42]

Although evidence of physical violence by hippies and drug users was rare, some officers referred to verbal threats against police, informants and undercover officers to make the case that hippies and drug users had violent tendencies. An undercover officer who worked in Yorkville in 1967 stated that he heard people "talking about killing policemen and assaulting people, or committing other offences." Although most officers believed that these were empty threats, one who worked in Toronto for five months disagreed, stating that "I have every reason to believe they would carry out their threats."[43]

There was one notable dissenting voice among the sixty-six officers who submitted reports. Reflecting on his experience and the verbal violence that he was subjected to when he was dressed as a hippie, an undercover officer in Winnipeg felt that youth often became violent because of how society treated them. "By letting my hair grow and wearing old clothes while undercover, I felt that the middle and upper class people thought of me as "scum" (…) I feel that a person who was without money and had to live in this environment for a period of time would turn on the common world and rebel for the rest of his life."[44]

Appalling Goals, Questionable Values, and Undesirable Social Expectations

RCMP officers had several sections in which they could describe hippies' goals, aspirations, values and attitudes toward education, established Churches, the state, family, and sexuality. These sections reveal a lot about what the RCMP considered legitimate aspirations, values and social expectations.

The word "none" succinctly summarizes the answer that most officers gave in assessing the life aspirations of drug users. They observed that people under surveillance had no daily routine and no regular schedule other than to take drugs, have sex, and promote their lifestyle. Many insisted on the fact that they lived day to day. An officer summarized the aspiration of hippies as "having a good time."[45]

Most officers depicted people under investigation as lazy and without inclination to physical work, unless they needed money to satisfy their drug needs, in which case they would get a job that lasted only long enough to earn the required money. An undercover agent who worked in Vancouver in 1968 had strong views on this issue: "I have never seen a true 'Hippie' doing an honest day's labour for his pay. Begging on the streets and selling the *Georgia Straight* paper seems a lot easier."[46] Some of the hippies lived off welfare cheques, prompting strong condemnations from officers who depicted them as parasites.[47] While noting that some hippies hoped to own a farm and grow marijuana,[48] a number of officers used the opportunity to ridicule hippies and their philosophy. Two other undercover officers concluded that drug users and hippies were dangerous because "by using drugs and disobeying laws they [would] also change things."[49]

Some reports made a distinction between "full-time" hippies and weekenders. Although the officers did not use harsh words to describe the weekenders' employment patterns, they deplored this choice of lifestyle anyway.

These negative comments on the part of RCMP officers reflect what Tom Lutz calls a "culture's repertoire of feelings about work." Since police officers valued work, the anti-work ethic rhetoric was very disturbing for them and triggered emotional and negative reactions.[50] However, one officer from British Columbia wondered if the lack of clear aspirations could be explained by the age of the drug users and hippies, since those he interacted with were teenagers still confused about their long-term goals.[51]

Furthermore, officers highlighted the fact that people under investigation did not follow any religion because they did not go to established churches. An officer who spent six months in Yorkville wrote: "I have never seen any of them going to church or even saying they were going."[52] It appeared that hippies rejected Christian institution-alized forms of worship. This was worrisome for officers who believed that attending church was the appropriate practice. But did hippies really become atheists or did they embrace other forms of religious belief? Some officers acknowledged that some hippies embrace other religious beliefs such as Buddhism or other Eastern religions.[53]

Participation in the political realm drew similar reactions. What RCMP officers considered to be proper political behaviour, such as voting and being engaged in the appropriate public issues, was rejected by hippies and their followers. An officer who worked in Yorkville in 1967 summarized the views on hippies expressed by many fellow officers: "They had no interest in sports, and they never talked about things normal people talked about. Their interests were the Vietnam War, sex and drugs, etc."[54] Hippies, their followers and other young people embraced issues such as the Vietnam War, amendments to drug laws or socialism. This focus prompted one officer to vent his frustration towards the broader society and how it handled its youth. "It seems to me that we are supporting a group of individuals whose political beliefs can only harm our country, should they get the means and the organization to become an influential force."[55] One of the officers who worked in Quebec identified the emergence of the "separatist problem" in that province as another worrisome issue.[56]

In his attempt to make sense of the youth rebellion, an undercover officer who worked in Kamloops, Kelowna and Vernon for ten weeks made a distinction between hippies and youth. Hippies, he said, rejected materialism and conformity because their prime concern was "their own happiness and freedom." Young people, on the other hand, were "in pursuit of fun and adventure, rebelling against their parents and other symbols of authority."[57]

Hippies opposed the state and its representatives, including police officers. They rejected authority and anyone who was symbolized it. Here is how an officer revealed his disdain for these attitudes: "They have no respect for the betterment of modern society and only criticize instead of working to improve it."[58]

Many officers who commented on the relationship of hippies with their families judged it negatively. According to them, hippies came from unhappy and/or divorced families and their family background explained their troubled behaviour. Others rejected their parents because they were authority figures.[59] Sometimes officers blamed parents for giving up on their parental responsibilities. They did not hesitate to hold them responsible for the drug problem since they did not stop their kids from using.[60]

Value judgments and unease about the sexual revolution and the redefinition of families surfaced as well. In the context of the Cold War and efforts to "reassert gender and sexual 'normality,'" officers used this rubric to denounce and condemn behaviours that were abnormal because they were "outside the 'normal' (...) social fabric."[61] Most officers concluded that hippies and their followers had a liberal attitude towards sexual relations. Was this liberalism welcomed by these officers? For most, the answer was no. Expressions such as "moral decay of one society," "free love without marriage," "loose morals," "little signs of morality," or "immoral attitude towards sex," were used to denounce the sexual revolution and liberal attitudes towards sexuality. One officer insisted that "some of the sexual acts [were] very perverted and on occasions, involve[d] their own children." Another questioned the meaning of love since hippies talked a lot "about sex but very little ... about love."[62] However, some officers offered a different perspective on sexual relations. One of them, who worked in a small university town in Nova Scotia for five months, stated that many individuals talked about sex but not much was happening.[63]

In his paper on the RCMP and the drug war in the 1920s and 1930s, Hewitt mentioned that officers paid attention to how women were treated by drug users, but also to the negative impact that drug use had on women's respectability. In the 1920s, "the image of the ultimate symbol of middle-class Anglo-Celtic masculinity, the Mounted Policeman, leading a moral crusade against hated and evil Asiatics, had a powerful resonance in Anglo-Canadian society."[64] The idea of the police as enforcers of the moral order was still present in the sixties. RCMP undercover officers had little respect for hippies since they did not comply, among other things, with the standard model of the male breadwinner. Moreover, officers felt that they had the higher moral ground when they commented on women's sexuality and how male drug users, hippies and drug traffickers treated their female companions. They accused the lazy, smelly, and disease-carrying hippies of sexually abusing women. They were "not ashamed to make love anywhere, especially while under the influence of drugs."[65] Others gave drugs to women before having sex with them.[66] At the same time, they asserted that some women would do anything to gain access to drugs, including sleeping with the first man they encountered. Consequently, sexual liberation—a motto used by the group under investigation - meant sexual exploitation in the eyes of the RCMP. The reference to "talk[ing] a lot about sex but there was little love" played well with those outside of the hippie and youth world who were uneasy about the sexual revolution. Officers argued that venereal diseases were a consequence of the sexual revolution, and that women were in danger of becoming prostitutes, incapable of finding true love, especially in the hands of drug traffickers willing to do anything to get money. Where fear of catching venereal diseases was not enough of a scare, some officers stated that many women as young as fifteen had sex under the influence of drugs.[67]

In his analysis of Yorkville, Stuart Henderson points out that, over time, many male hippies and other youth acknowledged their inability to fully understand the emergence of feminism and their casual attitudes towards women and sexuality. Furthermore, newspapers, politicians and other opponents to marijuana spread a narrative that insisted that hippies perceived women as easy sexual prey. Women were victims and unable to resist sexual advances by men. They became victims because of drugs that transformed them into sexual toys in the hands of male hippies eager to drug their victims and take advantage of them. Consequently, observations by RCMP officers reinforced the narrative of women as victims of drug male hippies.[68]

The officers' discourse on sexuality went beyond blaming young men and women. Some officers found evidence of mothers who were unable to assume their motherhood role. Two reports noted cases of mothers neglecting their young infants. In Vancouver, an officer wrote about a 16-month-old baby girl neglected by her mother. The baby was often stoned because she inhaled the marijuana smoke.[69]

The issue of homosexuality also surfaced in some reports. Some officers concluded that drug use sometimes triggered homosexual relations, which constituted a challenge to family values and "normal" sexuality. An officer posted in New Brunswick claimed that one man used LSD and became a homosexual. However, he specified that he "was not sure if it was due to LSD because he didn't have much contact" with him.[70]

The comments on goals, values and institutions reveal what the RCMP disliked about hippies. RCMP officers disclosed their disdain for individuals who did not believe in education since they themselves had to complete at least eight years of education before joining the force. Since 1944, potential RCMP recruits had to provide information about their family background, work experience, interests, activities, hobbies, inclination for sports, and ability to comply with RCMP training and discipline. The RCMP was also sending some officers to universities to improve their educational background. Hippies values differed from those held by RCMP officers since their lifestyles and attitudes were totally different. Hippies, unlike RCMP officers, did not have rules to follow, did not respect authority and did not have to go through a formal "training."[71]

Inducing Others to Become a Hippie

This section played on the fear that surrounded the discussion of drug use. In addition to concerns about drug addiction, there was the fear that drug users wanted to attract others to their lifestyle. The RCMP reports offered no reassurances to those who were already worried.

The police reports concluded that hippies and their followers were not inclined to help anyone except those who joined their movement. In their testimonies, officers argued that drug traffickers, drugs users and hippies did not care for others, but rather took advantage of them by selling them bad drugs and preying on innocent victims and women. This attitude constituted a societal danger since their goal was to seduce many into their way of living.[72] An officer who spent six months in Yorkville wrote that "these people lie, cheat and steal for their own gain, which always involve drugs, as they are interested in nothing else. They turn in members of their own cult for reasons of jealousy or money." Another reached similar conclusions: "They live immoral lives and they are unwilling to accept responsibilities of any kind. They have no pride in themselves and no consideration for their fellow citizens of Canada."[73] Or "[the] drug user will also induce young school children into the drug scene, in order that he may sell drugs to them and help him support his own habit."[74] Some officers made a distinction between hippies and drug traffickers and stated that the latter did not show consideration for other human beings since their goal was to sell as many drugs as possible.[75]

Besides the danger of "contamination" and propagation, young people observed by undercover officers constituted a threat because society was losing potentially valuable members. A drug user was "harming society in that he is depriving the community of what intellect or potential merit he has to offer."[76] If the federal government chose to legalize marijuana, it "would be the downfall of many young people in Canada."[77] Reflecting on his undercover operation, an officer alerted his superiors to the reality that "without regard to their ages, the entire group was unpredictable, unreliable and irresponsible and have an undesirable influence on an appreciable portion of our youths."[78]

Reflections on the RCMP Drug Narrative

Mary Louise Adams reminds us that efforts to construct normality during the Cold War era emphasized "appropriate gender roles" for men and women. Men would learn about their obligation to be breadwinners while women would learn to be good homemakers. Youth were also targeted since they were a source of social anxiety.[79]

In the sixties, some youths became active, militant and critical of social values and expectations. As a subset of youth, hippies captured media attention and were a source of social anxiety because of their lifestyle, cultural practices, values, ideals and demands. Given the context, the reports to the Criminal Investigation Branch from RCMP officers further fuelled this anxiety. These officers displayed a strong personal animosity toward hippies. Hippies, their behaviour, clothing, and other attributes were considered repulsive for their potential to corrupt impressionable youth.

Gathering information and reporting on the hippie phenomenon was not exceptional in the sixties. As Hewitt's studies of RCMP activity on university campuses have revealed, the force was very active and extended to attending meetings of the "Learned Societies." Since writing reports was part of the institutional culture, the reports on the Learned Societies, according to Hewitt, were "simply a case of reporting the facts with brief speculation occasionally thrown in,"[80] while in the case of hippies and drug users, comparable reports contained strong value judgments, depicting a bleak future for Canadians if hippies and their followers rose to positions of authority in society.

With these reports, the RCMP was able to update its drug narrative. The threat affected society at large because youth, the future leaders, were taking drugs. Two undercover officers who worked in Yorkville assessed the threat that drugs posed to young people as "one of the greatest problems we are faced with today," because they were "destroying themselves both physically and mentally."[81] Since marijuana use put its users in a "dreamy state of mind," there was a real danger that the entire society would wallow in a similar state if the marijuana habit became mainstream.[82]

RCMP officers believed that they had an obligation to send strong warnings about drug use and that their role was to prevent any attempts to accommodate hippies and their followers, especially their demands to liberalize drugs laws. Without providing much evidence, some officers concluded their reports by stating that marijuana was the gateway drug to heroin.[83] An undercover officer who worked in Toronto in 1967 insisted that "in most cases we must stop thinking of these people as young innocents, and start thinking of them as people who ignore the law and cause misery to others."[84]

This description of a bleak future was based on observations of various groups who were labelled as hippies. There was a notable lack of nuance in the information-gathering process that led to this dismal picture. Not much attention was paid to class, ethnicity, frequency of drug use, addiction levels, and other variables that might have produced a more complete image. Notably absent were direct references to ethnic groups, visible minorities, rural Canadians and anyone above 30 years of age. But hippies were an easy target, since social responses to them were already mixed. The RCMP's views of hippies, shared with the Le Dain Commission and other groups, increased the cause for concern of those with mixed opinions about this social cohort.

The RCMP drug narrative has some commonalities with the FBI, since it was shaped by work done by its American counterpart. In the sixties, student organizations, anti-war movements, and New Left groups were investigated by the FBI in order to assess the dangerousness of these groups. For instance, FBI undercover officers insisted in their reports that New Left activists neglected their "personal cleanliness, use[d] obscenities (…), publicized sexual promiscuity." These reports reflected the views of J. Edgar Hoover (first Director of the FBI), who argued in a May 1968 memo that "every avenue of possible embarrassment must be vigorously and enthusiastically explored."[85]

From time to time, some RCMP officers would dissent from the official drug narrative. Although most reports had a tendency to classify all drug users as hippies, some insisted on the diversity of the youth population. They discovered that there were several groups of drug users who had little in common with hippies. In fact, hippies were but one group among many others, such as youth delinquents, runaway adolescents, drug traffickers, members of biker groups, and youth in general. Even within the hippie groups, there were "true" hippies, part-time hippies who often had full-time jobs, and weekenders. On the issue of general appearance, officers reported to their superiors that the appearance of individuals varied according to their class origins, as young people from rich families tended to dress better. Others stressed the fact that some young people kept in touch with their families, especially if financial or legal assistance was required.[86] Some were tempted to conclude that the youth problem was temporary and would vanish because young people either matured or abandoned drug use "as the novelty wears off and [they] begin to know reality."[87]

Overall, the RCMP drug narrative did not integrate these dissenting voices. In the official documents and communications, such as the second brief submitted to the Le Dain Commission in March 1971, the RCMP had a clear message: drugs and in particular marijuana were dangerous.

Conclusion

The RCMP reports present us with a worrisome depiction of the drug scene at the end of the 1960s. They are filled with references to diseases, abject living conditions, and drug use. However, no clear distinctions were made among drug users. Who were the drug users? How many were there in Canada during this period? Were some ethnic groups more affected than others? What drugs did they use? How often did they use drugs? How many were addicted to drugs? Which behaviours could be attributed specifically to occasional drug users and which to regular use? Which behaviours were typical of drug addicts and marijuana users? The reports offered an incomplete portrait of drug users. Furthermore, the tendency to use the term "hippie" when "drug trafficker" was the more appropriate term was a clear indication that the RCMP's main priority in producing these reports was to reinforce its strategy of depicting hippies as a dangerous threat.

Although RCMP undercover officers reported on a variety of groups, including regular drug users, drug addicts, youth, part-time drug users, drug traffickers and hippies, it was the last group that dominated the reports. Why did RCMP undercover officers focus on hippies? The force engaged in a political and ideological battle to prevent the legalization or decriminalization of marijuana. It was critical to make the key elements of the battle accessible and comprehensible to Canadians. As the most easily identifiable group of drug users, hippies were a useful tool used by the RCMP in its campaign to demonize drug use. The RCMP's scare tactics were used in its presentations to the Le Dain Commission and various newspapers, while also providing ammunition to groups opposed to marijuana use. This drug narrative of the dangers of marijuana use was also routinely presented to politicians who were under pressure to take action on the marijuana issue.

The gathering of data on its citizens has accompanied the development of modern states. This has taken several forms, such as census data. In the case of the RCMP focus on hippies, it was noteworthy that the data were based on observations in the context of undercover operations, as part of a drug repression strategy, without any scientific basis. Since the RCMP was engaged in a cultural war with proponents of the counterculture movement, collecting data about them was crucial since this information became an ideological weapon. The fact that many hippies were not drug addicts did not matter to the RCMP. It was imperative that the force offer a clear picture of proponents of the drug revolution and what it would mean for society if drug users were successful in their demands. By depicting hippies in a negative way and casting them as stereotypical drug users, all drug use could be targeted and cast in a similarly negative light. According to the RCMP, hippies smelt bad, carried diseases, were lazy, and had no benevolent inclinations towards others except to attract others to their lifestyle, philosophy and cultural revolution. What good would be accomplished by legalizing marijuana, an important element of the hippie "platform of cultural and political change" if it meant validating the unpleasant hippie lifestyle? The society that RCMP officers wished to "perfect" would go into reverse gear.

It is ironic that the hippies' plea for changes in the drug laws was turned around by the RCMP as a reason in itself not to change drug laws. The RCMP effectively played on the anxieties expressed by groups towards hippies. It provided evidence, reassured those who felt uneasy about young people and their demands, and gave fresh ammunition to those who wanted to prevent changes to drug laws.

This episode is revealing when we compare the construction of the drug narrative of the sixties with earlier ones. A target had to be found. In the past, the drug issue was defined as a racial threat since drug users were associated with specific ethnic groups. In the context of the sixties, hippies became an identifiable group and the RCMP used them in its efforts to prevent change to drug laws. By making hippies a social threat, the RCMP added them to an increasingly long list of undesirables that included Leftists, homosexuals, trade union leaders, and members of the Black Power, Red Power and Quebec separatist movements.

Notes

1 An earlier version of my article was given at the New World Coming Conference, "The Sixties and the Shaping of Global Consciousness," Queen's University, Kingston, Ontario, June 2007. I want to thank Matthew Hayday, Colin Coates, and the anonymous readers of the *Canadian Historical Review* for their useful comments, suggestions and advice.

2 Report from Lloydminster, Saskatchewan, 20 October 1969, Library and Archives Canada (LAC), RG 18, volume 4833, file GC 310-10 supp B, vol. 2

3 Report from Toronto Drug Section, 7 November 1969, LAC, RG 18, volume 4833, file GC 310-10 supp. B, vol. 1.

4 Ward Churchill, *Agents of Repression: The FBI's Secret War against the Black Panther Party and the American Indian Movement* (Boston, South End Press, 1988); David Cunningham, *There's Something Happening Here. The New Left, The Klan, and FBI Counterintelligence* (Berkley, University of California Press, 2004); J. K. Davis, *Assault on the Left. The FBI and the Sixties Antiwar Movement* (Westport, Connecticut, Praeger, 1997); Martin A. Lee, *Acid Dreams: The CIA, LSD, and the Sixties Rebellion* (New York, Grove Press, 1985).

5 Steve Hewitt, *Spying 101. The RCMP's Secret Activities at Canadian Universities, 1917-1997* (Toronto, University of Toronto, 2002); Steve Hewitt, "Reforming the Canadian Security State: The Royal Canadian Mounted Police Security Service and the 'Key Sectors' Program," *Intelligence and National Security* 17, no. 4 (winter 2002): 165-184; Steve Hewitt and Christabelle Sethna, "Sex Spying:

The RCMP Framing of English-Canadian Women's Liberation Groups during the Cold War," paper presented at the *Debating Dissent: Canada and the Sixties Workshop Program*, Fredericton, University of New Brunswick, August 2008; Contributions of Steve Hewitt, Christabelle Sethna and Terry Pender in Gary William Kinsman, Dieter K. Buse and Mercedes Steedman (eds.), *Whose National Security? Canadian State Surveillance and the Creation of Enemies* (Toronto, Between the Lines, 2000): 91-109, 110-120, 121-128; Patrizia Gentile and Gary Kinsman, " 'Fiabilité,' 'Risque' et 'Résistance': Surveillance au Canada des homosexuels durant la Guerre froide," *Bulletin d'histoire politique* 16, no. 3 (printemps 2008): 43-58; Larrry Hannant, *The Infernal Machine: Investigating the Loyalty of Canada's Citizens* (Toronto, University of Toronto, 1995); Daniel J. Robinson and David Kimmel, "The Queer Career of Homosexual Security Vetting in Cold War Canada," *Canadian Historical Review* 75, no. 3 (1994): 319-345; Reg Whitaker, "Apprehended Insurrection? RCMP Intelligence and the October Crisis," *Queen's Quarterly* 100, no. 2 (Summer 1993): 383-406.

6 From 1946 to 1961, marijuana-related offences constituted 2% of all drug arrests. Catherine Carstairs, *Jailed for Possession. Illegal Drug Use, Regulation, and Power in Canada, 1920-1961* (Toronto, University of Toronto Press, 2006): 68.

7 Carstairs, *Jailed for Possession…*; Steve Hewitt, "While Unpleasant it is a Service to Humanity: The RCMP's War on Drugs in the Interwar Period," *Journal of Canadian Studies/Revue d'études canadiennes* 38, no. 2 (Printemps 2004 Spring): 80-104.

8 Commission of Inquiry Concerning Certain Activities of the RCMP, *Freedom and Security under the Law* (Ottawa, Second report, volume 1, 1981): 292.

9 Hewitt and Sethna, "Sex Spying…": 4. Cunningham argued that, in the United States, the FBI defined New Left supporters as subversive groups because they promoted new values that constituted a challenge to the status quo. Consequently, the main objective was to eliminate this subversive threat. Cunningham, *op. cit.*

10 Frédéric Monneyron and Martine Xiberras, *Le monde hippie. De l'imaginaire psychédélique à la révolution informatique* (Paris, Imago, 2008); Stuart Henderson, "Toronto's Hippie Disease: End Days in the Yorkville Scene, August 1968," *Journal of the Canadian Historical Association*, New Series. 17, no. 1 (2006): 205-234; David S. Churchill, "An Ambiguous Welcome: Vietnam Draft Resistance, the Canadian State, and Cold War Containment," *Histoire sociale/Social History*, 37, no. 73 (May 2004): 1-26.

11 Hewitt and Sethna, "Sex Spying…": 7.

12 Report from Halifax, 9 October 1969, LAC, RG 18, volume 4833, file GC 310-10 supp. B, vol. 1; Submission from Montreal, 13 November 1969, LAC, RG 18, volume 4833, file GC 310-10 supp. B, vol. 1; Report from Regina Drug Section, 13 November 1969, LAC, RG 18, volume 4833, file GC 310-10 supp. B, vol. 2; Report, No date, LAC, RG 18, volume 4833, file GC 310-10 supp B, vol. 2.

13 Report from Montreal Drug Section, 10 November 1969; Report from London Detachment, 12 November 1969, LAC, RG 18, volume 4833, file GC 310-10 supp. B, vol. 1.

14 F. G. Kilner, "Undercover Operation," *The RCMP Quarterly* 34, no. 3 (January 1969): 6.

15 Report from Halifax, 9 October 1969, LAC, RG 18, volume 4833, file GC 310-10 supp. B, vol. 1.

16 Report from Swift Current, 10 November 1969, LAC, RG 18, volume 4833, file GC 310-10 supp B, vol. 2.

17 McDonald Commission Report: 308.

18 Report from Saskatoon, 13 February 1970, LAC, RG 18, volume 4833, file GC 310-10 supp. B, vol. 1.

19 Report from Drug Squad in Ottawa, 24 November 1969, LAC, RG 18, volume 4833, file GC 310-10 supp B, vol. 2.

20 Report from Ottawa, 7 November 1969, LAC, RG 18, volume 4833, file GC 310-10 supp B, vol. 2.

21 Report from Vancouver, 6 November 1969, LAC, RG 18, volume 4833, file GC 310-10 supp B, vol. 2.

22 Report from Swift Current, 10 November 1969, LAC, RG 18, volume 4833, file GC 310-10 supp B, vol. 2.

23 McDonald Commission: 299; F. G. Kilner, "Undercover Operation": 6.

24 Carstairs, *Jailed for Possession…*: 93.

25 Report from Montreal Drug Section, 13 November 1969, LAC, RG 18, volume 4833, file GC 310-10 supp. B, vol. 1.

26 *Ibid.*

27 *Ibid.*

28 Report from Toronto G.I. Section, 10 November 1969, LAC, RG 18, volume 4833, file GC 310-10 supp. B, vol. 1.

29 Report from Montreal Drug Section, 18 November 1969, LAC, RG 18, volume 4833, file GC 310-10 supp B, vol. 2.

30 Report from Ottawa, 7 November 1969, LAC, RG 18, volume 4833, file GC 310-10 supp B, vol. 2.

31 See Margaret Hillyard Little, " 'A Fit and Proper Person": The Moral Regulation of Single Mothers in Ontario, 1920-1940," in Kathryn M. McPherson, Nancy M. Forestell, and Cecilia Louise Morgan., *Gendered pasts. Historical Essays in Femininity and Masculinity in Canada* (Don Mills, Ontario, Oxford University Press, 1999): 123-138.

32 Report from Vancouver, 17 November 1969, LAC, RG 18, volume 4833, file GC 310-10 supp B, vol. 2; Similar comments in report from the Vernon Detachment, British Columbia and report from the Chilliwack Subdivision, 7 November 1969, LAC, RG 18, volume 4833, file GC 310-10 supp B, vol. 2.

33 Report from Hamilton, 22 October 1969, LAC, RG 18, volume 4833, file GC 310-10 supp. B, vol. 1.

34 Report from Montreal, 13 November 1969; Report from Toronto Drug Section, 7 November 1969, LAC, RG 18, volume 4833, file GC 310-10 supp B, vol. 1.

35 Report from Montreal Drug Section, 18 November 1969, LAC, RG 18, volume 4833, file GC 310-10 supp B, vol. 2.

36 Report from Prince Rupert, British Columbia, 17 November 1969; Report from North B'ford City Detachment, Saskatchewan, 10 November 1969, LAC, RG 18, volume 4833, file GC 310-10 supp B, vol. 2.

37 Henderson, "Toronto's Hippie Disease…,": 205-234.

38 Report from Calgary Drug Section, 24 October 1969, LAC, RG 18, vol. 4831, file GC 310-10 (1969) part 1; Report from Saskatoon, 11 February 1970, LAC, RG 18, volume 4833, file GC 310-10 supp B, vol. 2.

39 Report from Winnipeg Drug Squad, 21 November 1969, LAC, RG 18, volume 4833, file GC 310-10 supp B, vol. 2.

40 Report from Chilliwack Subdivision, 7 November 1969, LAC, RG 18, volume 4833, file GC 310-10 supp B, vol. 2.

41 Report from the Vernon Detachment, British Columbia, LAC, RG 18, volume 4833, file GC 310-10 supp B, vol. 2.

42 Report from Winnipeg Drug Squad, 8 October 1969, LAC, RG 18, volume 4833, file GC 310-10 supp. B, vol. 1.

43 Report from Toronto Drug Section, 7 November 1969, LAC, RG 18, volume 4833, file GC 310-10 supp. B, vol. 1; Report from Parksville, British Columbia, 17 November 1969, LAC, RG 18, volume 4833, file GC 310-10 supp B, vol. 2.

44 Report from Winnipeg Drug Squad, 8 October 1969, LAC, RG 18, volume 4833, file GC 310-10 supp. B, vol. 1.

45 Report from the London Detachment, 12 November 1969, RG 18, volume 4833, file GC 310-10 supp. B, vol. 1.

46 Report from Vancouver, 14 November 1969, LAC, RG 18, volume 4833, file GC 310-10 supp B, vol. 2.

47 Report from Vancouver, 17 November 1969, LAC, RG 18, volume 4833, file GC 310-10 supp B, vol. 2.

48 Report from Saskatoon, 13 February 1970, LAC, RG 18, volume 4833, file GC 310-10 supp B, vol. 2.

49 Report from the Chilliwack Subdivision, 7 November 1969, LAC, RG 18, volume 4833, file GC 310-10 supp B, vol. 2.

50 Tom Lutz, *Doing Nothing. A History of Loafers, Loungers, Slackers, and Bums in America* (New York, Farrar, Straus and Giroux, 2007).

51 Report from Prince George, British Columbia, 13 November 1969, LAC, RG 18, volume 4833, file GC 310-10 supp B, vol. 2.

52 Report from the Toronto Drug Section, 7 November 1969, LAC, RG 18, volume 4833, file GC 310-10 supp. B, vol. 1.

53 Report from the Chilliwack Subdivision, 7 November 1969, LAC, RG 18, volume 4833, file GC 310-10 supp B, vol. 2; Report from Ottawa, 17 November 1969, LAC, RG 18, volume 4833, file GC 310-10 supp B, vol. 2. On the issue of hippies and religion, see Bruce Douville, " 'And We've Got to Get Ourselves Back to the Garden': The Jesus People Movement in Toronto," *Historical Papers. Canadian Society of Church History* 19, (2006): 5-24.

54 Report from the Toronto Drug Section, 7 November 1969, LAC, RG 18, volume 4833, file GC 310-10 supp. B, vol. 1.

55 Report from Cranbrook Detachment, British Columbia, 14 November 1969, LAC, RG 18, volume 4833, file GC 310-10 supp B, vol. 2.

56 Report from Montreal, 13 November 1969; J.G. St Denis referred to the emergence of separatism without associating the term problem, Report, 10 November 1969, LAC, RG 18, volume 4833, file GC 310-10 supp. B, vol. 1.

57 Report from Lillouet, British Columbia, 13 November 1969, LAC, RG 18, volume 4833, file GC 310-10 supp B, vol. 2.

58 Report from Prince Rupert, British Columbia, 17 November 1969, LAC, RG 18, volume 4833, file GC 310-10 supp B, vol. 2.

59 Report from Hamilton, 22 October 1969, LAC, RG 18, volume 4833, file GC 310-10 supp. B, vol. 1.

60 Report from Swift Current, 10 November 1969, LAC, RG 18, volume 4833, file GC 310-10 supp B, vol. 2.

61 Gary Kinsman, "The Canadian Cold War on Queers Sexual Regulation and Resistance," in Richard Cavell ed., *Love, Hate, and Fear in Canada's Cold War* (Toronto, University of Toronto Press, 2004): 114.

62 Report from Montreal, 13 November 1969, LAC, RG 18, volume 4833, file GC 310-10 supp. B, vol. 1; An officer who was involved in an undercover operation in Kamloops mentioned that there was no interest in marriage, No date, LAC, RG 18, volume 4833, file GC 310-10 supp B, vol. 2.; Report from Calgary City Police Department, 5 November 1969, LAC, RG 18, volume 4833, file GC 310-10 supp. B, vol. 1; Report from the Winnipeg Drug Squad, 8 October 1969, LAC, RG 18, volume 4833, file GC 310-10 supp. B, vol. 1; Report from the Owen Sound Detachment, 30 October 1969, LAC, RG 18, volume 4833, file GC 310-10 supp. B, vol. 1; Report from Lloydminster, Saskatchewan, 20 October 1969, LAC, RG 18, volume 4833, file GC 310-10 supp B, vol. 2; Report from Saskatoon, 13 February 1970, LAC, RG 18, volume 4833, file GC 310-10 supp B, vol. 2; Report from Vancouver, 14 November 1969, LAC, RG 18, volume 4833, file GC 310-10 supp B, vol. 2.

63 Report from Halifax, 9 October 1969, LAC, RG 18, volume 4833, file GC 310-10 supp. B, vol. 1.

64 Hewitt, "While Unpleasant it is a Service to Humanity…,": 88.

65 Report from Vancouver, 17 November 1969, LAC, RG 18, volume 4833, file GC 310-10 supp B, vol. 2.

66 Report from the Drug Squad in Ottawa, 24 November 1969, LAC, RG 18, volume 4833, file GC 310-10 supp B, vol. 2.

67 Report from the Montreal Drug Section, 18 November 1969, LAC, RG 18, volume 4833, file GC 310-10 supp B, vol. 2.

68 Stuart Henderson, *Making the Scene. Yorkville and Hip Toronto in the Sixties*, manuscript: 471 sheets.

69 Report from Saskatoon, 13 February 1970, LAC, RG 18, volume 4833, file GC 310-10 supp B, vol. 2; Report from the Cranbrook Detachment, British Columbia, 14 November 1969, LAC, RG 18, volume 4833, file GC 310-10 supp B, vol. 2.

70 Report from Chatham, New Brunswick, 23 October 1969, LAC, RG 18, volume 4833, file GC 310-10 supp. B, vol. 1.

71 Nora H. Kelly and William Kelly, *The Royal Canadian Mounted Police. A Century of History. 1873-1973* (Edmonton: Hurtig Publishers, 1973): 105-117.

72 Report from the Chilliwack Subdivision, 7 November 1969, LAC, RG 18, volume 4833, file GC 310-10 supp B, vol. 2.

73 Report from the Toronto Drug Division, 7 November 1969, LAC, RG 18, volume 4833, file GC 310-10 supp. B, vol. 1.

74 Report from North Battleford City, 11 February 1970, LAC, RG 18, volume 4833, file GC 310-10 supp B, vol. 2; Similar claim made by an officer from Kamloops, Report from the Vernon Detachment, British Columbia, LAC, RG 18, volume 4833, file GC 310-10 supp B, vol. 2.

75 Report from the Montreal Drug Section, 12 November 1969, LAC, RG 18, volume 4833, file GC 310-10 supp. B, vol. 1.

76 Report from Montreal, 13 November 1969, LAC, RG 18, volume 4833, file GC 310-10 supp. B, vol. 1.

77 Report from Hamilton, 23 October 1969, LAC, RG 18, volume 4833, file GC 310-10 supp. B, vol. 1.

78 Report from the Cranbrook Detachment, British Columbia, 14 November 1969, LAC, RG 18, volume 4833, file GC 310-10 supp B, vol. 2.

79 Mary Louise Adams, "Margin Notes: Reading Lesbianism as Obscenity in a Cold War Courtroom," in Richard Clavell ed., *Love, Hate, and Fear in Canada's Cold War* (Toronto, University of Toronto Press, 2004): 142.

80 Steve Hewitt, "Intelligence at the Learneds: The RCMP, the Learneds, and the Canadian Historical Association," *Journal of the Canadian Historical Association*, New Series, 9 (1998): 273.

81 Report from the Toronto Drug Section, 7 November 1969, LAC, RG 18, volume 4833, file GC 310-10 supp. B, vol. 1.

82 Report from the Montreal Drug Section, 18 November 1969, LAC, RG 18, volume 4833, file GC 310-10 supp B, vol. 2.

83 Report from the Montreal Drug Section, 13 November 1969, LAC, RG 18, volume 4833, file GC 310-10 supp. B, vol. 1.

84 Report from the Toronto Drug Section, 10 November 1969, LAC, RG 18, volume 4833, file GC 310-10 supp. B, vol. 1.

85 Davis, *Assault on the Left...,*: 46-47; Cunningham, *There's Something Happening Here...,:.* 92-100.

86 Report from the Montreal Drug Squad, 12 November 1969, LAC, RG 18, volume 4833, file GC 310-10 supp. B, vol. 1; see report from the Calgary City Police Department, 5 November 1969, LAC, RG 18, volume 4833, file GC 310-10 supp. B, vol. 1; Report from the North B'ford City Detachment, Saskatchewan, 10 November 1969, LAC, RG 18, volume 4833, file GC 310-10 supp B, vol. 2.

87 Report from Prince Albert, 24 October 1969, LAC, RG 18, volume 4833, file GC 310-10 Supp. B, vol. 2; Report from the Winnipeg Drug Squad, 21 November 1969, LAC, RG 18, volume 4833, file GC 310-10 supp B, vol. 2.

John Cleveland

Chapter	"Berkeley North": Why Simon Fraser Had

Chapter 6

"Berkeley North": Why Simon Fraser Had the Strongest 1960s Student Power Movement

The student power movement at Simon Fraser University (SFU), in the greater Vancouver area of British Columbia, was the strongest in 1960s English Canada by any measure: more students were mobilized and more power was won. This fact was universally recognized at the time as indicated by the decision of the 1968 conference of the Canadian Union of Students (CUS), the national English-Canadian federation of student associations, to adopt the 'SFU model' as the approach for all other campuses to emulate.

Why were SFU student radicals more successful both in mobilizing the mass of students and in winning decision-making power? To answer that question I employ the logic of comparing and contrasting cases to identify factors that were uniquely present (or absent) at SFU compared to other campuses. The comparisons are based on a detailed analysis of the contents of student newspapers on five campuses in different regions of English-Canada in the six academic years 1964-65 to 1969-70 (Dalhousie-King's, McGill, Toronto, Regina and Simon Fraser). This is supplemented by information on other campuses from the Canadian University Press (CUP) dispatches in the same period. I also draw on interviews with former student leaders and participant observation knowledge as a student activist from 1962 to 1966 at Dalhousie-King's, CUS organizer in 1966-67 and activist at SFU from 1967-70.

The answer lies in two major factors that distinguished SFU from all other cases. First, the Simon Fraser movement achieved more of a collective 'we' feeling in the student body than elsewhere by employing more participatory democracy structures for mobilization than other campuses did. They were also more consistent in demanding, winning and implementing more participatory forms of democratic power than others were. Arguably one might object that these factors are really symptoms of a movement that is more effective at mobilization and winning democratic power, too closely connected with what we are trying to explain to be treated as clearly distinct causes. This cannot be argued for the second factor which can be seen to be a set of structural realities that underlie the first: the weaker institutionalization of status differences at SFU, especially between faculty and students, which had a whole series of effects that gave students more leverage in winning battles with university authorities and created more space for participatory democracy.

The argument which follows begins by getting more specific about instances of the two main causes of SFU's relative success—more participatory democracy in means employed and ends sought and a weaker institutionalization of the power of faculty as a professional group over students. Next the baseline to which SFU is to be compared is sketched by providing a short overview of the overall 1960s student movement in English Canada. Finally we examine the four major conflicts that occurred at SFU and demonstrate how the two factors operate in each of them.

Weak Faculty Power at an Instant University

Simon Fraser was an 'instant university.' The right-wing populist Social Credit government, governing British Columbia since the Second World War as a merger of political forces to keep what the Socreds called the "socialist hordes" of the CCF-NDP opposition out of government, had underfunded higher education in what had been in the 1940s and 1950s a boom and bust blue collar natural resource extracting province. In the spring of 1963, Premier WAC Bennett appointed Gordon Shrum, the chair of BC Hydro and former physics head and graduate studies dean at the University of British Columbia, as chancellor of the new university and told him he wanted it operating within two years. SFU opened in September 1965.

Shrum personally organized the recruitment of faculty as well as the building of buildings. As the Canadian Association of University Teachers (CAUT) report of 1968 later asserted, in the first years SFU was to a significant degree operated as a quasi-"feudal" fiefdom of Gordon Shrum and the Board of Governors he dominated. Shrum also dominated the university president, Patrick McTaggart-Cowan, who was a former student of Shrum's and was treated like a subordinate. The CAUT Report also noted that McTaggart-Cowan had failed to act consistently as the representative of faculty and of autonomous faculty bodies to the Board and chancellor, acting instead more like the representative of the Board and Shrum back to the faculty or at best as an ineffective mediator between the two. Rather than being or appearing 'feudal' as the CAUT would have it, it is more accurate to say that SFU was structured so as to lay bare the fact that it was, like all modern universities, a capitalist corporation. It was operated by a system of professional collegiality but oriented to serving the interests of state and capital, what Clark Kerr referred to as a "multiversity." In most universities the existence of professional 'faculty power' masks this fact. At SFU the domination of the university by a group of mainly corporate lawyers and representatives of big business on the Board was highly visible, especially because they repeatedly and sometimes clumsily intervened to make decisions normally worked out in the modern university among senior faculty in faculty bodies and academic administrator posts.

The day to day academic decisions were made in the early years by a committee of heads, all recruited and appointed by chancellor Shrum, instead of chairs and deans elected or selected by collegial professional procedures. The Senate was made up mainly of administration, heads, appointed deans and lay representatives. Most important of all the Board did not agree with faculty on a system of hiring, firing, tenure, rank and promotion until forced to by the mobilization of faculty and students in the 1968 'CAUT crisis.' As a result there was a very underdeveloped status hierarchy among faculty. The large majority of faculty had neither rank nor tenure: in early 1968, only 77 out of 311 faculty had rank (33 full professors, 44 associate) with 160 classified as assistant professors and 74 as instructors with no agreed upon procedure for getting tenure protection.

In the absence of strong faculty-run departments and Faculties or even a faculty-controlled Senate independent of the Board and appointed heads, faculty ended up meeting together to deal with their differences with the Board outside the standard professional structures dominated by the higher ranks and divided by discipline and Faculty in other universities. In periods of conflict all faculty met together in a body called Joint Faculty which in effect was a kind of participatory democracy for faculty with no clearly defined leadership besides the Faculty Association executive—debate and decision-making took place in long plenary sessions of the whole faculty so that faculty ended up debating, deciding and acting as one with majority rule by the rank and file of faculty regardless of rank or discipline. Because of the Board's refusal to agree to a tenure system, the left faculty formed a Faculty Union in 1967 to challenge the perceived failure of the Faculty Association executive to stand up to the Board and by early 1968 had recruited over one third (120) of faculty into its ranks. This created a strong if still very much minority left bank within faculty and Joint Faculty meetings—its core was those without rank or tenure in the Arts Faculty. The graduate students organized a TA union which challenged the Graduate Student Association as the representative of their interests to the administration after the Board tried to fire five Teaching Assistants in the spring 1967 'TA incident' for off-campus political agitation. This forming of significant numbers of faculty and teaching assistant employees into unions was another sign of the very explicit feeling among many that the university was a corporation in which faculty were treated by a capitalist employer as employees rather than independent professionals and TAs were cheap labour with the justification that they were merely students getting a stipend instead of a salary and negotiated working conditions.

On top of all this, a large proportion of the unranked and untenured faculty were young—many were only ten years or so older than the youngest undergraduates and even closer in age to the graduate students and older undergraduates. The usually highly organized and institutionalized status barriers between faculty and students—and, equally important, among faculty—typical of the modern university were weak at SFU at least up until the end of 1968.

The fact that SFU was an instant university also had an impact on the nature of the student body and the (relative absence of) status hierarchies among students. Simon Fraser was set up very openly to be the university of the more working class Eastern side of Greater Vancouver. It is likely that most students were middle class or higher but there was a significant leavening of students from working class homes —the student newspaper record shows that there were battles among students in the early period over the attitude to take towards strikes and trade unions but the view that triumphed among the majority was clearly pro-labour. There were no professional faculties of medicine or law or engineering at SFU which typically provided the mass base for careerist pro-establishment conservative students at other universities of the period. Nor was there any existing entrenched student government and clubs elite.

Indeed there was no student government at all when SFU opened. Students had to create their own institutions from the ground up. In the first month two student papers competed, a mainly progressive one and a more conservative one, the latter aided by funding from administration sources. In a move that was to be typical of what followed, the two groups agreed that it was up to the student body to decide by a meeting, debate and vote. No such formal process occurred but the two papers, left and right, merged in order to create a paper that would serve the whole student community. With the exception of one semester in summer 1968, the editor of The Peak was never a radical and often was a self-described "conservative." However, the student paper consistently backed and promoted the student power movement and even treated the radical student groupings as a left flank within "our" movement to be criticized for its tactics but not its goals or demands. This process may also reflect on the class and status background of the student body as well as the influence of the broader political culture in the province. Unlike many other campuses, conservative students were as likely to be Socred right-wing populists as Liberal or Conservative parliamentary democracy elitists (the latter existed and were to spearhead the 'moderate' Student Councils that worked against student power especially after June 1968, revealingly by attacking the alleged excesses of participatory democracy—but they were still forced to allow mass student assemblies to continue to be the site of student debate and decision-making in periods of high conflict). Students who might be liberals elsewhere saw themselves as falling into the other camp in the provincial political culture, the 'socialist hordes' broad labourist left. Both 'left' and 'right' students quickly agreed that to build a "community" at Simon Fraser, both a student community seeking student power and a student-faculty community sharing power in order to build a "first-rate university" on the East side of town, the entire community had to be sovereign and had to debate and make all important decisions in mass meetings of the community.

In the first week students went about creating what they hoped would be an innovative style of student government by holding a mass student assembly in the open air mall at the physical center of the campus between the library, cafeterias, administration building and entrance to the Academic Quadrangle classroom and faculty offices building. It would be the site of much of the debate and action over the next five years. Some 250 students picked names out of a hat to choose a steering committee to draft a constitution. Various models were proposed and furiously debated in a series of mass meetings. Some proposed a parliament, others a United Nations. Finally a more conventional student association was created with a representative democracy Student Council but with one important difference. The mass membership meeting was to be sovereign, not just a place where Student Council decisions could be challenged and force Council to reconsider (as was the case for example at McGill and the University of Toronto) but a site for debating policies and making final decisions that overruled any decision of Council.

There were many other signs of a consensus across political lines (excepting the relatively weak non-populist establishment right) on the need to build a community through participatory democratic means. Despite repeated efforts by representatives of the UBC fraternities, supported by SFU athletes from the athletic scholarship built major sports teams and by a smallish group of students from more socially or political establishment family back grounds, the student body voted repeatedly to ban fraternities from recognition or support. The clinching argument was that the frats would create an elitist private community that would undermine the single public one. As early as 1966, while other student councils raised student fees in order to create a student owned and operated Student Union Building with the argument that it would strengthen student autonomy (the result being to make the Council a business with a significant student bureaucracy), Simon Fraser Council opted for an administration-funded Longhouse that would be equally open to faculty and students.

The insistence on building an inclusive community (which at various points was also extended to include non-management university employees, exemplified in the student support of employee strikes and unionization but also by the decision of the Political Science, Sociology and Anthropology or PSA department in 1969 to grant voting rights to their secretaries on some issues as well as voice and vote in some committees and in general assembly meetings) also meant a consensus among students against any signs of faculty acting like a professional caste apart. Separate faculty elevators had the lock-key mechanism soldered shut and the university president responded by opening the elevators to everyone. Left and liberal faculty set up an unofficial food committee in the first weeks together with students who had begun to use pressure tactics (pickets, a sit-in and boycotts as well as meetings with cafeteria employees to minimize negative effects on them). This was the first of several initiatives where left and liberal faculty and students worked together to achieve a better quality of facilities to serve the whole community. There was an ongoing battle over exclusion of students from the Faculty Lounge. Many faculty invited students into the lounge and eventually other students just went in on their own. The university president built a wall and posted a guard but eventually a small group of both faculty and students tore the wall down and it stayed down.

The notion of a single community where faculty mixed with students, albeit one where this was supposed to be confined to social mixing outside the classroom and university governance bodies, was also promoted from the top by the university president and by many not necessarily leftish faculty. A series of weekend retreat academic symposia were sponsored by the administration in the first years that drew faculty as well as students to debate how Simon Fraser should be built. Some of the retreats also included administration and Board members seeking to build bridges to both faculty and students with which they were in early and frequent conflict.

In sum, Simon Fraser was created with a weakly developed status hierarchy among both faculty and students and a related predisposition to build both a student and student-faculty community with participatory democratic structures. This had multiple effects which were to prove important in the rise and fall of a strong student power movement. First, up until June 1968 the large majority of faculty were without tenure or rank and saw themselves as vulnerable to dismissal by an apparently micro-managing chancellor and Board. Their exclusion from the usual professional control structures obliged them to use Joint Faculty and other participatory democratic structures to wage their battle for professional status and control.

Second, left faculty led this battle but even with the more liberal faculty who supported them and who shared in the 'myth' of Simon Fraser as 'experimental' and 'revolutionary' in building a faculty-student community, they were always a minority within faculty. To show other faculty that their more confrontational 'union' approach to winning tenure through insistence on collective bargaining an Academic Freedom and Tenure document (AFT) with the Board could work they had to be able to put more effective pressure on the administration. They needed to make an alliance with the students who could provide that pressure and a 'left flank.'

Third, in the absence of the usual structures of Senate, deans, chairs and faculty bodies dominated by the higher ranks and by those deferent to the higher ranks because they were aspiring to rank that constituted a legitimated authority of senior faculty rule, even many conservative and more rightish liberal faculty shared an immediate antagonist with the left students and faculty, one that was seen as 'external' to the academic community. That opponent was the business-dominated Board that they saw as non-legitimate power when deciding on academic matters, notably on hiring, firing, tenure and promotion matters that might affect them personally in an adverse way. In both of the major (and many minor) conflicts up to the winning of faculty professional power in June 1968 the majority of faculty supported the left student and faculty against the Board.

Fourth, after faculty won an academic freedom and tenure document, elected chairs and deans, a reformed Senate and above all a president (Economics professor and labour-management expert Kenneth Strand, elected chair of Joint Faculty) chosen from their own ranks by vote of Joint Faculty who pledged to implement the faculty professional control hierarchy, the majority of faculty no longer supported the student power movement and sided with the university president against them in the subsequent major conflicts.

Fifth, many of the left and left liberal faculty maintained the faculty-student alliance after June 1968 because they too ceased getting support from the majority of faculty. Rather than capitulate in their plans to build a more democratic university that experimented with progressive teaching-learning techniques and encouraged innovative and socially progressive courses and research , they chose to strengthen their alliance with the student power movement. The most notable example was the PSA department where the administration was blocking most of their appointments and was evidently maneuvering to find pretexts for dismissing some of the 'troublemakers.' They granted PSA students 100% student power in a system of parallel student and faculty plena, joint parity committees including committees for hiring, firing, tenure and promotion and mutual veto. Faculty in other departments were less radical but several granted parity on committees and significant student decision-making power outside the hiring-firing-tenure-promotion area; to include the latter would be to cross a big line, to challenged the very basis of a professional status group apart, with only the expert professionals allowed to make basic decisions about status. Only the majority of PSA faculty were willing to cross that line but their example inspired and strengthened the students and to a lesser extent the progressive wing of faculty in other departments to move at least part of the way in the same direction despite the new political environment among faculty overall.

Thus the student movement battles with the university establishment took on a different character before and after the winning of professional status faculty power in June 1968. The institutionalization of a faculty hierarchy to run Simon Fraser in the usual manner of a modern multiversity required the crushing of both the left student and left faculty and the separate and joint participatory democratic governance structures that they had led in building at SFU.

'Change The University First': The Common Strategy of the 1960s Student Movement in English Canada

Simon Fraser was in no way unique with respect to the ideology, goals, demands and tactics of its student movement compared to student activists on other campuses across English Canada. Indeed it shared those student power, New Left politics and approach to the 'process' of doing politics with student movements around the world. Like students on other English-Canadian campuses Simon Fraser also shared a de facto strategy, one which differentiated it from the strategies of at least the major student movements across the globe from the United States to Czechoslovakia to Italy to Japan and even China. Whereas all movements, in English Canada and elsewhere, sought to both 'Change the University' by winning student power in it and to 'Change the Society' by allying with progressive and often radical or revolutionary forces outside the university, in English Canada the strategy adopted in practice was 'Change the University First.' The basic reason, put simply, was that before 1968-69 there were very few militant let alone politically radical social and political movements outside the university to link up with in English Canada as there were in many other countries.

In Fall 1964, the French language Quebec university student associations withdrew from the pan-Canadian student federation and united with other post-secondary student associations in Quebec to form a separate student federation for the emerging 'Quebec nation,' UGEQ. At its founding congress, UGEQ adopted a declaration that it would be guided by a political philosophy of "student syndicalism." This meant that students were not children passively consuming education in order to later be active and productive members of society but they were "young intellectual workers," already adult citizens and already part of the economy as knowledge producers. This meant that they had both the right and duty to contribute to the catching-up 'development' of the previously under-developed new Nation by changing the university and by changing the wider society together with other progressive social forces. UGEQ positioned itself from the beginning as non-aligned in relation to Cold War international (student) politics. It embraced the idea promoted by the 'Quiet Revolution' Quebec City government of the Jean Lesage Liberals that one of the keys to the catching-up development of the Quebec nation was the "democratization" of access to post-secondary education.

Starting especially with the August 1965 annual congress, the Canadian Union of Students (CUS), the soon to be only English Canada (i.e. outside-Quebec) national student federation, made up of local student societies and their student councils, responded directly to UGEQ by declaring UGEQ to be a 'sister union' representing the students of 'what they conceived to be a distinct nation within Canada.' Instead of opposing the nationalist breakaway they chose to emulate it. CUS adopted its own Declaration of the Canadian Student as well as a policy for overcoming the social as well as financial barriers to higher education that it called 'universal accessibility." The Declaration was not full-fledged student syndicalism where the student movement was seen as part of a wider off-campus movement with the obligation to directly intervene off campus to promote social change. Nor did it explicitly conceive of students as 'young intellectual workers' and therefore explicitly conceive of student associations as 'unions' (although a number of campus student associations eventually did).

Rather the CUS Declaration said that students were fully adult "citizens" both in the university community and in the wider community. Therefore they had the right and duty as citizens to take stands on social and political change issues if not necessarily to directly intervene to actually pressure for those changes themselves. And student associations were therefore more to be thought of as student "governments," as vehicles of self-government completely autonomous from 'in loco parentis' control by the university administration or faculty. Those self-governing organizations were the vehicles for a group, students, that sought equal status in the government of the university. As citizens they also expected to at the very least 'speak truth to power' on wider social change issues as was the right and duty of any other citizen of Canada.

Given this philosophy a third key element of CUS policy (after being self-governing student-citizens that took stands on social change issues and seeking their version of democratization of access to higher education), first detailed as a priority objective at the August 1966 CUS Congress, was the commitment to 'democratizing the academic and/or university community' (the difference between the two being that the academic community was a 'community of scholars' made up of the student and faculty groups only whereas the university community was made up of potentially many 'estates,' or what ruling elites today like to call 'stake-holders,' which at the very least added 'administration' or management as a third group in governance). CUS called it "academocracy" for short but the mass media and most radical students usually called it "student power." By late 1967 this third goal had become the overriding one in campus struggles across the country.

In contrast, the francophone Quebecois student movement interacted with the Quebec separatist movement and developed modest links with an expanding and increasingly politicized labour movement led by the "de-confessionalized" formerly Catholic CSN labour federation that was already promoting the idea of a Second Front of union activism outside the workplace and collective bargaining in community organizing and political action by 1966 (but especially after 1968). Both student councils (rationalized by the University of Montreal and then Quebec national student union UGEQ philosophy of "student syndicalism," the philosophy that students were full citizens and not apprentice-citizens-still-growing-up-while-at-school and had the obligation to directly intervene to serve the emerging Nation in reforming and rebuilding the society) and student radicals established interventions to do community organizing of various kinds in poor and working class communities, albeit mainly in the summer with government funding of "community development" projects from the mid 1960s on.[1]

In the United States the civil rights/Black power/Third World peoples movement starting in the late 1950s and the Vietnam war particularly from early 1965 provided strongly influential off-campus movements that provided much of the stimulus to on-campus activism (for example, the original University of California Berkeley Free Speech Movement was sparked by resistance to a ban on civil rights movement supporting student groups setting up tables to recruit and raise money for the movement groups in the segregated South). In Italy the 1960s student movement arose at the same time as the revival of militancy in the labour movement fuelled in particular by the migration of Southern Italy youth to become workers in the fast-growing manufacturing industries of the North and the student movement adopted a "workerist" philosophy and sought to build worker-student alliances of various kinds well before the outbreak of the Hot Autumn strike wave of 1969. The French student movement had been politicized and radicalized and directed toward off-campus issues earlier than most by the impact of the Algerian war and drew on the relatively larger numbers of students with many years of political and organizing experience to great effect in sparking the May-June student strikes followed by worker occupations and a near general strike. Czech and Polish students battled for 'socialism with a human face,' Spanish and Portuguese students denounced fascism and many eventually joined in underground off-campus movements to overthrow the fascist regimes, Chinese Red Guards waged a Cultural Revolution and Japanese students fought battles with police to demand that Japan break its treaty and subjugation to "U.S. imperialism."

The English-Canadian student movement, including the movement at SFU and within PSA, took place in a relative vacuum. Yes there was the Quebec independence movement to provide off-campus context but that was geographically removed from most English-Canadian universities. There was a small 'red power' Native movement stirring by 1968-9. There was the beginnings of an independent Canadian trade union movement that helped stimulate labour militancy in the 1970s but it was barely begun by 1969. A middle class economic and cultural English-Canadian nationalism was on the rise in the late 1960s over very high and growing foreign (essentially US) ownership of Canadian manufacturing and resources and domination of mass media and cultural industries. This helped stimulate the creation of the sizeable Waffle Caucus in the social democratic NDP, a left-wing caucus calling for a left that was both 'anti-imperialist' by being Canadian nationalist and a supporter of party constituency groups joining with social movement groups in extra-parliamentary activism. But all of these movements only really emerged after 1968 and were more of a response to the New Left that had emerged on campuses and to 1960s social and political struggles around the world than they were a stimulus. Thus both the student power radicals and the PSA department at SFU were in a difficult position to actually carry out their wishes to engage in "community integration," to mobilize students and faculty to get involved in the struggles of popular groups in the wider society. There weren't that many high level off-campus struggles to integrate with. What in effect happened in English Canada was that a subsection of the students who had been politicized and radicalized in the context of the on-campus student movement opted by 1969-70 to move off the campus in order to integrate with disadvantaged social groups off campus and to take the initiative to become organizers of struggles in the wider community.

At the campus level, the main organizational units that were collective actors in the English-Canadian student power movement were: (1) the Student Council; (2) the Student Newspaper (weekly, or in the case of McGill and University of Toronto, daily on weekdays); (3) minoritarian activist groups with various names but I shall refer to them as SDUs or more informal militant or radical student groupings, usually organized but occasionally spontaneous; (4) mass Student Body meetings (official meetings of the Student Association convened by the Student Council or unofficial mass student meetings); (5) (mostly from Fall 1968 on) Departmental [Course] Unions (6) within university governance bodies like Senate or in committees set up jointly with faculty or with faculty and administration and others including Board or alumni or in non-decision-making university president advisory committees. The relative importance of each of these vehicles varied significantly from campus to campus and over time within the same campus. SFU was distinguished from all other campuses in according a central role to the fourth vehicle, the mass student meeting, as the body to which all of the other vehicles were ultimately accountable, but it too used all of these channels extensively.

The 1960s English Canada student movement operated more than many other countries did, and certainly for longer, for the whole 1964 to 1970 period, primarily within the framework of representative democracy student association structures. The Students for a Democratic University or SDU-type groups appear to have initiated fewer of the actions relative to student association structures compared to other countries (note the significance of the difference in the name from that of the SDS in the U.S.—in English Canada radical students emphasized with their choice of name that they were for a Democratic University rather than stressing the immediate goal of a Democratic Society). SFU is somewhat of an exception but even the Simon Fraser SDU operated as an activist group within the 'union' and, as will be noted below, generally subjected itself to the decisions of Student Assemblies, official or unofficial, even when planning civil disobedience and other militant actions.

At a national and regional level CUS (and the separate Canadian University Press news service of the student association funded student newspapers) played a key role as a clearinghouse for information about what was being tried on other campuses and for analyses developed at other campuses as well as by bringing together Student Council selected delegations at its annual Congress to debate and decide on campaigns and policies to be pursued at the campus level. It is no coincidence that the primary tactic of the political right on all campuses for defeating the left-wing student activists was to push for a referendum to get their student association to withdraw from membership in CUS.

The English-Canadian student movement is thus somewhat of an oddity. The student radicals shared the same ideology, goals, demands and tactics of left students around the world but they pursued a different short-term strategy of 'Change the University First.' This was because of the different environment external to the university in English Canada where left movements were only weakly developed before 1968-69. In saying this I am arguing that the focus on changing the university was not based on the fact that left students in Canada, in Quebec or in the rest of Canada, were any less motivated by an overriding desire to bring about radical changes in the wider society. This assertion is strongly supported by historical events: after the demise of the student power movement in 1969-70 many of the leading student radicals moved off campus and embarked on a career of left-wing activism that lasted for a large number at least through much of the 1970s and for many for a long time after that. Virtually none of them ever returned to the campuses to try to revive a student power 'change the university' movement. Nor did subsequent generations of student radicals ever do so although there was of course some on-campus activism and attempts to use student council and student newspaper structures and a Canadian Federation of Students to advance progressive causes including student-oriented ones like freezing tuition fees. It is notable however that most of these efforts such as those by radicals working in and around Student Council at Concordia and Guelph in recent years stressed off-campus 'change society' issues.

Simon Fraser took up the same issues and used the same mix of representative democracy and participatory democracy debating and decision-making processes and (almost exclusively non-violent, with the Sir George computer center burning being almost the only exception) range of tactics from committees and petitions to sit-ins, occupations and strikes. But it was clearly more successful in mobilizing a larger number of students into both debate and decision-making and in collective action and won much more in student power concessions from administration and faculty. Were there not major conflicts involving at times the mobilization of large numbers at other campuses? Yes there were, but nothing like the sustained high level of mobilization in the almost 24 consecutive months (SFU had a trimester system and hence a full summer semester) between February 1967 and December 1968 (there was a brief lull in the 1967 Summer of Love as SFU students directed their radicalism into developing a more intense youth counterculture) followed by another period of high mobilization during the PSA student-faculty strike of Fall 1969.

Many different campuses had one major confrontation, an occupation or a strike such as the January 1969 student strike at Regina Campus of the University of

Saskatchewan to oppose the attempt of the right-wing Ross Thatcher Liberal government to purge and censor the student newspaper. St Dunstan's students in PEI waged a successful strike to win an end to many in loco parentis regulations and some student representation. Loyola College students waged a militant and ultimately unsuccessful campaign of strike and sit-in over a period of weeks in 1969 to protest the firing of a professor (and then the threatened dismissal of 24 other faculty who had supported the protest which was beaten back) and piggybacked a list of student power demands. The Ontario College of Art waged a successful brief strike winning the sympathetic intervention of Education Minister Bill Davis who promised to reform the curriculum and the administration-governance structure. There was a sit-in in early 1968 at McGill in the president's office leading to arrests and a university disciplinary trial to protest the possible expulsion of a student journalist (John Fekete) for reprinting an "obscene" satire. Later there was a 'disruption' of a Senate subcommittee and a Board meeting in early 1969 but only the early 1968 action gained even significant student support (and the support was entirely passive and not translated into supportive action and was seen as weak by McGill radicals at the time). The latter actions polarized the student body and led mostly to a strong backlash against the student left creating an environment in which the administration was able to fire leading faculty and grad student radical Stan Gray without significant opposition.

At the University of Toronto there was a sit-in protest against Dow recruiters in Fall 1967, a Tent City on university grounds for a week or so at the opening of classes in Fall 1968 and an occupation of the administration building led by daycare parents and their children in spring 1970. Only Tent City actually mobilized large numbers in what was a quasi 'hippy' event and the daycare occupation came after the campus student movement was already effectively over. Yes there were a number of "ideological contestation" style disruptions organized by radical student groups at University of Toronto—such as the disruption of a speech by former University of California president Clark Kerr, disruption of some student orientation sessions in the colleges and disruption of several classes taught by U.S. State department linked political science professors—but they amounted to 'propaganda of the deed' by an exemplary vanguard at best and virtually all failed to mobilize significant numbers of students into sympathetic action. With the very qualified exception of Regina, the only real examples of sustained high mobilization of students behind left student leadership were among French-language students at the University of Ottawa and at the Universite de Moncton for more funding and faculty and courses in French and this is clearly more an expression of rising Acadien and Franco-Ontarian nationalism than it is of the overall student movement in English Canada. The Sir George occupation led by Black students, mostly from the West Indies, was also atypical and anyway was not a campaign that was sustained at a high level over a very long period.

The point here is not that there wasn't a great deal of political debate and confrontations of various kinds with the authorities on other English-Canadian campuses nor that the student movements did not engage large numbers of students ideologically and help politicize and radicalize many. Nor is it that the left student leaders were any less sophisticated or radical than at SFU. Indeed, it could be argued that the radical University of Toronto and McGill student activists had more developed social analyses and promoted more explicitly radical 'change the society beyond the campus' political ideas than the SFU radicals did. The point is that the SFU student left mobilized more students into more numerous militant actions and won more student power from the authorities over a sustained period than any other student left.

Were participatory democratic structures deployed at other campuses? Yes they were but sparingly, mostly only during the height of major conflicts and not always even then. Almost nowhere else except SFU (University of King's College on Dalhousie campus in Halifax is the only other example that comes to mind) was the mass student membership meeting made legally sovereign and used that way to actually make frequent important decisions relating to both policy and action. There were occasional large public meetings or rallies at other campuses but these were not sites for governance, for debates leading to binding decisions. Radical student groups used participatory processes for their own internal decision-making but that again is not the same thing as participatory democracy structures that directly engage the mass of students.

1960s student radicals shared the same basic perspectives on democracy across the country but only at SFU were the objective and eventually subjective conditions strongly favourable to the frequent use of mass meetings to debate and decide and above all to be the body to which all other student bodies were ultimately accountable. The main objective condition was that there was no institutionalized system of professional status faculty hierarchy at the instant university until after June 1968. The main subjective condition was the widely shared mobilizing 'myth' that the institution's goal was to build a high quality university that was experimental and democratic and socially progressive by building both a non-hierarchical student community and a student-faculty (and sometimes also university employee) community. The way to do that was to demand changes in decision-making structures that gave all members of the community the opportunity for direct participation and 'control from below' and to practice participatory democratic governance within the community raising those demands.

The Major Conflicts at SFU: How (Weak) Faculty Professional Status and Participatory Democratic Processes Explain Their Dynamics

While there were many relatively minor conflict situations pitting left students against the university authorities in the five academic years from 1965-66 to 1969-70 there were four major ones that achieved high levels of sustained mobilization and often resulted in significant gains: (1) the TA incident of February-March 1967; (2) the CAUT crisis which peaked with the aftermath of the CAUT censure of the Board and president in June 1968 but which actually included a series of conflicts from Fall 1967 on; (3) the raising of the 'four demands' for easier transfer and recognition of credits from colleges to university culminating in an occupation of the administration building, the calling of the RCMP to campus to arrest the occupiers and the week- long set of meetings to vote on a general student strike in support of the 'SFU 114'; (4) the non-renewals and denial of tenure to a large number of PSA faculty and the placing of the department under trusteeship for the crime of allowing student power over hiring-firing-tenure-promotion decisions that provoked a several weeks long strike of students and faculty in the PSA department with support strikes and support actions from students in many other departments (but not most other faculty or, in any effective way, from the moderate-led Student Council). There are many interesting lessons to draw from a close analysis of these conflicts but the goal here is the narrow one of providing a capsule summary of each event sufficient to show that the two major factors of a weak faculty professional status hierarchy and the predisposition to rely on participatory democratic mechanisms of mobilization explain key features of the way the events unfolded.

In particular, the analysis will look for evidence of the operation of the more proximate mechanisms of these two factors presented earlier: (1) the majority of faculty without rank or tenure felt that their chances of getting rank and tenure were under threat from the Board; (2) left faculty had to seek an alliance with the student power movement so that student action could put enough pressure on the Board on academic freedom and tenure issues to force them into a kind of collective bargaining relationship to faculty; (3) the majority of faculty, even many conservative or rightish liberals tended to side with left students and left faculty in major clashes with the Board up to June 1968; (4) after winning professional faculty power from the Board in June 1968 the majority of faculty turned against the left students and left faculty and supported the new faculty power university president in his campaign to reverse the democratization that gave students significant power; (5) that left faculty, especially but not solely in the PSA department, responded to the turn of the faculty majority away from support for further democratization by strengthening their alliance with the student power movement and seeking to extend democracy at the departmental and Faculty levels.

A strong test of the operation of all these factors would be evidence in support of the claim that the balance of forces changed radically between the before June 1968 and the after June 1968 conflicts. Before the institutionalization of a faculty hierarchy system, there was the building of a consensus among students across political lines (excepting the relatively weak establishment right) for a student community student power movement. There was also a less uniformly politically progressive but still generally solid majority of faculty ready to support a student-faculty alliance to promote the ideal of a student-faculty community that could wrest the making of all academic decisions from the Board. Both students and faculty operated frequently in participatory democratic structures of debate, decision-making and mobilization. After June 1968 the majority of faculty withdrew their support for a democratic student-faculty community and supported the making of decisions by and for faculty by the chairs, deans, senior faculty and above all the faculty power university president rather than by participatory democratic processes. Left students and left faculty continued to champion the same sort of changes and use the same participatory democratic processes (indeed they radicalized them further) and were still able to win the support of large numbers of students but the opposition of the faculty majority changed the dynamics and outcomes of the post June 1968 struggles.

A. The March 1967 TA Incident

The first major conflict between the SFU student movement and the authorities was the "TA Incident" in March 1967 in the second semester of the second academic year (At SFU there were three semesters per academic year—Fall, Winter and Summer). Students declared they would go on strike unless the Board reversed its decision to fire five teaching assistants (TAs) for off-campus political agitation that the Board saw as hurting the universities reputation in the 'community' (especially the business community but there was a general public backlash orchestrated by both the political police and commercial media). The majority of faculty including at least one key senior faculty member (Arts Dean and PSA head Tom Bottomore, the internationally famous scholar of Marx's work on stratification) backed the students. The Board reversed the decisions in a clearcut victory for the student and student-faculty communities. The issue was defined as one of interference with academic freedom and freedom of speech but many connections were made to wider issues.

The TA incident had at least two features that distinguished it from subsequent major conflicts at SFU and from most conflicts on other English Canada campuses. First, it began spontaneously when one of a group of TAs having morning coffee and tea in the cafeteria read out a story from the local newspaper about Peter Haines, a student at Templeton, a working class Vancouver high school, who had been suspended for writing a satire of the pretensions of a poetry teacher. Second, the decision by five TAs, most of them PSA MA students who had come to SFU from Britain to study under Bottomore, to go to the school to try to rally other students at the school to support Haines's right to student academic freedom was a decision to try to defend rights and liberties off-campus and had no connection to advancing any interests or change agenda of faculty or students on campus (beyond the defence of the same broad New Left political philosophy and student power principles).

Other features of the TA incident were to be echoed in subsequent SFU conflict events (although the last conflict, the Fall 1969 PSA department strike was a partial exception). First, the political initiative in framing an issue as one requiring action to challenge the authorities came from students (the intervention by the five graduate students and supporters at the high school over several days). Second, in a second stage of the conflict precipitated by a repressive response by authorities the main pressure placed on authorities to reverse their actions came as the result of mobilization and collective action (a strike call and mobilization by a strike committee, a student initiated and chaired rally and subsequent quasi sit-in outside the Board meeting) by students, not faculty. Third, left faculty organized among faculty in parallel and succeeded in solidifying the majority of faculty against the Board decision, in part by linking the firings to the professional self-interest of faculty in protecting their own academic freedom in the absence of tenure protection. Fourth, student and faculty radicals both tried to simultaneously widen and narrow the issues at stake. They sought to make links between the immediate narrow issues and wider issues of change in society (which tended to radicalize the analysis of the sources of the injustices and do more to "raise consciousness" and win a relatively small number of people to become radicals and activists). They also chose to connect the issues back to the more insular frame of 'changing the university' (which tended to broaden support to include various less or non radical groupings): what began as an issue of the rights of working class high school students and subsequently the right to free speech of graduate students facing discipline for off-campus political agitation was quickly reframed as a defence of the 'academic freedom' of TAs qua junior academics and linked by faculty as well as students to the Board's non-acceptance of the Faculty Association Academic Freedom and Tenure or AFT brief.

While the TA incident itself was a major media story over a period of a couple of weeks in March 1967 the confrontation between both left students and left faculty and university authorities had been building since SFU opened in September 1965. Four types of events had prepared the ground. First there were multiple instances where left faculty joined with students in pressuring the administration for changes that would make a reality out of the myth of SFU being a new kind of university committed to building a student-faculty community that would be innovative in exploring new approaches to teaching and learning. Left faculty supported several student efforts to boycott the cafeteria to pressure for changes in food quality and prices by setting up an unofficial student-faculty investigation committee. Many also applauded student action to sabotage separate faculty elevators by soldering the lock-out mechanism to the 'on' position. Many invited students into the faculty-only Faculty Lounge repeatedly and a few actually joined students in tearing down the Faculty Lounge wall that the university president had ordered erected so that a guard could keep students out. Large numbers of faculty opposed the granting to Shell Oil the right to build a gas station at the top of the Burnaby Mountain campus in a location where it blocked the view (a privilege granted because Shell put up some money towards the building of a men's residence). Almost no faculty joined in the civil disobedience blocking the machines clearing the Shell site (professors could be dismissed while students were unlikely to face serious discipline) in summer 1966. However, one philosophy professor (David Berg) wrote an open letter condemning the Board in strident terms for losing the confidence of the academic community over the Shell issue and called on them to resign. When a Board member counter-attacked in equally blunt language in print several other faculty came to the defence of Berg and supported his call for the Board's resignation. A reported 1,600 students and faculty, included a large number of the latter, participated in a "Shell Out" rally and march in Fall 1966. Several faculty were also active in a committee that tried to get the Board to authorize the construction of a University Village on the side of the mountain which they conceived of as being mainly cooperative housing. When plans for this looked to be delayed for several years, some faculty joined with a few dozen students to set up the radically communal New Westminister co-op.

A second type of event were multiple instances where students used collective action or even sabotage to challenge symbols and realities of status privileges accorded to faculty to make them socially separate from and symbolically superior to students. Some of those events were just mentioned. Others included a Park-In where the otherwise conservative Student Council president walked into the student cafeteria and led a couple of dozen students into the parking area to prevent the tow-trucks from towing illegally parked student cars. A garden was planted in an area next to the Theatre where a paved parking lot was to be built in an ultimately failed attempt to maintain a green campus in that spot. When Faculty Council tried to block publication of the student paper because of fear that a student would sue for critical comments made of her views on birth control by the student editor in an editorial the paper fought back and eventually published. When Faculty Council requisitioned photographs taken by the student newspaper photographer of a panty raid in order to prosecute the male student offenders the student paper refused saying that it would not and eventually that the photos had 'failed to turn out.' There were complaints about library policies and bookstore prices and the creation of a student operated cooperative bookstore on a shoestring to undercut the university one. Alex Turner, Student Council president in summer 1966 drove down to the site where some students were crossing the picket lines to do work normally done by striking Vancouver city workers to stand in front of them and ask them not to contribute to breaking the strike and was supported by his Council for doing so.

A third type of event that occurred frequently in the six semesters leading up to March 1967 were instances where students used participatory democratic structures to debate and decide upon policies and collective actions. This was the case for many of the student and student-faculty actions cited in the first two points. In January 1967, a chapter of the Student Union for Peace Action (SUPA) the New Left activist group was established on campus. It declared its attention to engage in educational activities and protests that would direct student attention to events and institutions both on and off campus that were "incompatible with democracy."

Finally, there were clear signs in the weeks and months before the TA incident that undercover "red squad" political police were engaged in both spying and harassment of SFU students and faculty. One event that appears to have stimulated this police action were the "pro-revolution" speeches made in conjunction of the University of Toronto Teach-In piped in over the phone lines to SFU among 150 other universities across North America. A second event was the founding of the Vancouver Committee to Aid American War Objectors by left faculty from both UBC and SFU. Right wing literature was distributed on campus claiming that there were many communists among SFU faculty in early 1967. The authors turned out to be prison guards at a nearby prison. Peter Morley, a PSA graduate student that had previously worked as a prison guard was approached in the parking lot by four undercover police officers who appeared to be about to ask him if he would be willing to do undercover work to report on the "communist" political inclinations and activities of faculty and students at SFU. On February 12 1967 PSA grad student Martin Loney was harassed and strip searched by the RCMP political police and narcotics squad together when he returned from a short visit across the border to a friend in Bellingham, Washington. On his way into the U.S. Loney had been asked whether he was a communist and whether there were a lot of communists at SFU. On his way back Loney was stripped naked by customs, had his car and personal possessions searched, his letters read and address book taken. He was held until the narcotics squad came and they followed him to his house and searched it for drugs. They found nothing but told Loney that "it would be in all of our interests" if he left Canada. Loney's political involvement had been in the Labour Party in Britain and as a student participant in the Committee of 100 outgrowth of the CND ban the bomb campaign. The whole incident was leaked to the media and the radio hotlines had a field day demonizing Loney as a "foreign agitator" and "dope-smoking hippy," the kind of person that was making SFU a hotbed of radicalism.

A month later, Loney and four other TAs read in the local newspaper about the suspension of Grade 12 student Peter Haines for publishing a parody of his teacher's efforts at poetry. On Friday March 10 they circulated an open letter at Templeton High School calling upon the students to support Haines's right to free speech. On Monday March 13 the TAs returned to the school to leaflet a call for a public meeting at lunch hour in the park across the street from the school where both SFU and Templeton students would speak. From 600 to 700 students attend the meeting. Football team members start fights in the crowd. Loney and a second SFU student Tom Tyre are ordered to leave by police and are later charged with creating a disturbance and released on $100 bail. On Tuesday March 14 Loney and Tyre are accompanied by a number of other SFU students who return to the park across from the high school to hold a silent vigil which turns into a silent walk on the sidewalk bordering the park. The police nab Loney and put him in a police car. He and a couple of others are charged with creating a disturbance. The sequence of events sparks a media frenzy.

On Thursday March 16 the Faculty Council votes to suspend the five TAs as students for one semester. A noon Student Council forum is held with the announced topic "Does the Faculty Council Have the Right To Take Any Disciplinary Action Against Martin Loney?." That afternoon, the SFU Board ignores the Faculty Council decision and, with minimal investigation of the facts, issues a press release announcing the "firing " of the five TAs. PSA head and Dean of Arts Tom Bottomore immediately announces his resignation as dean to protest the Board's action. On Friday afternoon, the Faculty Association votes unanimously to deplore the Board's action and call for the Board to accept the Academic Freedom and Tenure brief to reassure faculty that their academic freedom would not be similarly threatened. The meeting had begun with a debate "Should the Faculty Council Determine What Constitutes Legitimate Off-Campus Political Activity?." Also on Friday the Student Council meets to decide on a plan of action. Observers speak at the meeting. A strike is called to start Monday March 20 at 12:30pm if the Board doesn't rescind the firings, a deadline later extended to Tuesday noon to allow the Board to meet on campus Monday evening to receive delegations mostly from senior faculty and to debate the issue. Faculty and students speak at the all afternoon Monday rally. A letter signed by the presidents of all six student political clubs, including the right-wing government party, the Social Credit, declares their support for a student strike if the Board doesn't back down. Classes come to a halt as there are meetings of faculty and of TAs to vote on supportive statements that are then read out at the afternoon long rally. Many students stay on campus and eventually have a quasi sit-in outside the room where the Board is meeting. Shortly after midnight the Board announces that it has rescinded the firings and replaced them with "a severe reprimand" with no sanctions.

Key points show the operation of our two factors during the TA incident:

• It was initially an issue of left students agitating about democracy and rights and social justice in a society that claimed to be for these principles but whose practices often contradicted them. More specifically the issue of status equality, of students having the same basic rights as teachers/faculty in the classroom, was raised as the central point by the five TAs as a reason for their actions at the high school.

• The commercial media and both elite and non-elite people in the off-campus community understood this political point immediately and considered it to be the 'promotion of anarchy,' the undermining of parental, teacher and school administrator authority and control over, and the unrestricted right to discipline high school students.

• An important motivation that led first the Faculty Council (which suspended the five TAs as graduate students for one semester) and then the Board (who 'fired' the five as teaching assistants with the clear intent of removing them from the university permanently) to repressive action was pressure from outside the university and the desire to protect the 'reputation' of the university, but more particularly to persuade the government, business, potential donors and elements of the public that SFU was not being allowed to become a staging area for the export of social revolution into the wider community. There was hysteria in the community about the undermining of social hierarchies not only by 'outside agitators' (from outside the high school) but also by 'foreign agitators' (all five were British grad students) and indeed by persons perceived to be both 'communists' and 'drug-using hippies' because of the campaign that had been organized by local radio and TV to demonize the person labelled as the ringleader of the five TAs, Martin Loney, over a separate incident several weeks earlier.

- Both students and faculty immediately interpreted the denial of rights to the five graduate students and TAs as an attack on their rights and freedoms and both immediately begin to meet and debate how they should respond: at first separately and in parallel around the FA and SC, then by faculty participating in liaison committees supporting the student strike committee preparations and by faculty speaking in student organized and chaired rallies (individual faculty and groupings of faculty also applied pressure on the administration behind the scenes). Linking the firings to the Board's non-acceptance of the AFT brief served to broaden the base of support to include conservative and moderate liberal faculty but eventually the reframing of the conflict as an issue of academic freedom for faculty was adopted by the left students also in the post-mortem assessments (here the motive was to say that it was not just the 'liberal' issue of freedom of speech, which had now been won, but the issue that underlay it which had not yet been won, namely the lack of democratic decision-making power by the academic community in particular over issues of hiring, firing, tenure and promotions).

- Both faculty and students, but especially the students, used open and participatory democratic processes. The strike call is notably made by the Student Council not by a mass student meeting or by a referendum ballot. However, the Student Council is responding to the greater than expected level of anger of students at mass student meetings and its weekend meetings preparing the strike are opened to direct participation (and at times even voting) by student 'observers.' The main action carried out is a more or less continuous all afternoon rally of over a 1,000 faculty and students in the open mall area followed by Student Council supplied refreshments in the cafeteria as the strike committee and Student Council ask students to remain on campus. This leads to a quasi-sit-in outside the room where the

Board meets until just after midnight Tuesday March 21 1967. The pressure is the 'moral witness' of the entire 'community' acting as one.

• The Board likely backed down for at least two reasons. One is the success in engaging the mass of both students and faculty across status differences and political lines in a common public action and stand on the issue. The cost of refusing to reverse the decision would be high in terms of making certain that there would be increased conflict in future with both students and faculty. The other, at least equally important, was the indication from many of the elite and 'star' faculty who were already making SFU's reputation as a high-quality academic institution that they were included in this large majority. They made it clear that they might consider moving elsewhere if the SFU Board made the new university look like it was a backwards, 'redneck' kind of place where outside businessmen rather than faculty were in control.

B. The June-July 1968 CAUT Crisis

The second major conflict event was termed "the CAUT Crisis." It culminated in the summer of 1968 with the election of a radical Student Power slate to most positions on Student Council and the winning of both 'faculty power' (by decisions of the Board) and extensive 'student power' (by decisions of first Joint Faculty and then the newly empowered rank and file faculty in individual departments). It was the best of times and the beginning of a stimulating combination of both the best and the worst of times for the student and faculty lefts. Although the rapid and sweeping changes in power took place in late May, June and July of 1968, the CAUT crisis was really a period of sustained agitation and conflict, both behind the scenes and public, dating back to early Fall of 1967. Yet again while on the surface it might have appeared to outside observers that there was a sudden outburst, the period of highly dramatic and visible conflict and decision-making had a long pre-history of smaller scale conflicts that built up to the apparent sudden explosion. And again our two factors are key.

• Summer of 1967 immediately following the March 1967 TA Incident is a relatively quiet semester (although the Student Council and left faculty actively support the strike of university maintenance workers; the university president circulates a memo to try to slander the five TAs sparking a backlash among even senior faculty on Senate; and Senate, perhaps influenced by the student-faculty alliance in the TA incident, is the first in Canada to award [three] seats to student Senators, which is to prove to be important leverage for the student movement in later conflicts). It is the Summer of Love and much of the activity is about turning inwards away from political action to cultural issues and building a youth counterculture centered off campus in the emerging hippy community along Fourth Avenue in the Kitsilano neighbourhood of Vancouver. But it includes the expansion of the number of student residential communes and collectives everywhere including the two adjacent houses of the New Westminister Co-op.

- In Fall 1967, there is a beginnings of a revolt among faculty over the failure of the Board to accept their original AFT brief. One case brought matters to a head, the decision not to renew a relatively conservative Psychology professor Ken Burstein who had angered his appointed department head by agitating for a new head. The Burstein case stimulates the revolt for two reasons. First, the Burstein case brings the Board to clearly assert its right to ignore even faculty appeal committee decisions and to make final decisions on matters of hiring, firing, tenure and promotion instead of faculty bodies. Second, the Faculty Association waters down the AFT brief proposals without consulting the faculty membership. It is perceived as failing to be either tough enough with the Board or democratic enough with their members.

A special meeting of the Faculty Association on Wed Oct 18 1967 calls upon the Canadian Association of University Teachers (CAUT), in effect the national association of faculty associations, to investigate the reasons for the failure of negotiations with the SFU Board to result in an acceptable agreement on tenure and related matters. The SFU Faculty Association executive resigns to be replaced by another which is not notably different in political orientation but which is more careful to bring important matters to membership meetings. The lead in the revolt comes from left faculty who are also organizing a separate Faculty Union (the core of which is junior faculty in Arts without rank or tenure) which they hope will eventually win majority support, be certified and replace the Faculty Association. This puts further pressure on the Faculty Association executive to be more responsive to the grievances of junior faculty and to operate more democratically in order to maintain the allegiance of the majority of faculty.

Students are not fully aware of what is going on among faculty at this time and are more concerned with their own student power related issues and with the war in Vietnam (SFU students are prominent in the militant sit-ins at UBC against napalm manufacturer Dow Chemical). Students who have been sitting on a series of presidential advisory committees on matters such as cafeteria, student discipline and library express that they no longer believe that it is possible to win much change within such channels. The precipitating event is the rejection of the advice of several committees that had met for as much as two years by university president McTaggart-Cowan who then appointed a new super advisory committee, the Student Advisory Committee, to come up with a new report on most of the same issues.

An additional stimulus is the fact that one of the three students taking their seats as student Senators is the former leader of the radical SUPA group Sharon Yandle. She joins others in promoting a debate on how radical students should handle working within mainstream channels without becoming co-opted. Three main lessons are drawn in a series of speeches and articles in the student paper. First, one way to avoid being co-opted is to insist in the short term on students being granted non-token power in bodies that make decisions and that hold open meetings, not just voice in advisory bodies holding closed meetings. Second, even extensive student representation is not the goal in itself because on its own the reps will just 'join the club' of the elite decision-makers working for the supposed common good of the corporate university; rather the student reps must be held strictly accountable to mass meetings of their student constituency and simply convey the demands and concerns formulated by the mass of students. Third, student reps may sometimes collaborate with non-students to solve problems but that they must take their stand on all important issues by asking the question "Does this advance us further towards the long-term goal of direct participation and control by the mass of students in the running of the university?"

- In Winter 1968, left students regroup into the Students for a Democratic University or SDU (SUPA had dissolved itself formally in the summer of 1967). From the beginning they draw many left liberal students into their ranks around the emerging conflict over both the faculty issue of the acceptance of the AFT brief and the student power issue of university decision-making bodies holding open meetings and being accountable to the mass of both students and faculty. The SDU makes the Burstein case a very public issue with a series of leaflets and student body meetings. The Board announce that they will uphold the recommendations of the appointed heads and deans on Burstein instead of the decision of the elected faculty appeal committee. The SDU announces that it will do a 'walk-in' to the next Board meeting, thought to be considering Burstein and the AFT brief, where they will sit and observe the proceedings thereby forcing an open meeting.

Student Council votes to join in the action. The interim report of the CAUT investigation committee of February 14 1968 completely ignores issues of student rights and powers but also is strongly critical of the "feudal" administration system at SFU and the failure of the Board to agree to a tenure document along the lines recommended by CAUT, explicitly citing the Burstein as an example of a problematic policy. The Student Council president, also president of the campus Progressive Conservatives, resigns to protest the Council decision to support and engage in acts of civil disobedience.

Right-wing students surprise the Student Council and the student left by bringing a motion of impeachment to a student meeting in the mall on the eve of the Board walk-in which passes by 53% to 47%. Although there has been no notice of motion and the constitution requires a two-thirds majority, all of the mostly liberal and left students remaining on Student Council resign within 24 hours leaving only 'moderate' (and soon to be right-wing Student Council president elected in Fall 1968 in the backlash against the summer 1968 radicalism) ombudsman Rob Walsh as the legal representative of the Student Society.

The effect of the right's putsch is actually to stimulate a politically much wider mobilization. In the absence of a Student Council all decisions must now be made in mass student body meetings which for a period are held almost every weekday. Ten students ranging from right to left are elected to present two briefs to the Board during the walk-in. Many conservative and moderate liberal students join in the action. The populist conservative editor of the student paper declares that the student reps chosen by the student body to join in the walk-in and present a brief are representing 'all of us' not just the radical SDU (but including the SDU as the militant wing of 'our' student power movement). On March 5 1968 the Senate votes to accept the student-initiated policy of holding open meetings, the first in Canada to do so. It is apparent that a major factor in this decision is that some faculty on Senate see the need for an alliance with the students who can put pressure on the Board on their faculty power issues (although some voting for the reform may have been trying to cultivate a moderate student leadership to counter the left and liberal students with increasingly strong influence in Student Council and especially student body meetings).

Rob Walsh and the student right try frantically to reinstate the Student Council but instead students debate an SDU proposal to replace the Student Council with a participatory democracy system and a more liberal proposal for an expanded Council that holds more frequent membership meetings. These proposals eventually fail to get two-thirds support of a quorum of voters. Motions to call for the resignation of chancellor Shrum and university president McTaggart-Cowan also fail to get majority support but students are learning a lot about democracy and power.

In the late spring, a new issue emerges which will affect events in summer 1968 and beyond. PSA faculty announce that the administration has blocked their attempt to hire radical professor Andre Gunder Frank, author of many books on underdevelopment in the Third World being the result of the imperialism of the rich countries. It is the first publicized case of what will be a long string of blocked appointments over the next year or more. PSA faculty appeal to students and liberal faculty to donate money to hire Frank unofficially and set up a student-faculty committee within PSA. Left faculty are beginning to look even more than before to an alliance with the student movement. Fourteen PSA faculty approach the Senate with a request that it investigate "political discrimination" in the handling of its appointments. The right within Senate makes a spectacular counter-move by getting the Dean of Science to rise on the motion in Senate to read off a list of nine very vague charges that the PSA department itself has created a climate of political discrimination against students and faculty who don't buy into a radical line in PSA courses. He is unable to cite a single concrete example but the Nine Charges are the first public salvo in what will be a long 'witch hunt' culminating in the purge of left faculty within PSA in late summer 1969.

• The Summer 1968 semester begins with a smallish protest of a speech by Education Minister Peterson to convocation where he attacks the world-wide student power movement. Senate votes summarily to reject the PSA department's charges of political discrimination against its appointments. The most prominent of the radical five TAs in the TA Incident, PSA grad student Martin Loney, heads a Student Power slate that sweeps all executive positions and most of the seats on summer Student Council. They run on a very explicitly radical program promising to pursue a policy on campus of presenting demands for improvements in student services and student decision-making power but also on faculty-student issues like the blocked PSA appointments and the tenure issue to the authorities and holding regular student body meetings to decide on how to apply pressure to win concessions. They also state that they hope to link up with off-campus groups, including teacher and labour groups, to build a wider movement for radical reform in the province.

On Thursday May 30 1968, the second day of the second round of Student Council elections students learn that the CAUT Council has voted to censure SFU university president McTaggart-Cowan and the SFU Board for bargaining in bad faith on the tenure brief and for their "continued contravention of accepted principles of university governance" namely the refusal to let faculty make final decisions on matters of hiring, firing, tenure and promotions with the Board only rarely using its veto power.

Over 1,000 of the 2,400 students registered for summer semester meet the same day to debate and subsequently vote by secret ballot to adopt the Eight Demands for a democratic restructuring of the university to prevent the CAUT censure becoming a CAUT blacklist advising faculty not to accept positions at SFU. Many students worry about the perceived quality of their degrees.

Loney summarizes the majority sentiment among students: "To re-establish our name we must become the most democratic university in North America." The demands include abolition of the Board of Governors to be replaced by a restructured one with majority student-faculty control, a Senate that would become the main legislative authority and would be made up of students and faculty only, automatic due process and openness where required in all matters of appointment, tenure and promotion, democratization of departments along the lines of the CAUT report including the principle of a rotating chair with term appointments and the "striking of a committee composed equally of students and faculty chaired by a CAUT appointee to supervise the implementation of these reforms" (this last demand is pivotal because it is where the explicit demand for student-faculty "parity" is first raised).

University president McTaggart-Cowan calls a meeting of Joint Faculty on May 30 to discuss the CAUT censure. They adopt a motion calling for him to resign and begin a series of all day sessions of meetings of the entire faculty. On Friday May 31 a student meeting responds to the fact that the Board refuses to address its eight demands by putting two motions to referendum. On Tuesday June 4 the vote results are announced: a 1361 to 289 (89%) vote to call for the present Board to resign and a 967 to 706 (58%) vote for a week-long moratorium on regular classes, to stop earlier if the legislature agrees to an all-party committee to rewrite the Universities Act to establish democratic governance. In the middle of the voting the Board places McTaggart-Cowan on indefinite leave and attempts to get acceptance for an appointed acting president. Joint Faculty refuses this saying that it will name its own acting president to submit to the Board.

The Student Power Council decides that 58% is not enough to go on strike and this has the consequence of shifting the leadership of the movement to 'democratize' the university to regain CAUT approval to Joint Faculty whose meetings are attended or watched on closed circuit TV by hundreds of student observers, some of whom are on occasion allowed to speak. It also has the consequence of proving to faculty that the student power Council has the backing of its membership in its demands for real student power in a democratized university and that the radical students are offering them an opportunity to achieve radical reform through adoption of reforms by Joint

Faculty. The Storming of the Bastille is over for now and Joint Faculty is being asked to be the Estates-General with the Third Estate, the students, being outside its ranks but asking for various parity student-faculty bodies to carry out the reforms.

Two parallel committees of students and faculty are established both supposed to also meet jointly as parity bodies to negotiate compromises that can be accepted by vote of both students and faculty: a presidential search committee to pick an acting president and an Implementation committee to oversee the restructuring of governance bodies and to seek government introduction of changes to the Universities Act. There is some ambiguity in the Joint Faculty motions but it is the first enactment of what will become a guiding philosophy for SFU student power advocates: decision-making in parallel by separate student and faculty bodies that meet together to negotiate agreement in parity bodies with everything subject to mutual veto of student or faculty bodies.

The Board responds to Joint Faculty on June 2 with a Seven Points motion. It includes a promise to give early approval to a tenure document acceptable to the CAUT, to not unilaterally change recommendations from the president on academic matters, to accept early proposals from Senate on methods of appointment, tenure and functions of deans and department heads, to accept a new proposal on Burstein and to support the re-examination of the Universities Act with all parties consulted. Joint Faculty adopts a series of motions on restructuring university governance including "short term appointment by democratic procedures of all academic administration" and "the establishment of an exclusively academic Senate" but defers a motion for "reconstitution of the Board of Governors to give a majority to faculty and students." Instead a motion was passed supporting the elimination of the Board as a ruling body and the transfer of its powers to other existing bodies and for "a student-faculty committee to advise the Board until then."

The Board delays its response to the student Eight Demands but the Student Council does little. Some students occupy the Board room to maintain symbolic pressure, a quiet warning that students might use militant tactics again in the future. It does little to apply pressure but students with children involved in the sit-in eventually occupy a less-used part of the student cafeteria and set up the first university parent operated cooperative daycare later winning funding and a permanent site for it. In mid-June PSA students formed a departmental student union and proposed to faculty that the department operate on a full-scale parallel plena, parity joint committee and mutual veto system on all matters including hiring, firing, tenure and promotions. A solid majority of PSA faculty accepted the proposal with few modifications and began to apply it. On July 9 the CAUT signals that the Board's response is satisfactory and that it will lift the censure at a future meeting. On July 18 the Board finally publicly rejects all eight student demands and refuses to resign. It quietly drops its promise to use its good graces to get the government to introduce changes to the Universities Act.

Meanwhile the faculty search committee comes up with its candidate for acting president, Economics professor Kenneth Strand, a conservative on student power issues but solid in support of faculty professional power. The Board interviews him and signals that it finds him acceptable. The faculty committee renege on their commitment to subject their candidate to student scrutiny let alone a student veto and refuse to consider the student committee's candidate. The student committee splits and three of the five accept Strand on condition that he agree to step down after a year and after receiving vague promises from the faculty committee that they would seek something approaching the parity-veto procedure to choose the permanent president (a promise quickly abandoned afterwards). On July 30 Joint Faculty votes for Strand and the Board announces their appointment of Strand as acting president to the press the next morning. The Implementation Committee, which had made little progress in reconciling student and faculty views on democratizing governance (largely because faculty did not respond to the detailed proposals from the student committee), ends up making completely separate reports and proposals to their respective constituencies in Fall 1968.

Clearly the large majority of faculty abandoned its alliance with the student power movement the moment that the Board signalled approval of a 'faculty power' acting president, announced that it would allow a faculty-controlled system make final decisions on matters of hiring, firing, tenure and promotions subject only to rare rejections by the Board and would implement other features of professional self-rule such as elected chairs and deans when proposed to them by Senate. Note however that I am not making a reductionist and determinist argument that the behaviour of all faculty can be explained by the fact that most were without tenure protection or rank before the summer of 1968 and were looking toward qualifying for tenure and rank under a faculty-controlled system in the period immediately afterwards (which would naturally make anyone subject to that process more cautious about challenging the authorities until they were through the process). Obviously that cannot explain the choices made by the majority of PSA faculty or quite a few other left and left liberal faculty scattered in other departments after summer 1968 who only strengthened their support of the student movement. But I am arguing that the change in the

objective situation of a large majority of faculty with respect to rank and tenure before and after summer 1968 strongly influenced the stance of the majority of faculty
who were not left or left liberal. Before summer 1968, left faculty could often win
them to support challenges to the Board by mass student action. After summer 1968,
a large majority of faculty supported acting president Strand as he moved to repress
first the radical students and then the radical faculty.

C. November-December 1968: The 114 Occupation

The summer 1968 Student Power Student Council had an overall 'good reputation' in
many quarters despite a largely negative portrayal in the commercial media. It had
held back from waging a strike despite a 58% vote and refrained from pressure tactics
after that. It brought all of its policies that might be remotely controversial to student body meetings. While it was strongly supported on its student power agenda it
accepted defeat on motions that implied more radical political stands on issues beyond the campus. These included motions to donate money to the Black Panther
Party defence fund and a motion to rename the university after the Metis leader Louis
Riel instead of the racist colonizer Simon Fraser. The Student Council paid attention
to a host of concrete grievances in areas like library policy and food. It was widely regarded by even moderate conservatives to have provided 'good government,' highly
competent government and a government that actually lived up to its promise to
take issues to the members and abide by the results. The radical Council had won en-
dorsements from some labour unions for its policy of making university Boards more
representative of interests other than business. It had even attracted members of the
provincial legislature to campus to discuss changing the Universities Act and had elicited favourable comments from representatives of all parties even guarded ones
from members of the ruling Social Credit party.

All of this 'responsible' radicalism—holding back on the use of disruption tactics or attempts to mobilize large numbers of students and others in visible challenges to existing policies or illegitimate acts by authorities—did nothing to reduce
the extent of the repressive actions (criminal charges and mass firings) that the university administration, led by the newly appointed acting president Strand, would
prepare over the next months. The political right at both the student and administra-
tion-faculty level pursued a sustained campaign which had two main tactics. First,
right-wing or 'moderate' students sought to demonize the student left while the university president and some senior faculty allies sought to demonize left faculty, especially the core of that group in the PSA department. The new framing was that
moderate students and administration were for Change through Reason and the left

students and faculty were for Change through Intimidation: they were imposing a subtle type of totalitarianism especially through the use of participatory democratic structures which had the effect of intimidating into silence anyone who might wish to express disagreement with the radical orthodoxy (this provided convenient explanations for why Joint Faculty would have conceded parity-veto student power in early June 1968 or why the student power group, either SDU in spring 1968 or Student Council in summer 1968, repeatedly won massive support for radical policies and actions in meeting after meeting and vote after vote). Both moderate students and the a new conservative faculty majority supporting president Strand repeatedly sought to eliminate or reduce general meetings where extensive debate took place and tried to substitute voting by referendum with little or no debate.

The second main tactic was to work as under the radar as possible to build new institutions that could be used to establish a legitimated form of rule that included mechanisms for effective repression. At the faculty level this meant setting up all the institutions of decision-making by elected chairs and deans and bodies dominated by tenured faculty with rank to make decisions on the large majority of professors on renewals, tenure and promotions as well as on new appointments. Once in place, these structures would be used to block almost all appointments by PSA faculty and then to deny tenure, promotion or renewal to the majority of PSA faculty as well as various individual 'troublemakers' scattered across other departments. At the student level, the soon to be elected Student Council president Rob Walsh tried, and repeatedly failed, to get students to vote in referenda for new institutions that could be used to repress radical action by students, notably a new student society constitution that greatly reduced the authority of student body meetings and greatly increased the capacity of the Student Council president and executive to control things from the top-down and a joint faculty-student disciplinary body that could expel students or faculty for any acts of disruption.

In sum, the two tactics struck at precisely the two factors that I am arguing were the main sources of strength of the left movements among both students and faculty at Simon Fraser: first, to take away the participatory democratic structures that engaged the mass of students and faculty, especially the sovereign mass meetings conducting debates leading to policy stands or action; second, to end the unusual situation where junior faculty used their greater numbers to promote progressive ideas about teaching and research and democratic governance by constituting a standard professional hierarchy controlled by senior faculty (and to use that structure to purge all those faculty who held out against this and continued to support a democratic university controlled by students and faculty).

A great deal of this counter-insurgency had to be conducted by stealth, deception and dishonesty especially at the student level. Moderate students had to pretend they supported the same radical democratization goals as left students for the simple reason that a large number of students did, and time and again showed that they did. They had to pretend that they only disagreed about the means to those ends. At the beginning of the Fall 1968 semester, moderate Rob Walsh and a majority of other moderates won decisive victories to Student Council by declaring themselves `Moderates for Progress` through reason and hence ready to cooperate with the new university president Strand to reform the institution. Most of the students voting had not been on campus in the summer and were alienated from the radical language of oppression and power and confrontation and struggle that had become commonplace for those students who had directly experienced the CAUT crisis struggles of the spring and summer.

With left students largely out of power in the student government, the SDU, which had deferred to the Student Power Council in the summer, held a reorganizing meeting that attracted over 150 students. They decided that they would try to reorient the student movement by building it beyond the SFU campus in two ways. First they would look to raise issues on campus that made links to the class interests of workers and the interests of other disadvantaged groups in the wider society, issues that challenged the university as a business-controlled institution that served to replicate the social inequalities in society rather than undermine them, that served the dominant social groups rather than the poor and powerless. Second, they would work to actively construct alliances with off-campus groups starting by linking up with left student groups on other campuses.

A meeting of SDUs from several colleges as well as UBC and SFU was held on the weekend of November 9 and 10 1968. Students at Vancouver City College had been agitating for several weeks about the difficulty that large numbers of students were having getting accepted into SFU as well as getting the courses they had taken granted transfer credit. They charged that hundreds of students applying from the United States had been rejected apparently because they were deemed to be dodging the draft. Students from colleges, typically more lower middle or working class than those seeking transfer from other universities, were disproportionately denied admission or transfer credits. The SDUs decided to organize a joint campaign, led by the SDUs from UBC, VCC and Simon Fraser directed at SFU admission policies. Four demands were agreed to: (1) Freedom of transfer and automatic acceptance of credits within the BC public educational system; (2) An elected parity student-faculty Admissions Board; (3) The opening of all administration files [to investigate charges of conscious discrimination on either class or political grounds—surprising to even many radicals, files from administration filing cabinets would find their way into the student press after the student occupation which provided multiple dramatic examples of egregious discrimination of both kinds, including frequent RCMP background checks on student applicants and racist comments about things to do to stem the increasing number of foreign students applying especially from Hong Kong; (4) More money for education as a whole and equitable financing within post-secondary education (instead of most of the money going to UBC and SFU) including an end to the current school construction freeze.

The SDUs also agreed on an initial common action. On Thursday November 14 they drew 500 students, including contingents from UBC and VCC, to a rally outside the SFU administration building where students voted to adopt the four demands. Then a large number of students went into the registrar's office to present their documented individual cases of mistreatment and to ask for a new decision. Several hundred students did a "mill-in" action in the foyer of the registrar's office in support. University president Strand, accompanied by Registrar Evans, met them with a bull-horn. He told them they had a great issue and then said he categorically rejected all four demands. He referred the students to an Undergraduate Admissions Committee meeting that evening. Students attended but the committee, made up exclusively of faculty and administrators and normally meeting in closed sessions, voted that the demands were outside their terms of reference. After the students left the committee proceeded to adopt a substitute set of policy proposals that would be presented to Senate the next week. The students decided to meet on the weekend to plan an action for Wednesday November 20 when the Senate would meet in a special meeting on admissions issues called by petition of one of the student senators, Stan Wong, in response to the November 14 action and raising of the four demands.

Over the weekend preparations were made for presenting the four demands to the Senate and for various scenarios of follow-up actions, including at least a temporary occupation of the administration building, should they be rebuffed. The Senate voted to reject the four demands with almost no debate. Three hundred student observers walked out of the Senate meeting, met to decide on a course of action and occupied the administration building on the Wednesday night. On Thursday, the occupiers sent out students to speak in lectures to explain the demands and the occupation. Moderate Student Council president Rob Walsh called a mall meeting that he hoped would oppose the occupation. To his dismay 700 students voted over-whelmingly to endorse the four demands and the occupation itself.

The occupiers told president Strand that they would leave the building if he agreed to call a second Senate meeting to seriously debate the four demands. He re-fused and at 2am Saturday November 23 several hundred unarmed RCMP officers stood behind Strand as he spoke through a bullhorn telling students they had only a few minutes to leave the building or face arrest. The occupiers met, agreed that those with immigration status or other issues could leave and 64 students did but 114 stayed and, without resisting, were arrested and escorted one by one into waiting paddy wagons. At the jail the students were photographed and fingerprinted and re-leased on bail put up by sympathetic faculty and by the Student Council. They were charged with mischief against private property, an indictable offence punishable by up to 14 years imprisonment (later changed to trespass on public property punish-able with up to 5 years in jail).

Unlike most past major and minor conflicts with the university administration, this time the response of most faculty and most students sharply diverged. The Fac-ulty Association executive met on Saturday November 23 and issued a press release expressing full support for president Strand's calling of the RCMP onto campus to ar-rest the occupiers. They claimed that 158 out of 169 faculty contacted by phone had agreed with their statement. The Student Council met at 4am just after the bust and, with liberal moderate Stan Wong, former Student Council president, doing what President Walsh should have done, the Council voted to present five points largely drafted by Wong to a student body meeting on Monday November 25. On Monday Rob Walsh circulated a leaflet that flagrantly contradicted the Student Council's stand, calling on students to equally condemn SDU for the occupation and Strand for calling police on campus. Walsh's proposal was ignored and he quickly adapted and purported to support the five points while remaining vague on his stand on a student strike. There were long meetings of up to 2,000 students in the gym on Monday, Tuesday, Wednesday and Thursday (and hence a de facto strike since few students were attending classes).

Students voted for the first four points but not the fifth. They voted to urge Strand to convene Senate to discuss the four demands, asked Senate to create a par-ity body to investigate all administration files for evidence of political discrimina-tion, urged Strand to ask the Attorney-General to drop the charges against the 114 and asked Strand to assure the university community that the RCMP would not oper-ate any longer on campus. However on Thursday the results of a secret ballot on the fifth question, the calling of a general student strike starting the next Monday (the last week before final exams), were announced: students voted 2,428 to 1,181 not to go on strike. The 114 trials went ahead. Eventually 104 out of 114 pleaded guilty (but did not apologize for their actions) to a misdemeanour charge and a $250 individual fine. Several others pleaded not guilty and most received the same sentence. One student was sent to jail for three months because of an earlier conviction for speaking disrespectfully to a police officer who had been harassing a poor person in a restaurant. The repression worked to create fear and demoralization (and a considerable intensification of drug use, especially hallucinogenics, for a time) among many radical students. The SDU continued to agitate in the winter and summer of 1969 but there were no more major civil disobedience actions (although there a few small-scale ones).

D. The PSA Strike of Fall 1969

The last major conflict was the political purge of radical faculty who refused to go along with the institution of a standard professional hierarchy and insisted on maintaining and extending student-faculty democratic control where they had the authority to do so. The purge had been prepared carefully over a long period. The political police had been doing surveillance on suspected "communists" among faculty and graduate students since at least the lead up to the TA incident in Fall 1966 and Winter 1967. The belief that there were incorrigible radicals on the faculty had likely been a major consideration for the Board in refusing to accept the Faculty Association Academic Freedom and Tenure Brief, a refusal that led to the CAUT censure and crisis. Administration spokespersons were reported to have said more than once in that period that the Board felt that there had to be some "clearing out" of deadwood hired all too quickly in an instant university before a tenure policy could come into effect. The Board and president had been blocking PSA appointments since at least the AG Frank appointment of January 1968 but the blocking became more organized and systematic once Strand was appointed acting president in August 1968. In June 1968, the PSA faculty voted to accept proposals from the PSA student union that would soon create a system of parallel student and faculty plena with joint student-faculty parity committees negotiating policies to be voted upon by the two plena. This included committees and decisions dealing with hiring, firing, tenure and promotions. It was this action that was to provide the decisive opening for president Strand to orchestrate the purge.

Over the summer 1969 semester, departmental student unionism grew in other departments besides PSA and concessions of significant student power were won although not in the areas of hiring, firing, tenure and promotion. (It should be noted that the latter was not a "radical demand" in the view of students in the sense that the large majority of students who supported student power at all were enthusiastic supporters of having power in this area—in particular, even relatively conservative students wanted to have a say in what kind of teachers were hired to teach what kind of courses). On July 15 1969 the Dean of Arts Dale Sullivan announced that he was placing the PSA department under trusteeship. The parity-veto system in the area of hiring, firing, tenure and promotions violated university regulations and the whole parity-veto system would have to be dismantled. The PSA faculty had refused to do this in a vote on July 3. Over the next weeks, PSA faculty learned that most of them had been denied tenure, promotion or renewal by the University Tenure Committee.

Meanwhile the Board orchestrated the release of acting president Strand from his written promise not to stand for permanent president and appointed him permanent president. Professors in all three Faculties voted by large majorities to support releasing Strand from his promise. The Board organized a mail ballot of students between Summer and Fall semesters to pre-empt a Student Council plan to conduct a mass student meeting and then vote in the early Fall; a solid majority of students, not having heard any debate (most not enrolled in the Summer), voted to release Strand from his commitment. Strand had the mandate he needed to proceed with the purge of PSA faculty.

On Monday, September 22 1969, over 700 PSA students and faculty met in a combined General Assembly and voted to go on strike to demand the lifting of the trusteeship and restoration of the parity-veto system and a review of the University Tenure Committee decisions. Nine faculty were suspended for not teaching classes and action was eventually taken against others as well. Hearings for dismissal were announced. Left and liberal faculty in several departments adopted motions supporting PSA and its demands most notably in English and History. Students in the History and English departments voted to go on solidarity strike and picketed their own courses as well as joining in militant pickets to shut down "scab" replacement classes in PSA. Students in many other departments held strike votes and active students from each of these departments (Geography, Modern Languages, Philosophy, Biological Sciences, Education and even Economics and Commerce) provided support as individuals even though in most cases student referenda in their departments rejected a strike or did not complete the strike vote before the PSA strike was effectively over. Virtually all departmental student groups held debates between PSA and administration side spokespersons and all voted to support the PSA four demands. On October

2 over 200 Economics and Commerce students did this and also passed a motion after considerable debate stating, as the student paper reported, the central issue in this crisis is a defence of the right of student participation and we support the PSA department in its struggle to preserve this right for all students. When mostly conservative Economics and Commerce students adopt motions expressing sentiments like that you know that the support in the student body to hold onto and extend student power at the department level is rock solid.

The Senate voted 25 to 2 on October 6 to deplore the PSA faculty going on strike, to support the imposed new chair and to endorse the call of president Strand for a joint committee of CAUT and AUCC (the body of university administrations) to conduct an investigation of misconduct within PSA. The moderate Student Council president pressured the acting academic vice-president to convene a meeting of Joint Faculty on October 9. A motion was made to close the meeting, student observers would not leave and the chair ordered that a series of proposed motions be put to referendum without any debate. Multiple motions were eventually voted on by referendum over a period of about two weeks. The vote was 180 to 28 to 27 to support Strand`s call for an AUCC-CAUT committee to investigate PSA, 164 to 37 to 31 to commend Strand for following the procedures in the AFT brief in moving against PSA faculty and department (but to change them afterwards so they couldn't be used similarly against anyone else), 150 to 65 to 20 to decide most matters in future by referenda without holding Joint Faculty meetings for debate, 192 to 28 to 15 to close all future Joint Faculty meetings, 162 to 40 to 38 to deplore the action of PSA faculty in going on strike and, adding insult to injury, 115 to 98 to 22 to deny the suspended PSA faculty the right to participate in future Joint Faculty meetings [to plead their case] while still under suspension.

On October 23, the courts granted an injunction against picketing and 14 persons were served. On Friday October 24, the PSA General Assembly voted by a two to one margin not to defy the injunctions (which would have incurred jail sentences and fines). The strike was effectively over. On Tuesday, November 4 1969 the PSA General Assembly merged with students from the striking and supporting departmental unions in a Joint Assembly to vote to call off the strike. The student power movement had been defeated and the left faculty in PSA (and a few elsewhere on other pretexts) who had put their jobs and careers on the line in support of a democratic department teaching critical social science and serving the interests of social change for the poor and powerless were dismissed in what was likely the largest political purge of faculty in North American history.

The student body had stood solid in support of student power demands to the end. The change in the stand of the large majority of faculty from support for student campaigns in defence of academic freedom and freedom of speech and for the democratization of the university before June-July 1968 to opposition to both in the 114 occupation of November 1968 and the PSA strike of September-October 1969 was decisive.

Note

1 The extent to which UGEQ as a national student organization actually managed to mobilize students in 'change the society' struggles beyond the campus—and thus its differences from CUS and the English-Canadian radical student movement—should not be exaggerated. Certainly the student newspaper at the Universite de Montreal and to a lesser degree on other campuses promoted debate and reflection on Quebec nationalist and socialist ideas. The summer community organizing was effective at least in radicalizing many of the student participants if not in accomplishing much to set up ongoing social change movements in the communities where they had projects. UGEQ endorsed and mobilized some of its members to participate in some militant labour strike support pickets, marches for French-language rights (unilingualism) and demonstrations against the Vietnam war but it was a matter of endorsing the initiatives of others not leading and putting forward a policy, demands and calls to action. Above all the newly-created French language two year university colleges (or CEGEPs) and the College de Beaux-Arts achieved a high level of militant and sustained student mobilization.

The high point was the Fall 1968 occupation-strikes on multiple campuses over the demand for the opening of a new French-language university in Montreal to provide places to all the francophone CEGEP graduates. But this was on a higher education issue, albeit one that also posed the societal issue of the inequities between the privileges and resources accorded the English minority and the oppressed francophone majority in such areas as hospitals and schools. And it was this very mobilization that marked the beginning of the end of UGEQ (it dissolved into factions at its spring 1969 congress) because it exposed its incapacity to provide leadership to struggles beyond a single campus on either campus or societal change issues as well as its inability to resolve the internal crisis of 'process'—how to have student councils and the UGEQ leadership develop structures of participatory democratic debate and decision-making and still remain united and effective. UGEQ never took a position on separation at a Congress and was unable to participate directly in the main off-campus movement in francophone Quebec of the 1960s, the separatist movement. But UGEQ's failure to really implement the student syndicalist policy of intervening to contribute to the the development of a 'new nation' along a socially progressive path was not in vain. From 1968 on radical activist groups on most Montreal CEGEP and university campuses took up the banner and joined with municipal workers and the left-nationalist wing of the former RIN separatist group to participate in the FRAP campaign to unseat the mayor and especially in the community projects and committees (the CAPs or Political Action Commmittees) in the poor and working class neighbourhoods of Montreal which became the seedbed on radical societal change organizing on through the 1970s.

Anna Hoefnagels

Chapter **7** Native Canadian Activism and the
Development of Powwows in the 1960s

As one of the most public artistic expressions of Aboriginal culture in Canada, powwows showcase music, dance, arts and crafts, food, clothing and, in some ways, Native heritage and spirituality, in contexts that are open to Natives and non-Natives alike. Powwows can also serve as sites for cultural renewal and pride for participants, they are important for their role in sustaining traditional values and relationships (Huenemann 1992: 131), and they can also contribute to the healing of an individual, family and community (Warry 1998: 223). Powwows are also recognized as sites for First Nations people to celebrate their heritage in culturally meaningful ways, and as places where non-Natives can learn a bit about Native culture while enjoying the music, dance, food and crafts that comprise the powwow.

The powwow celebration gained in popularity and significance during the 1960s, in part due to the political climate of the time and the increased activism by, and awareness of issues challenging, First Nations people in Canada. Throughout the 20th century there were significant shifts in Native and non-Native relations in Canada, with an overall movement towards political organization, cultural revitalization and community and individual healing for and by First Nations people. The 1960s marks a significant period for cross-Canadian Native solidarity, as well as local or regional changes that fostered community well-being and pride in Native heritage. This period is also noteworthy for important developments in the powwow celebration: it was during the 1960s that existing social gatherings were reshaped in some Native communities to serve their own needs and interests; that powwows grew in popularity; and that various nations adopted the Plains-style music and dance that is now associated with the powwow celebration. Although the contemporary powwow celebration can be traced to the Warrior societies of Plains nations in the 1880s, powwows were not held in some regions of Canada until the mid- to late twentieth century, with some communities launching new celebrations today. This paper explores the factors that led to the political organization and increased activism of Aboriginal people in the 1960s, with a particular emphasis on the impact of the pan-Indian solidarity that resulted from Native involvement in the Canadian military during the World Wars, to illustrate the connections between precursors to the powwow, renewed "warrior prestige" and the development of powwows in the 1960s. I also explore the relationship between the political climate for Native Canadians during the 1960s and the developments in and decolonization of community gatherings, focusing on selected powwows held in southwestern Ontario. Drawing from fieldwork that was conducted in southwestern Ontario, interviews with powwow participants and organizers, and a review of relevant historical documents, this paper illustrates how powwows served to revitalize, and in some ways, decolonize Native culture in this region, especially during the 1960s. I argue that the increased awareness of the issues confronting Native Canadians prior to and during the 1960s, and the increased knowledge of powwows and related artistic expressions in other parts of North America, affected the popularity of these local gatherings while encouraging community members to organize and shape powwows to be meaningful cultural events in their communities.

Contemporary powwows in southwestern Ontario have a relatively short history, with many gatherings only dating back to the early 1960s, with new annual community gatherings launched since then.[1] For example, the powwow at the Walpole Island First Nation can be traced to 1955, the powwows at both Aamjiwnaang (Sarnia First Nation) and Wikwemikong can be traced to 1960, the Kettle and Stoney Point First Nation powwow dates back to 1970, Six Nations of the Grand River to 1980, and, for a comparison, the powwow at the Akwesasne Mohawk Nation, in southeastern Ontario, dates back to 2000. These powwows share many features with powwows throughout the rest of Canada, including a blend of social and ceremonial activities, music, dancing, crafts and arts vendors and a general renewal of Aboriginal culture and pride. It is generally agreed by powwow historians, participants and scholars that the origins of contemporary powwows can be traced to late 19th century war dances of various Plains Nations. As it will become clear later in this paper, the links between warrior societies, military involvement by Natives in the World Wars, and the resultant political organization and cultural renewal, directly impacted on the development and increased popularity of the powwow in the 1960s.

Adolf Hungry Wolf described the historic uses of war dances, writing:

[A] custom shared by American Indians of the past…was to work up courage and enthusiasm for war through dancing…The dancers pretended to
sneak around, their bodies often bent low, scouting for enemies and
searching the ground for signs. With their weapons they danced toward
imaginary enemies and fought with them, while whooping and yelling…If
the warriors returned from their war trails successfully, the women joined
them for victory dances (Hungry Wolf 1983: 4).

War dancing decreased in use and significance with the decline in warfare between
Native groups due to the establishment of reserves and the settlement of the Plains
region in the late nineteenth and early twentieth centuries, and so the importance
and roles of "the warrior" declined. At this time war dancing became primarily social
expressions, in which women and children were allowed to participate. Gradually,
these social gatherings spread beyond the Plains region and into other areas of North
America.

An important connection between 19th century war dancing and contemporary
powwows is the "warrior," soldier, or veteran which are highlighted in contemporary
powwow practices.[2] The status of "warrior" was re-legitimized through Native Canadian involvement in the military during the World Wars. Approximately 4000 status
Indians[3] volunteered for service during World War I (Dickason 2002: 307) and an estimated 6000 Aboriginal people enlisted in the military during World War II (Dickason
2002: 310). Native people who enlisted found that they were treated equitably and
that they were respected in the military, and they were also able to foster relationships with other Native recruits from across Canada. This resulted in a sense of solidarity amongst Aboriginal people across Canada, strengthening Native culture and
pan-Indian political organization. The First World War is recognized as an important
turning point in the unity of Native Canadians; historian Peter Schmalz indicates this
as he writes: "The seeds of pan-Indian consciousness were sowed when the war
brought Indians from across the nation into contact with each other for the first
time" (Schmalz 1991: 228). Indeed, Native involvement in Canada's military encouraged the revival and performance of significant cultural ceremonies and traditions
through the reinstatement of warrior status and prestige, which ultimately impacted
on the development and spread of powwows through the resultant cultural reawak-
ening, as explained by William K. Powers from his book *War Dance*:

Despite the early belief that Indian cultures were dying out, a number of
events occurred to strengthen rather than weaken Indian values, particu-

larly music and dance. First, World War I induced young American Indian men to volunteer for military service. The effect this had on native culture was to guarantee that many social institutions would maintain a sense of relevancy despite their anticipated degeneration and obsolescence. American Indians in fact had an opportunity to become 'warriors' again, thus permitting songs and dances related to war to retain a function within each of the Plains societies...the effects of World Wars I and II and, to a lesser extent, Korea and Vietnam, is that they gave American Indians the opportunity to reinforce cultural institutions that might have become dysfunctional. Indian soldiers who participated were regarded as heroes by their people and, in accordance with tribal custom, were publicly acknowledged through songs, dances, and giveaways. (Powers 1990: 50-51)

Native involvement in the military during the World Wars and other conflicts had adverse effects on their home communities, as their communities suffered economically and socially due to absence of many of their most able-bodied men and, in some cases, appropriation of reserve lands by the federal government. Upon their return, Native veterans were denied the benefits and supports given to non-Native veterans, leading to increased dissatisfaction on the part of Native veterans. However, through the enlarged social networks and cross-Canadian solidarity that resulted from contacts made through their military service, many Native soldiers gained an increased feeling of self-worth through decorations and commendations, and, having won the war alongside other Canadians, Native veterans felt they had proven their right to speak for themselves.

The pride and determination of many veterans resulted in a renewed sense of identity and autonomy, however, an important correlation can also be made between Native involvement in the military and increased political organization in Canada. Many veterans were involved in forming the Indian League of Canada in 1919, an organization which sought to improve conditions on reserves, foster solidarity amongst Native peoples across Canada and to negotiate co-operatively with federal government. Primarily focused in west, this group became known as League of Indians of Western Canada (in 1929), and it laid the foundation for Native political organization in Canada. Following the Second World War, other Native organizations were formed, including the Federation of Saskatchewan Indians (1958), the National Indian Council (1961), and the National Indian Brotherhood (1968) which was renamed the Assembly of First Nations in 1982 (Gaffen 1985: 72). These and other political organizations promoted greater awareness of the issues confronting First Nations people in Canada and also functioned as political institutions to strengthen First Nations communities. With increasing organization by Native peoples across Canada, the government grew uneasy, and in 1927 the Indian Act was amended, making it illegal for status Indians to organize politically or to retain legal counsel in pursuit of claims against the government. These restrictions remained in effect until 1951.

The political networking and establishment of various Native organizations during the first half of the twentieth also paralleled the increased activism by Native and non-Native individuals and groups that sought to acknowledge and rectify the issues and challenges confronting First Nations people in Canada and the United States. The 1960s was significant for Native populations across the continent due to the political organization, social activism and the general public's increased awareness of issues affecting Native people. For example, the Red Power Movement and the American Indian Movement both drew attention to the plight of Native people throughout North America, inspiring many people to learn about their heritages, and express their sentiments regarding the ongoing mistreatment of Natives. The American Indian Movement (or AIM), was founded in 1968 as a means of unifying Natives across North America and it fostered solidarity and a sense of pan-Indian identity, as it sought to "unite people in order to have an organized way of addressing recurrent and chronic problems that affect many different American Indian people and groups, rather than to blur their differences and to universalize indigenous experience" (Rich 2004: 71). Prominent master of ceremonies at powwows and musician Butch Elliott commented on the political climate of the 1960s, and the impact of AIM on Aboriginal people at this time, saying:

> Well the American Indian Movement was identified as a young organization, they were identified as youth, and they carried a lot of that…anger. All of a sudden they begin to realize that maybe there was something more…'maybe we should be more than we are,' and 'our condition should be better,' and 'why are we like this?' And there's actually very little publications about around that time, there's not a lot of books on the Indians and their experience…But, I think it was, you know that AIM [was] representative of the youth, and coming to the realization that all these things were going on, they'd seen all these problems that existed…Their actions started to get noticed, and you'd start hearing things about them, and [it]

really spread that people wanted to do something and realized that they could do something. All they had to do was just take the initiative to do it, and start standing up for themselves. You know we started dealing with issues like young guys wanted to wear their long hair, and that was against school policy…You had to deal with Social Service agencies that were taking kids. All those kind of heavy social pressures…You know, so you begin to question that, you begin stand up, you begin to feel good…in the late-sixties…that's where it really started to take hold. (Elliott 2007)

It is the cultural and political climate of the 1960s that fostered the adoption and adaptation of important gatherings for Native people throughout Canada, and North America more generally, leading to the adoption of the modern powwow and the decolonization of public "displays" of Native artistic practices. For example, due to their close proximity to non-Natives and ongoing assimilationist policies of the Canadian government, First Nation communities in southwestern Ontario had lost many traditional practices and customs and were taught to reject them as meaningful cultural expressions. As long-time powwow organizer and participant Glen Williams from Walpole Island said:

Indians…were taught…through residential schools that we were pagans…that it was devil-worship and stuff like this. And any Indian articles and stuff like that were destroyed, burned, we were not to handle it. And our language was beat out of us…there's a really large contingency here on Walpole Island, one of the largest from any other communities in Canada we're products of residential schools, maybe some 300 people that were sent to residential schools at one time or another. And that's not to say what they brought back from residential schools, and then it was put on to their children, the influences from that. And so there was that whole blanket, or that cloud, that hung over everybody at Walpole, that it wasn't a good thing, to dance and to sing. And so we were constantly up against this air there. And it was hard to get new people to come out and dance because they were our own people, Indian people, like they teased, you know, 'That's devil worship,' 'What are you going to do that for?'…To me it was pride, to me and my family. Because we were on the opposite of things, we tried to get this thing [the powwow] rolling…So anyway, we were battling that all the time, the attitudes, the attitudes and that sort of thing (Williams 2000).

Although Indian agents attempted to enforce the banning of traditional music and dance practices, according to Glen Williams (2000), traditional songs and dances had continued to be performed privately at Walpole Island until the 1950s, when the Indian Act of Canada was change to permit cultural expressions.

The musicians, dancers, organizers and other powwow participants with whom I spoke agreed that it was during the 1960s that powwows and similar gatherings in this area were reshaped to better suit the cultural needs of the local Native populations instead of serving the interests of non-Native audiences and Christian organizations. In terms of large Native social gatherings, the primary and immediate precursors to the powwow in this region included religious camp meetings and Native dance exhibitions akin to the Buffalo Bill and the Wild West Shows that were popular during the late 19th and early 20th centuries. At the Sarnia First Nation, former Chief of the Band, political activist, Men's Grass Dancer and respected Elder Fred Plain indicated that powwows gradually replaced the annual church camp meetings that had been imposed on the community by the United Church of Canada, indicating the 1960s as the period for this cultural renewal and the reshaping of community gatherings. Fred stated:

> …the actual beginning of the powwow in this community…actually found new life in the mid-60s. We advertised our powwow here. Now I think this year was the thirty-fifth, so that would take us back to 1965. I recall when the powwow first began…And the camp meeting was actually the forerunner of the powwow…I recall the first powwow they had here was in the mid-60s…we had a powwow I think in '62 or '63. So they've been going on ever since. And I recall at those powwows…the people would start coming, and…gradually, the religious camp meeting began to die away… they've given way to the powwow (Plain 2000).

As the main precursor to the Sarnia powwow, the annual Church camp meeting functioned as large social gatherings to Christianize those in attendance, yet these gatherings were reshaped or replaced to reflect the changing needs and goals of local participants and organizers. Indeed, drawing on local media in the 1960s, it appears that the first powwow at Sarnia First Nation took place on August 25th, 1962, and consisted of two "performances" of dances, one in the afternoon, the other in the evening. The local newspaper indicated that this was the first "performance of this sort at Sarnia reserve for white people," and a spokesperson stated that "the purpose in presenting the Pow-Wow was to preserve Chippewa traditions and culture and to inspire pride by the Chippewas in their own heritage and to educate white people in Indian lore and history" (Anonymous 1962: 9). While these sentiments continue to be echoed in modern commentary about powwows, the primary target audience is no longer "white people." Dance and music performances at early powwows at Sarnia were typically conducted by visitors from Mount Pleasant, Michigan, Toronto, Ontario, or from more distant Nations such as Blackfeet, Tawa and Muskegon. The prominence of visiting performers at early powwows at Sarnia is a trend that is common to many other gatherings in this region, due to the newness of the powwow and the inexperience of local musicians and dancers in powwow traditions at this time.

The connection between early powwows and Christian churches is also evident in the development of the powwow at Walpole Island. One of the oldest powwows in this region, this gathering can be traced back to at least 1955, when the Walpole Island Indian Fair took place on August 25th-27th. According to the local newspaper, this gathering included dance and craft displays, as well as a baby show, beauty contest, baseball games and a midway (Anonymous 1955: 7). The following year the paper referred to this gathering as the second powwow "to be held on the island in as many years," sponsored by Walpole Island's St. John the Baptist Anglican Church (Anonymous 1956:1). Complementing the information gleaned from local newspapers is the oral history of long-time powwow organizer and Walpole Island resident Glen Williams, who indicated that the community powwow evolved from staged dance performances that were held as fund-raisers for the local Anglican Church. He said:

> My uncle…was involved in the powwow when it was at the church grounds. It really wasn't called a powwow in those days, it was like a performance done by the dance troupe that was here…My uncle somehow became the organizer of that thing every year and what happened was they built a stage out in the field by the church grounds and they did these performances and demonstrated these dances on the stage. In twos and threes and fours and sixes at a time, and this was done as a fund-raiser for the church. All the monies went to the church, everything that was raised, or donations or anything like that. And eventually it evolved to inviting other dancers, like Oneidas from Muncey, and Oneida outside of London, and then we went further…And then they went on to invite people from Six Nations, what they called the dance troupe at the time and that was mainly a family too that went out and did those things. So we invited them down here and really, we would try here to give them a little bit of gas

money, just $5 or $10 for the gas tank just to get them back home and of course we'd have a nice feast with them too. But it was generally, it was really a good time. So that's how the powwow, if you can call it a powwow, it was an organized thing, that's when real organization came to it (Williams 2000).

Public displays of Native dancing in southwestern Ontario first took the form of dance troupes that traveled, and staged performances and demonstrations.[4] Staged dance performances, often for non-Native audiences, were one site where Native dancing was actually encouraged and fostered, even prior to the 1951 amendment to the Indian Act that had previously prohibited public music, dance and cultural performances. In an interview Butch Elliott reiterated the importance of these shows in the evolution of powwows, saying:

At one time powwows used to be…more like shows and stuff. There was stages, they used to dance on stages and stuff like that. And [powwow musician] Tefilo Lucero told me one time that down in the Detroit area, that nobody had regalia. A lot of those folks didn't have regalia at the time, and they rented them (Elliott 2000).

It is during the 1960s that the Plains-style music and dance that continues to be performed at powwows across North America was adopted into southwestern Ontario. In an interview, Glen Williams addressed the spread of Plains music into the lower Great Lakes region, while reiterating the historic role of the drum in peace negotiations:

And the western influence probably came over here probably just about the '70s, maybe around there, yeah. I'd say that, maybe '69, '68. And that came from Michigan way coming this way. And that's when we'd seen the big drum…And of course we knew that, and heard the stories orally, where the big drum had come from, it came from the western tribes, the Sioux, the Cheyenne, and it came through visions…And they were told that the drum was the sign of peace to all tribes, to the world or whatever it was at that time, whatever it happened to be. And that the Sioux and the Cheyenne were to take that word out and pass these…they were also taught songs that came with the big drum. And they were to take these songs and teach them to other tribes, and it was a symbol of peace, the drum was. And so that's how it all got started (William 2000).

Butch Elliott also commented on the music and dance precursors of powwows in southwestern Ontario,[5] similarly indicating the importance of the powwow for cultural revitalization in these communities in the 1960s and 1970s:

> [I]n southern Ontario and in through there…there were tribal dances… right up until the late 1800s. And for some reason after that, it took on a different form. It was done more theatrically, as an expression of culture. Because there was always…drums in my community hanging in the store or places, hand drums and different kinds of drums. But I never knew what they were…what it was when we were growing up, playing with a tom-tom or something like that. I mean it's always been with us, but I think we began to look at ourselves and how we should be using that, instead of putting it away, bring it out. And I think that's what happened in the Indian community in the '60s and '70s when people really began to go back to some form of expression. I think that's when the powwows became really meaningful…I think the powwow, the surge in powwows and dances and getting together has meant a lot in terms of really getting a grasp and a hold of who we are. And I've seen that, I've seen that in my lifetime. Not growing up with it as a child, and then later on finding out that there is this thing called a powwow, or this thing called a drum, and we used it as a very real part of the American Indian Movement and everything that we did…There was never a powwow at Cape Croker [when I was young]…I don't recall as a child ever going to a powwow like they do today (Elliott 2000).

Since the 1950s and 1960s, powwows held in southwestern Ontario have evolved from gatherings that served as shows for non-Natives in the form of church fundraisers and gatherings to reinforce the religious indoctrination of Native people, to become events meaningful to the community members themselves. Within this context of cultural revitalization and renewal, the powwow gained in popularity in southwestern Ontario and in other regions of Canada during the 1960s and 1970s, in part due to the acceptance of Native cultural practices such as the powwow and similar cultural expressions by the government during the late twentieth century; Fred Plain comments:

> And they [the government] couldn't stop the growth of the powwow. So it's recognized by them as just simply a part of the culture. And there's no

way they can stop it and in fact they encourage it now because they tell the
Canadian citizens that this is the life, the culture of the Aboriginal people.

The cultural revival that has been taking place since at least the 1960s in Native communities throughout North America has created a space for practices such as the
powwow, and, conversely, the powwow has served as a vehicle for this cultural revival. While powwows continue to be sites where non-Natives can watch, learn about
and participate in Native culture, the focus of modern gatherings is on the cultural renewal and celebration for Native participants and community members. From the
political activism and organization that characterized the 1960s, the reclamation of
control over Aboriginal cultural expressions and increased awareness of Native issues across North America, the powwow has become a site for the celebration of the
vitality and resilience of Native culture. While for many people powwows serve as a
reunion of friends and family and as an opportunity to meet new people from other
communities, for others they are places where they can celebrate, learn about and
take pride in their Native heritage, and reinforce connections with people from near
and far. The 1960s were particularly important for the political organization and cultural renewal for Native people across North America. It is also during this period
that communities, such as those in southwestern Ontario, claimed ownership over
their public celebrations, implementing changes to existing public gatherings that
had previously primarily served non-Native interests. Powwows played an important
role in the cultural revitalization that has taken place in Native communities since
the 1960s and, although powwows have changed since their inception, they are now
established celebrations with specific meanings, associations and importance to
people in these and neighbouring communities.

Notes

1 See Hoefnagels 2007 for more information on the development of specific powwows in this region.

2 See Hoefnagels 2001 for an exploration of the roles of veterans in contemporary powwows and the
   historic connection of powwows with warrior societies.

3 This figure does not include non-status Indians, Métis, and Inuit recruits.

4 In "Pan-Indianism in the Great Lakes Tribal Festivals," Gertrude Kurath commented on the acceptance of powwow music and dance in this region, focusing her analysis on the Iowa and Wisconsin tribes west of Lake Michigan, the Michigan Algonquins between Lakes Michigan and Huron.
   The only reference made to communities in this region of southwestern Ontario is to the Six Nations reserve east of Lake Huron: "the pagan Iroquois produce an August pageant; and Christian
   Iroquois put on Labor Day or October Fairs from Ontario to Nedrow, New York" (1957: 179).

5 An important factor that impacted on the current manifestation of powwows in southwestern Ontario is the travels that local people undertook in order to learn from other Native groups. Various people from communities in southwestern Ontario undertook travels to western Canada and
the United to attend powwows and learn strategies for hosting such an event, which they then
implemented at their own community gathering. Powwow organizer, musician and participant
Glen Williams recounted his family's role in learning and sharing western influences:

> ...[so]we began to travel, [my wife] and I, mainly in search of...I don't know if we were
> searching or not, I guess we wanted to gain knowledge I guess. We wanted to learn a lot about
> other Indian people throughout the U.S. and Canada. So we began to travel out west, we used to
> travel to Chicago and we'd come into contact with other Indians, some Sioux Indians there in Chi-
> cago, and there were Winnebagos, and then there was other Chippewas from Wisconsin and that
> area who'd come to Chicago, so it was a good gathering point there, to improve our knowledge
> about different things, celebrations and traditions and what other Indian communities were do-
> ing so we could come back and put them into our powwow, in our celebration, our days, our cele-
> bration days here. And then eventually we traveled further, the Canadian west. Saskatchewan,
> not so much Manitoba, but Saskatchewan, Alberta, and then down into Montana, the Dakotas,
> and then Nebraska and all through that area over there we traveled to learn more and constantly
> learning. And of course they had their celebrations out there...and we really enjoy ourselves out
> there at those things. And we really wanted to bring some of those, the things that we could
> bring, back over here too and have something likewise done here for the enjoyment of our peo-
> ple and so that's how we brought some of these influences over to our community, through our
> travel (Williams 2000).

By actively seeking knowledge and teaching about the powwow from other nations across Canada and the United States, people such as Glen Williams and his family were able to incorporate
new activities and ideas into their community powwow, shaping it to reflect the teachings they
had received in their travels.

References Cited

Anonymous. 1955. "Indian Craft, Dances, Baby Show Beauty Contest Planned at Walpole." *Wallaceburg News*, Tuesday, August 9, 7.

———. 1956. "Walpole Island Pow-wow To Hear Tom-tom Boom." *Wallaceburg News*, Tuesday, August 14, 1.

———.1962. "Pow-Wow To Get Encore." *Sarnia Observer*, Monday, August 27, 9.

Dickason, Olive. 2002. *Canada's First Nations*. Don Mills: Oxford University Press.

Elliott, Arthur (Butch). 2000. Phone interview by author. October 2.

Ewers, John C. 1964. "The Emergence of the Plains Indian as the Symbol of the North American Indian." Annual Report of the Board of Regents of the Smithsonian Institution, Publication 4613, Washington: U.S. Government Printing Office, 531-544.

Fowler, Loretta. 2005. "Local Contexts of Powwow Ritual," in *Powwow*, eds. Clyde Ellis, Luke Eric Lassiter & Gary H. Dunham: 68-82. Lincoln: University of Nebraska Press.

Gaffen, Fred. 1985. *Forgotten Soldiers*. Penticton, B.C.: Theytus Books.

Hoefnagels, Anna. 2001. "Remembering Canada's Forgotten Soldiers at Contemporary Powwows." *Canadian Journal for Traditional Music/Revue de musique folklorique canadienne* 28, 24-32.

———. 2007. "The Dynamism and Transformation of 'Tradition': Factors Affecting the Development of Powwows in Southwestern Ontario." *Ethnologies* 29/1-2: 107-141.

Huenemann, Lynn F. 1992. *Northern Plains Dance. Native American Dance: Ceremonies and Social Traditions*. Washington: National Museum of the American Indian.

Hungry Wolf, Adolf and Beverly. 1983. *Powwow*. Skookumchuck BC: Good Medicine Books.

Kurath, Gertrude P. 1957. "Pan-Indianism in Great Lakes Tribal Festivals." *Journal of American Folklore* 70, 179-182.

Plain, Fred. 2000. Interview by author. Sarnia, Ontario, July 6.

Powers, William K. 1990. *War Dance: Plains Indian musical performance*. Tucson: University of Arizona Press.

Rich, E. 2004. "Remember Wounded Knee:" AIM's Use of Metonymy in 21st Century Protest. College Literature 31/ 3 (Summer): 70-91.

Schmalz, Peter S. 1991. *The Ojibwa of Southern Ontario*. Toronto: University of Toronto Press.

Warry, Wayne. 1998. *Unfinished Dreams: Community Healing and the Reality of Aboriginal Self-Government*. Toronto: University of Toronto Press.

Williams, Glen. 2000. Interview by author. Walpole Island, May 12.

Kevin Brushett

Chapter *8*

Making Shit Disturbers: The Selection and Training of the Company of Young Canadian Volunteers 1965-1970

At the Twenty-fifth Annual Reunion of the Company of Young Canadians (CYC) former volunteer Dale Seddon reminisced that "when I joined the CYC, I was so straight I squeaked. I arrived at a Selection Weekend in Toronto wearing a suit and tie, clean underwear and socks, and shiny new shoes … What I heard, what I saw, was brand new to me, and the poetry of revolution filled me with admiration." Still," Seddon continued, "I was such a greenhorn, that, to this day, I have no idea how I ended up getting selected. From what people were saying I was the enemy… I emerged from training at Val David wearing beads and bells, headbands and ponchos earrings and torn jeans—an overnight hippy radical. My heart was loaded with the stuff of revolution, and I was out to gun down the lies my father had told me about the world.[1] Like hundreds of other idealistic young Canadians of his generation, Seddon responded to Prime Minister Lester B. Pearson call to join the Company of Young Canadians. In doing so, he became caught up in the debates both inside and outside the organization over the nature of its mandate. Would this new Company simply aid and assist existing social service organizations in delivering programs to Canada's poor and disenfranchised, or would it be an agent of social action and social change? By the time the first recruits and been selected and brought to Antigonish Nova Scotia for the first training section the more "radical" members of the CYC had decided that a community based "Alinsky-style" social action agenda would be the defining philosophy of the Company. Indeed, in the words of one volunteer who wrote to Prime Minister, CYC volunteers like Seddon were "to be shit disturbers … social change not service was to be our role."[2]

And yet the history of the CYC as a catalyst for social change has often been seen as one of failure. During its brief life as an independent government organization, the CYC constantly bounced from one controversy to another until late 1969 when the government finally decided to revoke its independence. In the intervening years, community projects came and went, and other than a handful of success stories, most achieved little more than slapping a few "band-aids" on the problems of poverty, powerless and prejudice. To some the CYC's failure was predictable; it was never more than a cynical ploy of the Liberal government to buy off discontented youth. For others the CYC's demise was largely self-inflicted. Most of these accounts have focussed particularly on the rocky relationship between the Council, the Ottawa staff and the volunteers in the field. All too often, they claim, volunteers were abandoned in their projects, with little guidance or even moral support from either the regional or head offices.[3] However, little attention has been paid to the role that volunteer recruitment, selection and training played in the troubles the CYC faced in achieving wider and deeper social change in Canadian communities.

Given that government funded hell-raisers, or as the media soon characterized them—a bunch of dirty hippies and adventure seeking beatniks—was a risky and in many ways revolutionary proposal, CYC leaders recognized that careful volunteer selection and proper training would be crucial to the organization's success and survival. Unfortunately, as the first training session at Crystal Cliffs (Antigonish, Nova Scotia) revealed, the Company was ill-prepared and the result was an unmitigated disaster from which the Company never really seemed to recover. What follows not only seeks to understand what happened at Crystal Cliffs (and beyond), but more importantly why the CYC was unable to make youthful idealists into successful community leaders of social action and social change. The answer to that latter question lies, I think, in large part to the inability of the Company to articulate a clear understanding of its own vision of community organization, social animation (or *animation sociale*), and radical social change and the characteristics of good community organizer. But , as the following pages will show, even if the Company had the ability and discipline necessary to impose such a vision it would have run up against the emerging generation gap within Canadian New Left over the very definition of these concepts and indeed the purpose of the Company itself.

The Road to Crystal Cliffs: Social Action vs. Social Service

The origins of the debate between social service and social action were present at the very creation of the CYC. Though Liberal politicians and backroom organizers spoke of creating a radical organization that would work with poor and disadvantaged communities to help them tackle the problems they faced, their working model was a domestic Peace Corps akin to the VISTA (Volunteers in Service to America) program organized by the Kennedy Administration. Under such a model, Company volunteers would "neither compete with nor absorb existing programs," but would work along side existing social service agencies. As the Leddy Report remarked, "the need for increased social action is obvious, and there are a number of areas in which the service of volunteers can be most helpful [however]... existing agencies don't have the resources." Hence the decision by the government to recruit, train and place volunteers in positions that would "increase their effectiveness and supplement their work."[4]

However, it was quite clear to many younger members of the Interim Committee that such a mandate would have very little resonance with young Canadians. For one, young Canadians, particularly those who saw themselves as radicals, bristled at the association of community development and the Peace Corps. To them the idea of a domestic Peace Corps, or its Canadian equivalent CUSO (Canadian University Students Overseas), was at best a hopelessly liberal "do-gooder" organization that would bring paternalistic and "middle class" solutions to the problems of poverty and disenfranchisement. At worst it smacked of imperialism, and perhaps even worse American imperialism, which by 1966 was manifesting itself in its most violent and destruction forms in the jungles of Southeast Asia. As Doug Ward, who was then head of the Canadian Union of Students (CUS) and a member of Canada's fledgling New Left organization, the Student Union for Peace Action (SUPA) remarked to his colleague and future CYC staff member Art Pape (also a member of SUPA):

> ... very clearly, the government does not ant any trouble at all with the Company. They see it as pure gravy, an excellent way to mobilize some of the awkward forces and power that youth today seems to be showing (the old 'get them swimming at the Y and they won't masturbate' approach). It is a nice programme and hardly anyone can be against it—*except the youth*.[5]

What the younger members of the Interim Committee such as Ward, Alan Clarke, Art Pape and Stewart Goodings, had in mind were Alinsky-style community development programs that Students for Democratic Society (SDS) had been running in various American inner cities since 1964. Known as Economic Research and Action Projects (ERAP) these community organization projects attempted to carry over the campus and civil rights activism that many SDS members had participated in for the previous two summers into poor northern inner-city neighbourhoods in an attempt to create an "interracial movement of the poor."[6] Despite the failure of most of the ERAP projects to create that movement, they captured the interest of SUPA members in Canada. By 1965 SUPA followed SDS movement from the ivory tower to the ghetto and had begun to organize communities across Canada from the black community in Halifax; to tenants in Kingston, Ontario; to Métis peoples in Neestow, Saskatchewan. Eventually, the CYC would sponsor those projects in the summer of 1965 in hopes of testing its approach and attracting future volunteers with expertise or at least experience in the field. In addition, to the influence of SDS and SUPA's activities, Clarke and Ward also had in mind the social animation projects run by the BAEQ in the Gaspe region of Quebec, which had real success in helping local people have a say in the economic development of their communities.

By early 1966 Clarke, Ward, and Goodings had successfully manoeuvred the Company leftward away from a social service ethos towards a philosophy that would see the Company's volunteers as catalysts for social change. As social *animateurs* they would reject the traditional "band-aid" solutions to poverty and other social problems. Instead, they were to be radicals in the sense of going to the roots of the problems in these communities and to help local people, identify and develop democratic solutions to the problems that plagued them and their communities. "Only when people [were] involved in the decisions that affect them," claimed Ward, "would effective and long lasting social change … take place."[7] If that meant disrupting existing social relations and occasionally "shaking the power structure," that is being "shit disturbers," then so be it.[8]

The move to the left was in many ways attempt to woo members of SUPA who viewed the CYC with a tremendous degree of suspicion and cynicism. How could a government run agency turn around and not only criticize it, but undermine the entire social order upon which in rested and depended for its legitimacy? To many SUPA members and others who saw themselves as political radicals those who defected to the CYC were in the words of Jim Harding, "Cash[ing] In [and] Drop[ping] Out."[9] To a degree the argument was valid, as Art Pape argued on when he left SUPA for the CYC, "[there was} four million dollars on the table and if we didn't pick it up somebody else is going to."[10] To Pape and other SUPA members who crossed the Rubicon to the CYC, it was more important that good work be done, or at least attempted, than to preserve some kind of ideological purity. For others in SUPA, the CYC as a hopelessly "liberal institution" that was "*not radical*, [but] … co-optive and [therefore] …cannot do 'real' community organizing."[11] Nonetheless, by 1965 it was clear that like SDS's experience with its own ERAP projects, SUPA's own community projects were floundering and only an influx of CYC cash in the summer of 1965 saved them.

Yet as much as Goodings, Ward, and Clarke courted SUPA they were also wary about the baggage that many of them might bring to the new organization. On the one hand, former SUPA members often matched the profile of the hip, young and committed radicals that they pictured the ideal CYC volunteer would eventually become. Many of them also had experience with community organizing which would help the CYC achieve the early successes they knew it would need to overcome the inevitable criticism that they were stirring up trouble where none existed. However, they also worried that a rapid influx of SUPA people would lead to charges that the CYC had been taken over by radicals and communists, charges that would waste Company time and resources trying to fend off. In this respect, Stewart Goodings noted in an article distributed to Canadian university campus newspapers that he hoped that the Company could make radical and significant social change without "falling into the hands of people who would wish to make it an ideological instrument."[12] He also admitted that he was very wary of the "predetermined assumptions" of SUPA members, which "very often get in the way of the problems and attitudes of the people in the community."[13] Others very much tried to make it clear that the Company would not reject anyone because of their political philosophy or ideology, and that the Company sought a wide range of "talented young people" who were willing to spend two years of their lives engaged in the "slow and painful process of getting the roots of the cancerous roots of [various] social problems."[14] Indeed, Company meetings held early in 1966 to decide on selection criteria made it clear that the CYC should avoid "extremists" and those with a "conflict of interest."[15]

Regardless of political philosophy, the shift from social service to social change required kind of volunteer that would be difficult to find among the population of young Canadians. Volunteers, the Company's Aims and Principles claimed, should be "independent, flexible—not under constant supervision—to exercise initiative and responsibility, invention and imagination." It also noted that volunteers would come to the community projects with their own prejudices, but hoped that they would be mature enough to "at least be aware of them" so that they would not think they were "bringing truth to communities." In this sense, the CYC was interested less in volunteers attitudes towards who were interested in social change than they were in those who were committed to "the methods and processes which are required for constructive social change."[16] In the words of Herbert Prefontaine, then one of Canada's few "experts" in the area of Community Development/Animation Sociale successful volunteers would need "a sense of mission" a well-rounded out education; emotional maturity; judgement; an over-riding interest in the well-being of other humans; a wide range of human relations skills; the ability to live in comfort with conflict and to provoke it when required; understanding for and respect of administrators and politicians but awe of neither; a sense of urgency; and a sense of humour."[17] This was a very tall order for an organization that originally conceived of having more than 1000 volunteers between the ages of 18 and 24 in the field by the end of its first year of operation. Indeed, many of those who left the provisional council after the Company changed its mandate from social service to social change, did so not only because they rejected the radicalism implicit in that transformation, but because they very much doubted that they company could find enough young people with the kind of traits Prefontaine had listed.

It would not be long before the doubting Thomases on the Interim Committee were proven right. Much of the early correspondence of the company highlights the profound disappointment with the abilities of the early applicants. By the spring of 1966, when the Company was gearing up to select and train its first cadre of volunteers, it had only received 1500 enquiries, of which only about 200 had formally filled out the 14 page application book. The application booklet asked them everything from their basic personal information, to their education and experience in community work, to their favourite books and television shows. Prospective volunteers were also required to undergo a number of psychological tests and an interview before they would be accepted into the company for training. After collecting the applications and test results from the first 178 candidates, many inside the company raised concerns about their calibre. According to an internal policy development paper "many of the volunteer applicants [did] not appear to have the necessary maturity nor experience to allow them to do useful work in community development." Jack Snell, a former SUPA member but now the Company's Ontario Regional Supervisor wondered whether those who were applying were "ready to "commit themselves to the slow painful process of [community development work] … can they spend long hours, days in communities learning from others" Or, he continued, were they "people who don't have this orientation, and who would be much more comfortable working in more structured situations in which a social agency, a Government department, or some other group would outline a set of specific tasks for them to carry out." Until then, many council members advised that the Company think long and hard about the types of projects it sent its volunteers to and that it "strike a decent balance in all areas of its operations; community development and social action, service to a variety of needs, recruitment of people with a variety of experience and abilities…."[18]

"What Happened At Crystal Cliffs:" *Lord of the Flies* Revisited

Of course the Company did not expect to unearth budding Saul Alinskys that it could immediately send into the field. So in early 1966 the Company began to plan a 6-week training session that would give its recruits an orientation to the Company and its aims, a program of sensitivity training, and some instruction into the basics of Community Development and Social Animation. Given that the Company was still in its infancy it farmed out the training to the Coady Institution and the Department of Extension at St Francis Xavier University located in Antigonish Nova Scotia. Both organizations had a long history of community development programs, including the training of Peace Corps, CUSO, VISTA, and even some civil rights volunteers. Led by Stanley Searle, who would conduct the sensitivity training, and Des Connor who would lead the community development segment of the course, the team from St. Francis Xavier envisioned a program that would give the volunteers "a systematic but flexible training in community development."[19] Some wondered, however, if social animation and community development were really teachable, especially in such a short period of time. Nonetheless, the company brushed those concerns to the side and forged ahead thinking that they setting out on a bold venture without precedent in Canada.[20]

On June 26 1966, when the Company assembled its first 56 volunteers at the Crystal Cliffs Camp in Antigonish for its inaugural training session the initial fears and anxieties about the qualities of the volunteers soon came back to haunt the Company. Unfortunately for both the company and its volunteers, what happened at Crystal Cliffs was an unmitigated disaster from which the Company never really recovered. As the CYC histories by both Margaret Daly and Ian Hamilton note, the first training session at Crystal Cliffs was "hastily arranged, uncoordinated, ill-conceived and utterly bizarre training session, which remained "painfully vivid in the minds of nearly everyone who went through it, near it, or even heard of it."[21] Within the first week, six volunteers abandoned the program. The first three left in the middle of the night when one volunteer escaped with his wife and child, the former of which who had come to believe that the water was tainted with LSD and that she could cause strange and intense sexual responses in others. Another young woman ended up in a psychiatric ward of a local hospital, diagnosed with schizophrenia. She was soon joined by a sensitivity trainer who had a mental breakdown just two days into the 10 day session.[22] By the time the six-week course was over, most volunteers stumbled out of Antigonish tired, relieved, full of radical rhetoric, but with very little practical organizing techniques or [information] about the communities they were to enter as volunteers.[23] As Stinson ruefully commented "the group which participated in the first Training Course, will disperse with no sense of unity, no common cause or value structure."[24] Indeed, only 42 of the first 56 were assigned to the projects, 6 abandoned the program, while another 8 were sent for further training; at the end of the two year contract, only 9 of the original 56 remained in employ of the Company.[25]

What had gone so terribly wrong? First and foremost, CYC officials paid little or no attention of the actual process of selecting volunteers. In the months leading up to Antigonish Company staff in charge of recruitment, selection and training were warned that the selection process was the most important factor in ensuring the success of its bold experiment in CD.

On the surface the 56 who arrived at Crystal Cliffs met the criteria expected of CYC volunteers. They were young, enthusiastic, idealistic, and ready to commit two years of their lives to the battle in the war on poverty in Canada. They came from all walks of life from all over the country.[26] Though most were university students, others included high-school drop outs, shoe salesman, draughtsman, professional engineers, school teachers, youth workers, a candidate for the United Church ministry, a radio disc jockey, and a "bearded ex-Army lieutenant who played the guitar." According to Michael Valpy, who recorded the session for the *Globe and Mail* (and who because of his attendance at the Crystal Cliffs subsequently became a public relations officer for the Company), "no more than a handful could be considered beatniks, radicals or hippies." Some of them like Lynn Curtis came because they thought it would be a "snow job" and were quite candid out their attempts to shake up the world views of the "bubblegummers" they expected to find. The rest were generally the straight middle class church going young people armed with little more than a vague humanitarianism to guide them.[27]

However, beneath the surface it was clear that at least one quarter and as many as one half of the original volunteers should have been weeded out before they even arrived at the inaugural training session. The application process proved to be the weakest link in the entire chain of events. The application booklet was supposed to collect as much information on potential candidates as possible. However, it became quite clear that the recruiting staff either ignored the information contained within or never properly assessed it. In fact, one young woman who made it to Antigonish, left her entire booklet empty save for the statement that she liked to watch the leaves fall in autumn. In addition, the women who suffered a schizophrenic breakdown had forged the signatures of her references, and those who could vouch for her were later determined to be "fallacious and unreliable."[28]

The psychological tests given to the prospective volunteers also revealed that many of them would be unsuitable *not only* as volunteers for social service type work, but particularly as "free agent" social *animateurs* who would be in remote locations with little direct support from the Company. The Company believed that its volunteers must be able to "tolerate stress, [loneliness], uncertainty, insecurity, and different behaviour patterns."[29] And yet, the initial psychological tests given to prospective volunteers were inadequate to measuring those qualities. No interviews were employed to better assess the tests scores or confirm their validity. Equally important, the company hired to conduct the DDT tests, a visual motor test that assesses ego functioning and the ability to deal with a loss of control, did not fully report "all angels of interpretation," or the "latent tendencies" of some of the volunteers. Even so, some of the reports were quite clear that certain volunteers were not to be put in stressful situations, such as ten days of sensitivity training with trainers who were not equipped to deal with serious psychological problems. To make matters worse, none of the training staff received any information on the volunteers, including their psychological assessments, until after the sensitivity training had finished. Only the presence of Dr Noel Murphy, a psychologist from St. Francis Xavier University, saved many more in the group from complete emotional and psychological collapse.[30]

Given the general disdain that many on the New Left held for psychology it is not surprising either that those responsible for the selection of the volunteers generally dismissed both the reports and the concerns they raised. After all, an anonymous author of a CYC document argued volunteers were naturally "screwy." They were "at the same time poet, revolutionary, madman and do-gooder? How can one person be naïve and wise, old and young, lazy, shiftless and hard working all at once? ... a volunteer is exactly this: a multitude of schizophrenic personalities tied together by some invisible, inexplicable bond...They do not fit. They are partially round blocks, and partially square blocks, and society has no holes, yet, into which they can comfortably fit."[31]

But many both inside and outside the movement warned about the high risk nature of attracting screwy personalities. For example, Bert Marcuse, the Executive Director of the Calgary Family Service Bureau warned the organizing committee as early as the summer of 1965 that "volunteers will offer themselves because, consciously or unconsciously, they will be seeking to meet their own ... emotional needs ... though a vicarious experience and will lack the emotional maturing and stability to function efficiently and selflessly in the type of work envisaged by the Company." Marcuse warned the CYC council members that "volunteers should be given a careful psychological and social assessment before being accepted as a volunteer in the Company."[32] If Bert Marcuse's opinions could be tossed as aside as those from the social service mafia those of Jim Harding should have been paid attention to. Harding remarked as early as 1964 that SUPA had "become a haven for neurotics and fanatics, people unable to cope with and manipulate reality." Another SUPA activist also noted that by 1967 SUPA it had become "a mixed bag of political activists and alienated youth," which meant that the organization had been as much a "quasi-therapeutic community for alienated kids' as it was a political movement.[33] In the aftermath of SUPA's decline it appears that the CYC took its place as the haven for idealistic misfits. Indeed, when asked what they would do if not selected for service in the Company, most volunteers couldn't give Dr. Murphy "any alternative."[34]

In the soul searching that occurred in the aftermath of Antigonish, Company officials believed that the high risk high payoff approach that it had taken with volunteer recruitment and selection should not have occurred at such a critical point in the CYC's history. Somewhat jokingly Wally Kubiski stated that in light of its recruiting practices the Company should change its name to "The Company of Hip, Radical, Turned-On Canadians," but it didn't generate much of a laugh with the rest of the staff. In fact, many were worried that harbouring weak, or in the terminology of the time, "hung up" volunteers, would not only be detrimental to the Company's work, but to the volunteers themselves. At a staff conference at Lévis, Quebec in November 1966 "staff members [not only] complained bitterly about the calibre of present volunteers … [but] almost unanimously agreed that the Company could no longer go on providing therapeutic havens for weak people in the field" Both Kubiski and Bob Oliveiro were clear that the time for "pussyfooting around" was over; the Company simply couldn't "afford to [continue] playing games with little boys and girls. Oliverio continued, "the problem is not lack of field support for the volunteers but a lack of staff ability to be firm and tough enough to stop hung-up volunteers from hurting themselves and others."[35] Ironically, the much disparaged Leddy Report, said exactly that; rejecting volunteers unsuited for the Company's work would be difficult, but that in the interests of its future, the Company needed "a set of criteria for selection and rejection, and apply them firmly as required."[36]

Of course ten days of sensitivity training in which the volunteers were thrust into without any structure, authority, and which was meant to challenge their perceptions of themselves and their world view only brought the latent psychological and emotional issues to the forefront. The T-group sensitivity sessions were intended to develop interpersonal skills such as listening, communication and consensus building. They were also intended to make volunteers more aware of their own "hang ups," to disabuse them of their middle class customs, and to make them more sensitive to the needs, desires, and problems of others. However, most of those who went through these ten days at Crystal Cliffs spoke of it as "[p]sychic conditioning gone right out of control," a "mind bending affair" that "tore them apart."[37] At the time, trainers and CYC officials brushed off some of the problems and conflicts that occurred in the T-group sessions as part of the normal reaction to the removal of traditional social barriers. As Dr Noel Murphy commented "It was a time for problems to come out... [and] when they do, defenses fall and all sort so insecurities are made apparent [and] the psychiatric problems held by anyone taking this course would have come out eventually, either here or later."[38]

The T-group sessions not only brought out volunteers' hang ups, but they became the first battlefield to test the Company's commitment to community organization as social change rather than band-aid style social service work. Radicals came to Antigonish intent on challenging the vague liberal humanitarianism of the middle class kids that the CYC would largely recruit. As Art Stinson noted, the radicals quickly took advantage of the lack of structure and authority because "shaking up the structure was what they knew best, and to which their skills were best adapted." The do-gooders among the groups were thrown off by the radicals and found it very difficult at least initially to articulate a response to them. Some of them quite consciously threw off their "middle class" baggage and joined the radicals. Others opposed them, but did so in a ways to avoid open conflict.[39]

In the meantime the idea of consensus, which was supposed to be used to build the "beloved community," was instead used to block almost every attempt to find it. Indeed, the idea of community itself became somewhat warped. As Stinson reflected: It was "a concept of a group with no structure, no mechanisms for action, no specialization of roles, individual "freedom," no rules, no discipline, acceptance of individual differences to the point of deviation and abnormality." "This system," he continued, "encouraged the breakdown of sexual morality, the accomplishment of bizarre acts of defiance (burning a cross), the rejection of outside sources of information, the elimination of most activities in which the leaders did not show up well (sports, singing, dancing) and the creation of physical exhaustion through sleep deprivation. As a result, he concluded, the leaders of the T-groups were "incapable to putting the pieces back together into 'a new and constructive structure' after breaking them up ... Anarchy reigned. Fear... derision and ridicule served as the methods of control for the new society."[40]

Quite ironically somewhere in all of this anarchy the volunteers did reach a certain level of sensitivity to each other that expressed the values of the beloved community. As volunteer Peter Mussallem noted "we found a feeling of sensitivity had been reached, we found a feeling of universality—a love orientation that seemed to transcend the existence of material boundaries."[41] The newness of the experience led us to believe that the propagation of a purely sensitive population should be guiding aim of the Company." Built on the infamous 60s motto "Make Love Not War" the new community soon was often "lived out" by volunteers. However, the concept of total love not only entailed a community that deprecated knowledge, skill and analysis, as Stimson argued, but it also tended to enhance an already romanticized view of the lives of the poor and disadvantaged.[42] It also led many to believe that the true purpose of the CYC was "the propagation of a purely sensitive population" and that "the Company of Young Canadians believes in a love-oriented society; one in which the values of individual morality are placed above the exigencies of technological economics."[43] While the organizers could appreciate these values and sentiments, they were not what they had in mind for successful tough minded community organizers.

At some point all agreed that the building of the beloved community had to end and the training of shit disturbers begin. The problem was that the T-group training had done such a good job 'turning on' the volunteers that it was very difficult to turn them off. As a result, many didn't want to leave the "unreal" community they had built over the previous ten days for the more prosaic concerns of how to find and develop leaders within a community. For those who did not adjust well or quickly to the T-group sessions, the rapid shift to the "reality" of what their future work in the Company would entail only left them even more frustrated. Somehow they believed they had been cheated out of attaining greater personal knowledge and feeling. Volunteers' reactions to introduction of structure, authority, and outside experts that characterized the CD sessions, brought into sharp relief the chasm of expectations between many of the volunteers and CYC leaders.[44] According to Bill Curry, the trainers and the staff "assumed that the volunteers were employees ... and that [even though] they were amateurs ... [they] ought to be professionals [who] had a job to do [which] was to fight the war on poverty." On the other hand, he noted "[t]he volunteers displayed an open contempt for professionalism and expertise. They implied that the world was already suffering from a surfeit of case-workers—an overburden of professionalism. They reiterated that since they were neither professionals nor employees, they had no objective, initially, more than simply going, in answer to invitations, and living in a community. They expressed the conviction (in the apparently

embarrassing terms of brotherly love that they were involved in a revolution, the nature of which is a reversal of traditional values and practices and which would result
in human potential being put ahead of all other allegedly practical considerations ...
the first reaction of the resource people was astonished disbelief ... followed by a
show of contempt to match that of the volunteers and they ridiculed the volunteers
as impractical, Utopian idealists..."[45] As a result, the CD sessions did not go very well,
and perhaps even worse, many volunteers did not even attend the CD sessions; attendance often barely reached half of the entire group.[46]

All in all, it was quite clear that the CYC had not done its homework in recruiting
and training the first cadre of volunteers. They had gone in with untested expectations
and assumptions both of young Canadians and the necessary qualities of a community
organizer and found them seriously wanting. For the most part, both the staff and the
trainers were unprepared for the rapidly changing attitudes of young people of the mid
to late 1960s who had become increasingly suspicious, if not hostile, towards all forms
of authority, structure, and expertise.[47] Many of them were quite clearly shocked at the
volunteers the CYC had recruited. Though they were quite taken by the idealism, the
sense of commitment and the "active spirit of revolt against middle class assumptions"
among many of the volunteers (although a significant portion retained their "hopelessly mixed up ... missionary or do-gooder complexes'), they were also quite often
taken aback by the aggressive, suspicious, and at times, paranoid, behaviour and attitudes of many of the volunteers, particularly the so-called radicals. CYC officials had
generally expected that the volunteers would be "unanimously ready and willing to
train' and that they would arrive with their same "love of freedom and ... carefree spirit
of venturesomeness." Instead they found "a widespread and morbid preoccupation
with security."[48]

The Fall Out from Crystal Cliffs

As the survivors stumbled out of Antigonish in early August 1966 to go to their projects, CYC leadership were certain that another Crystal Cliffs would not happen
again. Immediately, letters went out to prospective candidates for the upcoming
September training session in Moncton, New Brunswick advising them that their invitation to training did not constitute an automatic selection to the Company. Instead,
the files of all candidates would be re-examined, especially their psychological tests.
In addition, candidates were advised that they would be re-interviewed and those
who "were too immature or emotionally unstable or not interested in the kind of social change work to be done in CYC, will be counselled out."[49] The high risk, high payoff strategy employed at Antigonish was gone.

In addition to changes to selection procedures, the CYC also decided not to farm out training to outside persons and organizations. Instead, for the Moncton sessions, the CYC brought in a number of internal experts and advisors who could better get across the aims and principles of the Company. Two experts with a great deal of field training in the techniques of CD and *Animation Sociale*, Jacques Noel and Guy Beaugrand-Champagne, the latter of whom had extensive experience with the BAEQ, were brought in to conduct the training. Though sensitivity training was also part of the training programme it was greatly de-emphasized in favour of small group sessions built around the concepts and techniques of *Animation Sociale*, a brief three day field experience, and large group sessions to examine Company projects.[50] Indeed, if there was one thing that came out the experience of Antigonish it was the fact that the T-group sessions had basically created competing communities within the Company. As Art Stinson remarked Antigonish failed to get across that the "constant is the Company not the group." Otherwise the CYC would fail in "developing a team to work on series of related projects."[51]

Finally, in addition to taking on a greater responsibility for training volunteers internally, the Company finally decided to hire a full time staff member who was solely responsible for training and volunteer support. One of the chief causes of the Crystal Cliffs debacle was the fact that the work of the training committee had been very slip shod. According to committee member Richard Thompson, "the Training Committee had not been very meticulous in its recording of decisions up to that point, and it was not clear … who was responsible for implementing the [committee's]… decisions." He also noted that there was "no one on the staff whose primary responsibility is training."[52] To resolve this problem the Company hired Robertson Wood, a 30 year old psychology graduate from the University of Western Ontario. More important than his academic qualifications was his extensive experience with community and civil rights organizations. Before coming to the company Wood had worked as freelance writer, actor and worked in Mississippi with civil rights organizations, in Saskatchewan with SUPA's Neestow Partnership Project, and in Ontario as the organizer of SUPA's 1965 People's Conference in Kingston.[53] If nothing else Wood had "the street cred" that Des Connor did not. Whether that might actually turn volunteers on to the more mundane activities of community organizing remained to be seen.

Wood put the company selection and training program on a much more solid footing. He was highly critical of the Company's approach to training at both Antigonish and even at Moncton, even though he claimed that results there were "much more satisfactory … [and] came close to the expectations of its design." Both training sessions, according to Wood, put far too much emphasis on "introspection and developing "love," which only resulted in creating "sensitized but ineffective volunteers." Instead, Wood argued that the Company should put more emphasis on "communities ... what's happening there and how a volunteer can work with people to effect change in those places. "Animation and T-Group work," he continued, "are valuable for us, only if they are based on what we are doing and hope to do."[54] Indeed, the Company was quite clear that "training outside of the reality of the projects was having a negative effect on the trainees and eventually upon the projects where they were eventually going to put their training to work."[55]

The shift from centralized to in-field training occurred during 1967 Spring Training sessions. The new training regime would emphasize four elements: social investigation, learning by doing, community group or action organizing, group dynamics. Candidates were brought together at a camp near Packenham, Ontario, where a limited orientation to the Company and its goals and practices were given to volunteers. In addition, T-group sessions were conducted to "allow group to come together get oriented towards each other and the company before heading into the field." After the orientation sessions at Packenham, the group was then taken to Toronto for field experience. However, given the shaky nature of the projects, the company had to rely on more service oriented field experiences. To this end the Company secured two weeks of field experience on assignments from working on "Skid Row" in Toronto, to working with patients in the Ontario Mental Health Hospital, to working with inner city school children at the Duke of York School in Toronto's notorious Regent Park public housing project. During these field assignments volunteers were also supposed to attend debriefing sessions each evening to discuss their experiences with each other and with trainers to allow them to better understand the relationship with the theories of community development. Finally, all of the candidates spent a final two weeks at another camp in Val David, Quebec for further education on CD theory, organizational techniques and a chance to put their new experience and knowledge to work in designing their own project.[56]

Did Wood's reorganization of training and selection solve the problems that had plagued the first training sessions? At a general level, the answer must be yes. The 1967 Spring Training sessions experienced only one casualty out of more than 40 volunteers who went through the process. The company though still plagued by social misfits who applied for work in the company was better able to spot those with serious psychological problems, including one young man whom a psychologist's report described as exhibiting "free floating anxiety,... highly maladaptive behaviour, [and} complete unhappiness with his mode of life of uncertainty and hopelessness," before they arrived for training.[57]

However, those working in the field still complained about the quality of the volunteers sent into the field. Maeve Hancey, one of the successful graduates of the Antigonish session claimed that in her experience volunteers held "over simplified stereotypes," had a "lack of experience in living and in learning how to give and take," that was necessary in any community. She also claimed that many of them were not emotionally mature enough to handle the tensions that were a "permanent ingredient of volunteer [life]" and as a result they often interpreted "community crises as personal [ones]." Only older volunteers, she continued, seemed to be able to "accept the paradox of being comfortable with discomfort."[58] Hancey wasn't alone in her assessment. Dave Berner, who was also working in British Columbia noted that while the new in-field training program was the best training scheme available, his experience with many trainees was that though they were "turned on to an incredible degree and, ... were beautiful people, they had a number of perceptions and myths that really were pretty depressing." In the end, commented that "the orientation period was providing the equally strange results with people being very turned on to nothing." As a result, they were "not in any way, equipped to do the work."[59]

Even the trainees' were not sure they were cut out for the difficult life of a CYC organizer. Of course the commitment and the zeal for the Company and its work remained a potent attraction for many young Canadians. Others still simply expressed the desire simply to care for others and to be friends to the disadvantaged. But many of them also recalled that joining the CYC was an attempt to find themselves and their place in the world. A number of volunteers spoke of joining the CYC because "where else can one go to be real?" For many the CYC became place to experience individual growth first and foremost, rather than necessarily helping the disadvantaged solve their own problems, or social revolution. As Kim Moore, a trainee at Moncton who would eventually last no more than six months at her project in a downtown Toronto neighbourhood expressed that the Company was "an alternative school system—by all means take a field trip but don't call it field training." For many the Company became a rite of passage to the road to personal development. Again in Moore's words " ... you learn and then you drop out ... it's the healthy people who are planning to leave. I sort of feel I've passed through the company stage. I'm so happy. Now I know what I want to do."[60]

As in Antigonish volunteers still found it difficult to leave the training environment behind for the hard life of their projects. Again Kim Moore spoke on behalf of many volunteers when she claimed that the group sessions in training were some of the most intense and memorable experiences of her young life. As she remembered:

> We were packed so close … we were standing part inside each other's shells. The only way out was to expand the mind. And my mind opened a little further. The months since, in comparison, are diffused bloodless things. A lot has happened for me, but moments of intense feeling or of understanding are more random and scattered … Wake up with all its faults, the training session was where the real brewing happened … let things happen … Don't rip apart the aimless-seeming growth of talk and exchange between people… let people come close together … let them stay there and in love with one another … wonder for christsake let the new volunteers stay together for a time. Don't destroy.[61]

While not as poetic, other volunteers spoke of the "richness" of their training session experiences and the intense desire to continue those experiences by "all remain[ing] together in one big happy project." As a result, when many of them arrived in their field placements in Toronto, they retreated into their own shells. Just as in Antigonish, attendance at the more mundane debriefing sessions to discuss their field experiences was sporadic at best, ensuring that as one volunteer put it "a complete lapse of whatever commitment people in training had felt up to this time." Another volunteer Barrie Taylor, who had already been part of one of the Victoria based projects, remarked on the "inability of trainees to function in a non-structured environment where no organized schedule had been prepared." As one other volunteer put it, without a strong commitment "like getting up and going to work at 9 every morning …. we'll be useless to both ourselves and to the movement."[62]

In the end it was same approach to recruiting and training that brought Barrie Taylor to Moncton that eventually came to dominate the Company after 1967 with slightly more success. Instead of selection weekends or nationally based recruiting drives and centralized training. The CYC allowed individual projects to recruit and train their own volunteers on the project, after all the philosophy of the Company was volunteer control and the promotion of social change from within communities rather than imposed from outside. However, despite some individual successes there were problems with the decentralized system of recruiting and training. For one, it tended to exacerbate the growing tensions between the volunteers located in the individual projects and the Company staff in Ottawa. Because individual projects wanted the complete responsibility of selecting their own volunteers recruitment and training sessions became a place where such antagonisms were played out, sometimes right in front on prospective volunteers. Ian Hamilton notes that one such session in Toronto in 1968 weekend "highlighted the company's intellectual snobbery and the inability of staff to get along." Here, representatives of the Don Area Project, Ron Krupp and the Toronto Youth Project, Jim Kinzel wanted to get rid of Ed Smee a nationally renowned and well respected CD trainer who had volunteered his time and expertise to the Company. The rest of the selection weekend in Toronto broke down into petty jurisdictional and ideological pissing matches between the project volunteers and head office staff in Toronto. Similarly in Winnipeg in late 1967 another recruitment and selection session went off the rails when trainer Jackie Briskow failed to show up for the final selection meeting because she had become so dispirited with the quality and commitment of the volunteers. Despite Bristow's concerns all of the Winnipeg trainees were selected. Within six months all of the Winnipeg projects had shut down.[63]

Conclusion

In the end, the CYC never seemed to able to capture the vague idealism of young Canadians and turn them into hard headed community organizers that could mobilize communities for radical social change. To be sure there were some successes, David DePoe among the youth of Yorkville, Dal Broadhead in Alert Bay, and perhaps the most dramatic Bernard Muzeen who helped a poor Calgary neighbourhood fight City Hall and the Calgary Stampede to defeat the "renewal" of their neighbourhood. Yet while, many of these successes were due to CYC volunteers acting as "shit disturbers,"not one of them ever substantially altered the social structure of the communities in which they operated, let alone the nation. Moreover, many projects, even the successful ones, could be characterized as much as social service projects as social action ones. However, given the rather nebulous definition of community organization and social animation it was extremely difficult for those both inside and outside the Company to tell where social service ended and social action/social change began.[64] Indeed, an argument can be made that even the most "radical" Alinsky-style community organizing supports rather than challenges the status quo over the long term.[65]

Yet the experience of SDS, SUPA, and even Saul Alinsky was that making radicals, particularly from young people, would be a very difficult job even on the best of terms. As Harry Stevens, one of the Crystal Cliffs survivors wrote in an internal Company publication: "The Company wants supermen ya ya… Where is it going to get them? Where are natural training grounds in our present society for producing this sort of mature, tough, radical person?"[66] The Company's belief that it could transform well-meaning, humanitarian and "feelie" idealists, into hard–core effective organizers for radical social change represented both the strengths and the weaknesses of the entire New Left. On the one hand, it was premised on the sense of inclusion, openness, and full participation. All that mattered in some ways was that one's heart was in the right place that one was ready and willing to serve the greater cause of radical social change. On the other hand, the rejection of authority, organization, hierarchy, and perhaps most of all experience, meant that many volunteers ended up in the field with little sense of how to put their ideas into action. Whether six weeks of training could ever have changed that is a question that probably cannot be answered clearly. What was clear was that CYC officials, particularly the more "radical" members of the Council, such as Goodings, Clark and Pape, expectations were very high. They expected to find volunteers more like themselves—tough, committed, and perhaps most important "together." They also in many ways failed to recognize the rapid changes to youth and youth culture that had begun to take shape by the late 1960s.

What this paper reveals is that the making of shit disturbers was going to be very difficult when many of them simply didn't have their shit together. When the Company was first conceived, some spoke of it drawing on a new generation of young Canadians that Dr Charles Hendry of the University of Toronto School of Social Work called the "uncomfortable few." Here Dr Hendry was clearly thinking of the drafters of the Port Huron Statement who "looked uncomfortably at the world they were to inherit," but who were equally determined to meet the challenges not with contempt, but with "deep purpose, genuine commitment, unflinching courage and sincere faith."[67] What becomes clear from CYC records is that many of those attracted to the Company were not only uncomfortable with the society around them; many of them were obviously uncomfortable in their own skins. They looked to the CYC hoping to find a place where they would be accepted for who they were; they were, in short, looking for a comfort zone. But as the T-group sessions at Antigonish made all too apparent, the CYC wasn't the place where they would find it. Nor, was it really what the CYC wanted. And yet, the CYC sent mixed messages to young Canadians. The CYC's recruiting message to young Canadians was that it would be an organization of, by, and for them. Did that mean the CYC to be about personal development for volunteers or was it to be about the development of communities? Could it do both at the same time? Indeed, very early on in designing the selection and training procedures, one CYC council member remarked that the Company had to decide between two very different concepts: "whether one would select volunteers who would be good for the Company or persons for whom the Company would provide a good experience.[68] Even for those who were not completely "hung up" there was the worry that those who had not yet discovered life and their place in the world were would be difficult to mould into those who could change it. As Art Pape asked at one of these early staff sessions concerning recruitment and training "is one ever likely to be sensitive enough to be a creative catalyst [if one hasn't] left home between 10 & 20."[69] Unfortunately, to the detriment of both the volunteers and the Company as a whole, neither Stimson nor anyone else in the Company had an answer to that question.

Notes

1 Clara Thomas Archives and Special Collections (hereafter York Archives), Alan Clarke Fonds, File 35—Legacy of the CYC, Dale Seddon, "The Way it Should be" in *Intercom*, Vol. 26, #1 Newsletter of the Alumni of the Company of Young Canadians May 1992.

2 Cited in D Owram, *Born at the Right Time: A History of the Baby Boom Generation* (Toronto: U of T Press, 1996), 225.

3 Only two histories of the CYC have been written and both of those were authored by insiders not long after the government revoked the Company's independence. See Margaret Daly, *The Revolution Game: The Short, Unhappy Life Of The Company Of Young Canadians* (Toronto: The New Press, 1970); and Ian Hamilton, *The Children's Crusade: The Story Of The Company Of Young Canadians.* (Toronto: Peter Martin, 1970).

4 Library & Archives Canada (LAC) Records of the Company of Young Canadians (Hereafter Records of CYC), RG 116 Box 15, File 120 -01 -03 Organizing Committee Reports, A Report By the Organizing Committee of the Company Of Young Canadians to the Prime Minister of Canada (hereafter Leddy Report), 12.

5 Daly, *Revolution Game,* 14. Emphasis mine.

6 For more on ERAP see Kirkpatrick Sale, *SDS* (New York, Vintage Books, 1973), 62-76 and 85-99; Wini Breines, *Community and Organization in the New Left, 1962-68: The Great Refusal* (New York: Praeger, 1982); James Miller, *Democracy is in the Streets: From Port Huron to the Siege of Chicago* (New York: Simon and Shuster, 1987).

7 LAC, Records of CYC, RG 116, Box 15, File 120 J5—Interdepartmental Committee on Youth, Notes for a Presentation by Alan Clarke, Exec Director of the CYC to the Inter Departmental Conference on Youth to be held a the Tops Marina Motor Hotel—Smiths Falls, Ontario, March 25-26, 1968.

8 Bob Phillips cited in Gander, L.E. The Radical Promise of Public Legal Education in Canada (Edmonton: Legal Studies Program, 1999), Ch.5.

9 William Ready Division of Archives and Research Collections (McMaster University) (hereafter McMaster Archives), Company of Young Canadians Fonds (hereafter CYC Fonds), Box 4, File 12, Myrna Wood and Michael Rowan (with the assistance of Anthony Hyde and Linda Seese, "Notes

on the Nationalization of Saul Alinsky or "Community Organizing and the Company of Young Canadians." Emphasis in the original

10 Daly, *Revolution Game,* 31.

11 McMaster Archives, CYC Fonds, Box 4, File 12, "Nationalization of Saul Alinsky."

12 York. Archives, Alan Clarke Fonds, Box 40 File 1, News Service Canadian University Press, Jan 3, 1966, "Volunteer Control Still Possible CYC Worker"

13 LAC, Records of CYC, RG 116 Box 18 File 120—01 Organizing Committee—General Stewart Goodings to Don Roebuck, February 7, 1966.

14 York Archives, Alan Clarke Fonds, Box 21, File 15—Minutes and Memos 1966-67, Memorandum on Recruitment 29/7/67; LAC, Records of CYC, RG 116, Box 14, File 120 J1-3 Memo to the Members of the Interim Advisory Council and Members of the Staff of the Company of Young Canadians From Jack Snell, Ontario Regional Programme Supervisor, 5.

15 LAC, Records of CYC, RG 116 Box 13, File 120 C11, Committee on Selection, Training and Volunteer Support, Selection Committee, Qualities [of Volunteers], N.D.

16 CYC *Aims and Principles*

17 LAC, Records of CYC, Box 14, File 120 J3 – Committees interdepartmental Committee on Community Development—Survey of Training Programs Related to Community Development in Canada—Summary of Findings—Norbert Prefontaine March 1966)

18 York Archives, Alan Clarke Fonds, Box 41, File 3 Policy Development Paper June 20, 1966, and LAC, Records of CYC, RG 116, Box 14, File 120 J1-3 Memo to the Members of the Interim Advisory Council and Members of the Staff of the Company of Young Canadians From Jack Snell, Ontario Regional Programme Supervisor, 5.

19 York Archives, Alan Clarke Fonds, Box 41, File 3, Re: Comments on a Training Plan for Volunteers of the Company of Young Canadians, Crystal Cliffs, Antigonish, Nova Scotia, June 1966, May 13, 1966.

20 LAC, Records of CYC, RG 116, Box 14, File 120 J1-4 Minutes of the Interim Advisory Council April 15-17 1966, 3.

21 Quotes from M. Daly, *Revolution Game,* 40-41; and I. Hamilton, *Children's Crusade,* 13.

22 M. Daly, Revolution Game, 41-44; I.Hamilton, *Children's Crusade,* 13-18, Pierre Berton, 1967: The Last Good Year (Toronto: Doubleday, 1997), 172-185; Michael Valpy, "Stress and Strength at Crystal Cliffs," *Globe and Mail (The Globe Magazine),* August 6, 1966.

23 York Archives, Alan Clarke Fonds, Box 21, File 16, Newspaper Clipping – nd.

24 Stinson, "What Happened at Crystal Cliffs, 13.

25 Failure rates for CUSO and the Peace Corps ranged between 4 and 8 percent. Those for the Crystal Cliffs were in excess of 20%. See M. Valpy, "Are the CYC Brass Like a Groom at a Wedding, *Globe and Mail (Globe Magazine),* August 13, 1966, 3; York Archives, Alan Clarke Fonds, Box 42, File 5—Newspaper Clippings, "Farewell to Angst," *Time Magazine,* March 8, 1968; and M. Daly, *Revolution Game,*48.

26 As of May 20, 1966, the regional breakdown of the candidates accepted for training was as follows: British Columbia 10, Alberta 3, Saskatchewan 2, Manitoba 2, Ontario 26, Quebec 9, New Brunswick 1, Nova Scotia 1, Prince Edward Island 1. At that point no one from Newfoundland and Labrador, or the Northern Territories had been accepted, although there was very little interest from these regions as the Company had only received one application from Newfoundland and 2 from "the North." For the regional breakdown of applicants and volunteers as of the Spring of 1966 see LAC, Records of CYC, RG 116, Box 14, File 120 J1—Interim Advisory Council, "Summary of Volunteers." For suggestions on regional representation as a means of selecting volunteers see LAC, Records of CYC, RG 116, Box 183 File F, "An Appraisal of the 1st Training Project of the CYC, Crystal Cliffs, Antigonish, N.S." Appendix 1, Preliminary Report on CYC Training at "Crystal Cliffs by Dr. N Murphy, 1.

27 M. Valpy, "Stress and Strength at Crystal Cliffs," 6, 11.

28 M. Daly, *Revolution Game,* 41, LAC, Records of CYC, RG 116, Box 183 File F, "An Appraisal of the 1st Training Project of the CYC, Crystal Cliffs, Antigonish, N.S." Appendix 1, Preliminary Report on CYC Training at "Crystal Cliffs by Dr. N Murphy, 2.

29 York Archives, Alan Clarke Fonds, Box 41, File 11, Training Committee Meeting Monday August 15, 1966 "Notes," 12.

30 For the quality of the psychological testing see LAC, Records of CYC, RG 116, Box 185, File R, "A Report on the Selection of Volunteers – 2nd of 2 parts," SMA Inc., January 31, 1967; and York Archives, Alan Clarke Fonds, Box 21, File 19, "Summary of a Report on the Selection of Volunteers prepared by SMA INC," September 15, 1966, and on the lack of information available to the training staff see LAC, Records of CYC, RG 116, Box 183 File F, "An Appraisal of the 1st Training Project of the CYC, Crystal Cliffs, Antigonish, N.S." passim.

31 On the staffs' questioning of the morality of the tests see LAC, Records of CYC, RG 116, Box 185, File R, "A Report on the Selection of Volunteers—2nd of 2 parts," SMA Inc., January 31, 1967; LAC, Records of CYC, RG 116, Box 29, File 122-4-1, "What is a Volunteer?"

32 LAC, Records of CYC, RG 116, Box 18, File 120—01 Organizing Committee—General, Memo to CYC Organizing Committee From Bert Marcuse MSW Exec Director of Calgary Family Service Bureau, August 19, 1965.

33 D. Owram, *Born at the Right Time,* 231

34 LAC, Records of CYC, RG 116, Box 183, File F, "An Appraisal of the 1st Training Project of the CYC, Crystal Cliffs, Antigonish, N.S." Appendix 1, 7.

35 York Archives, Alan Clarke Fonds, Box 21, File 18, "CYC Nation," Edition 1 Dec 12, 1966.

36 LAC, Records of CYC, RG 116 Box 15, File 120 -01 -03 Organizing Committee Reports, "Leddy Report."

37 For the descriptions of the T-group sessions see M. Valpy, "Stress and Strength at Crystal Cliffs," 5; York Archives, Alan Clarke Fonds, Box 21, File 16, Anonymous Newspaper Clipping, nd.; and Box 21, File 30, P.N. Mussallem to Alan Clarke n.d., 2.

38 M. Valpy, "Stress and Strength at Crystal Cliffs," 6.

39 McMaster Archives, CYC Fonds, Box 4, File 13, Art Stinson, "What Happened at Crystal Cliffs?"

40 McMaster Archives, CYC Fonds, Box 4, File 13, Art Stinson, "What Happened at Crystal Cliffs?" Stinson's observations were generally supported by other observers at Crystal Cliffs, see LAC, Records of CYC, RG 116, Box 185, File F, "An Appraisal of the 1st Training Project of the CYC, Crystal Cliffs, Antigonish, N.S."

41 McMaster Archives, CYC Fonds, Box 4, File 2, "The Effects of the Antigonish Training Groups Upon the Evolution of the Aims and Principles of the Company of Young Canadians—A Subjective Report by Peter Nicholas Mussallem (Volunteer) August 8, 1966," 3.

42 McMaster Archives, CYC Fonds, Box 4, File 13, Art Stinson, "What Happened at Crystal Cliffs?"; LAC, Records of CYC, RG 116, Box 185, File F, "An Appraisal of the 1st Training Project of the CYC, Crystal Cliffs, Antigonish, N.S." Appendix 1, 4. For more on the way the romance of the poor by the New Left tended to inhibit action and analysis rather than sharpen it see Richard Ellis, "Romancing the Oppressed: The New Left and the Left Out," *The Review of Politics,* Vol 58, (1) (Winter 1996), 109-54; W. Briens, *Community Organizing and the New Left,* 139-146; and Jeremy Varon, *Bringing the War Home: The Weather Underground, the Red Army Faction, and Revolutionary Violence in the Sixties and Seventies.* (Berkeley and Los Angeles: University of California Press. 2004).

43 McMaster Archives, CYC Fonds, Box 4, File 2, "The Effects of the Antigonish Training Groups Upon the Evolution of the Aims and Principles of the Company of Young Canadians—A Subjective Report by Peter Nicholas Mussallem (Volunteer) August 8, 1966," 8.

44 LAC, Records of CYC, RG 116, Box 185, File F, "An Appraisal of the 1st Training Project of the CYC, Crystal Cliffs, Antigonish, N.S." *passim;* and McMaster Archives, CYC Fonds, Box 4, File 2, "The Effects of the Antigonish Training Groups Upon the Evolution of the Aims and Principles of the Company of Young Canadians—A Subjective Report by Peter Nicholas Mussallem (Volunteer) August 8, 1966, 5-6.

45 LAC, Records of CYC, RG 116, Box 185, File F, "An Appraisal of the 1st Training Project of the CYC, Crystal Cliffs, Antigonish, N.S." Appendix 2, Bill Curry "A Personal Evaluation of the First CYC Training Program, July 1-30," 13.

46 LAC, Records of CYC, RG 116, Box 185, File F, "An Appraisal of the 1st Training Project of the CYC, Crystal Cliffs, Antigonish, N.S.," Appendix 1, 6.

47 LAC, Records of CYC, RG 116, Box 70, file 445-1, "February Training, Prepared by Rob Wood" December 11-12, 1966, 2.

48 LAC, Records of CYC, RG 116, Box 185, File F, "An Appraisal of the 1st Training Project of the CYC, Crystal Cliffs, Antigonish, N.S." Appendix 2, Bill Curry "A Personal Evaluation of the First CYC Training Program, July 1-30," 5.

49 McMaster Archives, CYC Fonds, Box 4, File 2, "Notes of a Meeting of the Training Committee," August 15th 1966.

50 LAC, Records of CYC, RG 116, Box 70, File 445-1, "February Training," 2-3.

51 York Archives, Alan Clarke Fonds, Box 41, File 11, Training Committee, Monday August 15th [1966] "Notes," 6.

52 York Archives, Alan Clarke Fonds, Box 41, File 3, Richard Thomson to CYC Training Committee, September 14, 1966.

53 York Archives, Alan Clarke Fonds, Box 41, File 12 M. Valpy, "Media Kit sent to all news media across Canada—Section H Training," January 3, 1967.

54 LAC, Records of CYC, RG 116, Box 70, File 445-1 "February Training" N.D.

55 McMaster Archives, CYC Fonds, Box 4, File 2, Memo To Provisional Council From Richard Salter, Re Orientation, Training and Placement for Volunteers Recommendations for future policy,"

56 McMaster Archives, CYC Fonds, Box 4, File 2, "Training Memo- Rob Wood," May 4 1967.

57 York Archives, Alan Clarke Fonds, Box 40, File 16, Psychological Assessment of CYC Volunteer," by W.R. Clement Senior Research Scientist, May 30, 1967.

58 LAC, Records of CYC, RG 116, Box File 120 C12—Committee Project Planning, Evaluation and Research, Project Planning Evaluation and Research Committee Report Pacific Regional Projects, Sept 30, 1967, 6.

59 York Archives, Alan Clarke Fonds, Box 21, File 15, Memo to Rick Salter Re Next Training Programme Aug 18, 1967.

60 York Archives, Alan Clarke Fonds, Box 21, File 19, The Package—Ontario Region (newsletter Volume 1 Issue VII April 13, 1967.

61 York Archives, Alan Clarke Fonds, Box 21, File 19, The Package—Ontario Region (newsletter) Volume 1 Issue VII April 13, 1967.

62 McMaster Archives, CYC Fonds, Box 4, File 8, Feedback—To be the Way for Those Without A Way (CYC Volunteer Newsletter), March 4th-10th, 1967.

63 This section draws heavily on Ian Hamilton's analysis in *Children's Crusade,* 84.

64 See Kirkpatrick Sale for SDS's ERAP projects similar problems, Sale, *SDS*, 97.

65 Robert Fisher makes this argument quite persuasively in his book *Let the People Decide: Neighbourhood Organizing in America Updated Edition* (Twayne Publishing 1994), 63-65.

66 Stevens cited in M. Daly, *Revolution Game, 62.*

67 LAC, Records of CYC, RG 116, Box 18 File 120-01, "The Uncomfortable Few" Address prepared for 15th Annual Convocation of the University of Ottawa School of Social Welfare, St. Patrick's College Convocation Hall Ottawa Saturday May 29, 1965 by Professor Charles E Hendry Director of U of T School of Social Work. 4.

68 LAC, Records of CYC, RG 116 Box 18, File 120J1 -4, Interim Advisory Council Minutes, May 14 -15 1966.

69 York Archives, Alan Clarke Fonds, Box 41, File 11, Training Committee, Meeting Monday,

Kristin Ireland

Chapter 9

Our True North Strong and Free: The Sixties and Transsexual Sex in Ontario

In his widely-cited article "The Liberal Order Framework: A Prospectus for a Reconnaissance of Canadian History," Ian McKay argues against historians seeing Canada as a meaningless space on which events are acted out. Instead, he asserts that historians should see Canada not as a 'vacant lot' but as "the implantation and expansion over a heterogeneous terrain of a certain politico-economic-logic—to wit, liberalism."[1] In its most basic form, a liberal order can be understood as one that believes in the supremacy of the category 'individual.' In this model, 'the individual' is sovereign over her own body and mind and should be restrained only by voluntary commitments to God, or others, so long as pursuing her own freedom does not infringe on the freedom of other individuals.[2]

Furthermore, "the sixties" have been collectively defined in our popular memory as "The Swinging Sixties" because of the libertine attitudes that emerged. Enthusiasm toward a 'sexual revolution' and liberal attitudes regarding individual choice are generally associated with culture of the 1960s in both the United States and Canada.[3]

Thus, in a period generally defined as ideologically liberal, in a country thought to be a place that fostered liberalism, one would likely be lead to believe that the history of transsexuality in Canada, in the 1960s in particular, would be one laden with liberalist narratives. However, in this essay I will show that as sex reassignment surgery (SRS) became a somewhat obtainable option during the late 1960s and early 1970s, the 'right' of 'choosing' it was an almost nonexistent aspect of the ideological landscape from the point of view of medical professionals. In addition, this essay will explore how liberalist values worked historically in Canada to help and/or hinder the lives of transsexual people seeking SRS in the hopes of looking toward the future.

In the historiography on transsexuality to date in North America most of the literature has focused on the United States with the implied, if silent, assertion that the conclusions drawn can be transplanted unproblematicly on the Northern side of the border. However, Canada's healthcare system is different in some fundamental ways. In 1957 the Hospital Insurance and Diagnostic Act was put into practice which allowed funding from the federal and provincial governments to cover hospital stays and diagnostic treatments. By 1966, Lester Pearson and the federal Liberals had passed the national Medical Care Act which extended healthcare coverage to include doctor services. Consequently, when the University of Toronto decided to fund a study on transsexuality, in which those who passed all of the diagnostic criteria would obtain sex reassignment surgery, it was the Ontario government that covered the cost.[4]

It is perhaps important here to begin with a discussion of the terminology being used. In this kind of work the process of naming and defining is a complex task, fraught with potential problems and inconsistencies. Words such as Gender Dysphoria, transvestite, cross-dresser, transsexual, transexual,[5] transgender, trans-gender and trans-sexual,[6] transgenderist,[7] trans-identified, trans, transman, transwoman, two-spirited, female-to-male, male-to-female, male-to-male and female-to-female,[8] male-to-woman and female-to-man[9] (and the list goes on) have varying meanings in different contexts serving differing political and personal objectives. The discussion here will necessarily be limited as an entire book, or perhaps several books, could easily be dedicated to such a dialogue.

Historically some individuals have been heavily invested in policing the boundaries of these terms and others have been equally invested in blurring the distinctions. In the time period in which this project begins, the 1960s and 70s, the two words that were used with regularity are transvestite and transsexual (sometimes spelled transexual or trans-sexual). Doctors and other clinicians involved in the study and 'treatment' of transsexual people were very concerned with the perceived differences between transvestites and transsexuals.

The former, it was assumed, was sexually excited by wearing clothing of the 'opposite' gender, whereas the latter felt he/she was a member of the 'opposite' gender.[10] The discussion over terminology is much more important than simple semantics. If postmodern theory has taught us anything it is that language can have extraordinary power. My own perspective privileges the right of people to self-identify and therefore, in this project, I refer to individuals who sought out sex reassignment surgery as transsexual regardless of whether or not the medical professionals they saw deemed them to be 'true transsexuals.'

As well, to label a male-to-female transsexual person as a male transsexual instead of a transsexual woman is offensive. Within the context of the Toronto Psychiatric Hospital, which became the Clarke Institute of Psychiatry, in the 1960s and 70s greater emphasis was placed on the assigned sex of an individual rather than the lived-in gender.[11] Consequently, transsexual women are referred to as male transsexuals and transsexual men are referred to as female transsexuals. I have used the terms transsexual women to refer to male-to-female (MTF) transsexuals and transsexual men to refer to female-to-male (MTF) transsexuals. I have also used the pronoun of choice for all individuals who approached the Gender Identity Clinic if known. In quotations these pronouns and terms have been placed in italics to signify when they are problematic.

It is also necessary to problematize where transsexual people fit in the Liberal Order Framework during this perion. The 'individual' at the centre of this paradigm "not to be confused with actual living beings. Rather, 'the individual' is an abstract principle of the entity each one of them might, if purified and rationalized, aspire to become."[12] Because of their presumed collective identities, groups of people such as women, workers, ethnic minorities, Amerindians, and even Catholics have been partially or entirely excluded from the "burdens and responsibilities of full individuality."[13] Transsexual people inhabit a tenuous place in the conception of the individual. On the one hand, classical liberal assumptions might see them as not truly individuals because their 'disorder' would violate the assumption of rationality necessary to individualism. On the other hand, the right-to-choose philosophy inherent to liberalism may conceive of a transsexual person as someone with the individual right to ownership over his/her own body.

Understanding how a position focused around the liberal ideology of choice works is important to comprehending transsexual histories in the Canadian context.[14] Canadians became familiar with the concept of changing one's sex in the early 1950s when Christine Jorgensen achieved celebrity status upon returning from sex reassignment surgery in Denmark. Headlines such as "So womanly, glad hair is blonde, Christine says,"[15] and "A male two years ago, returns to U.S. as girl"[16] graced the pages of the *Toronto Daily Star* and the *Globe and Mail*.

Jorgensen was not the first transsexual, nor was she the first to be covered extensively in the media.[17] However, her story did make 'transsexual' a household word in the United States, as well as in Canada.

In the weeks and months that followed, 'blonde beauty,' Christine Jorgensen attained instant celebrity status. For some, Jorgensen served as a validation of their own identities by making a transsexual identity seem plausible. For others, she served as a spectacle as various media sources dissected her body parts, critiquing the degree of femininity each achieved. And still, for others, she caused fear and panic that soon untold numbers of biological males would haphazardly 'choose' to change their sex.

In 1955 Vancouver columnist Eric Nichols published a collection of his articles, titling his entire anthology after one article he wrote in response to Jorgenson. Nichols' argument was that living as a male was undoubtedly more grueling than living as a female; thus, if given the option, men would indeed rush to change their sex so that they could avoid shaving and paying gas bills.[18] He writes: "if enough more of these boys take the easy way out of baldness, tight collars and last chance at lifeboat, the H-bomb won't be needed. We'll be closed on account of alterations."[19]

In this article Nichols is not commenting on the experience of being transsexual but simply on the decision to obtain SRS. However, in his mind it seems clear that such a decision is a choice that one makes regarding one's own body without interference from outside sources. At the time his work was published, Canadian medical professionals were not yet performing SRS and so the only impediment faced by those seeking surgery was the availability of capital needed to travel to a country where the operations could be performed for a fee. The classic liberal assumption that all 'individuals' begin on an 'equal playing field' assumed that all who desired SRS had an equal opportunity to obtain it since raising financial capital was based on that person's hard work and fortitude.

Nearly eight years after Jorgensen's first public appearance, a number of clinicians met at the Toronto Psychiatric Hospital (which would later become the Clarke Institute of Psychiatry) to discuss the topic of 'trans-sexualism.'[20]

The clinicians met on October 25th 1960 with the intention of ascertaining what could, and should, be done 'about' transsexuals in Canada. The purpose of this meeting seems to have been to understand who could be counted as a 'true transsexual' and how best to 'cure' them. Based on a limited number of cases, these doctors made a number of generalizations about 'the transsexual.'[21]

Almost a decade later, in October of 1969, the University of Toronto announced plans for "a pilot study of the phenomenon of trans-sexualism and related problems of gender identity."[22] The press release that publicized the study defined transsexualism as "the conviction held by an individual who is in other respects biologically normal, of being a member of the opposite sex."[23] The original intent of the study was to "learn more about the phenomenon,"[24] not to advocate sex reassignment surgery.

By October 1970 the clinic closed its waiting list because 88 patients had already been referred (74 MTFs and 14 FTMs).[25] These 88 patients were subjected to a variety of tests and questionnaires which eventually brought the number down to 15 with four cases still being evaluated by 1973. In Stage I of the study 11 individuals did not fill out the questionnaire of their life history and were thus considered "dropouts."[26] A further 11 dropped out after completing Stage I by declining appointments or stating that they were not transsexual. After completing Stage II approximately one-third were rejected "as being unsuitable for further evaluation."[27] At this point seven additional individuals also dropped out.

Stage III was considered to be an extension of Stage II, in which "the family, spouse, and/or lover are interviewed in order to cross-check the information given by the patient."[28] Twenty-six individuals proceeded to Stage III where four more patients were rejected and three patients dropped out. The final phase, Stage IV, consisted of a demanding ten day evaluation. By this point, fifteen of the original 88 cases were still active and four more were still in the process of evaluation.

The psychiatrist in charge of the study, Dr. Betty Steiner, explained that by the time her report was partially published in 1973 "eight patients had undergone surgical sex reassignment, four male-to-female and four female-to-male (bilateral mammectomy and pan hysterectomy only). Three patients were waiting approval for surgery, and one was in long-term follow-up and was operated on in 1971."[29]

By restricting who was deemed to be a 'true transsexual,' and consequently who could or could not obtain SRS, the medical profession in Ontario limited the bodily autonomy of transsexual people. Individuals who approached the Gender Identity Clinic had to take a number of tests, of which it was possible to both 'pass' and 'fail', before they were allowed to officially enter into the program.

The clinic's policies were influenced heavily by Harry Benjamin's 1966 study The Transsexual Phenomenon, in which Benjamin classified 'true' transsexuals as heterosexual. He wrote:

> ...the sex relations of the male homosexual are those of man with man.
> The sex relations of a male transsexual are those of a woman with a man,
> hindered only by the anatomical structures that an operation is to alter.
> The sex relations of a transvestite are (in the majority) those of heterosexual partners.[30]

Consequently, admitting an attraction to women for MTFs or attraction to men for FTMs could call into question their transsexual diagnosis needed for access to sex reassignment surgery.

Kurt Freund, one of the doctors involved in the study at University of Toronto, developed a "phallometric test" to determine an individual's sexual preference. At the Second Interdisciplinary Symposium on Gender Dysphoria Syndrome, in 1973, Freund explained that the first 57 MTFs who applied for sex reassignment surgery at the Clarke Institute were given a sexual deviation questionnaire which automatically excluded five subjects because they admitted to being attracted to women and thus were deemed "transvestitic and heterosexual."[31] However, he feared that some of the subjects who denied being attracted to women were not being truthful and applied the phallometric test of sexual object preference.[32] The test "is based on a recording of penile volume changes while the subject observes pictures of various potential sexual objects."[33]

In her memoir, Dianna, the first transsexual to obtain SRS in Canada, describes her recollection of this particular test with disgust:

> The most distasteful test was when I had an apparatus attached to my penis. It consisted of a condom within a test tube that fitted snugly over my penis, this in turn was hooked up to a pressure gauge and the results were recorded in an adjoining room. As part of the test, I was shown a series of anatomical pictures of naked and clothed men, women, and children. When I realized just how personal, prying, and, in my estimation, degrading this was, I flung the contraption from my body, put on my clothes and, stomped from the room.[34]

Dianna further explains that Dr. Steiner advised her that she was a volunteer participant in the test and was not required to partake in anything.[35]

However, one can assume that many of subjects taking part in such tests did not feel that they were elective.

The female-to-male transsexuals who applied for sex reassignment surgery at the Clarke Institute were judged less on their sexual object preference, perhaps because there was no equivalent phallometric test to subject them to, and more intensely on their desire to take on the role of husband and father to heterosexually-identified women. In the video "Transsexual and Lesbian Couples," doctors Betty Steiner and Daniel Paitich introduced a number of female-to-male transsexuals who approached the clinic requesting sex reassignment surgery with their female partners. In the video Steiner and Paitich determined which couples they felt were heterosexual and which were homosexual. One of the participants, 21 year old Dusty, was deemed transsexual by highlighting his claim that he had an aversion to his own genitalia and abhorred his partners touching them. Dusty remarked, "when she's satisfied, I'm satisfied."[36]

In comparison, Paitich and Steiner concluded that another couple, Derek and Betty, were homosexual. They explained that Derek had legally changed his name but did not consider him eligible for sex reassignment surgery because both partners "enjoy sex and touching of the genitalia."[37] After interviewing a number of couples they concluded that "the lesbians allow genital touching—but in the transsexuals they orgasm from body friction and don't let the partner touch them."[38] The possibility that female-to-male transsexuals could be attracted to other men was not even broached.

Furthermore, when children were involved, the ability of the transsexual partner to take on the role of father was also used to clarify who counted as 'true' transsexuals. For instance, one female-to-male transsexual who approached the gender identity clinic was Evelyn. His partner Carol had a nine year old daughter who spent a lot of time with him but did not regard him as a father.

Without giving a specific reason why, Paitich remarked: "we feel that Evelyn is not a true transsexual."[39] In contrast, Al, who lived with his wife Pat, was referred to as "a good family man"[40] in a 1974 instructional video because he owned his own business and took on the role of a father to their five children (one Al gave birth to and four Pat gave birth to in previous relationships).[41]

In addition, the 'pass-ability' of transsexuals was also taken into consideration by the gate keepers who decided who was, and was not, suitable for sex reassignment surgery. One report created as a result of the 1960 meeting held at the Toronto Psychiatric Hospital praised MTF transsexuals who possessed, what they considered to be, feminine characteristics and criticized those who did not. For instance, one subject was described as "slender and graceful, his skin is smooth with scanty hair, his face mobile and expressive."[42] In comparison, another was described as having "an almost delusional belief that his figure is almost worthy of Marilyn Munroe and that, if given the chance to live properly, he would be a dark Spanish beauty. One suspects that this is almost psychotic and those who have seen him and read his correspondence concur."[43] The study concluded that perhaps, "if the total re-registration is not possible with all that may result from it, then operative treatment should not be considered at all."[44]

In comparison, the Gender Identity Clinic established in 1969 determined the ability of transsexuals to pass the 'real life test' by requiring them to work, go to school or volunteer full-time as their desired gender for a period of one to two years before being considered for surgery. The clinicians in Toronto who published results from the University of Toronto funded study reported that their subjects were more than happy to wait the allotted time. In one reference video a transsexual woman named Ali told the viewing audience that: "the climax part is living successfully as a woman before surgery."[45] In comparison, surgery "was like getting a tooth pulled," it "wasn't a big thing."[46] To clarify, Steiner asked: "so you don't regret the fact that you did have to wait and that you did have to establish your cross gender identity very firmly before you had surgery?"[47] To which Ali replied: "no I don't regret that."[48]

However, Canadian researcher Viviane K. Namaste tells a much different story. Namaste explains that in her interviews with transsexual people one of the biggest complaints that arose was the requirement of the "real life test."[49] The Gender Identity Clinic currently requires that people requesting sex reassignment surgery provide written documentation supporting their claim that they have lived in their chosen gender for two years. After one full year they become eligible for hormones.[50] Since 'passing' in public can be difficult for some without the assistance of hormones, many transsexual people seek hormones outside of the clinic through a family member (often without their knowledge), from a family doctor or on the street.[51]

The possibility that SRS could, although perhaps not should, be conceptualized as a choice, similar to a cosmetic procedure, was evident in discussions between Toronto medical experts as early as 1960. One of the doctors involved in the discussion held at the Toronto Psychiatric hospital asked the group: "what do you think of the parallel of the patient who asks for an operation on the nose and insists on having it done?"[52] Unfortunately, his question remained unanswered. However, a report generated from the meeting tells of a 29 year old Australian MTF who is "a typical case."[53] The 'early history' reads: "he expresses hatred or, and revulsion from , his masculine sexual organs and thinks he has a right to have them removed so that he can look anatomically female and can live as a woman."[54] Clearly, the doctors in this case were not advocating the transsexual woman had a 'right' to 'choose' sex reassignment surgery.

However, that was the way the woman herself was describing the situation. At no point during the study done in 1960 did the medical professionals articulate sex reassignment surgery as a viable 'choice' for individuals. In fact, the general conclusion seemed to be "that one cannot cure these people (in the ordinary sense) so why not treat them surgically and thereby remove their frustration, bitterness and uncertainty, thus making them happy and better adjusted citizens."[55] Of course, deciding who qualified to be 'cured' was not a decision that the individuals themselves could make.

A decade later, with the establishment of the Gender Identity Clinic at the Clarke Institute, the rhetoric was slightly altered. Instead of trying to 'cure' transsexualism, meaning convincing the individual to live in the gender role assigned at birth, the focus was on diagnosing who was, and who was not, a 'true' transsexual. Those deemed 'true' transsexuals could, if they 'passed' the extensive testing stages, obtain some form of sex reassignment surgery.

Across the border, Joanne Meyerowitz explains that in the United States, "in the 1960s the complicated process of redefining sex took place within a culture increasingly preoccupied by a 'sexual revolution,' by more liberal attitudes toward individual choice, and by revitalized human rights movements that insisted on social change in the name of justice."[56] In this vein, a few healthcare professionals in Jacksonville Florida, under the direction of Ira M. Dushoff, M.D., opened a private clinic called the Gender Identity Association. Their intent was "to create a total team, along university lines, in a private setting."[57] At the Second Interdisciplinary Symposium on Gender Dysphoria Syndrome in 1973 Dushoff explained that "rather than being in the untenable position of 'rejecting' anyone, the entire process allows the patients to sieve themselves."[58] Rather than defining, and enforcing, categorical boundaries of transsexuality, this clinic recognized that "a wide variety of transsexuals" were possible.[59] While patients at this clinic had to pay for their surgeries, it appears that the liberal ideology of choice, regarding what one does with one's own body, was much more present on the South side of the Canadian-American border during this period.

Conceptualizations of SRS as a legitimate choice one could make were not present in the work of medical experts in Ontario in the 1960s and 70s; however, that did not stop transsexual people themselves for imagining it in this way. During this era groups such as ACT (Association for Canadian Transsexuals) and FACT (Foundation for the Advancement of Canadian Transsexuals) emerged. Clearly frustrated by her inability to obtain SRS one anonymous ACT member wrote a letter in which she asked: "has society or the medical profession any 'right' to deny us a sex change?" The, seemingly rhetorical, answer is: "I think not."[60]

Imagining SRS as an individual choice generally entails comparing it to cosmetic procedures. In Canada arguments based on individual autonomy, and freedom-of-choice, are often easily accepted. The sociological textbook Gender in Canada, published in 1999, follows this kind of comparison when explaining the limited access to sex reassignment surgery in our contemporary period.

Nelson and Robinson write: "unlike those who would decide to undergo rhinoplasty (to surgically alter the shape or contours of one's nose), or breast augmentation, the would-be transsexual cannot be assured that their possession of sufficient money or medical coverage will entitle them to the procedure."[61]

In Canadian political theory, liberal values are generally "self-evidently good"[62] and everything else, which is presumably bad, is on the other side of the binary.

Thus, it can potentially be alluring for activists to use liberal ideology to argue against pathologization and for individual choice and autonomy. But let's work through this argument a little.

If individuals could choose sex reassignment surgery, like they can choose to alter their noses, the power invested in the Gender Identity Clinic would obviously be completely overhauled. This reality is probably the most tempting reason to embrace this discourse.[63] The gate-keeping procedures outlined above could potentially diminish and the hoops that individual transsexual people have had to jump through might be altered. In this kind of context, requirements such as mandatory counseling and the real life test could potentially be eradicated.[64]

My biggest concern with this conceptualization of SRS as choice is that it has the potential to create a consumer model of healthcare which perpetuates class privilege. The demedicalization of transsexuality would make surgery available only to those with the deepest pockets. Speaking of the Jacksonville Florida private clinic mentioned above in the early 1970s Dushoff argued that there was "no loading of the fee because of the unusual nature of this surgery."[65]

However, it is easy to imagine that such a reality could easily come into being.

In 1973 the American gay liberation movement forced the American Psychiatric Association to discontinue its categorization of homosexuality as a mental disorder in the Diagnostic and Statistical Manual (DSM) after much heated debate. The Dominion of Bureau of Statistics, which became Statistics Canada in 1971, published its Manual for the Classification of Psychiatric Diagnoses until the late 1970s which "listed homosexuality as a mental disorder."[66] However, the shift in ideology which stopped homosexuals from being assumed mentally-ill to being satisfied with their sexual orientation, made a huge impact on the self-perception of homosexual people.

Currently, international transsexual and transgendered activists are waging a similar battle.[67] However, one major difference between these struggles is that homosexual activists did not want to interact with the medical community in the hopes of obtaining surgery.[68] In 1997, the American group GenderPAC, Gender Public Advocacy Coalition, drafted a resolution to reform the medical diagnosis of Gender Identity Disorder (GID). One of the arguments put forth by GenderPAC is that "the use of psychiatric diagnosis to stigmatize those who want to modify their bodies or gender is an integral part of the systems of gender oppression, homophobia, and sexism, which seek to impose strict binaries and punish all transgression."[69]

There are numerous reasons to agree with this assessment. In the American context of privately funded healthcare, the government will never be paying for sex reassignment surgery. And, even though the technology has been around for decades, the majority of insurance companies and HMOS categorize SRS as an 'experimental procedure' and refuse to include it in their coverage.[70] Thus, while some argue in favour of maintaining the pathologized understanding of transsexual identities, in the hopes that sex reassignment surgeries will someday be reimbursed by private insurance companies, many others have decided the damage is not worth the potential benefit.

In the Canadian context, the public model of healthcare that holds the potential for sex reassignment surgery to be funded through the government must be recognized. The pathologizing of transsexuality has, at certain moments in Ontario's history, allowed the cost of sex reassignment surgery performed at the Gender Identity Clinic in Toronto to be covered by the Ontario Health Insurance Plan.[71] This argument does not assume that transsexual people should remain, uncritically, invested in this disease-model of identity. Instead, Canadians need to explore how this pathologization has worked north of the Canadian-American border before we accept American-based activist discourse as international. In the period studied here, the clinicians in Toronto held a great deal of power over the individual lives of transsexual people who sought out hormones and surgery through their enforcement of heterosexual norms based on regulated male and female roles and by implementing the 'real life test.' An exploration of how this power has been used historically is essential to facilitating new dialogue on future possibilities.

Today, transsexuals who approach the Gender Identity Clinic at the Clarke Institute of Toronto experience the institution somewhat differently. While much of the gate-keeping is still in place, the Ontario government is no longer paying for sex reassignment surgery. Patients who passed the diagnostic tests at the clinic between 1969 and October 1, 1998 had their surgeries financed by the provincial government. In 1998 the Conservative government in Ontario stopped funding SRS and claimed that the money was redirected to cardiac care.[72] Although, during the 1960s, 70s and until our present day, many transsexual people have utilized liberalist ideologies based on individual sovereignty to campaign for access to SRS, this essay has shown that it may have been the denial of such discourse by legal and medical professionals that allowed SRS to be paid for by the government. In some ways, it may be argued that not resisting the medicalized model of transsexual identities and campaigning instead for SRS to be publicly funded is a way to 'use the masters tools' to 'dismantle the master's house.'

By the close of the twentieth century, McKay writes: "liberal assumptions have been so successfully and massively diffused through the population that it is difficult to see."[73] In essence, talking about liberalism for Canadians is like fish talking about water—it is invisible, it is everywhere and it is seen as self-evidently good. This essay has shown that while transsexual individuals used liberalist arguments based on freedom-of-choice ideology in an effort to obtain SRS, the medical experts involved did not agree. Such a statement does not mean that these experts were necessarily working outside of the Liberal Order Framework since it may be argued that they saw transsexual people as not 'true individuals' in which case denying their bodily integrity would not be in conflict with maintaining the liberal order. Yet, arguments based on freedom of choice have found a fertile home in Canada.

Pro-choice activists have utilized catch-phrases such as 'my body, my choice' and 'keep your laws off of my body.' Those involved in the advancement and maintenance of such legislation have historically relied on liberalist beliefs which position women as "full moral agents with the right and ability to choose when and whether or not they will be mothers."[74] Canadian feminist Judy Rebick explains that this privileging of 'bodily integrity'[75] has been utilized "because freedom of choice is such a strong value in liberal democratic society."[76] Consequently, should transsexual people and their allies decide to utilize liberalist principles based on freedom-of-choice and ownership over one's body to argue for access to SRS they may find success if they decide that this reality would best suit their needs.

Understanding how these liberalist arguments have worked in the past is key to understanding in which directions future activism might focus. In "the sixties," a period most often characterized by its libertine attitudes, in a country where liberalism has been "akin to a secular religion or a totalizing philosophy,"[77] transsexual people were not granted complete sovereignty over their own bodies.

This reality raises two important questions: first, if such individual rights based ideologies could not take hold in "the sixties" when will they? And, second, just how liberalized were the "swinging sixties"?

Notes

1 Ian McKay, "The Liberal Order Framework: A Prospectus for a Reconnaissance of Canadian History," *The Canadian Historical Review* 81, no. 4 (2000): 620.

2 Ibid., 623.

3 For a discussion of when 'the sixties' actually took place see Andrew Hunt, "'When Did the Sixties Happen?' Searching for New Directions," *Journal of Social History* 33 (1999).

4 "OHIP covered cost of sex-change surgery," *Toronto Star*, January 28, 1974, The Clarke Institute of Psychiatry fonds, 5-10, A-2, Scrapbook: 1974, Centre for Addiction and Mental Health, Archives, Toronto (hereafter cited as CAMH).

5 For a discussion on the spelling of transsexual with one 's' or two see Riki Anne Wilchins, *Read My Lips: Sexual Subversion and the End of Gender* (Ithaca, NY: Firebrand Books, 1997), 15; and, Jason Cromwell, *Transmen & FTMs: Identities, Bodies, Genders & Sexualities* (Chicago: University of Illinois Press, 1999), 19.

6 Jean Bobby Noble writes trans-sexual and trans-gender "with hyphens to defamiliarize the way that these terms manipulate and produce gender difference by deploying what I will call an alibi of gender essence, an alibi provided by the sexologists and clinical psychiatry that authorizes interventions if the correct narrative is present." See Jean Bobby Noble, *Sons of the Movement: FTMs Risking Incoherence on a Post-Queer Cultural Landscape* (Toronto: Women's Press, 2006), 17.

7 This term was coined by gender researcher and transgenderist Virginia Prince. Originally, she intended it to signify a person who lived in the 'opposite' gender but had not obtained sex reassignment surgery. More recently, however, transsexuals have been included as a sub-category of transgenderists.

See Gordene Olga MacKenzie, *Transgender Nation* (Bowling Green, OH: Bowling Green State University Popular Press, 1994), 2.

8 Male-to-male and female-to-female are sometimes used in recognition of the fact that the person never felt in accordance with the gender assigned at birth. See Leslie Feinberg, *Trans Liberation: Beyond Pink or Blue* (Boston: Beacon Press, 1998), 43.

9 Gordene Olga MacKenzie uses these terms to "more accurately reflect the state of a genetic male or female living in the role of the other gender, part-or full-time. Refusing to use the widely accepted and medically derived terms male-to-female and female-to-male, commonly used to describe transsexuals, cross-dressers and transgenderists, questions the promise of biological transformation and the medical and cultural emphasis on the genitals as indicative of gender roles." MacKenzie, *Transgender Nation*, 2.

10 See Virginia Charles Prince, *The Transvestite and his Wife* (Los Angeles: Argyle Books, 1967). Marjorie Garber argues that although doctors spent a great deal of time ascertaining the differences between transsexuals and transvestites, the individuals themselves did not always see such distinctions. See Marjorie Garber, *Vested Interests: Cross-dressing and Cultural Anxiety* (New York: Routledge, 1992), 3; see also Charlotte Suthrell, *Unzipping Gender: Sex, Cross-Dressing and Culture* (Oxford: Berg, 2004), 4.

11 The Toronto Psychiatric Hospital became the Clarke Institute of Psychiatry in 1966.

12 McKay, "The Liberal Order Framework," 625.

13 Ibid., 626.

14 The concept of 'choice' here refers not to the experience of being transsexual but to the possibility of 'choosing' sex reassignment surgery.

15 "So womanly, glad hair is blonde, Christine says," *Toronto Daily Star*, December 2, 1952.

16 "A male two years ago, returns to U.S. as girl," *Globe and Mail*, February 13, 1953.

17 Joanne Meyerowitz, *How Sex Changed: A History of Transsexuality in the United States* (Cambridge, Mass.: Harvard University Press, 2002), 4.

18 Eric Nichols, *Shall We Join the Ladies?* (Toronto: The Ryerson Press, 1955), 31.

19 Ibid.

20 "Discussion: Trans-Sexualism at Journal Club. T.P.H. October 25, 1960," 1960, The Clarke Institute of Psychiatry fonds, 4-04, E-1, *Medical Literature*, CAMH.

21 Torontonian, Dr. Ball collected 23 cases but it is unclear how many individuals were seen by the other doctors participating in this meeting. "Discussion: Trans-Sexualism at Journal Club. T.P.H. October 25, 1960," CAMH.

22 "University of Toronto studying trans-sexualism," *Toronto Star*, October 20th, 1969, Clarke Institute of Psychiatry fonds, 5-10, A-2, Scrapbook: 1969, CAMH.

23 "University of Toronto to study why men want sex-swap operations," *The Telegram*, October 20th, 1969, Clarke Institute of Psychiatry fonds, 5-10, Scrapbook: 1969, CAMH.

24 "University of Toronto plans study on trans-sexualism," *Globe and Mail*, October 21, 1969, Clarke Institute of Psychiatry fonds, 5-10, Scrapbook: 1969, CAMH.

25 B. Steiner and D. Paitich, "The Toronto Gender Identity Project: A Preliminary Report," In *Proceedings of the Second Interdisciplinary Symposium on Gender Dysphoria Syndrome*, eds. Donald Laub and Patrick Gandy (Stanford, CA: Stanford University Medical Center, 1973), 73.

26 Ibid.

27 Ibid.

28 Ibid.

29 Ibid., 74.

30 Harry Benjamin, *The Transsexual Phenomenon* (New York: Warner Books, 1966), http://www.symposion. com./ijt/benjamin/chap_02.htm#Sex%20orientation%20scale%20(S.O.S (accessed March 5, 2006).

31 Kurt Freund, "A Comparison of Transsexuals and Non-transsexual Homosexual Males," in *Proceedings of the Second Interdisciplinary Symposium on Gender Dysphoria Syndrome*, 28.

32 Ibid.

33 Ibid.

34 Dianna pseud., "Once I was a Man. Behold I am a Woman," as told to Felicity Cochrane (New York: Pyramid Books, 1972), 203.

35 Ibid.

36 Robert Gilder, Dir., "Transsexual and Lesbian Couples," commentary by Daniel Paitich and Betty W. Steiner, VHS (Toronto: Faculty of Medicine, University of Toronto, 1975).

37 Ibid.

38 Ibid.

39 Ibid.

40 Robert Gilder, Dir., "Transexualism," commentary by Daniel Paitich and Betty W. Steiner, VHS (Toronto: Faculty of Medicine, University of Toronto, 1974).

41 What is more disturbing about this assessment is that, a year later, in a different video, Al described his 13 year old son as "hard to handle" and admitted: "I beat the living shit right out of him and it doesn't make a difference." See Gilder, Dir., "Transsexual and Lesbian Couples."

42 "Transsexualism or Eonism: a Morpholigal, Psychiatric and Psychological Study," 1960, The Clarke Institute of Psychiatry fonds, 4-04, E-1, *Medical Literature,* CAMH.

43 Ibid.

44 Ibid.

45 Robert Gilder, Dir., "Changing Faces: disorders of gender identity," commentary by Betty W. Steiner, VHS (Toronto: Faculty of Medicine, University of Toronto, 1979).

46 Ibid.

47 Ibid.

48 Ibid.

49 Viviane K. Namaste, *Invisible Lives: The Erasure of Transsexual and Transgendered People* (Chicago: University of Chicago Press, 2000), 196.

50 Ibid., 198.

51 Ibid., 160-161.

52 "Question Period," 1960, The Clarke Institute of Psychiatry fonds, 4-04, E-1, *Medical Literature*, CAMH.

53 "Transsexualism or Eonism: a Morphological, Psychiatric and Psychological Study," CAMH.

54 Ibid., 6.

55 Ibid., 31.

56 Meyerowitz, *How Sex Changed*, 7.

57 Ira M. Dushoff, "Economic, Psychological and Social Rehabilitation of Male and Female Transsexuals Prior to Surgery," in *Proceedings of the Second Interdisciplinary Symposium on Gender Dysphoria Syndrome*, 197.

58 Ibid.

59 Ibid.

60 Anonymous Letter, 1972, Association for Canadian Transsexuals, 284, Canadian Lesbian and Gay Archives, Toronto.

61 E.D. Nelson and Barrie W. Robinson, *Gender in Canada* (Scarborough, Ontario: Prentice Hall and Bacon Canada, 1999), 28. By using the term 'would-be transsexual' Nelson and Robinson seem to be implying that a transsexual person can only actually become transsexual through sex reassignment surgery.

62 McKay, "The Liberal Order Framework," 629.

63 However, private clinics in the United States (and perhaps in other places) still sometimes withhold hormones and surgery to people who label themselves as gay or lesbian. See Cromwell, *Transmen & FTMs*, 124.

64 Yet, I have to agree with Patrick Califia here that I am "not so sure that people who want plastic surgery of any kind should not first seek out counseling." See Califia, Sex Changes, xxvi.

65 Dushoff, "Economic, Psychological and Social Rehabilitation of Male and Female Transsexuals Prior to Surgery," 200.

66 Kinsman, *Regulation of Desire*, 290.

67 See Zachary I. Nataf, *Lesbians Talk Transgender* (London: Scarlet Press, 1996), 11; Kate Bornstein, *Gender Outlaw: On Men, Women, and the Rest of us* (New York: Vintage Press, 1995), 119; Patrick Califia, *Sex Changes: Transgender Politics,* 2nd ed. (San Francisco: Cleis Press, 2003), 263-64.

68 Patrick Califia, *Sex Changes: Transgender Politics*, 2nd ed. (San Francisco: Cleis Press, 2003), 6.

69 Gender Public Advocacy Coalition, "GenderPAC Board Endorses GID Reform," GenderPAC, http://www.gpac.org/archive/news/notitle.html?cmd=view&archive=news&msgnum=0058 (accessed April 1, 2006).

70 Califia, *Sex Changes*, 263.

71 The cost of sex reassignment surgery varies. According to the Ontario Human Rights Commission's working policy on gender identity, in Toronto, female-to-male surgery costs approximately $10,000 to $12,000 and male-to-female surgery costs approximately $18,000. The 1996 British Columbia law reform project on human rights and the transgendered community estimates that SRS for MTFs is between $5,000 and $10,000 and FTM SRS ranges from $20,000 to more than $60,000. See Ontario Human Rights Commission, "Towards a Commission policy on gender identity." However, it is unclear here what surgeries are being incorporated. For instance, a MTF transsexual may undergo a variety of procedures including vaginoplasty, breast augmentation, electrolysis and shaving of the Adam's apple. A FTM transsexual may seek phalloplasty (skin grafts are used to construct and attach a penis), metaidioplasty (the clitoris, enlarged by testosterone therapy, is partly cut loose so that it can perform more as a penis), chest reconstruction surgery and hysterectomy. SRS that has historically been considered for public funding in Ontario has been limited to vaginoplasty, metaidioplasty and potentially phalloplasty; see Egale Canada, "Sex Reassignment Surgery (SRS) Backgrounder," Egale Canada, http://www.egale.ca/index.asp?lang=E&menu=34&item=1086 (accessed April 16, 2006).

72 Alexandra Gill, "Ontario decision to halt sex-change surgery payments challenged," *Globe and Mail*, May 4, 1999.

73 McKay, "The Liberal Order Framework," 630.

74 New York Pro-Choice Coalition, "Abortion—Every Woman's Right," in *Feminist Frameworks: Alternative Theoretical Accounts of the Relations between Women and Men*, 3rd ed. eds. Alison M. Jaggar and Paula S. Rothenberg (Boston, Mass.: McGraw Hill, 1993), 50.

75 See Janine Brodie, "Choice and No Choice in the House," in *The Politics of Abortion*, eds. J. Brodie, S.A.M. Gavigan, and J. Jensen (Toronto: Oxford University Press, 1992), 72.

76 Judy Rebick, "Is the Issue Choice?" in *Misconceptions: The Social Construction of Choice and New Reproductive Technologies*, vol. 1, eds. Gwynne Basen, Margrit Eichler, and Abby Lippmen (Hull, Que.: Voyageur Publishing, 1993), 87.

77 McKay, "The Liberal Order Framework," 623.

Barbara Godard

<table>
<tr><td>Chapter
10</td><td>Quebec, the National Question and
English-Canadian Student Activism in the
1960s: The Rise of Student Syndicalism</td></tr>
</table>

As an elated organizer entered the residence dining hall for a late lunch, he was greeted with the news that J.F. Kennedy had been shot in Texas. His heart sank not just with the knowledge of Kennedy's assassination and all that might presage, but with the realization that Kennedy's death would be headline news for weeks to come, eclipsing any media attention to the unprecedented event that had just taken place in Toronto in November 1963. Consequently, the extensive mobilization which had brought 3000 University of Toronto students into the streets to "March for Canada" would have limited political impact. Everything was over, he thought. Nonetheless, despite his doubts, this event was not the ending. Nor was it the beginning. The March, however, crystallized a turning point in student affairs. As the nexus of a web of related activities, the demonstration epitomized the innovations of 1963-1964 at the university, a year whose "watchword" was "change," as the Vice-President of the Students' Administrative Council (SAC) described it in her year-end report (McMahon 1). Over the course of that year, in response to a crisis in the National Federation of Canadian University Students (NFCUS) which mirrored what was generally considered "the greatest crisis" in the body politic (Royal Commission 13), the English-Canadian students in Toronto began to adopt the "syndicalisme" that Quebec students had long advocated, understanding the role of the student to be that of citizen as well as member of the academy. By the end of a decade of extraordinary student activism around the world initiating yet further changes, the student would become a citizen *in* the academy. Student activism focused then on issues of university governance, no longer on the future of the Canadian nation state as it responded to the force of rising Quebec nationalism.

Periodization of the 1960s must avoid the pitfalls of both nostalgia and abjection with their attendant "commemorations of glories" and "public confessions" of "missed opportunities," warns Fredric Jameson, by focusing on the possibilities of a "determinate historical situation" in all its ruptures and contradictions (Jameson 178). A decade in which "everything seemed possible" was nonetheless caught up in a "dialectical process" in which the apparent "liberation" of energies was intertwined with the "domination" of "late" capitalism's spread of "universal industrialization" into the Third World (Jameson 207). With hindsight, the 60s will be remembered as a period of global systemic transformation which ended in the worldwide economic crisis of 1973-74 with a secondary break occurring around the time of economic recession in 1967-68 (Jameson 205). To these overlapping phenomena in the dialectics of US history, must be added a third with particular force north of the 49th parallel; the conjuncture of multinational corporate capital with US foreign control which was undergoing unprecedented expansion in Canada during the period 1958 to 1964, coincident with the crisis.[1] The "First World 60s," Jameson contends, had "Third World beginnings" in the cultural nationalist models of liberation of decolonization movements in British and French Africa and Latin America. With an accelerating pace in the 1950s and 1960s, revolutions overthrew colonial masters as previously subordinate peoples coming to self-consciousness sought to control their destinies and affirm their collective identities as subjects of history.[2] Among these, the "dialectic of cultural and linguistic independence" in Quebec is one of the more "dramatic examples" of the contradictions of the "Fanonian model of struggle" (Jameson 190). The victory of Slave against Master reaches a limit in its search for a collective identity. Yet to sustain this newly acquired sense of cohesion, it needs to maintain an outside other through a secessionary logic that proliferates fragmentation. Whether what began in Quebec as a "révolution tranquille" was pre-eminently cultural or economic, and how this dialectical relation might manifest itself in political terms, remained a matter of debate and division throughout the decade within and without Quebec.

Drawing an analogy with other peoples in the process of decolonization, the FLQ (Front de libération du Québec) *Manifeste* of April 1963, proclaimed that the people of Quebec have had enough of subjection to "la domination du colonialisme" and will throw out the "impérialistes qui vivent de l'exploitation des travailleurs du Québec" (qtd. in Fournier 40). The triumph of the FLN in Algeria in 1962 lent conviction to the analyses of revolution in Frantz Fanon's *Les damnés de la terre* (1961) and of colonialism in works by Albert Memmi (1957) and Jacques Berque (1964) focusing on the Maghreb which provided a theoretical framework for the Quebec independence movement.[3] However, it was the example of Fidel Castro and Che Guevera in Latin America, with the liberation of the tiny island of Cuba from the claws of US imperialism, which convinced Quebec separatists that they too could succeed in a revolutionary struggle. As contacts with Cuba multiplied during the 1960s, following René Lévesque's interview with Castro as he passed through Montreal in April 1959, the Cuban revolution along with the American civil rights movement remained the most influential models for Quebec *indépendantistes*.[4] "Nègres blancs d'Amérique," as Pierre Vallières called them, expanding on the trope of the "roi nègre" articulated by André Laurendeau and Paul Chamberland to name the puppet-like Quebec provincial premiers (Chamberland 20), Québécois were subject to the domination of US economic imperialism like American Black activists. In an age of rising expectations for full time employment and a panoply of new consumer goods, francophones were the third lowest income-earning group within their own province. *Indépendantistes* came to recognize that the colonialism to which they were subject was not just *political* subordination to English-Canada but also *economic* domination by American global capital. Revolution can only be "nationalist," Paul Chamberland declared in *Parti Pris*, but it must begin with the radical reconstruction of socio-economic structures. It will only be social "si elle vise à détruire les puissances d'oppression qui aliènent la majorité de la nation: le capitalisme américan et anglo-canadien, et même canadien-français" (Chamberland 16). As Gilles Bourque, a later editor of *Parti Pris,* revised the *étapisme* in this account of a complex situation: the Canadian bourgeoisie "playing a subaltern role in the imperialist chain" under English and American capital "was always forced to deal with regional bourgeoisies which had their own political apparatuses in the Provinces" (Bourque and Legaré 216). What ensued in the 1960s, according to Bourque, was a struggle between competing hegemonies in a bourgeois rather than a socialist revolution.

In their support of the nationalist aspirations of Quebec, English-Canadian students learned not only how to act as citizens within the political arena but came to recognize the constitutive contradictions of their own situation of "mastery" in which, as future managers of branch plants, they, too, were under the domination of American economic imperialism. In freeing Quebec, they could forge links across progressive groups to free Canada too. At least that is what is implied in a statement prepared by the Combined Universities Campaign for Nuclear Disarmament (CUCND) for its final conference in December 1964 when, discussing "The Student and Social Issues in the Nuclear Age," it expanded the scope of its treatment of domestic policy from a critique of militarism to the question of Quebec's growing separatist movement which presented an opportunity to re-examine "the goals of Canadian society" ("The Student" 12). In a welcome "broadening [of] its perspective" (Gonick 12) beyond the narrower concerns of the "peaceniks" (Lloyd-Jones 6) to advocate non-alignment in foreign policy and to investigate the roots of poverty at home, the draft statement for the conference focused ten out of sixteen domestic issues on the national question and the impact of "Quebec's quiet revolution" in revealing the "problematic state" of Canadian politics. The situation demanded "a renewal of social imagination and action" ("The Student" 12). "[A]ction oriented" this "impressive group of young Canadians" was, keen to know more about the power structure of their country (Gonick 12).[5] In most narratives of the 1960s (Kostash, Levitt, Reid), the 1964 meeting in Regina marks the beginning of the New Left in the attempt to develop a broader political analysis than anti-nuclearism as the basis for transforming social institutions. SUPA (Student Union for Peace Action) emerging out of this meeting became synonymous with the student movement (Laxer 281) which, in turn, was linked to the generation of baby-boomers arriving at the universities in the mid 60s. Contradictorily, in view of their opposition to nuclear weapons, they were beneficiaries of the expansion of the universities in the Cold War competition over outer space in a post-Sputnik era.

The student organizers of the Regina conference belonged to an older generation, born during the Depression and the early years of WWII, who came of age in the 1950s under Cold War tensions and decolonization's rapid transformations of the global order. Some had been following the dynamics of international power through participation in student organizations, such as the Model United Nations among Toronto high schools and WUS (World University Service) coordinated by NFCUS. Among its various activities with the Third World, WUS organized summer study tours for students to recently decolonized countries such as Pakistan (1963) and Algeria (1964). This generation was the first to raise the questions of Quebec separatism and Canadian nationalism which have been acknowledged as the specifically Canadian aspects of the New Left that distinguish it from the American movement where the national question played no role (Levitt 160-61, Kostash xii). Representatives from Quebec were among the "resource people" in the workshop on "Nationalism Today" at the Regina conference, especially Richard Guay from the Université de Montréal, Vice-President of the newly formed Union générale des étudiants du Québec (UGEQ). Moreover, Doug Ward, one of the principal organizers of the 1963 "March for Canada," also attended in his capacity as head of external affairs of CUS (Canadian Union of Students) and may well have been responsible for inclusion in the draft a statement linking the issue of Quebec nationalism to a critique of the industrial-military complex.[6] SUPA did not translate this principle into action, however, leaving the question of Quebec within the Canadian nation state to others, especially to CUS and CUP (Canadian University Press) where an experiment with "sovereignty-association" had been underway for several years, the context for the 1963 "March for Canada" at the University of Toronto.

The Quebec connection was significant, nonetheless. The radical shift of the peace movement articulated in "The Student and Social Issues in the Nuclear Age" was a new orientation to action, "student syndicalism," identified as an important "new policy" by the Toronto-based peace publication, *Sanity*, in its report on the conference ("A New" 7). Syndicalism, topic of workshops on "Students in Society," whose facilitators included Richard Guay of UNEQ and Howard Adelman, SAC's Finance Commissioner, was deemed "possibly the most unique idea" to be adopted in Regina, an idea as yet relatively new in the English-speaking world although it had "recently made advances in Quebec" ("A New" 7) and at the University of Toronto. Stewart Goodings, a past president of CUS and Toronto graduate student, also highlighted "student unionism" as the dynamic new force emerging in 1964-65 in students' relation both to their "immediate community—the university, and the wider social context" (Goodings 5) which he connects to SUPA-led demonstrations in Toronto and Ottawa (March 1965) in solidarity with civil rights workers in Alabama. Instead of Quebec, SUPA turned to groups disadvantaged by poverty or racialized minority status as the primary agents of social transformation. This tendency which was derived from US New Left projects, along with a distrust of institutional structures characteristic of individualism (Gray 49), positioned SUPA more within the horizon of American radical perspectives than within the struggles of traditional left movements in Canada against exploitation by American capitalist imperialism. Indeed, the New Left Committee, which briefly succeeded SUPA in the summer of 1967, avowed that SUPA's failure derived from its "inability to develop a coherent analysis of the structure of modern capitalism and of its specific characteristics in Canada" (Laxer 282). The committee determined to advance the student syndicalist programme by aligning more with Canadian socialist traditions. In contrast to what Stanley Gray considers the "individualistic, issue-oriented and periodic activism of the 'new left'" (Gray 49), the syndicalist perspective advocates a collectivist orientation to politics, adopting a broad approach to social change. James Laxer observes the same tension when he contrasts the refrain, "UGEQ was still building student syndicalism," to English-speaking Canada where "the torch did not fall to a new generation this year [1965-66]" as a fleeting series of actions "flashed onto the scene ... only to disappear the next" ("Where" 5).

The student intellectuals-in-formation who were mobilized to take a collective stand on the future of the nation, viewing the situation as a crisis requiring urgent intervention, had close interaction with Quebec and a consequent awareness of the gravity of the implications of the changes occurring there.[7] Those most attuned to the divergences in understanding the nature and function of student life separating the two communities were in constant dialogue with their Quebec counterparts in the organizations under stress, NFCUS and CUP (Canadian University Press). By 1964 both had mutated into CUS and UGEQ and CUP and PEN (Presse étudiante nationale) respectively, the introduction of "Union" in the associations' names signalling the new syndicalist orientation. The Briefs submitted by these organizations to the Royal Commission on Bilingualism and Biculturalism in 1965 give the fullest account of the students' awareness of and responses to the "problem of Canadian unity" (Laxer and Fortin 1), offering a history of the long-term relations between the two cultural communities within these organizations and culminating in the mutual recognition of their autonomy and desire for continuing collaboration. Co-authors of these Briefs were the President of CUS, Doug Ward, and of CUP, Jim Laxer, who in 1963, in their respective positions as President of SAC and Features Editor of the *Varsity*, had been co-organizers of the University of Toronto "March for Canada."

Together, the Briefs give an account of longstanding social and cultural divisions between French and English-speaking students which arise in part from the different organizational and funding structures in higher education that remains a provincial matter, but also from different conceptualizations of student associations with a continuing tension between providing student services (typical in English-speaking Canada) and promoting awareness of pressing social issues (desired in Quebec). Beyond the purely linguistic, these differences led to the development of two autonomous organizations. Bilingualism was nonetheless a source of frustration since it remained "institutional and theoretical," rather than yielding "concrete results" (Laxer and Fortin 4): all the correspondence of CUS and the news service of CUP were produced in English, provoking a response from the Quebec student papers that "nous en avons assez soupé du bilinguisme théorique" (qtd. in Laxer and Fortin 4). The predominantly anglophone organizations were slow to respond to demands for French-speaking staff. What pushed the papers to withdraw from CUP was less a matter of "translation" than of "content," according to the Brief (Laxer and Fortin 5). In part, the different focus arises from organization of the Quebec educational system in which, unlike the other provinces, universities were post-graduate institutions offering more specialized or professional instruction for the graduates of the

classical colleges, later of the CEGEP. Founded by Gérard Pelletier in 1943, La Presse
nationale étudiante (PEN) had provided technical services for student journalism at
the college level. However, at its Congress in 1960, PEN's statutes were modified so
that it began to carry out research, becoming a "centre of thought" to generate ideas
and advance common interests (Laxer and Fortin 3). Making little use of CUP's press
releases written in English, the French-speaking newspapers found it difficult to jus-
tify paying the relatively high fees for CUP membership. More importantly, the decision of the Quebec university newspapers to join PEN in November 1963 reinforced
student unity in Quebec within the framework of student syndicalism, of which PEN
had been an initiator, conceiving student journalism as a means for advancing the
student condition through social and national action (Laxer and Fortin 8). Combining
the activities of a student organization with a trade union's action at the political
level, a syndicalist perspective recognizes that student problems are fundamentally
social problems and adopts a broad political approach to socio-economic change.

The Brief prepared by CUS traces an equally long history of diverging philoso-
phies about the function of student organizations with a persistent tension between
an English orientation to pragmatic service provision and a French preference for
structure and political action, a debate which intensified after 1956 when Laval University proposed a division of responsibilities between the regions and the national
office. An additional recommendation, that the French university students and classical college students organize themselves into a Federation that would become one of
two federations forming the Confederation of Canadian University Students, dele-
gated to the French universities for further study, would return to haunt NFCUS at its
end in 1963-64 as the Kenniff committee struggled yet again to find structures to balance regionalizing and centralizing forces in light of Quebec demands for a more politically engaged association. The call for an organization that would be "a dynamic
and forceful vehicle for social change" in both university and society was raised as
early as 1947 in a report to the NCFUS conference by its president that year, Maurice
Sauvé, who advocated adoption of the "Charte de Grenoble" which greatly influenced student organizations in Europe in the post-war period (Ward et al. 5).
Adopted by the Union générale des étudiants de France (UNEF) at its 35th Congress in
April 1946 when its membership swelled with young people returning to studies interrupted by imprisonment, deportation or work in the resistance movement, the
Charter broke with the corporatist and apolitical stance of the past to align students
with workers whose rights had been defined earlier in the century in the Charte
d'Amiens. The Charter's first article declared the student to be "un jeune travailleur

intellectuel" (Bouchet). In exchange for rights to its material support, the young intellectual worker has responsibilities to develop his "technical skills" for the benefit of society. Above all, as an intellectual, the student has a duty to search for truth and the freedom which is its guarantee. Indeed, as the seventh and last article enjoins, it is the student's "most sacred mission" to "defend liberty against oppression" (Bouchet). UNEF pressed for, and finally obtained in September 1948, an extension to students of the system of social security enjoyed by French workers. Their demands for a salary and for sharing in university governance were not answered. From 1950, however, UNEF supported the "aspirations and demands" of students in the French colonies, exemplifying in this the Charter's enjoinder to solidarity with young people throughout the world, as they engaged actively in anti-colonist struggles during the Algerian war for independence (1956-62) (Monchablon 79-80).

Throughout the 1950s, French Canadian student leaders continued to be interested in the creation of an organizational structure that would foster an effective student movement to communicate the student's views to government and the general community. The task of any National Union of Students, as Sauvé conceived it, would be to "promote the rights of a student and to awaken their consciousness to the correlative duties." Syndicalism aims to expand the "common points on which a united stand can be taken" (Ward et al 6). Especially at the Université de Montréal the need for a charter continued to attract interest throughout the 1950s with a review of the question published in *Le quartier latin* in December 1952 which called for a "Fédération Nationale" that would be the sole representative to government "making known the intentions of Canadian students gathered into *syndicat*s with all the advantages offered by the situation: Recognition by government and university authorities of our legitimate demands and the legal means at the disposition of all unions so that their demands would be respected" (Ward et al 8). The Montreal students, influenced by the success of their counterparts in France, nonetheless understood the French example to be less "a theory for application than the opening of new horizons" (Neatby 161). Stimulated by their individual and joint presentations with NFCUS to the Massey-Levesque commission which pressed for changes in the structure and funding of university education, the AGEUM carried out a statistical study of Montreal students that revealed the class-based economic determinants of access to education. Drawing on this data, the AGEUM prepared a brief to the provincial Tremblay Commission on fiscal matters in February 1954 which, in explicitly syndicalist terms of the need to support "intellectual work," presented a demand for a "pré-salaire" comparable to the subsidies of Russian students. Additionally, the

brief called for the Quebec government to hold a federal-provinical conference to develop more equitable tax policies that would provide better funding for higher education in the province (Neatby 178-79). Despite their alternation between provincial
and federal arenas that led the AGEUM to quit and rejoin NFCUS in this decade, the
Montreal students became the principal "porteurs du flambeau réformiste au sein de
la FNEUC"—the most "*nfcus-minded* de tout le Canada" (Neatby 162, 160). Four years
later, the Montreal students pressed their demands for better funding of universities
more radically, organizing all the student associations in the province to prepare a
brief which exposed the broader socio-economic factors in the elitism of these institutions. Frustrated in the attempt to present this brief to Duplessis, the coalition conducted a referendum on all campuses and declared a one day strike on March 6 1958,
followed by a months'-long sit-in at the premier's office requesting a meeting. Although their demands for better funding were not answered, the strike was judged a
success because of the wide-spread support it received from the media, trade unions
and Quebec intellectuals (Neatby 228). For Daniel Latouche, this strike "marks the
turning point" when student syndicalism makes its entry into Quebec society: Quebec students have been "set[ting] the pace of the student movement" in North America which the "progressive wing" of CUS belatedly tried to copy (Latouche 113-14). In
April 1964, Quebec students again pressed the demand for free education with a
march on Quebec during a Dominon-Provincial fiscal conference, repeating with a
different issue the gesture of the Toronto students the preceding November.

Only in 1962 did NFCUS draft a Charter in an attempt to align the objectives and
principles of French and English speaking students which had been steadily drifting
apart over the previous decade. As the Brief to the Laurendeau-Dunton Commission
explains, the draft reiterated the principles of student syndicalism without referring
to the structures of NFCUS which had increasingly become the matter of fractious debate and periodic withdrawal from NFCUS of different member universities (Ward et
al 20). However, after heated discussions at universities across the country, the draft
was rejected by three of the four regional NFCUS groups, passing in Quebec only after
impassioned debate and amendment by the English-speaking universities in that region (Ward et al 20). Although in March 1963 a Provisional Committee had been
formed to establish a framework for a Union générale des étudiants de Québec which
would integrate the classical colleges with the universities, Quebec student leaders
continued to press demands for restructuring NFCUS at its October 1963 Edmonton
Congress along the lines of two separate organizations for each cultural group who
would remain sovereign, but assign certain duties and resources to a superstructure

uniting the two, the Confederal Canadian Union (Ward et al 22). The Structures Commission worked to give institutional shape to these demands over the course of the 1963-64 academic year, but its recommendations were never discussed, since the Quebec universities signalled their intention to withdraw from CUS before the annual meeting in September 1964, determined to found an alternative to its "corporatist" or guild-like structure (Favreau 83). In November of that year, they would meet to form UGEQ at which time they signed the Charte de Grenoble, annotated for the Quebec context by Serge Joyal. "Student unionism defends the economic and social interests of the student," making him "aware of his power in the social, political and economic realms," while stressing his "solidarity with all segments of society" (Joyal 20). The student thus participates fully in the "present Quebec revolution" when the university is no longer marginal to social and political life. The student has a duty to fight against all forms of exploitation, intolerance and discrimination, but especially as apprentice intellectual to work for the democratization of the university by presenting as an objective "universal, free education" (Joyal 21). UGEQ received official recognition from CUS at its September 1965 meeting in Lennoxville, Quebec. At its second congress in November 1965, UGEQ established an office of Internal Syndicalist Affairs to affirm the desire of the students expressed in a resolution to work for "the radical transformation of Quebec society" (Favreau 84).

Written after the withdrawal of Quebec students into autonomous organizations, these Briefs highlight the role of NFCUS and CUP as "a laboratory for the efforts of young people of both language groups to find a successful and fruitful modus-vivendi" (Ward et al 1). This history, they propose, would be of "value to the Royal Commission" in assessing the "prospects for *biculturalism*" (1).[8] In its final report, NFCUS's Structures Commission affirmed the "principle of dualism" insisting that the English Canadians must recognize this principle ungrudgingly and give it their full respect while the French speaking students must not isolate themselves within a narrow linguistic community but cooperate with English speaking colleagues. In their Brief, CUP and PEN highlight the concrete steps being taken for such cooperation which include the joint writing of the Brief where they quote the optimistic comments about friendship and collaboration made in response to the participation of the President of CUP at PEN's annual convention in November 1964 and the return visit of the President of PEN to CUP's conference the next month. Subsequently, the two executives met to coordinate exchanges of daily press releases and other documentation of interest to the two organizations and their members in the aim of "stimulat[ing] a clear and objective understanding of the real issues of the Canadian problem on both sides" (Laxer and Fortin

12). This close collaboration, Fortin and Laxer suggest, is possible as a direct result of the autonomy of the two organizations (12). Consequently, they caution against the endorsement of a facile concept of "unity" which overlooks the social, economic and political complexities of a "multi-national country" and advocate "organizational separation along national lines" (Introduction np). In the two decades following WWII, the student organizations had worked out ways of giving concrete expression to the principle of "sovereignty-association" which had brought them to take up a position in the key political debates of the 1960s.

The crisis which manifested itself in student organizations with the announcement of an impending split in March 1963 was precipitated by unsettling events in the wider political arena which led the members of the Royal Commission on Bilingualism and Biculturalism to observe that the nation was "passing through the greatest crisis in its history" (Royal 13). At the beginning of March, Pierre Bourgault called for a "révolution sociale" to accompany "l'indépendance" which the RIN (Rassemblement pour l'indépendance nationale) would now pursue through the electoral route, having restructured itself as a political party from the movement launched with a Manifesto in 1960. A few days later, his words were echoed in the news release of the FLQ (Front de libération du Québec) which punctuated them with bombs detonated at three armories. These first explosions were followed quickly by other bombings and attempted bombings of symbols of federal authority, the statue of Wolfe on the Plains of Abraham, the federal tax building, the central train station and the Quebec-Montreal railway line where Prime Minister Diefenbaker's train was scheduled to pass on his electoral campaign. The independence movement had become a more forceful presence in both parliamentary and revolutionary arenas exerting considerable pressure on the Lesage liberal government which had taken power in 1960, initiating a new post-Duplessis era. "Le grand noirceur" had been banished with the winning slogan, "Il faut que ça change" which, in turn, had been replaced by the call to become "Maîtres chez nous" with which the Lesage government had been reelected in 1962 on a mandate to nationalize Hydro-Québec. A social if not socialist revolution was underway in Quebec, although who had the right to use force in advancing it was as yet a moot point. In the federal election in process in the spring of 1963, a minority Conservative government was replaced by a minority Liberal government among whose first tasks in July 1963 was to establish a Royal Commission on Bilingualism and Biculturalism to respond to the troubled state of Quebec by inquiring into "the existing state of bilingualism and biculturalism in Canada" and make recommendations for the development for the future of Confederation on the basis of "an equal partnership between the two founding [peoples]" (Royal 180). Adopting a syndicalist stance, CUS determined that students would be active participants in this process by presenting briefs to the Commission through both national and individual university associations.

In this conjuncture of imminent schisms in both student and national bodies, SAC moved at an Extraordinary meeting of Council on September 26 1963 to establish a "French Committee" to be called the Temporary Committee on Canadian-Canadien Relations or Le Comité Temporaire du Conseil Administratif des Etudiants pour les Relations Canadiennes-Canadian. As one of its responsabilities the committee was charged with preparing a brief for the Royal Commission. While no formal document was presented, members of the committee had opportunities to express their views informally to the commissioners at some of the organized events. Although there was a French Canada Week at the University of British Columbia, a bilingualism week at Sir George Williams and a CUS regional conference at the University of Western Ontario in January 1964 on contemporary Quebec, the number and variety of activities at the University of Toronto involving students in discussions about current Quebec politics far exceeded those at any other English-Canadian university. Over the next six months the Committee mobilized the entire campus through a number of interlocking networks—political clubs, disciplinary associations, college publications—in seminars, debates and articles informing students about the history and current situation of French Canada. This extended form of Teach-In (before the term had been invented) was preparation for the "March for Canada" of November 22 1963 when a Brief was presented to Premier John Robarts shortly before a Dominion-Provincial Fiscal Conference calling on him to "think of the welfare of Canada" and to "maintain an understanding and flexible attitude" during the conference to the problems presented by Quebec. This petition was prefaced by an expression of the students' deep concern for the "future of Canada" which has manifested itself in the recognition of the importance of "le fait Canadien français" as the Canadian Union of Students had recently done (SAC minutes Nov 13 1963). The President of SAC, Douglas Ward, was an ex-officio member of the Committee whose Chair, Richard Pope, was a member of SAC's External Affairs Committee. Eventually numbering about forty people, divided into sub-committees, the initial members drawn from participants in the Carabin exchange also included students from a seminar on Quebec nationalism taught by History professor, Ramsay Cook. Among these was the Features Editor of the *Varsity*, Jim Laxer, who also served on the executive of the University of Toronto NDP. Through these different networks, the Committee carried out an active campaign of consciousness raising on the historical roots and contemporary manifestations of Quebec nationalism which climaxed with the gathering of 3000 students at Queen's Park. This demonstration was not listed in the original mandate of the Committee which instructed members to carry out a general watchdog and coordinating function on matters relating to French Canadian affairs, advising SAC on these matters and translating its correspondence with French speakers, as well as acting as publicist for the work of SAC to the French-language press. Among the assigned responsibilities of the Committee was the "establishment of a library of relevant reading materials," while another was to carry out the "regular study" of French language media in order to communicate its information to Council and other interested parties in the university. Throughout the decade, these would remain the principal activities of the Canadian-Canadien Committee, especially the gathering and disseminating of news from Quebec in the pages of the *Varsity*, along with the organization of lectures, conferences and cultural performances.

These events unfolded at a dizzying pace over the course of the 1963-64 academic year. At Victoria College, the 105th Debating Parliament deliberated on the question "Canada should be Bilingual" in October 1963, while two debaters from the Université de Montréal were victors in a Hart House debate in February 1964 when the motion was defeated that "This house deplores Quebec's current aspirations. Prof. Ramsay Cook conducted a series of seminars on English-French relations in Canada for the campus NDP during November 1963, while the campus Liberals focused a meeting in the same period on biculturalism and the constitution. When it came time to hold elections for the Model Parliament a month later, the party positions on confederation were solicited and spokespeople for the four political parties held a debate on bilingualism. André L'Heureux, secretary of the Quebec Socialist Party, gave a talk on "The Future of Confederation" during October. The Political Science department was also actively involved for Prof. Paul Fox gave a talk on the Quebec crisis on November 20th alongside the organizers of the March. And R.S. Blair of the economics department wrote a position piece in the *Varsity* outlining the dominion-provincial fiscal relations in question (15 November 1963, 1). The pace of events in the second term was as intense, as the Canadian-Canadien Committee invited a number of prominent figures from Quebec as visiting speakers over the course of two weeks in February and organized the Current Canada Seminar on the question of Confederation for the weekend in mid February between them. The positions on the issue of Quebec separatism varied considerably; historian Michel Brunet, speaking on "Canada's Unity and French-Canadian Survival" and Jacques-Yvan Morin, talking about the "Bicultural Problem and the Future of Canadian Federalism" were more sympathetic to the separatist cause than journalist Solange Chaput-Rolland, noted for her dialogue with her "Dear Enemy," anglo-Montrealer Gwethelyn Graham, who suggested love and understanding would bridge the cultural divide. Certainly, a concern for a diversity of perspectives was evident in the selection of speakers for the weekend seminar which included Charles Taylor from McGill and MLA René Levesque. F.R. Scott was also present in his capacity as member of the Bilingual and Bicultural Commission, inviting those present to submit briefs and receiving them informally in conversations with students. Even faculty supported the student concern to promote better understanding of Quebec by inviting Quebec historian, Fernand Ouellet, to give the 18th annual Gray Lecture. The Canadian-Canadien Committee concluded its presentation of Quebec perspectives on a different note with the first appearance in English Canada of renowned chansonnier, Gilles Vigneault, on stage at Hart House Theatre.

A similar mix of lecture by recognized experts on Quebec and student presentations and debate was the format of the many interuniversity seminars and exchanges that year. Members of the Canadian-Canadien Committee had a number of opportunities to interact directly with the leaders of the Quebec student movement. Richard Pope and Charles Beer were SAC representatives to the 7th annual Congrès des affaires canadiennes at Laval University early in November 1963 on the topic of "Les nouveaux québécois," while Archie Campbell, Bill Harris and Beer were the Toronto delegates to the Current Canada Seminar where their defence of Quebec's right to succession lost in a debate to the University of Windsor students supporting Canadian unity. Under the leadership of Richard Pope, the Carabin exchange with the Université de Montréal was transformed from its previous weekend-long party into an intellectual forum with presentations by students, as well as by David Lewis and Peter Gzowski, on "Quebec: Revolution or Evolution." Only students fluent in French were selected for the exchange which impressed the Montreal visitors to Toronto at the end of November. Among them, Michel Beaulieu, editor of *Le Quartier latin*, extended his relations with the *Varsity*, his byline on subsequent articles published there listing him as the "*Varsity*'s Montreal correspondent" as he reported on the Ottawa Dominion-Provincial fiscal conference and the December march of Université de Montréal students on the Trans-Canada Air Lines offices to protest their recent airplane purchase as well as their discriminatory language policy (January 6 1964, 4). This proved a more peaceful protest than the Gordon Affair two years earlier against the language policies and their economic effects at Canadian National Railways. A parallel exchange that weekend involving engineering students from Toronto and Montreal was also considered a success. As the *Varsity* editorial of the following week observed, "le dialogue de ces deux universités peut-être très important pour fournir un bon exemple du contact anglo-français" (2 December 1963, 4).

This stance of active listening to "what Quebec wants" characterized the majority of activities organized at the University of Toronto that year, even those of the *Varsity* which was nonetheless influential in advancing the concept of student syndicalism. Reports were published on the many events taking place on campus along with commentary by members of the Canadian-Canadien Committee on the status of the French language in Quebec and its absence in the teaching of French at Toronto. The *Varsity*'s key role, however, was its publication of a series of ten articles on "Canada in Crisis" with contributions on the challenges to confederation from many different positions, geographical as well as political. Voices of the anglophone minority in Quebec, the Acadian minority in the Maritimes, as well as those of the west, were intermingled with differing views from Quebec which included those of an FLQ member imprisoned for the April bombings of the Westmount armory (18 November 1963, 1), as well as Michel Beaulieu, author of the second in the series called a "provocative explication" in the brief synopsis which follows the French text (30 October 1963, 4). Beaulieu explains why he advocates separatism, feeling that the current situation is condescending to Quebec which has a vibrant culture, whereas the rest of Canada controls the economy. He is dismayed not only by the betrayal of Quebec politicians serving in the federal government, but also by the demand in Montreal to "speak white" rather than his mother tongue.[9] Provocative the text may have been politically to those who could read it. Provocative it most certainly was in its untranslated French. Some of the articles were written by the series editor, Jim Laxer, including the first which framed the series as "A tale of two cities," Montreal and Toronto in necessary dialogue (28 October 1963, 5), and the final one which prepared for the March—"The moderate must act" (20 November 1963, 4). "The sane voices of compromise and reason," he urges, must make themselves heard in the debate to make it clear that they are "concerned about the future of Canada." Nowhere in all this deliberation on Quebec is there an explicit discussion of syndicalism which remains implicit in the significance of the subject matter, as is evident in the first editorial of the year, "A time for decision" (27 September 1963, 2). The reason for the split developing in NFCUS, the editorial explains, is because "the French Canadian Students have discovered their status as citizens in a democracy and are acting accordingly." It is time for English speaking students to decide between "involvement or non-involvement in the issues of their time. We hope they have the courage to act in a responsible manner." In the final editorial, the year's activities are summarized: "the March for Canada, the change in the CUCND from a protest body to a positive action group, the formation and subsequent achievements of the Canadian/Canadien Committee, the continued negotiations with Simcoe Hall for student autonomy, and on and on ..." Stressing the foundational nature of the year, the editorial concludes that "all these happenings appear as manifestations of an English-Canadian awakening of the type which occurred in French Canada two years ago" and so offer "promise for the future" (13 March 1964, 4). Would this extended dialogue be enough to change the course of Canadian politics? Or of the student movement?

What indeed were the Toronto students advocating in the "March for Canada"? Given the wide range of positions on the political crisis that had been presented on campus that fall, there was reason to be sceptical about what the March meant other than that students were uncertain about the future. More of them participated in this demonstration than in any other on university funding during the decade, but that may have been because the organizers of the March drew on the material support of the old guild style student association—the "hustler's handbook" or student telephone directory—to urge students personally to attend. In the weeks prior to the March, editorials in the *Varsity* stressed the importance of participating on a non-political basis to indicate their concern as "citizens of this country" (13 November 1963, 4). As a final urging, the editorial of November 22 stressed that missing a lecture was not important when "[t]he future of Canada lies in the hands of the youth of Canada" who have "an opportunity to shape" it today (4). In his speech at Queen's Park at the head of the large group of students, Douglas Ward was more explicit about the syndicalist philosophy of the March when he described it as "catching up on a student involvement and commitment which has spread to us from our French-Canadian contemporaries; and as one of them has noted, we students are perhaps apprentice-doctors, and apprentice-engineers, but we are not apprentice citizens" (25 November 1963, 5). The concerned students do not propose solutions but wish the premier to be responsive to the "challenges, in the light of a new Quebec" and so act to prevent the establishment of a border between two countries. Although the left wing political clubs had been most active in fostering dialogue on campus about the subordinate position of Quebec in Canada, the explicit positions taken in the March endorsed no socialist revolution but at most exemplified a competition of hegemonies in which youth challenged the reigning elite.

In the fall of 1964, student syndicalism became more overtly connected to the question of Quebec. The Canadian-Canadien Committee fulfilled a promise made by Charles Beer the preceeding year at Laval and organized the annual conference on "The Changing Face of English Canada" to examine the political dilemma of Canada from the opposite perspective in order to help Canadian unity by casting light on English-speaking Canada's identity. "Is there a Homogeneous English Canada?" was the question asked by speaker Blair Fraser and with the geographical and ethnic diversity of the participants, the outcome seemed to be a resounding no. The inclusion of a Ukrainian senator and Acadian from New Brunswick complicated the situation for the closing speaker, Pierre Laporte, addressing "The Prospects for a United Canada." Claude Ryan and Solange Chaput-Rolland, speaking on a panel on the "Arts in English Canada," moderated by Robert Weaver of the CBC, were other French speakers whose presentations were more easily followed by the participants from thirty universities with the aid of simultaneous translation. Observers from the Royal Commission were also in attendance. This was the major activity of the Can-Can Committee that year and by the time it took place at the end of October 1964, the attention of student activists had turned to Quebec where police violence against peaceful student demonstrators protesting Queen Elizabeth's visit to Quebec city has raised the stakes for syndicalist actions. Moreover, the decision to leave CUS by Quebec universities over their refusal to support a federal student loan plan, was headline news in the first issue of the *Varsity* (23 September 1964, 2). The *Varsity* continued to make Quebec a focus of attention, publishing an article by Maurice Sauvé, by then a Liberal cabinet minister of forestry, who proposed that English Canada should "Welcome Quebec Revolution" since an economically strong Quebec would benefit all of Canada (30 September 1964, 5). A different view by sociologist Tony Bond prophesied that "Quebec will separate" since French Canadians of Quebec think of themselves as "a nation," whereas English Canadians consider them "a large majority" (9 October 1964, 21). In between these two opinion pieces, the *Varsity* observes that "SNCC will try again at U of T" (2 October 1964, 18) and published a report by one of the Toronto students to visit Cuba on a summer study tour which highlighted the "social revolution" ongoing there. The focus of student activism was moving south. For the remainder of the fall it stayed focused on Quebec with a visit of Pierre Maheu, co-editor of *Parti Pris* speaking on November 5 to the Socialist Club on the class basis of the "quiet revolution," following up on a contact first established by the Canadian-Canadien Committee the previous spring. Similarly, a committed separatist, Giles Grenier of RIN, was an invited speaker during the Harvard Exchange in November, sign of the more radical orientation among Toronto students toward Quebec politics. A more "radical brand of nationalism" was prominent in Quebec student organizations too, as a November meeting in Montreal of PEN voted for "a resolution calling for Quebec to work towards becoming an independent, republican state" (*Varsity* 16 November 1964, 1). The same weekend in Montreal delegates from universities, classical colleges, technical and normals schools met to found UGEQ on which occasion they adopted the Charte de Grenoble, a "conception of student syndicalism" that will make the Union a powerful, radical force in Quebec (16 November 1964, 1). The first of many articles on syndicalism over the next few months, it highlights the orientation toward "political, economic, social and cultural progress" for all in the French Canadian Nation. In preparation, working papers were written by Richard Guay on international policy and by Serge Joyal on "Student Syndicalism in Quebec." Both would play a significant role a few weeks later in Toronto and Regina as a more fully articulated understanding of syndicalism moved from Quebec through English Canada to the English-speaking world.

As the *Varsity* reported on the arrest of student protestors of Berkeley's Free Speech Movement in California (4 December 1964, 1), it announced an upcoming seminar on student action organized by the campus NDP to "study how the new ideas evolved by the student movement in Quebec can be applied to English Canada" (14 December 1964, 2).

As Gord Laxer, coordinator of the seminar expands a few days later, the "philosophy of student action is part of a larger philosphy—that all citizens must take an active interest in their community in order for it to be vibrant and free" (18 December 1964, 21). Students not only have a right but a duty to act upon questions of concern to their community. Among the speakers at the seminar were Robert Panet-Raymond, vice president of UGEQ, Jim Laxer, vice-president of CUP and graduate student at Queens, Ken Drushka past editor of *Varsity*, Howard Adelman of the Campus Co-ops, and Art Pape, national chairman of CUCND. A number of these speakers would travel to Regina a week later to participate in the CUCND conference there, possibly repeating some of their talks, as in the case of Adelman's presentation on "The Philosophy of Student Syndicalism." For the seminar in Toronto, David Lloyd-Jones prepared a translation of Serge Joyal's "Le syndicalism au Québec" and later wrote about syndicalism for the University College *Gargoyle*. The translation served as a background paper for the Regina conference, then in March 1965, was published in *Canadian Dimension*. It circulated later as an offprint with *Canadian Dimension* on its cover, surfacing in documents related to a SUPA conference on student syndicalism for western Canadian universities held at Fort Qu'appelle, Saskatchewan in May 1966, for which Richard Guay was on the mailing list. By the end of 1966, the translation of Joyal's text was being distributed in the pamphlet collection of SUPA.

With the escalation of the war in Vietnam, campus activities at Toronto focused on the annual Teach-Ins from the fall of 1965. Members of the Canadian-Canadien Committee continued to be interested in student syndicalism most frequently in their capacity as journalists for the *Varsity* or as External Affairs Commissioner for SAC which called on them to attend meetings of UGEQ. With the schism of the student unions and the cancellation of the Carabin exchange by Université de Montréal students in the fall of 1965, contacts with Quebec students were no longer as frequent or sustained. By the academic year 1968-69 the question of Quebec in the future of the nation had been replaced at the University of Toronto by a concern with the liberation of the student from the authority of the academy. SAC was running a Free University, F U of T, with courses ranging from Anarchism and Black Magic to Women's Liberation, and attempting to persuade the professors' association to join them in resisting the Board of Governors to ensure student-faculty parity on the Commission on Governance being established. The Canadian-Canadien Committee continued its activities of sponsoring speakers on campus, less clearly linked to the Committee in announcements of events than in the past. It organized what was now called a "Fête annuelle," rather than a conference, stretched out over a couple of weeks in February with Quebec theatre, films and speakers, in what had become primarily a cultural rather than political event, following the practice of the preceding year. An election meeting advertised for later that month to select a new executive for the Committee seems to have been unsuccessful, for the 1968-69 Chair cannot remember there being any successor. Glendon College was the sponsor of a conference, "Quebec: Year Eight," in November 1967, on a much larger scale but of similar structure to the conferences held at the University of Toronto in 1964. The action had passed elsewhere and the question posed at the beginning of the decade as to whether Quebec's subordinate status was cultural or economic was being addressed in diverse ways in different political forums both parliamentary and movement based.

Réné Lévesque's decision to leave the Liberal party in November 1967 to found the Mouvement Sovereignté Association, then the Parti Québécois, created scissions in many separatist groups, such as *Parti Pris*, as the call to unite in the cause of independence through electoral politics divided those who put independence first from the more radical left who envisaged a socialist alternative. The disbanding of the RIN was decisive in this regard when its members swelled the number of adherents to the PQ. The possible threat of an independent Quebec achieved through democratic processes was countered in the spring of 1968 on the election of Pierre Elliot Trudeau as leader of the Liberal party. For those who understood the problem of Quebec in a purely cultural framework, the advent of a bilingual Québécois as Prime Minister enabled them breathe a sigh of relief that they no longer had to stand up for Canada. The first volumes of the *Report of the Royal Commission on Bilingualism and Biculturalism* came out in July 1967 and focused on regimes of language rights with recommendations for linguistic equality, which Trudeau moved quickly to recognize (at least partially) in the Official Languages Act of 1969.

In Ontario, the Advisory Committee on Confederation continued its work on Franco-Ontarians until 1971 to carry out research and policy development in response to the changing face of the Canadian polity. Established in 1965 under the leadership of Ian MacDonald, this committee initiated planning for French language services, especially in the areas of education and the law, although never the full bilingualism that some of its members desired, especially those members of the subcommittee on culture and education, including language. Charles Beer, a founding member of the Canadian-Canadien Committee served as secretary to this subcommittee and in 1968 was lent to the Ministry of Education to do research for the person responsible for implementing the governement's French language public school system (Stevenson). Twenty years later he would become Minister of Francophone Affairs responsible for implementing the French Language Services Act. He had been mistaken in November 1964 in thinking that everything was finished. For him it was only the beginning. Archie Campbell, another of the founding members of the Canadian-Canadien Committee, had just left the Ontario civil service where he had worked in the Attorney-General's office on the implementation of a French language court system in the province. Possibly this is the one concrete outcome of the March for Canada in 1963, that John Robarts heard the students and recognized them as the voice of the future.

Co-optation by power was not the only way the question of Quebec continued to play out in the political arena. Within the traditional instances of power it had been the NDP which, from the beginning of the decade, had been most inclined to recognize the cultural duality of Canada. Indeed, the concept of "sovereignté-association" had been developed by some of its Quebec members in the Parti social démocrat before they joined the PQ. At Queen's University, Jim Laxer, yet another founding member of the Canadian-Canadien Committee would have an important role in articulating a left position on Quebec nationalism in the Waffle Movement on the margins of the NDP (Smart). The demands of the left for radical socio-economic transformation were not satisfied by the triumph of the "petite bourgeoisie technocratique," as Gilles Bourque called the PQ (Bourque and Legaré 191). The implications of student syndicalism for establishing alliances with other unions of workers was not much explored by the University of Toronto activists who had been initially so responsive to the idea. However, with the "Operation McGill Français" in March 1969, students grouped around the *McGill Daily* linked up with UGEQ and many other militant socialist groups in Quebec with the support of Michel Chartrand and the Conseil central des syndicats nationaux de Montréal (CSN) to mobilize 15,000 people, including some members of the Toronto Canadian-Canadien Committee, to demand that rich and powerful McGill, fortress of the anglophone capitalist establishment, become a second French university in Montreal to provide more opportunities for the francophone majority surrounding it. Relations between French and English Canadians took a different turn with the rise of a new phase of Quebec separatism in the 1970s which developed a political framework for it to attain greater cultural if not economic autonomy.

Notes

1 Already in Canada by 1962, over 60 percent of the mining and petroleum industry and over 50 percent of the manufacturing industry were foreign owned (Kostash xvi).

2 Jacques Berque, an ethnologue, had a direct influence on Quebec movements as a Visiting Professor at the Université de Montréal in 1962 (Fournier 23).

3 Although in 1933, only three countries in Africa were independent, by 1963 thirty-four of them had broken their colonial bonds, declared Martin Luther King in affirming the urgency of a new black politics (Fournier 52).

4 As early as August 1959 a group of students from the Université de Montréal travelled to Cuba (Fournier 33). Georges Schoeters, who returned to Cuba shortly afterwards to work on agrarian reform, would a few years later co-found the FLQ whose members sought refuge or exile in Cuba throughout the 1960s and 70s. Maps of Cuba and posters of the revolution decorated the offices of the Association générale des étudiants de l'Université de Montréal (AGEUM) around 1963 as reported by former University of Toronto students Douglas Ward and James Laxer of their visits to their counterparts, Pierre Marois and Michel Beaulieu, in student government and journalism (personal communication, May 2007).

5 Cy Gonick, editor of *Canadian Dimension*, was one of the "resource people" at the Regina conference for the workshop on Social Issues and Peace. Dimiti Roussopoulos, editor of *Our Generation*, was a resource person for workshops on Canadian Foreign Policy.

6 A copy of the draft statement, "The Student and Social Issues in the Nuclear Age," along with press reports of the conference commenting on student syndicalism are held in the Douglas Ward

Fonds at the William Ready Archives, McMaster University. Ward was a resource person for workshops on Student Organizations along with his fellow University of Toronto student, Arthur Pape, national President of CUCND.

7 Many who became involved in the various related actions of 1963 had participated during the 1950s in the Visites Interprovinciales spending the summer in Quebec families or had taken summer courses in French at Laval, Trois Pistoles (UWO) or St. Pierre et Miquelon (U of T). Many had participated in the longstanding U of T exchanges with Quebec universities, the Carabin weekend with Université de Montréal and the St. Michael's College-Laval exchange, or SCM (Student Christian Movement) workcamps which in the summer of 1964 initiated a bilingual work camp in Montreal (SAC Congrès; "SCM" 6). In these contexts, or when participating with students from Quebec in the international summer seminars of WUS or the International Union of Students, University of Toronto students had become aware of considerable cultural differences between the student communities of Quebec and Ontario.

8 These longer briefs reiterate the key point of the short text presented by CUS to the preliminary hearings of the Royal Commission, November 7 1963.

9 Michel Beaulieu, later a well-known poet, also wrote an essay, "The Church and French Canada," translated by Liora Proctorand Rene Forsey Marquis, for "Revolution (part 2): The Revolution at Home," special issue of the University College magazine, *Gargoyle* 11 (February 1964): 2-5.

Works Cited

"A New Policy, student unionism accepted," *Sanity* (February 1965): 7.

Berque, Jacques. *Dépossession du monde*. Paris: Editions du Seuil, 1964.

Bouchet, Paul. "La Charte de Grenoble." [1946] URL: http://unefparis8.wordpress.com /2008/03/02/la-charte-de-grenoble/

Bourque, Gilles and Gilles Dostaler. *Socialisme et indépendance*. Montreal: Boréal Express, 1980.

Bourque, Gilles and Anne Legaré. *Le Québec: La question nationale*. Paris: Librairie François Maspero, 1979.

Chamberland, Paul, "Aliénation culturelle et révolution nationale," *Parti Pris* 2 (novembre 1963): 10-22.

Favreau, Robert, "The Quandary of l'Union générale des étudiants du Québec," *Our Generation* 5, 1 (1967): 93-101; Rpt. in *Québec and Radical Social Change,* ed. Dimitrious I. Roussopoulos. Montreal: Black Rose Books, 1974. 82-90.

Fournier, Louis. *FLQ: Histoire d'un mouvement clandestin*. 2e ed. Montréal: Lanctôt, 1998.

Gonick, Cy. "Students and Peace," *Canadian Dimension* 2, 2 (January 1965): 12.

Goodings, Stewart, "Students and Social Action," *University Affairs/ Affaires universitaires* (April 1965): 5-6.

Gray, Stanley, "The Troubles at McGill, " in *Student Power and the Canadian Campus*, ed. Tim and Julyan Reid. Toronto: Peter Martin, 1969. 48-55.

Jameson, Fredric, "Periodizing the 60s," in *The Ideologies of Theory: Essays 1971-1986: The Syntax of History*, vol. 2. Minneapolis: University of Minnesota Press, 1989. 178-208.

Joyal, Serge, "Le syndicalisme au Québec." Union générale des étudiants du Québec, Founding Conference, November 12-14 1964; "Student Syndicalism in Quebec," trans. David Lloyd-Jones and Sharon Vinesacker. *Canadian Dimension* 2, 3 (March 1965): 20-21.

Kenniff, Patrick et. al. "Report of the Commission on Structures." July 1964. NFCUS/CUS Fonds, William Ready Archives, McMaster University, Box 4.

Kostash, Myrna. *Long Way from Home*. Toronto: James Lorimer & Co., 1980.

Latouche, Daniel, "The Quebec Student Movement. Radicalism, Syndicalism, Reformism, Revolution, Realism, or What?, in *Student Protest*, eds. Gerald F. McGuigan, George Payerle and Patricia Horrobin. Toronto: Methuen, 1978. 113-131.

Laxer, Gordon, "NDP to confer on syndicalism" *Varsity* (18 December 1964): 21.

Laxer, James, "Where has the student movement gone?" *Varsity* (24 January 1966): 5.

Laxer, James, "The Americanization of the Canadian student movement," in *Close the 49th parallel etc. The Americanization of Canada*, ed. Ian Lumsden. Toronto: University of Toronto, 1970. 277-286.

Laxer, James and Pierre Fortin. "Brief presented to the Royal Commission on Bilingualism and Biculturalism by the Canadian University Press and Presse étudiante nationale," September 1 1965. James Laxer Fonds, York University Archives, 1999-046/001 (06).

Levitt, Cyril. *Children of Privilege: Student Revolt in the 60s*. Toronto: University of Toronto Press, 1984.

Lloyd-Jones, David, "A Different Kind of Year," *Gargoyle* 11 (April 1965): 6-8.

McMahon, Mary Pat. "Vice-President's Final Report" (SAC 1963-64). Student's Administrative Council Fond, University of Toronto Archives, A 70-0012/016 (01).

Memmi, Albert. *Portrait du colonisé précédé du Portrait du colonisateur*. Paris: Buchet/Chastel, 1957.

Monchablon, Alain, "L'Apogée d'un mouvement syndical (1944-1962)," in *Cents ans de mouvements étudiants*, ed. Jean-Philippe Legois, Alain Monchablon and Robi Morder. Paris: Editions Syllepse, 2007. 71-81.

Neatby, Nicole. *Carabins ou activistes? L'idéalisme et la radicalisation de la pensée étudiante à l'Université de Montréal au temps du duplessisme*. Montreal and Kingston: McGill-Queen's University Press, 1999.

Quebec Year Eight; the Glendon College Forum 1967. Toronto: CBC, 1968.

"Resolutions, NFCUS Congress 1962." NFCUS/CUS Fonds, William Ready Archives, McMaster University, Box 83.

The Royal Commission on Bilingualism and Biculturalism. *Preliminary Report*. Ottawa: Government of Canada, 1965.

SAC Congrès des affaires canadiens, November 1963. SAC Fonds, University of Toronto Archives, A72-0023, Box18, File 8.

SAC Brief to Premier, Minutes of SAC 4th meeting, 13 November 1963, p .5. SAC Fonds, University of Toronto Archives, A70-012, Box 16, File 1.

SAC Carabin Exchange 28-30 November 1963. SAC Fonds, University of Toronto Archives, A72-0023, Box 17, File 16.

SAC Report on Seminar on Student Syndicalism, 13-16 May 1966. SAC Fonds, University of Toronto Archives, A72-0023, Box 26, file 24.

"SCM fights binational problems," *Varsity* (7 December 1964): 6.

Smart, Patricia, "Queen's University History Department and the Birth of the Waffle Movement," Paper presented at New World Coming, Queen's University, June 16 2007.

Stevenson, Don. "John Robarts' Advisory Committee on Confederation and its Impact on Ontario's Language Policy." In *Légiférer en matière linguistique*, ed. Marcel Martel and Martin Pâquet. Québec: Les Presses de l'Université Laval, 2008. 183-189.

Vallières, Pierre. *Nègres blancs d'Amérique*. Montréal: Editions Parti Pris, 1968.

Ward, Doug, Patrick Kenniff and Richard Good. "Submission of the Canadian Union of Students to the Royal Commission on Bilingualism and Biculturalism." September 14, 1965. NCFUS/CUS Fonds, William Ready Archives, McMaster University, Box 88.

Pat Smart

<table>
<tr><td>Chapter

11</td><td>Queen's University History Department
and the Birth of the Waffle Movement</td></tr>
</table>

In March 1971, the Security Service of the RCMP, in a brief on the Waffle group submitted to the Solicitor General of Canada Jean-Pierre Goyer, noted that:

> The prime aim of the Waffle Group within the NDP is the establishment of an independent socialist Canada to be achieved through the existing structure of the New Democratic Party. The Waffle group hope to change the NDP from within and radicalize the NDP socialist policies. Considering the Waffle group as a whole, it is felt they will be a viable political force within the NDP.[1]

The RCMP has provided us here with an accurate description of the aims of the Waffle group; unfortunately, however, they were wrong about the viability of our group within the NDP. The following reflections about the Waffle is as much a memoir as an objective analysis: their aim is to provide a personal look at this Left nationalist group, a unique blend of movement and party politics which had a significant impact on Canadian politics in the late 60s, and at its links with the Queen's University History department.

I should probably start with an explanation of the group's strange name. In one of the meetings held to draft our manifesto "For an independent socialist Canada," which was to be presented as a resolution at the federal convention of the New Democratic Party in Winnipeg in September 1969, there was heated debate on exactly what position we should take on foreign ownership, and one member of the group commented that he would rather "waffle to the left than to the right." The term was picked up in a Globe and Mail editorial when the manifesto was publicly released a few months later, and the rest is history. The Waffle has been discussed in a number of theses, articles and books, and was the subject of many newspaper articles and editorials at the time the group was active; but no one has ever documented the details connected with the fact that six of the original twelve people who drafted its mani-

festo were Queen's students, three of them graduate students in the History depart-
ment. The three History students were Jim Laxer, Lorne Brown and my husband John
Smart; the other three were their wives: Krista Maeots, Caroline Brown and myself.
Two other key founding members should be mentioned, though they had nothing to
do with Queen's: Gerry Caplan, Stephen Lewis's best friend and a close friend of the
Smarts through University of Toronto History Department and NDP connections, and
Mel Watkins, a young professor of Political Economy at the University of Toronto,
who had recently authored an explosive report on foreign ownership for the Canadian government. Watkins had come back from his graduate studies at MIT a thor-
oughgoing continentalist, but was radicalized by the legacy of Harold Innis and the
presence of C.B. Macpherson and Abe Rotstein in his department, as well as by
George Grant's *Lament for a Nation*, which he says he read for the first time to see how
many mistakes he could find, but was unable to put it down when he realized how
right it was.[2] Grant's thesis was that Canada had historically been a place where resistance to liberal technological capitalism was a real possibility and an essential part of
the fabric of our culture, but that this was no longer possible since the defeat of the
Diefenbaker government in 1963. But to get back to Queen's…

When we arrived in the mid-sixties, the Queen's History Department was growing and changing rapidly. Until then it had been relatively small in size and not particularly political. Fred Gibson, a brilliant Canadianist and senior professor in the
Department, had ties to the Liberal Party. Arthur Lower, just then entering his years
of retirement, had been for years an intellectual gadfly on the Canadian scene but
was not publicly tied to any particular political party. But among the newer faculty
there were several active New Democrats : Syd Wise, Donald Swainson (who at one
point took a year's leave from the department to return to his native Manitoba to advise Ed Schreyer's new NDP provincial government), Gerry Tulchinsky and George
Rawlyk. Professor Tulchinsky's brother, Dr. Ted Tulchinsky, was a public advocate for
medicare and leader of a movement to create community medical clinics in Canada.
He was one of the progressive doctors who had gone to Saskatchewan in 1962 to
practice medicine during the doctors' strike against the province's new medicare
scheme, and he married Tommy Douglas's younger daughter. George Rawlyk had
worked for the NDP in Nova Scotia and Ontario, and even after he came to teach
full-time in the History Department.he remained a key advisor to Donald MacDonald,
the leader of the Ontario NDP.

Into this mix came the three new graduate students already mentioned. Lorne
Brown was a strong Saskatchewan NDP socialist; John Smart was an active NDPer who

had managed Stephen Lewis's first run for the Ontario Legislature and earlier been a member of David Lewis's campaign team in York South; and Laxer, who had been brought up as a Red Diaper baby and has recently published a memoir of his childhood under that title,[3] had been active in the student movement at University of Toronto and headed Canadian University Press for a year before starting his Ph.D. at Queen's. Through Lorne and Caroline Brown, we had an introduction to the generosity, radicalism and confidence of Saskatchewan socialist culture, quite different from anything we Ontarians were familiar with; as for John Smart, he was already president of the NDP riding association for Kingston and the Islands by the time the Waffle began in 1969, and active in municipal politics. What Laxer brought to the mix in addition to his student activism was a strong sense of the possibility of a new Canadian nationalism, which he translated into action during the 1966-67 academic year by setting up a student-run seminar called "The Seminar on Canada," which soon became popular among the history graduate students and many from other departments. Soon a number of us were meeting off campus, hatching the strategy for a left nationalist takeover of the NDP and starting to put together ideas for the manifesto "For an independent socialist Canada," large parts of which were drafted in the living room of our apartment at 228 Johnson Street, in a house which we took pride in recalling had once belonged to Sir Oliver Mowat, the Liberal Premier of Ontario from 1872 to 1896.

The main idea of the manifesto was that Canada could not remain an independent country unless it was also a socialist country, and that socialism could not be achieved without Canada's independence from the United States. The logic of that interconnection is laid out in the 26 points of the manifesto, which include: the aim of transforming the NDP into the parliamentary wing of a larger movement; the statement that "the American Empire is the central reality for Canadians [and that] it is an empire characterized by militarism abroad and racism at home"; an insistence on the need to nationalize the Canadian resource sector in order to take control of our economy; an affirmation of the key role of the Canadian working class and the labour movement in building an independent socialist Canada; and a two-nations position on Quebec which I'll elaborate on in a moment. As I recall, the most controversial aspect of the manifesto for many was the use of the term "American Empire," perhaps an easier target than some of the manifesto's radical content.

My own memories of the beginnings of the Waffle are very much tied up with Quebec, for at the time I was a Ph.D. student in the French department at Queen's, totally immersed in the novels of Hubert Aquin and the left nationalist fervour that had produced them. Central to the new understanding of Quebec I was developing were the ideas of the new independentist and socialist journal *Parti pris*, produced mostly by students from the University of Montreal who were themselves heavily influenced by the anti-colonialist writings of Albert Memmi, Jacques Berque and Frantz Fanon. I was probably typical of many Canadian students of Quebec culture in that I found in that culture a passion and sense of identity that seemed lacking in my own; and per-haps typical of Canadian students as well in the fact that I really didn't know very much about our own culture and literature. At the University of Toronto, where I had done my undergraduate work in Honours English and French, there had been only one course that touched on Canadian literature. It was called "American and Cana-dian literature," and in it we became thoroughly familiar with the work of Emerson, Thoreau, Poe, Henry James, Fitzgerald and Hemingway, and then—about two weeks before the final exam—were given a quick run-through of the poetry of E.J. Pratt. In French, the only Quebec content was a half-credit course for honours students in the final term of fourth year.

As I recall, my understanding of the parallels between our own struggle and that of Quebec began to take shape during some long walks with Jim Laxer in Macdonald Park near the Queen's campus, on lovely fall afternoons when we probably should have been in class. We talked about George Grant, whom I was just starting to read, and about the ideas of *Parti pris* and the huge impact they had had on the politicization of Quebec culture. A few months later, when I read Dennis Lee's great poem *Civil Elegies* (1968), I finally saw in our literature a passion, despair and yet re-fusal to despair about the nation we were trying to give birth to which echoed exactly the sentiments I was discovering in the novels of Aquin. Lee's poem is prefaced by the following lines from Grant: "Man is by nature a political animal, and to know that citi-zenship is an impossibility is to be cut off from one of the highest forms of life."

It was Laxer who had the greatest influence in shaping the Waffle position on Quebec and in convincing us of the importance of Quebec in our political agenda. A key figure in the Quebec-related student demonstrations that had taken place at the University of Toronto in his undergraduate years, he had done his Queen's M. A. the-sis on the nationalism of Henri Bourassa, which in spite of its eccentricities contains a "two-nations" position not unlike the one the Waffle would adopt. (In fact, Bourassa's position in 1911, that Quebec should be represented in Ottawa by its own political party, prefigures the present day Bloc Québécois). The paragraphs on Que-bec in the manifesto stated that "there is no denying the existence of two nations within Canada, each with its own language, culture and aspiration"; that "English Canada and Quebec can share common institutions to the extent that they share common purposes"; that "an English Canada concerned with its own national survival would create common aspirations that would help to tie the two nations together once more"; and finally that "socialists in English Canada must ally themselves with socialists in Quebec in this common cause." "Two nations, one struggle," the manifesto says. Unfortunately the experience of the following years would lead to the recognition that such a position on Quebec would never be wholeheartedly endorsed by the NDP, given the party's base in Western Canada, although by taking the strong position that we did, we did manage to get the party to adopt a slightly watered-down version of it at its 1971 federal convention.

But why work through the traditional party system at all? Kingston was a hotbed of radical left politics in the 60s, and certainly members of SUPA and the SCM, as well as Joan Newman Kuyek's Association for Tenants' Action Kingston, which was working with the poor and disenfranchised of the city's north end, were scornful of us for working through the NDP. But Smart and Brown and others were longtime NDPers, and Laxer had by now become convinced that the student movement in Canada had become totally Americanized, with civil rights and anti-Vietnam politics its central focus, and that the only way to bring about change was to work within the party system. I remember him explaining to me during our walks in the park how one of the main differences between the political cultures of Canada and the U.S. was the fact that unlike the Americans we had a left-wing party to work within, as well as a strong working class tradition brought here mostly from the British Isles. As he would later write, "Today's student movement still bears the stamp of American influence. It has been unable to formulate a political strategy relevant to Canadian society."[4]

However, to get anywhere within the party we had to get our manifesto passed as a resolution by as many riding associations as possible in order for it to have strong support at the Winnipeg convention. And we first had to pass it in our local riding association, as well as winning enough votes to get some of us elected as delegates to the convention. Not an easy task when our riding association also contained Professors Swainson, Tulchinsky and Rawlyk. The meeting was packed to the rafters with new NDP members we had signed up, including almost all the graduate students from the History department, and there was passionate debate and disagreement between the History department professors and students. The manifesto passed, and Wafflers won several delegate positions. A few days later, there was a very angry late night call to our house from one of the History professors, complaining about some of the procedures of the meeting.

When the manifesto was circulated in the NDP in the summer of 1969, it met with a positive response well beyond what we had expected. Between 400 and 500 party members signed it publicly, while more than 20 constituency associations passed it and its associated resolutions and asked that they be debated at the federal convention. The Provincial Council of the Saskatchewan NDP endorsed it, and at the convention their leader, Woodrow Lloyd, voted for it. The signatories of the manifesto also included NDP MLAs in Saskatchewan, Manitoba and British Columbia (including Dave Barrett), as well as the leader of the Nova Scotia NDP, Jeremy Akerman.

At the convention, 35% of the delegates voted for the Waffle Manifesto and nine Wafflers were elected to the federal executive or Federal Council of the party. Waffle resolutions on foreign ownership, NATO, women in the party and extra-parliamentary activity received significant support. The convention debate on the manifesto was televised and the CBC ran a TV documentary by filmmaker Ralph Thomas called "What's Left?" in the days before the convention.

By the end of 1969 the Waffle had given the NDP a strong left wing and made it respectable to talk about socialism, nationalism and Quebec within and outside the party. As the *Toronto Star* noted, "The Canadian people have been provided with a more distinct political alternative and, of even more importance, an alternative that is more strongly nationalist. A convention that can make a claim like that can't have been a complete bust.[5]

After the convention, the Waffle group stayed together as a caucus within the NDP, as well as writing about our ideas in *Canadian Dimension*, *Canadian Forum*, *Last Post*, *This Magazine is About Schools* and in local papers. We went on radio and TV, and held public meetings, rallies and teach-ins on the issues we cared about. We had a newsletter and eventually a small newspaper. There were Waffle groups meeting across the country, working hard to develop and disseminate our ideas, but also to strenghten the NDP at the constituency level. In March 1970 we held a major teach-in on "The Americanization of Canada" at the University of Toronto, with speakers including former Finance Minister Walter Gordon and the Quebec labour leader Michel Chartrand. In April the Toronto Waffle organized a massive campaign against the closure of the Dunlop Canada plant in east Toronto. In fall 1970, the Saskatchewan Waffle ran Don Mitchell of Moose Jaw for the leadership of the provincial party, as a successor to Woodrow Lloyd (who had angered his party's right wing by supporting the Waffle). That September we held a series of successful rallies across the country protesting energy exports to the United States, and in the same month, Jim Laxer's influential book *The Energy Poker Game* was published. Tommy Douglas told the Ontario NDP convention in October 1970 that every New Democrat should read it.

It was at that Ontario convention that Stephen Lewis was elected provincial leader and the seeds of the Waffle's destruction were planted. The Waffle showed remarkably policy and organizational strength at the convention, with a third of the members elected to the provincial executive being Wafflers, including Queen's students Jim Laxer, John Smart and Krista Maeots. It was one thing to cause a bit of disturbance in the federal party, but to threaten control of the party in Ontario, the home of the Lewis family and the site of the union base of such people as Lynn Williams of the Steelworkers and Dennis McDermott of the Canadian Autoworkers, was another kettle of fish. NDP documents which later became available reveal that it was at this point that the traditional leadership began discussions about how to put an end to the Waffle in the NDP.[6]

Before that happened, however, the fight for the federal leadership began. Jim Laxer, by then a 28 year old sessional lecturer in Canadian History at Queen's, was chosen to be the Waffle candidate and waged an incredibly strong campaign, much of it focussed on Quebec, as these were the months of the FLQ crisis and the War Measures Act and its aftermath. Laxer came second on the final ballot of the April 1971 convention, ahead of both Ed Broadbent and John Harney, with 612 votes to David Lewis's 1046. After the convention David Lewis made it clear he would make no concessions to the Waffle, but in fact the party had changed by then, and NDP rhetoric and policy reflected that fact. During the 1972-1974 period of minority government when the NDP held the balance of power, the party was certainly influenced by Waffle ideas in the demands it made on the Liberals, even though the Waffle had left the party by then. The creation of Petro-Canada, the Foreign Investment Review Agency, the Canadian Development Corporation, and to some extent the "Corporate Welfare Bums" NDP campaign theme of 1972 all bear the mark of Waffle influence.

Within fourteen months of the 1971 federal convention, the Waffle had, to all extents and purposes, been expelled from the NDP. The action was taken at a meeting of the Ontario NDP Provincial Council in Orillia in the spring of 1972, where the Waffle was accused of operating as "a party within a party" and its members were forbidden henceforth to publish their newsletter or communicate among themselves in any official way. Ironically, the committee which made these recommendations to the party was headed by Gerry Caplan, one of the original authors of the Waffle manifesto. Shortly thereafter, after much painful debate, the Waffle group decided to leave the party and try to operate as an independent organization, the Movement for an Independent Socialist Canda, which eventually became a shortlived political party.

For two years we operated outside the party, and without the hook to reality that the NDP had provided we soon descended into the sterility and futility that have been the fate of so many left intellectual formations before and since. We did hold public meetings, and publish articles and books; and we ran three Waffle candidates in the 1974 federal election, all the while trying to organize what we called "the grassroots." But once we were no longer part of the NDP we became more interesting to academic Marxists, and spent much of our time in interminable discussions, in which any attempt to argue a position based on the need for Canadian independence was branded as "bourgeois nationalism." In Ottawa, one of our active and influential members was a former Saskatchewan socialist, and we somehow found ourselves locked into the position that we should be spending most of our time organizing the dairy farmers of the Ottawa Valley against Kraft Foods. That and other differences eventually led to a painful split between the Toronto and Ottawa groups, which were effectively all that was left of the Ontario Waffle at that point. The final breakup of the Waffle, in my mind at least, was an all day confrontation between the two groups in Toronto which I sat through in tears, aware that some of my closest friendships were dissolving in the arguments about abstractions that neither side was willing to compromise on. It was the fun and the friendships as well as the passion for country that had held us together, and I think for many of us their disappearance was a devastating loss. By the end of the seventies most of us had drifted back into the NDP, but the passion was gone, both from us and from the party.

In conclusion, the Waffle was a key part of the left nationalist consciousness that grew up in Canada in the late 60s. Because of the urgency and wide popularity of the national question, it came closer to bridging the age-old gap between intellectuals and the working class, party and movement than most left groups have been able to do. By the end of the seventies, other groups—notably the Committee for an Independent Canada—had picked up on the nationalist aspirations we had articulated, and they, along with a number of individuals who had been in the Waffle, made significant contributions to the Liberal government's ill-fated National Energy Policy. The socialist side of our agenda disappeared and has not been heard of since. In the academic world, Waffle ideas and individual Waffle members played a key role in the emergence of Canadian Studies programs and in the rediscovery of Canadian political economy.[7] As for the NDP, there is little left in its policies of our positions on the economy or on Quebec. In the 1988 Free Trade election, it was the Liberals under John Turner who picked up on and profited from Canadians' desire for independence from the United States, while NDP leader Ed Broadbent argued vaguely that the important issues were the social demands of "ordinary Canadians." And not much has changed since. But, to quote my husband John Smart, on whom I have relied for a great deal of the information in this paper, "the Waffle gave us a brief glimpse of what a New Democratic Party with guts, brains and a soul could have been like and what it could have done for Canada."[8]

The connection with the Queen's History department was perhaps accidental, but perhaps not. I used to wonder at the time why so many of the people I knew who were conscious of the possibility of political change and committed to this country were historians, but those characteristics may be what drew them to the discipline in the first place. As well, the combination of an excellent department, the companionable atmosphere of a university town and the zeitgeist of the age were probably what gave us the energy to spend late nights in nicotine-fuelled meetings, honing our ideas and strategies, and then go home and work on our academic assignments before (at least in our case) getting up in the morning to look after our kids. It was so much fun. We thought we could change the world, and maybe in some small way we did. In any case, I think the Queen's History department should be proud of this part of its past.[9]

Notes

1 Quoted in Report of the Commission of Inquiry Concerning Certain Activities of the Royal Canadian Mounted Police [Macdonald Commission] *Freedom and Security Under the Law*, Second Report, Vol. I, August 1981, p. 483.

2 *Canadian Dimension*, 52.

3 James Laxer, *Red Diaper Baby: A Boyhood in the Age of McCarthyism* (Vancouver: Douglas & McIntyre, 2004).

4 "The Americanization of the Canadian student movement" in *Close the 49th Parallel* (ed. Ian Lumsden)

5 *Toronto Star*, 3 November 1969.

6 See John Bullen, "The Ontario Waffle and the Struggle for an Independent Socialist Canada: A Study in Radical Nationalism," M.A. thesis, University of Ottawa, 1981; and Bullen's article "The Ontario Waffle and the Struggle for an Independant Socialist Canada: Conflict Within the NDP," *Canadian Historical Review*, Vol. 24, No 2 (1983), 188-215.

7 See Rianne Mahon, "The Waffle and Canadian Political Economy," *Studies in Political Economy* 32, Summer 1990, p. 187 ff.

8 "The Waffle's Impact on the New Democratic Party," *Studies in Political Economy* 32, Summer 1990, p. 177.

9 Presented at the conference *New World Coming: The Sixties and the Shaping of Global Consciousness*, Queen's University, June 16, 2007

Gillian Helfield

| Chapter *12* | A Time for Change: The Sixties and Cinéma direct in Québec |

The 1960s was a period of profound change that engendered numerous and diverse social, cultural and political movements. Each of these movements in their own turn were fraught with conflicts and contradictions, characterizing the spirit of this momentous age, as well as codifying its history for ensuing generations. As noted by film historian Richard Barsam, during the 60s the co-existence of a traditional culture and a counter-culture signaled simultaneously a secure postwar world and yet one whose values were under attack. One witnessed, on the one hand, social progress and a quest for peace"; and on the other, "social decay and outbreaks of violence at home and abroad" (Barsam 1973:299). Due to these conflicts, historical accounts of this period also tend to be inconsistent with one another, describing the 60s alternately as a "momentous decade and a slum of a decade" (Anderson 1985: ii), "an age of unquenchable spirit, and an age of rubbish" (ibid).

Ironically, what is most consistent throughout the 60s is its pervasive climate of change, which launched a "rise of revolutionary politics" (ibid) throughout the Western world. This was particularly true in Québec, which experienced a 'revolution' of its own in the 1960s, known as the *'révolution tranquille'* or 'Quiet Revolution.' This revolution was triggered by a change in political leadership in the 1960 provincial election. The victory of the Liberal Party, which brought to an end the eighteen-year régime of the *Union nationale* party under its authoritarian chief Maurice Duplessis,[1] marked a significant turning point for Quebec, as indicated by its electoral slogan "it's time for a change" (Durocher 1988: 1813). The Liberals' victory in the 1960 provincial election struck a decisive blow against the conservative establishment, composed primarily of Church, State and bourgeois business interests (both Anglo-American and Francophone), which had held French Québec in their grip for over two centuries (McRoberts and Posgate. 1980:73-75). Key social and economic reforms were legislated which aimed to enable Québec to catch up to the rest of North

American society and the first world, taking its place as an autonomous nation in its own right. And although the term 'revolution' may now seem exaggerated, its continued popularity and usage speak to the tremendous shift in Québécois society during this period, when "everything came under scrutiny, and everything was discussed " (Durocher 1988: 1813).

> Everywhere there was a new self-confidence, a new sense of direction, and a new sense that Québec people were highly competent and qualified, capable of developing an advanced, modern, technological society based on their own resources and their own abilities. This alone was a major revolution from which much else was to flow (ibid).

The most prevalent arena for this new age of open debate was Québécois culture, including French Canadian art, literature, theatre, music, and especially the cinema. The 60s importantly testified to a 'revival' or 'renaissance' (Barsam 1973: 299) of documentary cinema. As noted by Paul Arthur, film history shows us that documentary cinema tends to become more prominent during periods of crisis (Arthur 1993:108). For example, the Hollywood social documentary arose first during the 1930s and the Great Depression. In the 1960s, social documentary arose again in the form of *Cinéma vérité*, which attached to documentary realism a new desire for 'truth.' This desire emerged as part of a reaction against the lies and obfuscations promulgated by authoritarian regimes throughout World War II, as well as against the 'classical' documentary conventions by means of which the political ideologies and doctrines of those regimes had been powerfully propagated. In this new political and cultural context, documentary cinema via *Cinéma verité* was able to produce a new vision of the world and a new relationship to 'the real.'

In keeping with the 60s' spirit of *'ouverture'* or opening up to new ideas, French Québec was also interested in exploring its connections to and establishing its position within the global Francophone community. Of particular significance was the effect of the world-wide process of decolonisation taking place at this time. Quite simply, what was happening socially and politically in Québec—the emergence of a distinctive cultural and national identity—could be explained and justified by the fact that it was happening elsewhere in the world at that same time, in other nations similarly seeking autonomy from the dominant cultures that had colonised and controlled them.

Also in keeping with the spirit of *'ouverture,'* the 60s in Québec were marked by two other important events: the Montreal World's Fair of 1967, known as 'Expo 67' and the creation of the Montréal Expos, the professional baseball team named for the World's Fair, which in 1969 was admitted to the American National League. Both these events were an important source of pride and identity for Québec, which now was able to successfully compete in the 'major leagues' with other first-world nations.

In the cinema, documentary found its own distinctive expression in the work of francophone filmmakers working at the National Film Board. Their films, which collectively formed the *Cinéma direct* movement, came out at the height of the Quiet Revolution, and explored Québec's colonial and post-colonial experiences as well as its burgeoning Francophone subjectivity and identity. As such these films are thought to be instrumental not only in the birth of a new wave in French-language cinema in Québec, but also in the awakening of a Québécois 'national' consciousness (Coulombe and Jean 1991: 107).

The Cinéma direct films which I feel most effectively reflect the 60s' spirit of change are a small group of sports films produced by the NFB and aired on Radio-Canada TV as part of the television series *Temps present* ('Present Tense') between 1957 and 1964, also known as the "Golden Age" of Canadian documentary.[2] These films include *Les Raquetteurs* (Michel Brault, Gilles Groulx, Marcel Carrière, 1958), *La Lutte* (Michel Brault, Claude Fournier, Claude Jutra, Marcel Carrière, 1961), *Un jeu si simple* (Gilles Groulx, 1964), *Golden Gloves* (Gilles Groulx, 1961), and *Margaret Mercier, ballerine* (George Kaczender, 1963). The filmmakers intended only to deliver direct *reportages* of their subject material, without overt sociological or political motives. And yet, by making "visible the complex and changing face of French Canadians" (Morris 1984:291), the films became an aesthetic and political turning point (Véronneau 1987:37) for Québécois cinema and for Québécois cultural representation in general.

The most distinctive features of *Cinéma direct*, which relate to its significance both within the Quiet Revolution, and 60s' cinema in general, are its use of the hand-held camera, and the filmmakers' interactive, participatory approach to their subject matter. The new film technology liberated the filmmakers from the physical and aesthetic constraints of studio filming, and from conventional documentary practices associated with the National Film Board and the colonizing presence of the Anglophone Establishment in Canada and Québec. Moreover, the hand-held camera left the filmmakers free to follow close behind the on-screen characters, to venture into their immediate sphere and to present the action from 'the inside.' Their immediate physical presence and involvement in the scene was clearly signalled by the sound of their voices asking questions, or by the camera's position in the midst of the action. Taken together, the new technology and interactive approach enabled the filmmakers to represent a uniquely and specifically Québécois subjectivity, by expressing changes taking place not only in Québécois society, but also in the image that the Québécois had of themselves as a people and a nation.

For example in *Les Raquetteurs*, the manifesto film of the Cinéma direct movement which profiles a gathering of snowshoeing clubs in Sherbrooke Quebec, the camera runs alongside the snowshoers, joins the circle of majorettes twirling their batons, and gets into line with the marching band on parade. Similarly, in *Golden Gloves*, the mobile camera mimics the on-screen characters' movements and gestures, bobbing and weaving in imitation of the boxers training for their upcoming bouts. This mobile technique creates a sense of physical synchronicity between the camera and the on-screen characters, which in turn expresses on a deeper level the socio-cultural synchronicity between the filmmakers and the society they're filming.

But also importantly, constant movement on screen captured by the mobile camera approach effectively captures the forward movement, of Québécois society throughout the 60s. Even in rare moments in which the camera remains in one spot, continual movement leaves little opportunity for the eye to rest anywhere: either the camera pans or tilts over the object of its gaze, or else the object itself moves. In *La Lutte,* which depicts a night of professional wrestling at the Montreal Forum, there are scenes in which the camera lingers on the wrestling fans in the audience, their bodies and faces alive with movement as they gesticulate, grimace, yell, chew their snacks, puff their cigarettes or blow raspberries at the referee. Even the background seems to be in constant motion. In the wide shots of the crowd and the ring, action is simultaneously captured on three different planes, in the foreground, the midground and the background, making the entire shot seem to ripple and writhe with movement.

In a very large sense, these films function as cinematic expressions of 'movement-as-change': the montage techniques which accentuate movement between shots, suggest that the movements within the shots, captured by the mobile camera, actually transcend the bounds of the picture frame. Sequences frequently begin in the middle of the narrative action. These films often cut on motion as well, which serves to maintain the forward flow and direction of action. In *Margaret Mercier, ballerina*, which profiles a principal dancer with the Québec-based Grands Ballets Canadiens, or in *Un jeu si simple*, which showcases team practices for the Montreal Canadiens hockey team, this technique maintains the forward flow, thus maintaining the forward flow and direction of action. Both films also alternate between different kinds of shots, juxtaposing static shots with moving shots of athletes or performers, even using jump cuts in such a way as to heighten the impact of the action itself, making both the athlete and the shot appear to burst into motion.

In conclusion, these sports films are an important manifestation of the spirit of the 60s that equally marked Québécois society and culture. The films are landmark examples of the experimentation taking place within the *Cinéma verité* movement which characterized not only 60s documentary, but also 60s filmmaking at large. As well, the films remain remarkable for their ability convey a sense of the revolutionary changes taking place in Québéc at this time, and to render in cinematic form the images and sounds and movements of an evolving society and an emergent new nation.

Notes

1 Maurice Duplessis held office twice in Québec: first, from 1936-1939, and again after the war, from 1944 until his death in 1959.

2 *Temps présent* was not a produced as a series in the usual sense of the term. Rather, it is the title that has been given to this group of films that were made by the NFB and subsequently organized into a series of screenings or airings for Radio-Canada, the French arm of the CBC. For this reason, the films have never been released or distributed as a series by the NFB. They are only available under their own individual titles.

Works Cited

Anderson, Terry H. 1995. *The Movement and The Sixties*. New York: Oxford University Press.

Arthur, Paul. "Jargons of Authenticity" in Michael Renov. 1993. *Theorizing Documentary*. New York: Routledge.

Barsam, Richard, M. 1973. *Non-Fiction Film: A Critical History*. Bloomington/Indianapolis: Indiana University Press.

Coulombe, Michel and Marcel Jean. 1991. *Dictionnaire du cinéma québécois*, New, Revised and Expanded Edition. Montréal: Éditions du Boréal.

Durocher, René. "Quiet Revolution," *The Canadian Encyclopedia*, 2nd Edition, Volume III. Edmonton: Hurtig, 1988.

McRoberts, Kenneth and Dale Posgate. 1980. *Quebec: Social Change and Political Crisis*. Toronto: McClelland and Stewart,

Morris, Peter. 1984. *The Film Companion*, Toronto: Irwin Publishing.

Véronneau, Pierre. 1987. 'Résistance et affirmation: la production Francophone à l'ONF 1939-1964.' *Les Dossiers de la Cinémathèque*, Numéro 17. Montréal: Cinémathèque québécoise/Musée du cinéma.

Chris Harris

| Chapter **13** | Canadian Black Power, Organic Intellectuals and the War of Position in Toronto, 1967–1975 |

Introduction

This research seeks to explore the organizational and educational development of those who led the Canadian Black Power movement from 1967 to 1975—a watershed period of radicalism under-represented in current scholarly literatures. I will clarify the role of African-American vanguard organizations in the expansion of Toronto's Black Left; in doing so, I will rely on ideas from Antonio Gramsci's (1971) *Prison Notebooks*, in which he identifies the centrality of a revolutionary party in the formation of working-class organic intellectuals (communist activists) actively engaged in an anti-capitalist war of position in civil society.[1] I contend that the U.S. Black Power movement led the ideological development of *Black-Working-Class Organic Intellectuals*, the pioneers of Canada's first African-liberation movement.

During the 1960s and '70s Toronto's Black Left grew rapidly under the influence of the Black Panther Party, League of Revolutionary Black Workers, and African Liberation Support Committee (ALSC). From 1967 to 1971, Canadian Black revolutionaries were inspired by the Panthers and League inviting them periodically, to help educate and organize Toronto's Black working class against Canadian imperialism. The Panthers and League helped Toronto Black Power organic intellectuals understand their own experience of *internal colonialism*[2] as an oppressed national minority in Canada —a White settler imperialist nation. Then from 1972 to 1975, the Toronto chapter of the ALSC was organized to build material support for national liberation movements in southern Africa.

The Role of U.S. Black Power in the Production of Canadian Black Power Organic Intellectuals

Canadian Black Power was influenced by U.S. activists who came to live in Canada during the 1960s. In 1967, African-American Black Power activist, Norman "Otis" Richmond came to Toronto to protest his induction into the Vietnam Draft at the age of 21, and worked alongside local Black radical youth and elders to organize Canada's first Black Power organization. Prior to his arrival, Richmond recalls studying and organizing a Maoist Study Group with future Panther leaders Bunchy Carter and Masai Hewitt, as a student in Los Angeles that same year:

> As a native of California, I studied at the Los Angeles City College in 1967. I went to school with Bunchy Carter. At that time I joined a Maoist study group, and we had close relations with Bunchy who brought Eldridge Cleaver to speak to us at a local community centre, when he had just got out of prison. There was also Masai Hewitt, who joined our study group but soon after became a leading Panther as well … When our group merged with the Panthers by the end of 1967, Bunchy became Minister of Defense, and Masai, the Minister of Information. (Richmond:2007:5)

In Toronto Richmond helped found the Afro-American Progressive Association (AAPA) with Jose Garcia, an Arubian Trotskyist in the Communist League, and other revolutionary-nationalists from the U.S. The organization was called "Afro-American" because the leadership adopted Malcolm X's view that all people of African descent in the Western Hemisphere were the descendants of African slaves in the Americas (Richmond:2007:2). During that early period, Richmond met elder and Toronto Black left pioneer Lenny Johnston, who joined the AAPA soon after its formation. Johnston was the first African-Canadian to join the Communist Party of Canada (CPC) in the late 1930s. When the AAPA was formed, Johnston worked at the CPC's bookstore and co-founded Third World Books and Crafts in 1968 with his wife Gwen. Soon after the AAPA was formed, Johnston left the CPC to join the organization because of the party's refusal to recognize the national oppression suffered by Blacks in Canada. Third World Books was Toronto's first independent Black bookstore and the headquarters of the AAPA from 1968 until its demise in 1971. It was also a popular meeting place for Black Power organic intellectuals and others in the Black Community to discuss the politics of anti-colonialism in Canada, Marxism, African History, and participate in local grassroots organizing (Harris:2005:60).

The AAPA began a war of position in African-Canadian civil society by organizing rallies and international solidarity campaigns in support of U.S. Black Power, attended by hundreds in the Black community. Representatives from the Panthers and League were invited to educate African-Canadians about their struggles against U.S. imperialism and the possibilities of building a similar movement in Canada. On April 2, 1970, the AAPA sponsored a rally featuring two Panther leaders. The meeting was attended by 200 African-Canadians who came to hear the Panthers speak about their struggle against white imperialist hegemony in America. In commenting on the success of this event to help Blacks understand the politics of African-Canadian colonization and liberation, an AAPA member observed:

> As far as the Black community is concerned I think the opportunity to meet some members of the B.P.P.; the opportunity to experience two hundred beautiful Black people under one roof have reinforced the hopes of a lot of Black people who have become disheartened by the previous apparent lack of unity that was displayed in Toronto. We intend to work much harder to try to bring about an even stronger and broader base of unity among the Black community through education and we hope that our other Brothers and Sisters will do the same. ("Panthers speak in Toronto," 1970)

As a revolutionary vanguard party, the Panthers played a significant role in the development of organic intellectuals in the AAPA leadership, who in turn pioneered their own model of anti-colonial education, hundreds of African-Canadians underwent during this period.

The AAPA also organized solidarity events with the League to debate their ideological tensions with the Panthers. On November 13, 1970, a rally was organized featuring League spokesperson, Edward Cooper. At the event Cooper spoke about the League's ideological differences with the Panthers. Although the League organized the Detroit chapter of the party, the two organizations separated over ideology by this time. Cooper criticized the Panthers for laying too much emphasis on mobilizing the Black lumpen street element against the police, which only brought further repression in African-American communities ("Pan-Africanism and Socialism," 1971). According to Richmond, the two organizations had tactical differences over which class force should be mobilized to advance the revolutionary process in America: "While the BPP held the lumpen proletariat up as the leaders of the Black revolution, the League maintained the Black working class were the natural leaders or vanguard of that struggle" (Richmond, 2004:7). Ideological tensions between the Panthers and League remained unresolved during the Black Power era.

The AAPA's international solidarity events with the League and Panthers revealed their lack of ideological clarity and inability to fully comprehend the contradiction of Canadian imperialism and African-Canadian colonization. As a lesson in historical specificity, Rodney warns against modeling one's own liberation project after the example of successful foreign movements because each national context has its own particular race and class contradictions:

> People are searching for answers, but to be frank, sometimes searching for them in somewhat uncreative ways, because it really isn't creative to turn around to somebody else and ask what is the answer ... There is a tendency to believe that somebody somewhere has the key ... (1990:82)

It is true that there was a certain lack of originality in the war of position Toronto Black Power organic intellectuals initiated in the late 1960s however the AAPA is credited for recognizing the similarities between the national oppression experienced by Blacks in the U.S. and Canada. Since the Panthers embodied a far more advanced revolutionary-nationalist praxis, it is not surprising the AAPA followed their ideological orientation without addressing the specificity of African-Canadian colonization.

By 1969 AAPA organic intellectuals were divided over the politics of Black-Nationalism. Richmond recalls how internal disputes split the organization into a revolutionary-nationalist (Marxist) and conservative nationalist wing:

> While I was there, a struggle between people who wanted to be more Marxist and Black Nationalist, began to split the organization ... and from that point on, the Nationalists formed a youth group called the Black Youth Organization (BYO). And Jan Carew, Jose Garcia, and Lenny Johnston formed a Marxist group called the Black Liberation Front. (Richmond: 2007:1)

Due to internal sectarian differences the AAPA split into two separate Black Power organizations in1971: 1) Black Youth Organization (BYO); 2) Black Liberation Front of Canada (BLFC).

One concrete gain that came out of BYO was the establishment of a united front between Left-wing and Right-wing Black Power organizations in Toronto. On July 26, 1970, BYO formed an alliance with the AAPA and Sundiata and Ebony Services. After a public debate that lasted for three hours in which the three groups tried to establish a common program, a united front was established to coordinate their efforts to empower local Black working-class youth through: 1) the implementation of a bridging program to increase Black student enrollment at George Brown College; 2) the formation of an African cultural community center to deliver programs to African-Canadian youth ("Blacks form United Front," 1970).

After the AAPA split, organic intellectuals in the BLFC continued to advance a Black liberation agenda in Toronto. The BLFC was launched in July 1969 with the first issue of *Black Liberation News*, as a Leninist vanguard organization concerned with increasing the race and class-consciousness of African-Canadians by educating them about Third World Revolutions. The BLFC's monthly newspaper carried articles ranging from critical coverage of the Vietnam Revolution and the struggle for Palestinian liberation, to monthly updates on the Panthers. Black Power organic intellectuals in BLFC also produced *Black Liberation News* to educate the Black community about the role of Canadian imperialism in exploiting the natural resources and labor of South Africa, Jamaica, Guyana, and Brazil (BLN:July 1969).

In the summer of 1969, the BLFC implemented a summer program for working-class African-Canadian youth that consisted of Black History classes, a film series, and guest speakers. They also offered tutoring for Black students to help them improve their academic performance (Ibid).

On July 25-27, 1969, the organization held a rally against police brutality at Rochdale College, where they organized a Citizens' Review Board to increase police accountability and charge officers guilty of excessive use of force (Ibid). At another rally, there were guest speakers from the League, who spoke about the political-economy of racism in the U.S., and the relationship between African-American and African-Canadian liberation movements (BLN:August 1969:1).

The contradiction between revolutionary-nationalists and conservative nationalists in the U.S. began to develop locally when influential conservative leaders came to Toronto. For example, Amiri Baraka (Leroy Jones) spoke at the historic Black People's Conference at Harbord Collegiate, February 19-21, 1971, and encouraged the 2,000 delegates in attendance to undergo an "internal revolution" still narrowly defined as cultural nationalism. *Contrast*, a local Black independent newspaper reported the following coverage of Baraka's keynote address:

> Addressing an open session on Saturday, February 20th, Brother Baraka said an internal revolution would require Black people to get themselves sorted out, to remove themselves from a mental commitment to slavery, relate themselves to their point of origin and develop a Pan-Africanist attitude … Dealing with the question of Black unity, he said that as African people we must focus on our African heritage as this is the only unifying source. (*Contrast*, March 6, 1971: 1)

Before he converted to Maoism in the mid-70s, Baraka was a conservative nationalist who perceived the struggle strictly in racial terms. Ideological divisions between revolutionary Marxists and conservative nationalists led to the decline of Canadian Black Power in the early '70s.

Black Power Organic Intellectuals and The Two-Line Struggle Within Toronto ALSO

Following the example of the U.S. leadership, Toronto Black Power organic intellectuals advanced ideologically by supporting the national liberation movements against Portuguese colonialism in Southern Africa. In 1971, U.S. Black Power leader Owusu Sadauki experienced an ideological transformation from cultural-nationalism to Marxism-Leninism upon his return from traveling to the liberated zones in Mozambique to consult with Somaro Machel, leader of the Front for the Liberation of Mozambique (FRELIMO). Kelley affirms the Sadaukai-led delegation to Mozambique to meet with FRELIMO, and their engagement with Cabral a year later in America transformed U.S. Black Power into a revolutionary Pan-African movement:

> FRELIMO's president Samora Machel and other militants persuaded Sadauki and his colleagues that the most useful role African Americans could play in support of anticolonialism was to challenge American capitalism from within and let the world know the truth about FRELIMO's just war against Portuguese domination. A year later, during his last visit to the United States, Amilcar Cabral, the leader of the anticolonial movement in Guinea-Bissau and the Cape Verde Islands, said essentially the same thing. (Kelley, 2002: 104)

In May 1972, the U.S. ALSC[3] was established, with a Toronto chapter organized by local Black Power organic intellectuals to build material support for the following national liberation movements in southern Africa: FRELIMO, the African Party for the Independence of Guinea and the Cape Verde Islands (PAIGC), and the Popular Movement for the Liberation of Angola (MPLA). They did this by organizing the annual African Liberation Day (ALD) demonstrations in major cities throughout the Caribbean and North America on May 27, 1972.

Thanks to the organizing efforts of Toronto ALSC, 3,000 African-Canadians attended ALD '72.[4] The event was held at Christie Pits, re-named "Henson-Garvey Park" to memorialize the historic Black leaders, Marcus Garvey and Josiah Henson.[5] The keynote speaker was Canadian Black Power leader Rosie Douglas who spoke alongside U.S. ALSC leaders, Julian Bond and John Conyers[6] (Johnson:2003:489). Guest speakers educated the community on the relationship between the western imperialist conquest of Africa and the national oppression experienced by Blacks in Canada; and the centrality of mass mobilization to overcome this oppression. ALD '72 was the first serious attempt of African-Canadians to protest in solidarity with oppressed nations on the continent (Black Labor, May 24, 1975:6). The success of this first demonstration was exemplified by the expansion of the ALSC which grew from an annual international solidarity campaign into a dynamic revolutionary Pan-African movement in the U.S., Canada and Caribbean (Johnson:490).

In 1974, a two-line struggle emerged in the U.S. branch of the ALSC, eventually dividing the movement in Toronto. Ultimately, the ideological struggle between Marxists and Nationalists; and Maoists and Soviet Marxists, lead to the collapse of the organization in 1975 due to ultra-left sectarianism. In the last year of the movement, ALD '75 split into three different demonstrations organized by each of the three Toronto ALSC factions (Richmond:2002:14). The ideological struggle within the U.S. branch of the ALSC, in turn, led to the development of a similar tension in Toronto where many local organic intellectuals experienced a qualitative leap in their revolutionary consciousness by adopting Marxism-Leninism. The Marxist/Nationalist debate within Toronto ALSC represented a significant shift because it demonstrated the majority of leftists within the organization were beginning to challenge capitalism and imperialism in addition to White settler hegemony.

The transformation of Black Power organic intellectuals from narrow Nationalism to Marxism-Leninism resulted from the Marxist/Nationalist debate at the ALSC's first national conference at Howard University in 1974, entitled *Which Road Against Racism and Imperialism for the Black Liberation Movement* (Johnson:492). The conference was attended by 800 delegates from across North America and the debate centered on a question central to the progress and unity of the movement: which ideological faction will lead the African-American Revolution? The right-wing saw ALSC as a Black Nationalist organization that sought to unite all Africans, continental and Diasporic against White supremacy and European dominance. Meanwhile the left-wing saw the ALSC as an anti-imperialist organization that must mobilize material support to help advance Socialism in Africa. In an article in the May 1975 issue of *Black Labor*, an independent Toronto Black Power newspaper, the object of the ALSC Marxist/Nationalist debate was to achieve ideological clarity and discourage right-wing nationalists who had devised a "pure race theory" of African-American liberation without any anti-capitalist analysis:

> ... a number of discussions emerged concerning the ... two ideological
> lines within ALSC, representing two different theoretical positions, two
> different sets of concrete programs based on two different class realities.
> One was a pure race theory, and the other a theory of class struggle with a

correct analysis of racial oppression with a programme of mass involvement based on the necessary leadership of the black working-class. These
positions were clearly brought to the fore at the ALSC conference held in
Washington, D.C. in May 25-26, 1974 with the Toronto African Liberation
Support Committee supporting the latter. (Black Labor:May 1975:6)

The Marxist faction dominated the debate and many conservative nationalists left
the U.S. organization. When Canadian delegates returned, they spearheaded the debate in the Toronto ALSC; and the Marxists became hegemonic in the organization.

By 1974, the Toronto ALSC had entered a new phase of ideological struggle
where members were divided over the Sino-Soviet conflict.[7] As in the rest of the International Communist movement, Toronto ALSC split into two ideological camps engaged in a two-line struggle between China and the USSR. The debate centered on
which country was the legitimate leader of the Socialist bloc in the post-Stalin years,
with China claiming authority because the USSR degenerated into state capitalism.
One group of Toronto ALSC organic intellectuals adopted Maoism while the other,
Soviet Marxism. Richmond contends Maoism was more appealing than Soviet Marxism because China was recognized as a former colonial nation, whereas the Soviet
Union was falsely perceived to be a "White" imperialist nation:

> … we loved Mao Tse Tung because Mao wasn't White. So he was supposedly
> a Marxist, but he wasn't White so we came to Socialism through a Chinese, as
> opposed to Marx, Engels, or Stalin or Trotsky and those white dudes because
> we probably wouldn't have studied Scientific Socialism if it wasn't for Mao
> Tse Tung—because Mao Tse Tung wasn't considered white at that time. We
> were still very much anti-white. And we were anti-Soviet because we didn't
> know at the time that the Soviet Union was a multi-national nation-state, we
> just thought everybody was white. So, I mean that's how naïve we were, being
> born in America … at least I was. (Richmond, 2002:2)

This later period in Canadian Black Power was characterized by intense debates during
organizing meetings and study groups where Maoist and Soviet Marxists took positions on which country was providing the most aid to the African liberation forces in
the Portuguese colonies. Toronto ALSC's Maoist faction blindly supported the groups
that received aid from China, although those groups, like the United Party for the National Union for the Total Independence of Angola (UNITA), tended to be more reactionary.[8] On the other hand, the Soviet Marxist faction supported the USSR because
they aided the real vanguard forces in Portuguese Africa[9] (FRELIMO, PAIGC, MPLA).

In its fourth year of existence, sectarianism soon engulfed Toronto ALSC caus-
ing the organization to go into decline, with each clique merging with different Maoist and Soviet-backed communist parties on the Canadian Left. In 1975 the Maoist
faction formed a party-building cell called the Black Study Group (BSG), which studied and debated Lenin and Stalin's writings on the national question in an effort to
develop a theory of internal colonialism for Blacks in Canada.[10] Their aim was to unify
with other oppressed nationalities and White Maoist groups to build a new
multi-national communist party; however the group disbanded within a year. Meanwhile, in January 1975 the Soviet-faction led by Rosie Douglas formed the short-lived
Black Workers Alliance (BWA)—a revolutionary black labor organization that struggled for Black workers' rights in the workplace (Auguste:1975:2).

BWA organic intellectuals were also involved in organizing Black Power rallies
to educate the Black working-class about liberation politics. African Marxist Scholar
and Activist, Walter Rodney spoke at a BWA conference in Toronto on May 2, 1975,
attended by 700 people. Rodney addressed the relationship between Black Liberation and Socialism alongside Amiri Baraka; Dudley Laws who at that time was the
leader of Toronto's Universal African Improvement Association (UAIA), spoke about
the relationship of Black Power to the legacy of Marcus Garvey. Rodney clarified the
revolutionary Pan-Africanism and anti-imperialism of the ALSC and discussed its relationship to the Vietnam Revolution and the revolutionary process in Southern Africa,
which had dealt significant blows to U.S. imperialism (Black Workers Alliance:1975).
Rodney continued the process of organic intellectual development in Canada by participating in the BWA as a leading ideologue. The BWA also sponsored a series of
events throughout 1975 that featured Douglas who was fighting to remain in the
country after being charged for leading the 1969 Sir George Williams Rebellion.[11]
When the BWA disbanded by the fall of 1975 most of its members had joined the CPC.

The major reason for the decline of Toronto ALSC was the internal weaknesses
of the Canadian Black Power leadership, still in their early stages of ideological matu-
ration. Maoist in the BSG and Soviet Marxists in the BWA failed to identify their common interests to build a dynamic African-Canadian liberation organization in
Toronto. Mao stated that contradictions among the people should be handled differently than those between the masses and imperialism; namely through criticism and
debate that strive to unify opposing groups on the Left so that a higher level of unity
may be achieved (Mao:1966:322). Because Maoists and Soviet Marxist organic intellectuals in Toronto ALSC did not see their common interests as an oppressed national minority, they split it into two separate organizations which both degenerated

into ultra-left sectarianism within six months. Toronto ALSC failed to achieve organizational autonomy so it suffered greatly when U.S. Black Power went into decline.

In defense of the organic intellectuals who developed as Marxist-Leninists during the Canadian Black Power era, I turn to Rodney's critical reflection on the ALSC experience, which concluded that despite their limitations, the debates advanced the struggle for Pan-African liberation in North America:

> Although there are many criticisms that I have of the character of the current debate, one must come out very clearly at the beginning and understand that the debate itself is another facet of the liberation movement, irrespective of the validity of the arguments or however misguided some people participating in it may be. I think this must be got very clearly, because there are some people who would not like to have a debate in actual fact, because the debate is raising questions about the nature of the capitalist system … that is part of our revolution. (Rodney: 1990:94)

For many, those debates confirmed the idea that capitalism was the root cause of Black national oppression in North America.[12]

The Role of Gender Contradiction in Black Feminist Organic Intellectual Formation

Black working women were rarely to be found in the leadership of U.S. or Canadian Black Power organizations although they did play an important role as rank-and-file organizers. The AAPA, BYO, BLFC and Toronto ALSC did not include Black women in their leadership, and although they did perform subordinate roles their issues went largely under-recognized so that a Black patriarchy disguised as Black working-class unity could be maintained. Toronto organic intellectual Dionne Brand recalls how her black feminist consciousness initially developed as a negation of the sexism in local Black Power organizations alongside other emerging Black Feminists:

> In the black liberation movement in Toronto there was a group of … very forthright women who would call down guys on certain questioned [such as] … the idea that the revolution had to come first and then they'd deal with women's issues. We discussed what was more important, black struggle or black woman's struggle … I started to think that my role wasn't to support black men to establish a black patriarchy. (Rebick: 2005:131)

By the early 1970s, Black women challenged men who wrongly perceived women's liberation as a deviation from the struggle for African-Canadian liberation against White imperialist hegemony.

Black Feminist organic intellectuals questioned gender contradictions in the movement by writing in Toronto's independent Black press. The following article in *Contrast* a pioneering Toronto Black Feminist argued that since Black women during slavery played a leading role in ensuring the race's survival, they were qualified to lead the struggle for Black Power alongside men:

> There is no question today that the resources which initiated and established modern industrial capital were the Slave Trade and the enslavement of Black people in the Americas. Neither is there any doubt that these same Black people are the architects of social change and a new humanity. Among the architects there has always existed women like HARRIET TUBMAN, MAMMY PLEASANTS and SOJOURNER TRUTH, who played valiant roles in the struggle to end oppression. Let me make it quite clear ... Our women were plowed into slavery and were found to be as equally efficient and profitable as the men. And it seems to me that that is the only equality they have ever known ... Our women have acted as domestics and concubines to white society, and as soldiers and protectors to Black society. ("Need for Pan-African Ideology," 1971)

This article confirms Black Feminism was the product of female Black Feminist organic intellectual resistance to Black patriarchy in the movement. Similarly, the BWA paper *Black Labor* also contained Black Feminist articles in a section called "Perspectives on the Woman Question."[13] These newspaper articles indicate that Black Marxist Feminist cultural production was at best marginalized in the war of position led by Toronto Black Power organic intellectuals during the '60s and '70s.

Conclusion

The Canadian Black Power leadership developed as organic intellectuals by setting up organizations, rallies, and protests from 1967 to 1975. Socialist consciousness did not emerge spontaneously in the Canadian Black Power movement; it was brought to the movement from *without* by U.S. Black Power's leading vanguard organizations, the Panther and the League, African Marxist ideologue Walter Rodney, and elder Toronto organic intellectuals Lenny and Gwen Johnston at Third World Books. As members of the AAPA, the BYO and the BLFC (1967-1971) organic intellectuals established the first Black Power organizations in Canada. When former AAPA, BYO, and BLFC organic intellectuals joined the Toronto ALSC, their leadership experienced a qualitative leap during the 'African Liberation' phase of their ideological development

(1972-1975) by participating in the Marxist/Nationalist ideological debates that raged within the organization. The tension between Marxists and Nationalists, and later Maoists and Soviets, was never resolved and Toronto ALSC degenerated into ultra-left sectarianism with half of its leadership splitting into the Maoist BSG and the remaining forming the short-lived Soviet BWA.

The war of position waged by Canadian Black Power from 1967-1971 in the AAPA, BYO, and BLFC advanced to a new stage of ideological development with the formation of Toronto ALSC in 1972. In the Toronto ALSC, Black Power organic intellectuals advanced ideologically through their participation in the Marxist/Nationalist debates spearheaded by U.S. branch of the organization over the relevance of Marxist-Leninist ideology to the African-American Revolution. By building material support for the national liberation movements in Southern Africa from 1972 to 1975, Toronto Black Power organic intellectuals advanced their war of position in civil society and staged the largest anti-imperialist mobilizations in African-Canadian History.

The war of position initiated by Canadian Black Power from 1967-1975 was a watershed period for the development of the Left in Toronto and created a small group of organic intellectuals who have remained active in Toronto Black Radical movements in the proceeding decades. Most of the Black Power leadership who developed during that era went on to become leading anti-racist and Black labor activists for contemporary organizations like the CPC, Black Action Defense Committee (BADC), the Coalition of Black Trade Unionists (CBTU), the Black Women's Congress and the African Liberation Month Coalition.[14]

Notes

1 Gramsci developed his theory of hegemony and Communism in the 1920s as he was trying to figure out why the socialist revolution failed to develop in the western industrialized nations. The result was an expansion of Lenin's theory of state hegemony (coercive power) to encompass the state and civil society. In 1924, Gramsci expanded his thesis on the strategy and tactics of communist parties in the west further by stating that Bourgeois ideological and cultural hegemony within the working-class institutions of civil society was a huge barrier to the development of the revolutionary working class movement:

> The direct determinism that moved the Russian masses in the streets to revolutionary assaults was complicated in Central and Western Europe by all the political superstructures created by the greater development of capitalism; it rendered mass action slower and more cautious, and therefore demands from the revolutionary Party a system of strategy and tactics much more complex and long range than those used by the Bolsheviks between March and November 1917. (qtd. in Hamrin, 1975: 77)

According to Gramsci, a long protracted *war of position* consisting of communist education, mass cultural reform, class alliances and anti-capitalist mobilization *against* bourgeois hegemony was necessary for communist parties to gain control of the working-class movement and
lead it towards socialism. *Bourgeois hegemony*, which is the capitalist elite's consensual control of
the working-class and oppressed nationalities; is exercised through the social, cultural, religious,
labor, communications (mass media) and educational institutions of bourgeois civil society
which appear to be autonomous; but nevertheless, serve the political interests of the ruling class
by propagating and legitimating bourgeois ideology in all areas of life. For Gramsci, the war of
position was a necessary precondition of the dictatorship of the proletariat, which could only be
achieved once the working-class attained *proletarian hegemony* in civil society.

From 1967 to 1975, Toronto Black working-class organic intellectuals in the Canadian
Black Power leadership, waged an internal war of position in African-Canadian civil society
against Canadian imperialism and white bourgeois hegemony through the formation of international solidarity campaigns, rallies, study groups and anti-imperialist protests which became the
catalyst for the formation of a Black liberation movement against Canadian imperialism.

2 Inspired by the anti-colonial national liberation movements against European colonialism and imperialism in Africa during the 1950s and 1960s, the theory of internal colonialism was initially es-
poused by Malcolm X and Martin Luther King, Jr. in the civil rights movement to explain the racial
oppression of African-Americans (Bohmer:1998. This framework which saw racial oppression as
colonial oppression was developed further by U.S. Black Power in the late 1960s by Stokely
Carmicheal and Charles V. Halmilton (Student Non-Violent Coordinating Committee) in Black
Power that referea argued African-Americans were an oppressed nation that required political independence and economic independence (1969).

3 When the U.S. Black Power movement went into decline in the early 1970s, the leadership debated
how to re-build the movement after it was defeated by the FBI's successful counter-insurgency
program COINTELPRO, which undermined the African-American Revolution in the 1960s. These
discussions inspired the leadership of former Black Power organizations to unite and rebuild a
Black revolutionary united front that mobilized all the progressive elements in the Black community regardless of their class background rather than solely focusing on the black working-class
majority and growing underclass in the urban centers of North America. In 1971, the African Liberation Support Committee (ALSC) emerged as a united front, uniting African-Americans from
the grassroots to politicians in the U.S. Congress (Johnson, 2003). The ALSC chapters in the U.S.
as well as Canada (Montreal and Toronto) consisted of a broad united front of cultural nationalists and revolutionary-nationalists who came together to build material support for the national
liberation movements against Portuguese colonialism in southern Africa during the 1970s.

4 In 1972, ALD was attended by 30, 000 in Washington; 5,000, San Francisco; 6,000, Dominica;
10,000 Antigua; 3,000, Grenada. See Front Story, "African Liberation Day," Contrast, June 15,
1972.

5 Josiah Henson (1789-1883) was an African-American slave born in Kentucky who eventually escaped through the Underground Railway to Ontario at the age of 40. Henson played a leading
role in establishing the most successful economic African community in Ontario, as a minister

and laborer who bought 3,000 acres of land and built a saw mill and produced timber exported all over the world. As a result, he built a school to educate runaway slaves, brought over 200 slaves to freedom, and constructed a waterway between Dresden, Ontario and Detroit, that became a federal waterway. See, Contrast (June 15, 1972: 8).

6 Rosie Douglas was a leader of the Black anti-racist student rebellion at Sir George Williams (Concordia university), Montreal, Canada, 1969. Julian Bond was a founding member and Communications Director, Student Non-Violent Coordinating Committee (for more information see www.ibiblio.org/sncc/). John Conyers, is a Democratic Congressman, Detroit, Michigan.

7 In 1963, the Chinese published The Chinese Communist Party's Proposal Concerning the General Line of the International Communist Movement (June, 1963). Soviets responded with Open Letter of the Communist Party of the Soviet Union (ended up being last formal communication between the two parties). By 1964, Mao claimed that there was a counter-revolution in the Soviet Union and the Dictatorship of the Proletariat was conquered by a rising bourgeois class (represented by Kruschev) that restored capitalism and historically arose from the ranks of the Soviet State bureacracy that was the ruling class since the victory of the Socialist Revolution. Although the Sino-Soviet split began as a two-line struggle in the international communist movement between the two dominant parties, it soon divided the entire communist movement into two ideological 'war of position' (imperialist Canada) and 'war of movement' (in colonial Africa) against each other factions. For example, China had antagonistic relations with the so-called Soviet satellite states that came to power in Africa during the mid-70s. Source: Source: Wikipedia.org/wiki /Sino-Soviet_split.

8 UNITA was formed in 1966 when its leader, Jonas Savimbi broke with FNLA to form it. FNLA (1957) conservative African-Nationalist; (China's reactionary foreign policy was a result of the two-line struggle between the USSR in the '60s and '70s resulted in its lending material support to a conservative bourgeois-nationalist Liberation to eliminate the Soviet-sponsored MPLA, although that was the true vanguard of the people. UNITA's leadership comes from the Ovimbundu Tribal group and its policies were formally Maoist although it was aligned with South Africa and later U.S. Imperialism in the '80s. Source: Wikipedia.org/wiki/UNITA (free encyclopedia)

9 A united front of progressive anti-colonial political groups who formed the Front for the Liberation of Mozambique in 1961 as an anti-Portuguese guerilla political party and began armed struggle civil war against Portuguese colonialism in September 1964, and became independent June 25, 1975. Source: Wikipedia.org/wiki/Mozambique (free encyclopedia)

10 Through various conversations with some elder activists in Toronto's Black working-class community the history of the African-Canadian Black Power Movement was recovered.

11 On January 31, 1975 Douglas spoke at 334 Queen St. West about the BWA anti-racist campaign to appeal his deportation order set for the following week ("Douglas to Speak," 1975). Douglas also spoke out against Ottawa's racist immigration policy that sought to deport him back to Dominica for his leadership in the Black student rebellion. On another occasion, Douglas spoke at a BWA rally for Black History Week 1975, entitled "A Tribute to Malcolm X." The event commemorated Malcolm on the 10th anniversary of his death on February 21 at St Michael's All Angels Church Hall ("Black History Week," 1975). On May 11, the BWA held a rally at the Ethiopian Or-

thodox Church attended by 300, to protest the police murder of 15 year-old Michael Habib (Black Labor: May 24, 1975).

12 In a discussion with the Institute of the Black World (IBW) at the University of Massachussetts, May 1, 1975, Rodney offered the following reflection on the Marxist-Nationalist debate emerging out of ALSC and its significance to the African liberation project in North America.

13 To give an example of the type of articles written by Black Power women, in the May 24, 1975 edition, there was an article on women in the MPLA, the Angola People Army. the BWA advocated Black working women's participation in African Communist wars of movement as the only means of alleviating race, gender, and class oppression from their lives:

> For black women and other women of colour under capitalism ... They are oppressed not only as workers and as women, but also as members of 'minority' races. They are in many ways the most downtrodden, and are subjected to forms of contempt; humiliation and degradation ... Women who had experienced similar or worse conditions were only able to realize a change in their situation by participating actively in the national liberation struggles and fighting to overthrow capitalism. ("ALD, Past and Present," 1975)

14 Many of the BWOI's who were active in the City's Black Power movement went on to become founding members of the Black Action Defense Committee, Black Music Association, Anti-Apartheid efforts in the '80s and the Communist Party of Canada in the '70s and '80s. Note, Interview with Owen Leach, December 2003.

List of References

August, A. (1975). Why a Black Workers' Alliance, *Contrast*, p.2.

Black Labor. (1975, May 24). A.L.D. past and present, 1(2), p.6.

Black Labor. (1975, April 24). Demonstrate! African liberation day, 1(2), p.5.

Black Labor. (1975, May 24). Blacks fight back against racism, 1(2), p.1.

Black Liberation News. (1969, July). History and aims of BLFC, 1(1), p.1.

Black Liberation News. (1969, July). BLFC summer program, 1(1), p.3.

Black Liberation News. (1969, August). BLFC seminar demands citizens control ofpolice, 1(2), p.1.

Boyd, H. (1998). Radicalism and resistance: The evolution of black radical thought. *Black Scholar*, 28(1), 43-53.

Brohmer, P. (1998). African-Americans as an internal colony: The theory of internal colonialism. Online: www.academic.evergreen.edu/b/bohmerp/internalcolony.htm

Contrast. (1970, April 4). Panthers speak in Toronto, p. 10.

Contrast. (1970, August 15). Blacks form united front, p. 4.

Contrast. (1971, December 1). Pan-africanism and socialism, p. 13.

Contrast. (1975, Jan. 31). Douglas to speak, p.4.

Georgakas, D. and Surkin, M. (1998). *Detroit: I Do Mind Dying; A Study in Urban Rebellion* (2ⁿᵈ ed.). Massachusetts: South End Press.

Gramsci, A. (1971). *Selections from the prison notebooks of Antonio Gramsci*. NewYork: International Publishers.

Hamrin, H. (1975). *Between bolshevism and revisionism: the Italian communist party, 1944-1947*. Stockholm: Scandinavian University Press.

Harris, C. (2005). A gramscian historical-materialist analysis of the informal learning and development of black working-class organic intellectuals, 1969-1975. Unpublished Master's Thesis, University of Toronto.

Johnson, C. (2003). From popular anti-imperialism to sectarianism: The African liberation support committee and black power radicals, *New Political Science*, 25 (4), 477-507.

Lewis, R.C. (1998). *Walter Rodney's intellectual and political thought*. Detroit: Wayne State University Press.

Rebick, J. (2005). *Ten thousand roses; The making of feminist revolution*. Toronto: Penguin.

Richmond, (2002, July 17). CKLN Interview by Harris with Richmond (pgs. 20).Unpublished raw data.

Richmond's (2004, July 8). Mumia Abu Jamal's new book a must read. *Share*, p. 7.

Richmond, N. (2007). *The political biography of Norman Richmond* (UnpublishedArticle). Toronto: Black Action Defense Committee (BADC).

Rodney, W. (1990). *Walter Rodney speaks; The making of an African intellectual*. New Jersey: Africa World Press.

Tse Tung, M. (1966). *Quotations from Chairman Mao*. Peking: Peking Foreign Languages Press.

Erin Morton

| Chapter 14 | "Eight Days Before the Election": Politicians, Culture Industries, and Folk Art in Nova Scotia |

Introduction: New World Coming

In the spring of 2007, I attended an interdisciplinary conference at Queen's University entitled "New World Coming: The Sixties and the Shaping of Global Consciousness." At this conference, I presented an early version of this chapter in a session called "Art and Activism: Populism and Revolution," sharing the stage with two colleagues who gave papers on site-specific protest during the 1960s Chicano civil rights movement in the U.S. and on the global circulation of Latin American revolutionary images. After listening to my colleagues' excellent presentations on these intricate stories of local resistance enacted on cultural terms, I—as a visual culture historian of Atlantic Canada—immediately felt in over my head. When I chatted with a friend about the uncertainly I felt at having my work slotted into this panel, since I had proposed a paper on the resistance strategies of what is conventionally known as "folk art" production in Nova Scotia, he laughed and said: "Well, of course, everyone knows that art in Nova Scotia just doesn't have the same revolutionary potential of art in Mexico and Latin America." Since I was experiencing a particularly low moment of self-confidence in my own research project, I agreed—and my colleague looked horrified: he was, of course, as a good Canadian historian himself, only kidding about his comments on the revolutionary potential of visual cultural production in Atlantic Canada. And deep down, despite my own moment of self-doubt about the contemporary relevancy of my project in the age of global analyses, I knew that he was right: what Ian McKay calls "the dramatic, revolutionary, contested, difficult, and contingent process" of the historical expansion of liberalism across Atlantic Canada too contained moments of popular resistance—and these moments are still relevant to studying this region today (McKay 2000b).

My experience at this conference reminds me of the fact that there is a contested albeit pervasive narrative in the tradition of Canadian national/ist historiography when it comes to Atlantic Canada. At its most basic level is the idea that marginalized regions such as Atlantic Canada produce "peripheral" ideas from "peripheral figures," especially when compared to the dominant traditions of national/ist histories located in the Québec–Windsor corridor (McKay 2000b, 100). More recently, the Atlantic Canada case seems to fall short when compared to triumphant narratives of local resistance to the neoliberal enlistment of popular culture by global market forces in diverse geopolitical regions such as Latin America and South Asia.[1] Indeed, cultural historians who study Canada have much to learn from this literature when it comes to articulating our own local stories about the widespread economic and historical changes that have occurred globally since the 1960s. And so we seem to be at an impasse, a tenuous moment in writing cultural history in Canada, after generations of Canadian history students have long debunked older narrative frameowrks such as Donald Creighton's Laurentian thesis.[2] Similarly, the metropolis-hinterland tradition in Canadian national/ist historiography, which saw constructions of Canadian region, east and west, and posited the western frontier movement as a masculine, innovative expansion and which establishes Atlantic Canada as a feminine, tradition-laden counter-frontier, has also undergone rigorous critical analysis over the past twenty years (Forbes 1978; McKay 2000b). So why do those of us who study Atlantic Canada need to be continually reminded of the lasting effects of these ontologies of region? In order to read such dominant narratives in Atlantic Canadian historiography against themselves, this chapter will take Ian McKay's sound advice in abandoning the idea of writing a particular story as part of a larger Atlantic Canadian synthesis. McKay has effectively argued that it is no longer desirable or possible to produce an integrated narrative that every resident of the region can somehow read themself into (2000b). By employing McKay's more "problem-centred, bridge-building approach" to Atlantic Canada studies, I would like to focus here on the "logical and historical conditions of possibility as a specific project in a specific time and place" (2000b, 91)—specifically, the nascent stages of global culture industry[3] as it relates to rural Nova Scotia.

In this case, these conditions of possibility surround the use of art practice as a mode for resistance to the social structure and conditions in late twentieth-century rural Nova Scotia. I take as my primary example here the state enlistment of "folk" art at a particular historical moment during the 1970s, which demonstrates the way such popular culture forms are often "doubly enrolled" in two competing yet interrelated systems (García Canclini 1988, 486; Guss 2000). Popular culture, as historian Michael Denning argues, "is neither simply a form of social control nor a form of class expression, but a contested terrain" (2004, 98). Keeping this in mind, this chapter examines a moment in the career of Collins Eisenhauer (1898-1979), a self-taught artist from Union Square, Nova Scotia, in relation to the larger context of collecting "folk" art in the province. In 1974, Eisenhauer displayed a series of wooden sculptures called *Political Figures* (fig. 1) on a makeshift float in a local Canada Day parade. "[The audience] took it as an insult I guess," Eisenhauer remembers. "It was eight days before the election and they thought I was hitting at the politicians, but I wasn't" (quoted in Huntington and Stewart 1976).

Figure 1: Political Figures (Pierre Trudeau, Robert Stanfield, David Lewis and Gerald Regan) by Collins Eisenhauer, 1973-74. Photo © Canadian Museum of Civilization, artefacts 75-913; 75-914; 75-915; 75-916, photo S76-3004.

After parading his life-sized sculptures of David Lewis, Gerald Regan, Robert Stanfield, and Pierre Trudeau, Eisenhauer sold Political Figures to a local collector and the works were subsequently circulated in the Art Gallery of Nova Scotia's (AGNS) first nationally touring exhibition in 1976. The Eisenhauer case demonstrates the complexity behind popular culture forms, as a contested terrain between cultural producers and cultural institutions, and how the dissemination of popular cultural production from Nova Scotia took on new importance for the local state in the developing global culture industry of the 1970s. In order to explore Eisenhauer's staging of a particular artistic event in Nova Scotia, which subsequently took on national significance when a federal museum purchased Eisenhauer's sculptures, I examine the implications of "folk" art collecting during what social historian Arthur Marwick calls "the long decade" of the 1960s (1998)[4]—a historical moment that for the first time made apparent the now commonly acknowledged appropriation of culture for the marketplace (Rifkin 2000) and left artists such as Eisenhauer without strong authority to control the meaning behind their production.[5]

Collins Eisenhauer and the Rejection of All Things "Rotten"

Since his death, Eisenhauer has become one of Nova Scotia's most well-known "folk" artists, largely due to the widespread domestic and international circulation of his work by private collectors and Canadian cultural institutions since the 1970s. In 1976, the AGNS in Halifax organized and toured Eisenhauer's work as part of a seminal survey of contemporary folk art from the province. The exhibition, entitled "Folk Art of Nova Scotia," was the first of its kind—the first treatment of the visual cultural production of those economically disadvantaged, rural Nova Scotia artists who were long imagined to be "folk" by the province's middle-class cultural producers. It was through this decisive exhibition that the AGNS first publicly labeled Nova Scotia's self-taught, rural artist as producing "folk" art, which is all the more significant since this exhibition also represents the newly established provincial art gallery's first nationally touring exhibition. In his seminal study on antimodernism and cultural selection in twentieth-century Nova Scotia, McKay argues that countless cultural figures of influence employed the poetics and politics of folklorization as a way of understanding the province's culture and history (1994). This process involved rewriting the history of Nova Scotia's subaltern classes, who urban cultural producers came to understand as "the passive recipients of tradition, not its active shapers" (McKay 1994, 21).

This familiar trope of folklorization, in which cultural producers enact the "folk" as a social and cultural category to understand Nova Scotia's rural poor, is crucial to understanding how the AGNS categorized the work of artists such as Eisenhauer. As visual culture historian Lynda Jessup argues, categories for understanding visual images and material objects such as "tourist," "primitive," "folk," and "craft" serve to "reformulated and naturalize social relations in the field of cultural production" (2001, 4)—in this case, the cultural traditions of a romanticized, rural underclass. Although these processes of myth-formation and cultural invention have helped to establish rural Nova Scotians such as Eisenhauer as the passive recipients of tradition, existing interviews with the late artist clearly demonstrate that saw his art practice as means to comment on the world around him. Despite the AGNS's pervasive construction of contemporary folk art as a remnant of pre-modern, anti-industrial tradition in the province, in many ways Eisenhauer resisted the parameters set forth for him by collectors and curators. By using his artistic practice as a way to stage what was perhaps an act of protest, but which was definitely a sign of conscious political activity on July 1st, 1974, Eisenhauer provides an important case to consider how state cultural institutions such as the AGNS developed "folk" art as a category of artistic expression in Nova Scotia—a process that hinges on the state enlistment of popular art forms to establish the province's isolation from capitalist modernity.

When Eisenhauer mounted his Canada Day parade float in New Germany, Nova Scotia, he made the four life-sized wooden *Political Figures* especially for the occasion. In a 1979 interview that he conducted with *Artscanada* magazine, Eisenhauer describes how he conceived of the idea for the float a year leading up to the event:

> On the first of July in New Germany they used to have a sort of Fireman's Parade and people would take things there, trimmed up, and make a celebration of it. Well, I had a wagon and a pair of ponies [in 1973] and I took them up there with no trimmings, nothing, and I got lost. I mean I felt so foolish. So on my way home that's when I stated planning for next year. That's where the politicians come in. I materialized them in my mind and I started working from there (Eisenhauer quoted in Donaldson 1979, 21).

After a solid year of work, on July 1st, 1974, Eisenhauer set off in his horse and wagon from his home in Union Square to the parade site in New Germany, a thirty minute drive by car, and carried with him four wooden renderings of the most prominent Canadian political figures of the day: Federal Liberal leader and Prime Minister Pierre Trudeau, complete with a plastic rose in his lapel; former premier of Nova Scotia turned leader of the official Progressive Conservative federal opposition, Robert Stanfield, clutching a banana; a smiling federal New Democratic Party leader David Lewis; and, in a painted plaid suit, Nova Scotian Liberal premier (soon to be majority leader) Gerald Regan carrying a whip—presumably to be used on the horses that carried him in the wagon (fig. 1). Eisenhauer seated Stanfield and Trudeau across from each other at a card table, flanked by Regan and Lewis, who we can imagine giving input on the game that took place before them. Carried in the back of Eisenhauer's wagon, the four painted wooden sculptures—now collectively know as Eisenhauer's *Political Figures*—acted as one of many floats in New Germany's 1974 Canada Day parade before eventually retiring as lawn ornaments in Eisenhauer's front yard, and then being purchased by Murray Stewart, a local art collector.

In 1975, a year after Political Figures debuted in the parade, a more prolific collector in Nova Scotia came into contact with Eisenhauer. The AGNS credits Chris Huntington as establishing a cultural "resurgence" of folk art production in Nova Scotia (Martin 1994), through his position as a wealthy U.S. antique dealer turned patron who spent thousands of dollars collecting work from self-taught artists such as Eisenhauer between 1974 and 1993. Looking at Huntington's practices of cultural selection in conjunction with his methods of providing artistic direction to rural Nova Scotian artists helps to better situate *Political Figures* within the province's history of collecting, specially since Eisenhauer produced these politically charged sculptures before he came into contact with Huntington. This is important to consider, since Huntington was always interested in policing the boundaries of authenticity by selecting works that he perceived to be uninfluenced by the tourist trade (which often led artists to repeat popular objects and produce work in serial form to meet the tastes of their tourist patrons). According to this hierarchization of folk art objects, Eisenhauer's art production was valuable because Huntington ensured it remained divorced from modern phenomena such as tourism, which the collector perceived as corrupting folk art production by turning artists' wares into tourist commodities.

Huntington made his thoughts on the popularity of contemporary folk art with tourists during the 1970s well known, distinguishing between his own interventions into an artist's creative process and those of visiting tourists:

> You have to be as sensitive as you possibly can. You certainly don't tell [the artists] what to do and you don't ask them to "make another one of those" because you know that you can sell it. That's the biggest problem I see in the whole folk art thing, is the mass production aspect of it and … [the artists are] nice people and they want to satisfy you or somebody else and they get victimized by that (Huntington quoted in *Folk Art Found Me*).[6]

Despite the fact that such "mass production" was the result of a situation in which an individual artist would simply produce certain works on commission for buyers or dealers, Huntington maintained that the demand to repeat the same subjects over and over again devalued the quality or authenticity of their art practice. Huntington's collecting practices in Nova Scotia during the 1970s were prolific and the objects he purchased from rural artists came to form most of what now exists as the AGNS's folk art collection. Between 1974 and 1993, Huntington became the most prominent liai-

son between Nova Scotia's self-taught artists and major Canadian cultural institutions that were interested in collecting the best of what Huntington had to offer.

I argue that the historical moment in which this occurred is particularly significant, since, as economist Jeremy Rifkin points out, it was at the beginning of the
twentieth century that "the arts—and artists—were [first] appropriated for the marketplace" (2000, 144). As a result, cultural producers were

> … left without a strong voice to interpret, reproduce, and build on [their]
> own shared meanings. The significance of this capitulation didn't become
> obvious, however, until the 1960s. By the time Andy Warhol unveiled his
> reproductions of Campbell's soup cans and other products as works of art,
> the transition from traditional culture to consumer culture was far along.
> Art, once an adversary to the values of the marketplace, was now its pri-
> mary apostle and the main communicator of its values (Rifkin 2000, 144).

Historical perceptions on mass culture since the middle of the twentieth century
have helped show how popular cultural forms became, what Denning describes as
"contested terrain structured by the culture industries, the state historical apparatuses, and the symbolic forms and practices of subaltern classes" (2004, 98). As
one of the sites where class struggle is most centrally engaged, notions about
what constitutes popular and mass culture have too been transformed since the
economic circumstances of late capitalism. During the 1960s, the moment between the culmination of modernity —when capitalist investment in culture ensured that mass culture forms won out over all others—and the nascent stages of
neoliberal globalization is palpable. It is important then to recognize the historical factors that allowed Huntington and Eisenhauer to interact in the way that
they did, fostering what was no doubt a mutually beneficial relationship but also
one that helped to promote Eisenhauer's work in an economic climate hungry to
capitalize on popular culture forms.

Chris Huntington and the "Resurgence" of Nova Scotia Folk Art

The market for folk art in Nova Scotia is intrinsically connected to this history of commodity forms and class formations. It is also deeply related to what Frederic Jameson
describes as "the cultural logic of late capitalism" and commercial antimodernism in
Nova Scotia (1984; Denning 2004; McKay 1994). As Joan Donaldson, a writer for
Artscanada magazine, pointed out with regards to Eisenhauer's work in 1979, "There is
a genuineness here, a rejection of all he sees as 'rotten' in today's world, of half-truths

and fancy ways. His joy is in the making, in the creation" (1979, 22). Similarly, writing in 1977, Marie Elwood of *Canadian Collector* suggested "Rural isolation and long winters conspire to provide the opportunity for the folk artist to produce his works. Since they are not bound by tradition or livelihood to their art, their work truly represents them and their habitat" (1977, 31). As Huntington himself puts it, referencing his own tendency to guide and influence artists such as Eisenhauer to produce particular kinds of things,

> It's not always the best work, that stuff they did before they were ever contacted by a human being or by civilization or by the mainstream of art, or whatever. It isn't always the best, sometimes the best came at the end after this information has been stuffed through their heads and they filtered through and they make what they can out of it (Huntington quoted in *Folk Art Found Me*).

At this moment, in 1970s Nova Scotia, the economic hardships of artists such as Eisenhauer must have been apparent to Huntington when he visited their homes to collect new and interesting objects. Such struggles, however, were continuously credited with producing the seemingly unique social and economic circumstances that allowed folk art production in Nova Scotia to flourish the in first place (Martin 1997).

In 1976, Huntington conducted a series of interviews, which he later published segments of in the catalogue for "Folk Art of Nova Scotia." During one such interview, Huntington spoke with Eisenhauer about the benefits of creating new and "interesting" work. Huntington discussed Eisenhauer's financial struggles in relation to how Eisenhauer's artwork sales were able to subsidize a lifetime of underemployment, a practice that Huntington elides here to focus on the artist's pure creative impulses:

> Chris Huntington: How do you see yourself as an artist?
>
> Collins Eisenhauer: [laughing] No good!
>
> CH: Come on now! Give me a serious answer to that because obviously you've had a lot of interest. I mean there's a growing interest in what you're doing and you have to take it pretty seriously. You must be really pleased to have gotten as far along the ladder as you are.
>
> CE: I am pleased. It's helped me out a lot financially.
>
> CH: Well it's helped you out financially, but how about spiritually? Do you think all this interest in your carvings encourages you to work and make different things?

CE: Yes it does.

CH: Do you think you're going to be famous some day?
CE: Oh I wouldn't know.

CH: You don't know. You'll leave that up to us?
CE: I would like to be.

CH: I think you've got a pretty good chance. I think it depends … on what you make between now and when you close your eyes for the last time. You know the problem is as we discussed before, you made so many of the same things, so many swans [(fig. 2)].

Figure 2: Swan by Collins Eisenhauer, c. 1977. Photo © Canadian Museum of Civilization, artefact 77-290, photo S85-3694.

You've already made a lot of things, but I think consistently you're making the most interesting things you've ever made now. That's my feeling. I think you made wonderful things in the past, but you know you made a lot of things that are kind of stereotypes, you've seen one, you've seen 'em all sort of thing. …
CE: There aren't too many artists I don't think that would start out at first with the best thing they ever did.

CH: No, I think those early swans you made were certainly as good as anything you ever made. … I mean, obviously your talents are just as strong as they ever were … It's one reason why I'm happy you're no longer making chickens [(fig. 3)] by the dozen, because that was a waste of … energy.[7]

Figure 3: Rooster by Collins Eisenhauer, c. 1975. Photo © Canadian Museum of Civilization, arte-fact 77-385, photo S83-535.

CE: Well it wasn't, because it helped me to live—helped to keep me living.

CH: Oh yes, all I'm thinking is the whole body of your work is as good now and you're getting more money for things and you're making a broader range of stuff. And it will be interesting to see what the future has in store (Huntington and Stewart 1976).

Huntington's conversation with Eisenhauer suggests that an artist's economic struggle was not a viable reason to begin mass-producing "stereotypes" in order to sell multiple items at lower prices to tourists. Rather, Huntington encouraged Eisenhauer to move away from creating multiples of the same subject (swans or chickens) and towards large-scale figures that, for Huntington, were a better representation of the broad range of Eisenhauer's work (Huntington and Stewart 1976). According to Huntington, the exhibition "Folk Art of Nova Scotia" was an opportunity for audiences to see "the best rooster or the best cat," exposing Eisenhauer's potential to be collected in fine art circles and not just by tourists alone (Huntington and Stewart 1976).

In 1997, the AGNS surveyed Huntington's vocation as a "folk" art collector. As part of his research for the accompanying exhibition catalogue, guest curator Ken Martin interviewed Huntington about the first visits he made to the province during the 1970s. Driving through Nova Scotia to stock his lucrative business in Maine, Ezra Peters Antiquities, Huntington remembered: "It was so beautiful. I just said, 'Why don't we leave this [Ezra Peters] chapter right behind and see what happens, and have a little adventure'" (quoted in Martin 1997, 8). And so, in 1974, Huntington and his then wife Ellen sold their business in Maine and auctioned off their massive personal collection to move to Eagle Head, Nova Scotia (Martin 1997). "Of course," Huntington later wrote, "we did not know very much about our adopted environs; but, in hindsight, we were, no doubt, the right people at the right place and time. It did not matter that we knew little of Nova Scotia's cultural history. ... One could not say that we witnessed or partook in a renaissance, because practically no artistic tradition had existed here" (1984, n.p.). Huntington's experience in Nova Scotia, like that of many collectors before him, began abruptly with this "sudden discovery" of local culture (Martin 1997, 6).[8]

As Huntington became increasingly aware of the self-taught artists living in rural Nova Scotia, he began collecting their work as part of his wider interest in antiques, collectibles, and fine art.[9] After quickly making contact with artists through local residents, and with his initial knowledge of the work of Collins Eisenhauer, Huntington made connections with, and began purchasing pieces from, Albert Lohnes and Charlie Tanner, among others.[10] These artists were retirees, most were former fishermen, wood carvers or other manual labourers, and, according to Martin, Huntington tracked them all down "in the nick of time" considering their advanced years (Martin 1997, 9). One of the first artists to truly impress Huntington, Tanner was "discovered" by Huntington when he stumbled across some figures on display in a nearby yard (Martin 1997, 9-10). "By now, Huntington was on a roll. The big question, he later explained, was 'how many more Charlie Tanners were there out there behind those weathered doors?' He began to look for them all" (Martin 1997, 9).[11] His interest sparked, Huntington thus became an avid collector of contemporary Nova Scotia "folk" art and, following local cultural selectors before him, imagined that this work was on the verge of disappearance.[12] Since these sel-taught artisits, most of them elderly, would only produce a limited number of objects and during his time in Nova Scotia, Huntington consistently "snapped them up, for there would be no more" (Martin 1997, 10).[13]

Huntington proceeded to post advertisements around the province to seek out these aged artists and began purchasing items from most who answered his call, "even when he was unimpressed by their initial offerings, expecting better things tomorrow" (Martin 1997, 11). To explain what he considered to be a unique form of art production that was certain to disappear, Huntington marked these artists working in the 1960s and 70s in generational terms. He thought that a combination of cultural and economic circumstances were converging in the work of these senior artists, who came of age at "a time when traditional skills of working with one's hands carried over into a time when pensions allowed people for the first time the leisure to express themselves artistically" (Huntington quoted in Martin 1997, 11). These apparently unique regional circumstance found in Nova Scotia's supposedly isolated rural areas allowed these artists, Huntington felt, to develop their own creativity—especially since, as retirees, they now had plenty of time to spare. All of these artists, according to Martin, were "ethnically diverse and isolated ... intelligent, oblivious to academic rules, yet propelled by a need for personal expression" (Martin 1997, 11).

By 1975, Huntington had spent upwards of $40,000 on his purchases from Nova Scotia's self-taught artists (Martin 1997, 12). According to Martin, such a significant financial investment in contemporary Nova Scotia "folk" art made Huntington "integral to the growth of the genre" (1997, 12). By intentionally and unapologetically manipulating the work of the artists he collected from, Huntington directly influenced the production of a handful of artists that he alone is credited as discovering. Martin describes Huntington's relationship with the artists he patronized at length, by highlighting the active role Huntington took when commissioning certain pieces for his own collection:

> From the start, Huntington had deliberately influenced his charges, a practice that folk-art purists find controversial, to say the least. When an artist was serious about finding buyers for his work Huntington was ready with topical advice and, if necessary, art supplies. He was tactful enough to moderate his criticism, but he firmly gave artists directions he thought would stretch their talent—and make money. For example, he urged carver Harry Wile to undertake a Noah's ark complete with menagerie. Or take the case of Donald Manzer, who answered a Huntington advertisement [quoting Huntington]: "Manzer showed up in my driveway in Eagle Head with a bunch of little carvings in a bigger cardboard box[.] ... I said, 'You know, if you could make something a little bigger than this, I think there really might be a market for some life-size carvings.'" Manzer readily complied.
>
> Or consider Clarence (Bubby) Mooers, whose sculpture *Penelope and Poodle* [(fig. 4)] became a highlight of the 1976 exhibition ["Folk Art of Nova Scotia"]. "Penelope" was not an artistic accident but the result—at least in part—of Huntington's expressed wants. Explaining market realities to another carver in 1976, Huntington confided that he had been unimpressed with Mooers's early work, but he [quoting Huntington] "kept going there, kept expressing interest in what he was making. And the last thing he made was really wonderful. It's a life-size figure of a nude woman and a poodle dog. It ... can be sold for quite a bit of money. But if I hadn't stuck with him, he would have never made that." Even so, there was another problem with Penelope [quoting Huntington]: "I said, 'Look, I love the figure, but those breasts are just too big[.] ... They get in the way of the thing! They've got to be smaller.' He never got 'em as small as I wanted, but he got 'em down to a reasonable size. If you overdo something like that, people will never really look at the figure." Other nudges to carvers: Avoid gulls (not enough humour), think big (large carvings are more salable), and avoid repetition (every piece should be fresh). [Quoting Huntington] "Everyone has [carved] ox teams in Nova Scotia," he admonished carver Ray Fancy. "That's just what you shouldn't do. But a baseball player would be a nice subject" (Martin 1997, 14-15).

Figure 4: Penelope and Poodle by Clarence Mooers, c. 1976. Photo © Canadian Museum of   Civilization, artefact 77-373.1-3, photo S79-7010.

Such direct instructions from Huntington undoubtedly led Manzer, Mooers, and Fancy to develop certain subjects, abandon others and, most importantly, entrenched the idea that Huntington, as dealer, was a crucial participant in the artistic process.

As Huntington oversaw each step of these artists' practice, he established himself as both the direct link between artist and gallery and between object and consumer. He became increasingly irritated when tourists visiting Nova Scotia purchased folk art directly from artists, which he felt kept market prices low and paid artists less than their pieces were worth: "I believe that anyone looking for Nova Scotia folk art would be better off to buy from me because I always had the best pieces. It really didn't work out that way, however" (Huntington quoted in Martin 1997, 19). He maintained further that dealers such as himself were all that stood between "opposing values—the greed of modern society and the naïveté of people who have lived close to the land or sea, worked their asses off all their lives and ended up with very little except their humour and their talents" (Huntington quoted in Martin 1997, 19). In this way, Huntington perceived himself to be the purveyor of cultural truths in Nova Scotia, speaking on behalf of rural residents in order to maintain regional traditions that might otherwise be lost.

Moments of Refusal

This history of Huntington's collecting practices in Nova Scotia begs a number of questions. For instance, as Denning posits, "do any cultural forms escape the logic of the commodity? Is there a political or oppositional art? ... Was there a cultural practice in the face of reification" (Denning 2004, 105)? If modernism and mass culture developed together under the conditions of late capitalism, then, as Denning argues, they might also come to an end together as the culture industry changes—despite the fact that through capitalist investment in culture "mass culture has won. There is nothing else" (2004, 103). Huntington's experience in Nova Scotia certainly did not influence the creation of Eisenhauer's *Political Figures* directly, since the artist conceptualized and produced these works long before Huntington made Nova Scotia his semi-permanent home in 1974. Yet, an important relationship between Eisenhauer and Huntington ensued, particularly in terms of the way Huntington influenced and supported Eisenhauer's work. There is no doubt that artists such as Eisenhauer became well known amongst Canadian museum professionals in and after the 1970s because of Huntington's patronage and the way the collector helped to circulate the artist's work. But it is also important to consider here the way that Eisenhauer used hias own art practice in his local community. There is a disjuncture between Huntington's vision for Eisenhauer's art practice and Eisenhauer's own political motivations for his work. Fredric Jameson lays out this quandary plainly by arguing that there is "authentic cultural production" that draws "on the collective experience of marginal pockets of the social life of the world system" (1979, 140; quoted in Denning 2004, 105). Jameson simultaneously suggests that a politicized artistic practice is not a choice but a problem: "you do not reinvent an access onto political art and authentic cultural production by studding your individual artistic discourse with class and political signals" (1979, 140; quoted in Denning 2004, 105).

It is clear that most discussions of the enlistment of popular culture by non-community forces have, until now, largely surrounded concerns about the state (Guss 2000). As Denning observes:

> No popular cultural practices is necessarily subversive or incorporated; it takes place in a situation, becomes articulated with a 'party' in Gramsci's sense: an organized way of life, an alliance of class formations, a conception of the universe, a historical bloc which creates the conditions for political use of reading, the conditions for symbolizing class conflict (2004, 111).

It is within this context that I will offer a few final remarks regarding Eisenhauer's art practice and Huntington's circulation of Eisenhauer's work, which I read here as examples of the expediency of culture—in other words, the use of culture to achieve a particular objective (Yúdice 2003). According to literary scholar George Yúdice, although battles for cultural rights to representation are certainly defined by histories of unequal power relations, there are ways to discuss the incorporation of cultural objects for the global marketplace while, at the same time, examining the significance of popular culture forms for local communities. Yúdice argues that this is because, under the conditions of globalization, all cultural forms become managed bureaucratically at every conceivable level—from production to collection to distribution and beyond (2003).

Following Yúdice's argument, I want to expand the notion of expediency beyond a means to attaining an end that is convenient but considered to be immoral, which would read collectors such as Huntington as taking advantage of artists such as Eisenhauer for their own purposes. This kind of understanding is not only limiting, but, as Yúdice points out, also "implies that there is a notion of right that exists outside of the play of interests" (2003, 38). Yúdice explains his argument most effectively when he posits a performative understanding of the expediency of culture, which both absolves Huntington as the villain in this process and allows one to read Eisenhauer's own agency in cultural and social constructions such as those implicit in folklorization. "A performative understanding of the expediency of culture," Yúdice suggests, "focuses on the strategies implied in any invocation of culture, any invention of tradition, in relation to some purpose or goal" (2003, 38). I read Eisenhauer's staging of his *Political Figures* in relation to this, as one of those "little, personal acts of resistance" that McKay describes as *moments of refusal*, in which someone suddenly sees through the liberal order's appearance in the Canadian state—identified in this case as middle-class cultural producers' invention and reinforcement of the "folk" as a cultural and social category—when one begins to speak out loud about the system's "unspeakable truths" (2005, 71; 103).

Certainly, I would argue, by parading his politicians eight days before the election, Eisenhauer was pointing to some of these unspeakable truths on his own terms. If nothing else, he made clear that he was quite capable of negotiating both a venue for his own art practice and his creative engagement with Canadian politics. As part of Huntington's interview with Eisenhauer for the "Folk Art of Nova Scotia" exhibition, Huntington inquired about the *Politicians* and asked: "How did the people like them?" to which Eisenhauer replied: "they took it as an insult I guess... It was eight days before the election and they thought I was hitting the politicians but I wasn't." In reference to the audience that day, Eisenhauer remembers that "they didn't laugh at me quite and I didn't laugh at myself because I had something to show" (quoted in Donaldson 1979, 22). Indeed, Eisenhauer did have something to show. The National Museum of Man (now the Canadian Museum of Civilization in Ottawa) purchased Eisenhauer's *Political Figures* in 1975, the first example of contemporary Nova Scotia "folk" art in its permanent collection. A year later, the AGNS chose the four sculptures of Trudeau, Stanfield, Lewis, and Regan as the cover for the seminal "Folk Art of Nova Scotia" exhibition, which toured nationally from 1976 to 78. As a result of this exhibition, Eisenhauer's *Political Figures* came to be a prominent marker in the circulation and dissemination of Nova Scotia "folk" art as a category of artistic expression.

In the catalogue that accompanied "Folk Art of Nova Scotia," the exhibition's curators outline the unique cultural circumstances of the province as follows: "Folk art is produced by artists who are self-taught.... Many of these carvers are carpenters, or combine the hand-skills of farm and sea, reminding us that a craft artisan tradition has contributed to folk art. Rural isolation and long winters conspire to provide the opportunity for the folk artist to produce his works. Since they are not bound by tradition or livelihood to their art, their work truly represents them and their habitat" (Folk art of Nova Scotia 1976, n.p.). Of no surprise here, perhaps, are the curators' attempts to embed their definition of "folk" art as Nova Scotia's indigenous cultural production along with some invented essence of regionality—as if the creative inspiration of artists such as Eisenhauer arose from the land and sea of the province itself.

In reference to Eisenhauer in particular the catalogue notes, "The folk artist approaches the task of carving without an academic knowledge of the craft of sculpture. He solves his many technical problems intuitively and with a simplicity and directness that is part of the appeal of his work" (*Folk art of Nova Scotia* 1976, n.p.). The catalogue goes on to read, "When asked what he thought about the 'Politicians' being owned by the National Museum of Man in Ottawa Collie replies: 'Well, it made me feel quite happy that they had gone some place where somebody would see them … It made me feel as though a little more somebody" (*Folk art of Nova Scotia* 1976, n.p.). The exhibition catalogue effectively serves to remove any agency from Eisenhauer as cultural producer, particularly in relation to the politically motivated subject matter that this piece employs. Eisenhauer as artist is not, for instance, analyzed as staging a protest about the 1974 election, nor is he questioned about the reasons behind choosing these politicians as subject matter. More than Eisenhauer as "folk" artist, the limited media coverage of the parade in New Germany explains that the *Political Figures* themselves inspired a reaction because, to quote one reviewer, "it was close to election time, and Maritimers can be a conservative lot, and there was some muttering about poking fun at politicians" (Donaldson 1979, 22). Despite the fact that AGNS curators, Huntington as patron, and journalists have historically read Eisenhauer's parade float as a act of "poking fun" at the politicians he rendered, the artist himself has clearly countered such notions. He wasn't poking fun and, in fact, the conceptual planning behind the politicians series is embedded with a keen sense of irony—particularly, in my reading of the works, with regards to Eisenhauer's depiction of Robert Stanfield, who is shown as he is famously remembered, calmly eating a banana while he waited for the 1967 Tory leadership results.

I am not necessarily interested in pointing out the subtle nuances of political commentary implicit in Eisenhauer's *Political Figures,* though there are many that I think could be read quite obviously. Rather I find Eisenhauer's series engaging because of the moment they help to illustrate in Canadian cultural and political history and because of the way, as objects of visual culture, they have historically been used as a resource in Nova Scotia to promote an indigenous provincial folk culture for a variety of purposes—a process that is intertwined with the ongoing efforts of cultural producers and the state tourist industry in Nova Scotia to promote positive ideas about the province, as well as to elide provincial histories of economic decline and a perceived sense of political conservativism. As Yúdice argues, "there is an expedient relation between globalization and culture in the sense that there is a *fit* or a *suitability* between them." Globalization involves the dissemination of symbolic processes, which increasingly drive economics and politics, and, to quote Malcolm Waters, guides the fact that "material exchanges localize, political exchanges internationalize, and symbolic exchanges globalize" (Waters quoted in Yudice 2003, 29). The manner in which such exchanges operate and interact was, in Nova Scotia at least, particularly visible eight days before the election.

Notes

1 Clearly, as historical understanding of regional interaction in a global marketplace develops, the function of places such as Canada's east coast might be studied in ways that are more specific and contextual—in other words, in ways outside of their relationship to dominant historical narratives based in central Canada. In addition to challenging historically contingent national/ist narratives, this approach also disrupts limiting binaries within the current moment of globalization, among them those cultural anthropologist Richard Wilk describes as the perceived "polarities of global hegemony and local appropriation" (2002, 194).

2 Creighton's authoritative argument of Canada's development as a nation suggests that modernization and economic expansion flowed between metropolises through the St. Lawrence River system alongside fur, timber, and wheat. Creighton's writing was among that which set forth the most prominent English Canadian history writing of the 1930s and 40s (Creighton 1937).

3 These transitions in the way culture functions in capitalist economies from the first half of the twentieth century to present day are mirrored in what Scott Lash and Celia Lury describe as Adorno's worst nightmare come true (2007). Horkheimer and Adorno's theory of culture industry—in which, as Lash and Lury explain, culture "became objective like any other commodity" through the emergent, widespread capitalist economy that developed under the conditions of modernity (2007, 3)—is one of the primary sources associated with the development of disciplinary cultural studies in the 1970s (Adorno 1991; Horkheimer and Adorno 2002). Subsequently, Horkheimer and Adorno's arguments on culture industry have long been debated by those who argue that culture is not only a site of domination but also of resistance (Lash and Lury 2007; Hall et al. 1980; Hall and Jefferson 1993). Lash and Lury situate this debate historically, by building on the arguments of classical cultural studies to examine the modern culture industry as a particular moment that has passed since these questions about counter-hegemonic opposition first emerged. While arguments advanced surrounding examples of domination and resistance to the culture industry were no doubt correct at the time, in Lash and Lury's minds, "since the time of critical theory *and* since the emergence of the Birmingham tradition in the middle 1970s—things have changed" (2007, 3). Culture, Lash and Lury suggest, has taken on "a different logic" as mod-

ern culture industry transformed to *global* culture industry, giving culture "a fundamentally different mode of operation" (2007, 3).

4 Marwick posits not simply a "'long sixties' but of that period being divided into three distinctive sub-periods, 1958-63, 1964-8/9, and 1969-74" (1998, 8). As music historian Kenneth Gloag points out, "Although the 1960s were, and in retrospect remain, a very distinct cultural moment, it is obvious that neither the beginning nor the end of the decade can automatically be seen to delineate a discrete historical and culture period" (2001, 98). It is with this in mind that I examine the historical circumstances surrounding Eisenhauer's *Political Figures*, since while the artist created the series in 1974, the sculptures are, in my mind, politically bound in subject matter and culturally bound in context to processes of cultural expediency that become most apparent in the 1960s.

5 Rifkin explains this historical shift from industrial to cultural capitalism as a process in which "old institutions grounded in property relations, market exchanges, and material accumulation are slowly being uprooted to make room for an era in which culture becomes the most important commercial resource, time and attention become the most valuable possession, and each individual's own life becomes the ultimate market" (2000, 11). In this way the cultural sphere is being absorbed into the commercial sphere, although as Rifkin points out "the commercial sphere always has been derivative of and dependent of the cultural sphere … because culture is the wellspring from which agreed-upon behavioural norms are generated" (2000, 11). Yet when the commercial sphere risks devouring the cultural sphere—as Rifkin argues it is—"it threatens to destroy the very social foundations that give rise to commercial relations" (2000, 12). Achieving a balance between these two realms is, according to Rifkin, the most challenging task of the current era.

6 This and several of the following Huntington quotations are taken from the 1993 National Film Board documentary *Folk Art Found Me*, which interviewed the collector and several of the artists he patronized. I should be noted that, as McKay shows, the connection between the tourist state and the construction of a "folk" identity in Nova Scotia is not something that suddenly emerged at the time Huntington began collecting there. As McKay notes, "insider" support for tourism in Nova Scotia was linked in the early twentieth century to provincial patriotism. However, criticisms of cheaply produced souvenir items in shops around the province were evident, usually because such objects were seen to crowd "authentic" Nova Scotian products with things that were not manufactured in the province. As McKay's analysis shows, this was often coupled with handicraft workers in Nova Scotia attempting to compete in the souvenir trade by producing cheap souvenirs themselves, which was widely encouraged by cultural producers such as craft bureaucrat Mary Black. See McKay 1994, 194-199.

7 For simplicity's sake, I have edited part of Huntington's actual conversation in which he states: "Its just a matter of, you know it's one reason why I'm happy you're no longer making chickens by the dozen, because that was a waste of, seems to be a waste of energy."

8 The majority of Martin's research for this exhibition was derived from personal interviews with Chris Huntington and his second wife Charlotte McGill, who maintain a private archive of information from Huntington's career as a collector. Martin cites this source as the "Hunting-

ton-McGill Collection, Blockhouse, Nova Scotia," which Huntington describes as a "rough" compilation of his many years of activity as a collector (Chris Huntington, e-mail to the author, 9 Mar. 2005). The interview Martin conducted with Huntington has since been lost (Chris Huntington and Charlotte McGill, e-mail to the author, 18 Mar. 2005; Ken Martin, e-mail to the author, 30 Mar. 2005). For this reason, I reference this interview entirely through this valuable secondary source. Unless otherwise indicated, all Huntington quotations cited in Martin are taken from this particular interview, which was conducted in May 1996.

9 Huntington notes that, in fact, he and McGill are "not more interested in folk art than in fine art. In fact, we are less so. It's just that it is by far the best that was here when I moved to Nova Scotia in 1974 and was still the best when Charlotte and I married in 1984. And, it was still vibrant, if fading, ten years later" (Chris Huntington and Charlotte McGill, e-mail to the author, 9 Mar. 2005).

10 Martin mentions that the Huntingtons often admired Eisenhauer's work in Murray Stewart's antique shop, another collector based in Nova Scotia. For more on Stewart, see Cliff Eyland and Susan Gibson Garvey, 1994, *Uses of the vernacular in Nova Scotian art*, Halifax: Dalhousie Art Gallery, 15.

11 Martin's quotation of Huntington is here taken from Huntington's introductory essay in the catalogue to the exhibition, "Charlie Tanner 1904-1982: Retrospective," which was shown at the AGNS in 1984.

12 See for example McKay's discussion of Helen Creighton, a collector of what were regarded as traditional Nova Scotia ballads, who was largely responsible for elevating Nova Scotia folklore to a position of cultural prominence beginning in the 1920s. McKay also outlines the career of Mary Black, the chief inventor of behind the invention of a handicraft tradition in Nova Scotia that led to the development of such a prominent cultural symbol as the Nova Scotia Tartan. See McKay 1994, Chapters 2-3.

13 Many artists, among them Samuel Bollivar, Charlie Tanner and Harry Wile, were quite elderly at the time Huntington contacted them and suffered from ailments that prevented them from producing many works after the 1970s.

References Cited

Adorno, Theodor W. 1991. *The culture industry: Selected essays on mass culture.* Ed. J.M. Bernstein. London: Routledge.

Appadurai, Arjun. 1996. *Modernity at large: Cultural dimensions of globalization.* London and Minneapolis: University of Minnesota Press.

Creighton, Donald. 1937. *The commercial empire of the St. Lawrence, 1769-1850.* Toronto: The Ryerson Press; New Haven: Yale University Press.

Denning, Michael. 2004. *Culture in the age of three worlds.* London: Verso.

Donaldson, Joan. 1979. An Eisenhauer portfolio. *Artscanada.* 230/231: 20-22.

Elwood, Marie. 1977. 20th century Nova Scotia folk art. *Canadian collector.* 12.1: 31-34.

Folk art found me. 1993. VHS. Directed by Alex Busby. Halifax: National Film Board of Canada and Wisdom Teeth Productions.

Folk art of Nova Scotia: A travelling exhibition of 20th century folk art of Nova *Scotia*. 1976. Halifax: Art Gallery of Nova Scotia.

García Canclini, Néstor. 2001. *Consumers and citizens: Globalization and multicultural conflicts*, trans. George Yúdice. Vol. 6 of *Cultural studies of the Americas*. London and Minneapolis: University of Minnesota Press.

García Canclini, Néstor. 1988. Culture and power: The state of research. *Media, Culture and Society*. 10: 467–497.

Gloag, Kenneth. 2001. Situating the 1960s: Popular music—postmodernism—history. *Rethinking history*. 5.3: 397-410.

Guss, David M. 2000. *The festive state: race, ethnicity, and nationalism as cultural performance*. Berkeley: University of California Press.

Hall, Stuart, Dorothy Hobson, Andrew Lowe and Paul Willis, eds. 1980. *Culture, media, language: Working papers in cultural studies, 1972-79*. London: Centre for Contemporary Cultural Studies, University of Birmingham.

Hall, Stuart and Tony Jefferson, eds. 1993. *Resistance through rituals: Youth subcultures in post-war Britain*. London and New York: Routledge.

Horkheimer, Max and Theodor W. Adorno. 2002. *Dialectic of enlightenment: Philosophical fragments*. Ed. Gunzelin Schmid Noerr. Trans. Edmund Jephcott. Stanford, CA: Stanford University Press.

Huntington, Chris and Murray Stewart. 26 April 1976. Interview with the wood carver Collins Eisenhower [sic]. Tape-audio. Chris Huntington Collection, HUN-A-3 (XII-A-4), Box 202, Acc. No. 77-79. Canadian Museum of Civilization Archives.

Jessup, Lynda. 2001. Antimodernism and artistic experience: An introduction. In *Antimodernism and artistic experience: Policing the boundaries of modernity*, ed. Lynda Jessup, 4-9. Toronto: University of Toronto Press.

Lash, Scott and Celia Lury. 2007. *Global culture industry: The mediation of things*. Cambridge: Polity Press.

Martin, Ken. 1997. Chris Huntington and the resurgence of Nova Scotia folk art, 1975-1995. Halifax: Art Gallery of Nova Scotia.

Marwick, Arthur, 1998. *The sixties: Cultural revolution in Britain, France, Italy, and the United States, c. 1958-c.1974*. Oxford and New York: Oxford University Press.

McKay, Ian. 1998. After Canada: On amnesia and apocalypse in the contemporary crisis. *Acadiensis* 28.1: 76-97.

McKay, Ian. 2000a. The liberal order framework: A prospectus for a reconnaissance of Canadian history. *The Canadian historical review* 81.4: 617-645.

McKay, Ian. 2000b. A note on 'region' in writing the history of Atlantic Canada. *Acadiensis* 29.2: 89-101.

McKay, Ian. 1994. *The quest of the folk: Antimodernism and cultural selection in twentieth-century Nova Scotia*. Montreal and Kingston: McGill-Queen's University Press.

McKay, Ian. 2005. *Rebels, reds, radicals: Rethinking Canada's left history*. Toronto: Between the Lines.

Press Release. 17 February 1978. "Folk Art of Nova Scotia" comes to the National Gallery. "Folk Art of Nova Scotia" Exhibition Files, dossier 4, Box 88, EX 1609, National Gallery of Canada Library and Archives.

Rifkin, Jeremy. 2000. *The age of access: How the shift from ownership to access is transforming capitalism*. London: Penguin.

Yúdice, George. 2003. *The expediency of culture: Uses of culture in the global era*. Durham: Duke University Press.

Wilk, Richard. 2002. "Learning to be local in Belize: Global systems of common difference." In *Development: A Cultural Studies Reader,* eds. Susanne Schech and Jane Haggis, 194-208. Malden, MA: Blackwell.

ALSO AVAILABLE from BLACK ROSE BOOKS

PARTICIPATORY DEMOCRACY

Prospects for Democratizing Democracy

Dimitrios Roussopoulos, C.George Benello, editors

A completely revised edition of the classic and widely consulted 1970 version

First published as a testament to the legacy of the concept made popular by the New Left of the 1960s, and with the perspective of the intervening decades, this book opens up the way for re-examining just what is involved in democratizing democracy.

With its emphasis on citizen participation, here, presented in one volume, are the best arguments for participatory democracy written by some of the most relevant contributors to the debate, both in an historic, and in a contemporary, sense.

> The book is, by all odds, the most encompassing one
> so far in revealing the practical actual subversions
> that the New Left wishes to visit upon us. —*Washington Post*

Apart from the editors, contributors include: George Woodcock, Murray Bookchin, Don Calhoun, Stewart Perry, Rosabeth Moss Kanter, James Gillespie, Gerry Hunnius, John McEwan, Arthur Chickering, Christian Bay, Martin Oppenheimer, Colin Ward, Sergio Baierle, Anne Latendresse, Bartha Rodin, and C.L.R. James.

DIMITRIOS ROUSSOPOULOS was a prominent New Left activist in the 1960s, locally and internationally, and is the author and/or editor of some eighteen books, most recently *Faith in Faithlessness: An Anthology of Atheism*.

C.GEORGE BENELLO (1927-1987) taught sociology at Goddard College in Vermont until his untimely death. He was author of *From the Ground Up: Essays on Grassroots and Workplace Democracy*.

2004: 380 pages
Paperback ISBN: 1-55164-224-7 $24.99
Hardcover ISBN: 1-55164-225-5 $53.99

OF RELATED INTEREST

POLITICS OF OBEDIENCE and ÉTIENNE DE LA BOÉTIE

Étienne De La Boétie and Paul Bonnefon

Introduction by Murray N. Rothbard

In his *Discourse*, La Boétie delves deeply into the nature of tyranny and into the nature of State rule: why do people, in all times and places, obey the commands of government? Apart from the complete text of *Discourse of Voluntary Servitude,* this edition includes a comprehensive 100-page biography by Paul Bonnefon.

> It is ironic that the works of Machiavelli, advisor to rulers, should enjoy widespread currency, while the libertarian La Boétie is muted. Hopefully, publication of his 1550 *Discourse*, with its superb introduction by Murray Rothbard, will right the imbalance. —Stanley Milgram

ÉTIENNE DE LA BOÉTIE was a sixteenth-century political philosopher. PAUL BONNEFON is the author of *Oeuvres Complètes Étienne de La Boétie* (*Complete Works of Étienne de La Boétie*, 1892).

2006: 160 pages, paper 1-55164-292-1 $19.99 ✳ cloth 1-55164-293-X $48.99

THE FRENCH LEFT: A History and Overview

Arthur Hirsh

Consisting of a new evaluation of the intellectual history of the contemporary Left in France, this book is an important contribution to understanding the debates that have had an international influence.

> Hirsh's gift for compression and clarity provides us with a fine itinerary of the New Left in France. He reconstructs and makes more accessible the ideas of Sartre, Henri Lefebvre, Cornelius Castoriadis, and Andre Gorz, including the tensions among them…and he dissects the relations between the work of these theorists and the great events of 1968 in France.
> —Paul Breines, Boston College

> In this truly admirable book, Arthur Hirsh does the near impossible: he presents opposing ideas with clarity and without bias… *The French Left*, one of the very best works I have seen for some times, will not soon be surpassed.
> —Herb Gintis, University of Massachusetts

> Hirsh's work is of the greatest interest. —*Canadian Journal of Political Science*

253 pages, paper 0-919619-23-6 $12.99 ✳ cloth 0-919619-24-4 $41.99

ALSO AVAILABLE from BLACK ROSE BOOKS

THE NEW LEFT

Legacy and Continuity

Dimitrios Roussopoulos

As the contributors to this anthology revisit the sixties to identify its ongoing impact on North American politics and culture, it becomes evident how this legacy has blended with, and influenced today's world-wide social movements, in particular, the anti-globalization movement, and the 'Right to the City' movement: the successes and failures of civil society orgnisations as they struggle for a voice at all levels of decision-making are examined, as are the new movements of the urban disenfranchised—the homeless, the alienation of youth, the elderly poor.

Apart from evoking memories of past peace and freedom struggles from those who worked on the social movements of the 1960s, this work also includes a number of essays from a rising generation of intellectual and activists, too young to have experienced the 1960s firsthand, whose perspective enables them to offer fresh insights and analyses.

> An eclectic mix of memoir and commentary that accents the legacies of the 60s rebellious youth, and the continuities of the political dissent and oppositional challenges of that decade. —*Canadian Dimension*

Contributors include: Dimitrios Roussopoulos, Andrea Levy, Anthony Hyde, Jacques Martin, Mark Rudd, Katherina Haris, Gregory Nevala Calvert, Natasha Kapoor, and Tom Hayden.

DIMITRIOS ROUSSOPOULOS was a prominent New Left activist in the 1960s, locally and internationally. He continues to write and edit on major issues while being a committed activist testing theory with practice.

2007: 224 pages
Paperback ISBN: 978-1-155164-298-7 $19.99
Hardcover ISBN: 978-1-155164-299-4 $48.99

OF RELATED INTEREST

CANADA AND RADICAL SOCIAL CHANGE

Dimitrios Roussopoulos, editor

Outstanding essays from the radical journal *Our Generation* have been brought together to form a contemporary view of priorities for social change in Canada.

   1973: 270 pages, paper 0-919618-09-X $5.99 ✳ cloth 0-919618-10-3 $34.99

QUÉBEC AND RADICAL SOCIAL CHANGE

Dimitrios Roussopoulos, editor

Perceptive essays on radical movements in Québec politics by Québéc analysts.

   1974: 210 pages, paper 0-919618-51-0 $5.99 ✳ cloth 0-919618-52-9 $34.99

QUÉBEC LABOUR, revised edition

Preface by Marcel Pépin

Marcel Pépin, former president of the Confederation of National Trade Unions, provides a lively introduction to the 1972 CNTU manifestos.

   1972: 251 pages, paper 0-919618-15-4 $7.99 ✳ cloth 0-919618-14-6 $36.99

---

send for a free catalogue of all our titles

C.P. 1258, Succ. Place du Parc

Montréal, Québec

H2X 4A7 Canada

or visit our website at http://www.blackrosebooks.net

to order books

In Canada: (phone) 1-800-565-9523 (fax) 1-800-221-9985

email: utpbooks@utpress.utoronto.ca

In United States: (phone) 1-800-283-3572 (fax) 1-800-351-5073

In UK & Europe: (phone) London 44 (0)20 8986-4854 (fax) 44 (0)20 8533-5821

email: order@centralbooks.com

Printed by the workers of

for Black Rose Books

imprimerie **gauvin**